TAHITI NUI

P9-CJW-330

Tu-nui-ae-i-te-atua. Pomare I (1802).

TAHITI NUI

Change and Survival
in French Polynesia
1767–1945

COLIN NEWBURY

THE UNIVERSITY PRESS OF HAWAII
HONOLULU

Copyright © 1980 by The University Press of Hawaii

All rights reserved.

Manufactured in the United States of America.

Library of Congress Cataloging in Publication Data

Newbury, Colin W
   Tahiti Nui : change and survival in French Polynesia,
1767-1945.

   Bibliography: p.
   Includes index.
   1. Tahiti—History. 2. Tahiti—Colonization.
I. Title.
DU870.N48   996'.211   79-23609
ISBN 0-8248-0630-1

The pencil drawing of Pomare I *(frontispiece)* is by
J. W. Lewin (1770-1819) and is reproduced from the
collection of Father Patrick O'Reilly. The drawing "A
View of Port Royal (Matavai) Bay" is reproduced by
permission of the British Library Board. The reproduc-
tion of the watercolor painting of "The Harbour &
Town of Papahitie" is from the Peabody Museum. All of
the other illustrations, unless specified, are from the
O'Reilly Collection.

For Father Patrick O'Reilly,
Bibliographer of the Pacific

CONTENTS

ILLUSTRATIONS

FIGURES

MAPS

TABLES

PREFACE

IN THE LITERATURE of the Pacific Tahiti holds a special place. There is solid documentation on the European explorer's view from seaward and on Europe's appreciation of that view—from the end of the eighteenth century to the modern tourist industry's exploitation of the South Seas image. More recently, too, reprints of older works on the oral traditions and ethnology of Tahitians have been supplemented by archaeological evidence for settlement patterns in the eastern Pacific and a revision of our thinking about the navigational techniques that may have guided the first people there. A summation of scholarly rediscovery of the island and its inhabitants has been magnificently presented in Douglas L. Oliver's *Ancient Tahitian Society.*

There are few interpretations of the period of nineteenth-century European contact with Tahiti, however, though the missionary period and events leading up to French occupation have featured prominently in detailed and specialized works by Dr. Niel Gunson, Professor W. P. Morrell, Léonce Jore, and J.-P. Faivre. Not till after 1945 did the period of French rule and its consequences for Tahitians arouse a limited amount of investigation into the politics of local government in French Polynesia and socioeconomic changes resulting from the development of local markets and intensive investment in the economic infrastructure of the nuclear testing program of the 1960s.

It is easy to emphasize the structural changes that have taken place between the late eighteenth century and the mid-twentieth. It is more difficult to trace the continuities that have been a feature of contact between islanders and alien visitors and settlers for over a century and a half. Some of the drama at the beginning and end of that period has obscured significant adjustments, accommodations, and, above all, the slow creation of new social groups within Tahitian society—groups that, to a great extent, are the political and economic legatees of the institutions of government, business, and the churches evolved during the early period of missionary and French tutelage.

Advances in the history of other island groups in the Pacific —more particularly the Hawaiian Islands, Western Samoa, Fiji, Tonga, and New Guinea—have drawn attention, too, to parallel developments in the exploitation of resources and in systems of administration used to regulate and arbitrate Pacific markets. Compared with historical insights obtained into the operations of traders, labor recruiters, companies, and officials in these islands and archipelagoes, the French territories, including the more advanced industrial economy of New Caledonia, are *insulae incognitae*; and works in English or French dealing with their societies concentrate heavily on the age of exploration and the activities of the first settlers.

An interest in those activities and encouragement by the late Professor J. W. Davidson, head of the Department of Pacific History at the Australian National University, led me to begin this study over twenty years ago. Since then, the eventual thesis on French administration in eastern Polynesia has been revised and expanded, along with my own academic interests in other societies in Africa. Materials not available to me in the 1950s—particularly on the economic history of the region—have been located and are open to students. A curiosity about the complex correlation between markets and the exercise of political authority in other societies under European rule has also led me to reexamine some of the methods, assumptions, and conclusions I reached earlier. But I still owe a considerable debt of gratitude to the Australian National University, which materially assisted my first exploration of French Polynesia in the archives of Australia and Europe and in the field. I have also gained more than I can say from the insights of the late Richard Gilson and J. W. Davidson into Samoan history, from the work of Niel Gunson on the first missionaries, and from Professor H. E. Maude's pioneer study of early Tahitian trade. It is impossible for a historian not to be also in the debt of social anthropologists; and I have learned to ask questions raised by the later studies of Bengt Danielsson for Raroia and Professor Ben Finney for Tahitian socioeconomic behavior.

Consequently, the emphasis in this book is more on the economic interchanges that have characterized European contact with Tahiti and adjacent islands and much less on formal patterns of government and administration. For that contact resulted in a crude market, as a working compromise, in 1767. By the date of the Second World War, Tahitian markets absorbed the produce of most of the region under French rule and had been closely integrated into the political economy of the colonial power. But this integration was a relatively recent development, under French rule, giving rise to a dependency and to a class of Franco-Tahitian intermediaries which differed from nineteenth-century Tahitian society in important ways and which was to play an enhanced political and commercial role after 1945.

Throughout these interchanges a constant theme in Tahitian history has been land as a valued resource; and within the limits of our very partial understanding of Tahitian land tenure, I have stressed the place of attitudes to resource zones (including transferable estate) at critical periods at the outset of French occupation and in nineteenth and early-twentieth-century investment in commodity exploitation. It could not be claimed, however, that evidence on land tenure or on trade is readily quantifiable in terms that would be essential to a thorough economic history of the period; and historians of other developing societies will recognize familiar problems in using qualitative data to describe continuity and change. We are, however, fortunate in having a reasonably complete set of business records for an important commercial enterprise up till 1914, and I have used a German firm as an example to illustrate a number of themes related to commodities, credit, and the advancement of Tahitian intermediaries within the structure of a colonial "peripheral" economy linked to world markets.

Given this emphasis, I have deliberately omitted much material on the pre-European and early European period (some of which is published elsewhere). My debt to researchers who have labored to construct an ethnographic baseline will, however, be abundantly clear in the first two chapters.

The title, too, has been chosen in the knowledge that to purists it refers only to the larger northern part of the island. But "greater Tahiti" could be held to encompass, both eponymously and in quite mundane ways, the outlying islands and atolls of the region, their inhabitants, and their institutions of government, business, and the church. It is part of the argument of this study that a concentration of market exchanges at the main port accelerated the adaptation of local Tahitians to a cash economy from a relatively early period. Tahiti has long been a central place.

Thus, while important regional variations exist in the history of French Polynesia and are (I hope) acknowledged in this study, the emphasis is on the regional assimilation of local societies to the capital through the operation of a variety of economic, legal, and linguistic factors over some six generations of improved communications and four generations of French rule.

From the outset, a number of scholars, librarians, and officials have assisted in special ways. They cannot all be mentioned here; but I wish to record my gratitude to Josephine Nordmann Salmon, Aurora Natua, the late H. Jacquier and Paul Doucet, François Kruger, Irene Fletcher, and Father Patrick O'Reilly. Finally, my wife has assisted me untiringly through the many years of revision, particularly with the more difficult sections of German commercial records. For the use made of these and all other materials and for the conclusions I am responsible.

Oxford, October 1978

CHAPTER 1

THE MARKET
AT MATAVAI BAY

ALONG THE PENINSULA at Teauroa (Cook's Point Venus) on the
north shoreline of Tahiti a beach of black sand curves round for
about half a mile to the foot of Tahara'a or One Tree Hill. Behind
the beach a stream once emptied the floodwaters of the Vaipopo'o
River into the sea; and the river itself still winds back over the plain
of Ha'apape district to the foothills of the Tua'uru Valley under the
mountains of Aora'i and Orohena. The stream has long since disappeared, for the plain was drained for nineteenth-century plantations. But as late as the 1860s a giant tamarind tree—reputedly
planted by Cook, but more probably by an early missionary—
towered at the end of the peninsula, where the monument to the navigator still stands. For it was on that spot that Cook's men set up
their tents to make their observations in 1769 two years after the
European discovery of Tahiti by Captain Wallis. Later a house was
built on the bank of the stream during Captain Bligh's second visit
in 1792. For the first British missionaries who landed in 1797, it
served as a storeroom and shelter until its destruction in the political upheaval that followed this settlement.

Thus Matavai Bay enfolds much of the early history of European contact with the most important island of eastern Polynesia,
that constellation of marine peaks and atolls scattered over a million square miles of Pacific Ocean. Other islands of these archipelagoes were discovered earlier, from the end of the sixteenth
century, by Europeans. In some, such as the Marquesas, the results
of their passage were much more disastrous for Polynesians, while
others in the Tuamotu were relatively undisturbed till late in the
nineteenth century. Yet in all the numerous inhabited groups that

eventually became part of French Polynesia, Tahiti and its port gained a special significance: they became the central place for a maritime culture in a region which has been profoundly influenced by the development of a commercial and political capital at Pape'ete.

By the end of the eighteenth century, all the passes and harbors of the northwestern coast of Tahiti and many at Mo'orea and the Leeward Islands had been roughly charted by the seamen of another maritime civilization. The bay became an occasional port of call for naval vessels and merchantmen plying between the China coast, the Indies, the Americas, and New South Wales. Made famous by the publications of Wallis, Cook, and Bougainville, the curve of Teauroa Peninsula offered good shelter in easterlies; wood, water, and provisions were reputed to be plentiful at most seasons of the year for a vessel at anchor inside the banks of coral reef that gird all the inlets at Matavai, Wai'amo, Pare, Taunoa, and Pape'ete; the inhabitants were hospitable; and if the preference of seamen determined that the main anchorage would shift by the early nineteenth century to Pape'ete, some 6 or 7 miles to the west, nevertheless the ground rules for the earliest commercial transactions between the *popa'a*, or strangers, and the *ta'ata fenua*,[1] or natives, were laid down on the beach at Matavai.

Such exchanges of produce, ideas, and people were, of course, not new in eastern Polynesia. The Tahitian dialect is short of words connoting buying and selling;[2] but the term for a market, *ho'o ra'a*, and its verbal form, appear in the earliest European word list collected by the Spanish visitors to Tahiti in 1772.[3] They also noted terms for the payment of debts, for a bargain, and for deception and theft. The almost universal experience of the first Europeans to trade at Tahiti was that their possessions were redistributed as much by stealth as by exchange.

They recorded, too, that long-distance trade was carried on by the chiefs of the Taiarapu Peninsula with Me'etia Island some 70 miles to the east.[4] Tahiti and Mo'orea were in frequent communication with the Leeward Islands 90 miles to the northwest and, less frequently, with the northern Tuamotu. Some of this trade undertaken by double canoes may reflect a growing demand in the 1790s for pearls, pearl shell, coconut oil, and hogs at Tahiti, where there was a reexport of European goods. But it is certain that commercial imperialism was indigenous. For the chiefs of Pare and Arue in northern Tahiti exploited Tetiaroa Atoll as a kind of proprietary colony which specialized in the export of fish and coconut oil for imported provisions; and there is evidence that the island of Makatea had become tributary to the same chiefs by the beginning of the nineteenth century.[5] There is evidence, too, of exchanges arising quite simply out of endowment or technical specialization in production. The islands of Borabora and Taha'a traded a surplus of coconut oil and vegetable dyes for the bark cloth which was one of the Windward group's principal manufactures. The best canoes were reputed to be made in the Leeward Islands and were purchased for war and trade at Tahiti.

It is also clear that the interchange of goods and services among the islanders was carried on in the form of gifts as well as barter.[6] Like many of his fellows, Cook's astronomer, William Wales, found these donations to importunate "friends" a costly business and resolved to "proceed by the less noble and generous though perhaps more just and equitable way of Barter & Trade."[7] Even for chiefs, property accumulation was often a temporary state of relative wealth impaired by constant demands on their generosity; and, if stored, their goods were not immune from pillage, whatever their status. On the other hand, the social and political benefits of redistribution to kin and followers were well understood when Europeans enlivened the market with an unprecedented range of manufactures and added new possibilities for political and social advancement.

THE TERMS OF TRADE

However much the more picturesque aspects of this exchange touched eighteenth-century imaginations and gave rise to legends of agreeable intercourse, the initial contact between Tahitians and Europeans, when Wallis's *Dolphin* touched at Matavai Bay on 21 June 1767, was prosaically similar to other clashes between seamen and islanders. Desperate for fresh water and supplies Wallis's men committed the ship's boats to sounding out a hostile shore.[8] They were in a poor position to bargain; and the few canoes that came alongside "behaved very insolently, none of them would trust any of our men with any of their things untill they got nails or toys from them, then several of them would push off and keep all and

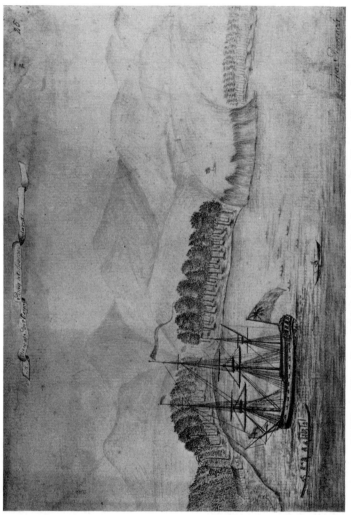

"A View of Port Royal (Matavai) Bay." Pen drawing by George Pinnock.

oythers caried their insolence so high that they struck several of our men."[9]

It is possible that Tahitians had long since learned of the loss of Roggeveen's *Afrikaanische Galei* in 1722 at Takapoto in the Tuamotu and hoped for a similar windfall. Their intention to cut out the ship became clear enough, though they showed no experience of the consequences of European firepower at this stage. For an island that was to earn a worldwide reputation for hospitality, this was a poor beginning. Worse was to follow. Harried by several hundred canoes and jeered at for their weakness, the shore party under the master of the *Dolphin* opened fire on the boldest of their tormentors, killing one and wounding another. The lesson was temporarily sufficient to stimulate trade the next day, when the mere leveling of a musket "or even of a spye Glass at them" encouraged canoemen to "give Value." But there were to be more desperate moments. The *Dolphin* ran onto a shoal at the mouth of the bay, and her guns were fired to disperse attacks while a safe anchorage inside the reef was found. Undeterred, the Tahitians loosed a bombardment of "stones lyke hail," and the ship fired rounds of grape which blasted their canoes and took a heavy toll of life.

Thereafter, the initial bloody contact settled into a truce and a measured appraisal of the advantages to be had. On 26 June, under cover of the ship's guns, a ceremony of annexation was performed on the peninsula and a pennant was hoisted on a long pole at Teauroa Point. This event aroused keen interest; and after some reciprocal ceremonial on the part of the Tahitians, the pennant was removed to be incorporated into the *maro ura* regalia of the paramount chiefs of the southwestern districts of the island.[10] The meaning of Wallis's act, if correctly guessed, was not accepted, though the symbol of European authority was clearly thought worth keeping.

Thus in the short space of five days the inhabitants of Matavai and neighboring districts were introduced brutally to the rules of alien commerce, to a totally new level of technology, and to a strange but suggestive indication of permanent settlement. They had reacted with hostility but without entirely rejecting what they saw. Not until 27 June did Wallis's men succeed in making their point, when some seventy or eighty large canoes, capable of holding up to a thousand men, were systematically holed and damaged to discourage treachery.

Until 28 July, when the *Dolphin* sailed, both sides exercised a measure of restraint over the ship's crew and the commonality on the shore. Loss of life by long-range gunnery and the destruction of valuable war canoes in such numbers could not be tolerated as a price for risky stratagems. In any case, there were other ways of gaining visitors' artifacts. Shore parties were offered "several very handsome Young Girls."[11] News of their perfections dissolved much of the current hostility, roused the sick from their torpor, and initiated a commerce (the *Dolphin*'s master calls it the "old trade") which the "Liberty men" soon fixed at the rate of "a thirty penny nail each time."

There are several aspects of this early trade in all its forms which became permanent features of European contact with Matavai Bay. First, as one of Cook's men noted six years later, the sanction of force, held in reserve, kept order in the marketplace, where:

> We had seldom less than four or five hundred of the Natives of All Ranks & sexes round our little Encampment, and I did not fail to profit by the Opportunity of trying and studying their tempers & disposition with the Utmost Attention. It may surprise some to be told that an extent of 60 Yards in front, and near 30 in depth, was guarded from such a body of People by only 4 Centinals, with no other lines to assist them, but a rope stretched from Post to Post, & that often so slack as to lay on the ground; but it is nevertheless true, and so effectually that none of us ever received the least insult or incivillity from any of them, nor did any of them come within our lines without leave: so terrible did Capt. Wallace make the sight of a Gun to the Inhabitants of Otahitee![12]

Cook had occasion, when exasperated beyond his usual endurance by thefts, to order punishments. But not till the early years of the nineteenth century did Tahitians again, because of their own exasperation with the results of European contact, attempt to seize a European vessel or offer a real threat to foreign settlers on the island.

Moreover, there was a marked tendency toward price inflation resulting from excessive demand. At the outset in 1767 the market price on 22 June had been "a twenty pene nail for a Hog of about twenty pound, a tenpeny for a rosting pig, a sixpence for a Fowl or some fruit, but all of them seemed most fond of nails."[13] A week later the gunner complained of "a hundred per cent" increase "owing to the Liberty men, who gives too high a price for all sorts of curiositys that they deal in."[14] A visit by the chief of Papara, Purea, and a friendly reception on shore served to increase the quantity of goods exchanged, but the new price levels remained high. The dexterity of the crew in acquiring nails from stock also inflated the prostitution rates, which rose in value by about double.

Clearly, a commerce which threatened to draw the fastenings of every cleat on the ship and condemned men to "lie on the Deck for want of nails to hang their Hammocks" demanded regulation. After an inquiry, sanctions were enforced. Ship's brokers were appointed under the supervision of the gunner as "Market man."

Over the next thirty or forty years of European contact the range of goods expanded to include a greater variety of cotton, arms, and ironware. Tahitians overcame their initial dislike of spirits; and by the date of Vancouver's visit (1791–1792) several of the chiefs had an addiction to brandy.[15] But all the visitors were obliged to enforce elementary rules on their crews and on Tahitians, at least until their vessels were provisioned. Some, like Cook in 1769, noted that seasonal shortages affected the pattern of trade. After two months, the supply of coconuts and breadfruit dried up; hogs were few; and by the third month the market had almost ceased to function because the "season for bread fruit was wholly over and what other fruits they had were hardly sufficient for themselves, at least they did not care to part with them."[16] Prices increased still further, though William Wales in 1773 shrewdly guessed that withholding against such a rise might have accounted for some of the shortage, "as they knew it was Hogs we most wanted, it is probable they might keep them up, as we did our Axes to increase the price."[17] Any nail under 4½ inches "was of no Value" in the fruit trade; and, noted Cook, "we could not get a Hog above 10 or 12 pounds weight for any thing less than a Hatchet, not but what they set great Value upon spike Nails but as this was an article many in the ship were provided with the women soon found a much easier way of coming at them than by bringing provisions."[18] Despite this inflation, however, the market was orderly and managed by Joseph Banks.

Market procedures were similar at Tautira, where the Spanish seamen bartered during their second visit in 1774. Gift exchanges between chiefs and officers at one level prefaced a more mundane exchange from canoes and a certain amount of deception of the crew by Tahitians.[19]

By the date of Cook's second voyage, red feathers—mostly parakeet feathers—were added to the list of staples and functioned as currency. Trade also began to take on the appearance of a "sortings" exchange with a variety of items being included in the transaction. By 1777, for ritual reasons perhaps, red feathers were more prized than ever.[20] The chief of Pare-Arue, Pomare I, paid ten hogs for a Tongan headdress made from them; and the returning Raiatean, Omai, paid for a canoe purchased from a principal chief in feathers imported from Tonga. For a time, the European visitors used a medium of exchange which enabled them to transact the most profitable bargains since their discovery of the island.

They also made less obvious innovations which had important consequences. To offset periodic shortages, Cook, Bligh, and Vancouver, as well as the Spanish at Tautira, distributed seeds and livestock—citrus fruits, vines, root vegetables, maize, the papaya and the pineapple, goats, and hogs.[21] Of these imports the Spanish hogs flourished best. In 1777 Cook noted that they were "of a large kind, and have already improved the breed originally on the island."[22] The English navigator made his own contribution to this investment in resources, and Omai was given a boar and two sows.

We have no way of knowing whether Tahitians deliberately set about raising quantities of such livestock for sale to Europeans at this early date. (They were perfectly capable of enclosing sections of land for other productive purposes.) It seems more likely they allowed the new stock to interbreed and run wild, exercising restrictive controls over capture and slaughter for ritual, for consumption by chiefs, and for export. On the whole, pork was not consumed by commoners in Tahitian society.[23] There were abundant sources of protein on the shoreline and from deep-sea fishing;[24] and the hog would seem to have been reserved for gifts, trade, and religious ceremonial.

Whatever the reason, there are indications that the shortages of the early 1770s were made good by the 1790s, when Lieutenant Portlock reported:

> We got a good supply of hogs and every other article of food and much more reasonable than might be expected when we consider the Quantity that must have been taken off by the different ships, we got

a fair Hog weighing 150 Pounds for a sixpenny or an eightpenny hatchet; we get 10 or 12 heads of breadfruit for a Sheathing nail and as many Cocoanuts for a Sheathing nail also—this I think cheaper than we found it when here in the Resolution and Discovery.[25]

The news of this ready supply soon reached the struggling colony at Port Jackson when Vancouver dispatched his storeship *Daedalus* from Nootka, at the end of 1792, for a cargo of hogs landed at New South Wales early the following year.[26] The pork trade became for Tahiti what the sandalwood trade was about to become for Hawaii: a source of wealth and a potent catalyst for social and political change.

The two decades following the last of Cook's voyages saw a marked increase in the number and frequency of European visits to Matavai. In all, some twenty-three vessels called between 1788 and 1808. Six of these were government expeditions under naval captains who, like Lieutenant Hanson of the *Daedalus*, had more to do with commerce than with showing the flag. At least six vessels were British whalers which first arrived in 1792—the forerunners of a more important and more numerous traffic of whalemen in the 1820s. The rest were private merchantmen of various sorts: partnerships engaged in the Northwest Coast fur trade, company ventures from Macao, private ventures from Chile and Port Jackson. One vessel—the *Duff* in 1797—brought a novel cargo of missionary settlers to join the small number of deserters and shipwrecked seamen who found their way to Tahiti, adding to the Tahitians' experience of the earliest European community to live among them from 1789 to 1791—the *Bounty* mutineers.

As H. E. Maude's researches have shown, the growing dependency of the Matavai market on New South Wales was most marked in the years 1801 and 1802. Thereafter there was a lull (with only one cargo of pork collected for Port Jackson) before shipments again increased rapidly to four and five a year in 1807, 1808, and 1810.[27] In all, both Leeward and Windward groups would seem to have exported about 3 million pounds of salt pork to New South Wales over a period of twenty-five years (1801–1826). In return, the islanders were paid a variety of hardware, tools, haberdashery, clothing, arms, and ammunition.

The last items were not new (Cook had supplied Omai with a few pistols and muskets when he settled him at Huahine in 1777) and they may even have temporarily tipped the balance in local conflicts between chiefs of the Leeward Islands.[28] It is also certain that chiefs set a high value on small stocks of arms and ammunition and made careful inquiries about their manufacture and the preparation of gunpowder. Persons who could service firearms, whether Europeans, Hawaiian, or Tahitians who had been abroad, were particularly valued as auxiliaries. There is ample evidence of conflicts arising from the theft of firearms.

But a sense of scale is needed before the connection between the "arms traffic" and political changes in island society is pressed too far. It is an oversimplification of Tahitian history to ascribe the eventual paramountcy of one set of tribal chiefs to the favor of Europeans and the acquisition of stores and arms from the pork trade.[29] The arms traffic was quite small: the manifests of imported cargoes in 1801 and 1802, when the early pork trade with New South Wales flourished, list only six "Stand of Old arms," eight muskets, and four pistols.[30] Bligh in 1792 listed only twenty-seven muskets and twenty-one pistols for the whole of Tahiti, though undoubtedly there were others at Mo'orea and in the Leeward group, and more were to be acquired from traders and whalers who called from the end of the century.

The descriptions we have of Tahitian warfare at this period, however, do not suggest that firearms were a decisive factor; rather they were a continuous source of contention which was not immediately removed. When the district of Matavai fell out with neighboring districts in 1792 over the plunder of money and arms from the shipwrecked crew of the *Matilda*, ten or twelve days of skirmishing ensued, and some of Bligh's officers left firsthand accounts:

> They had rather a serious set to with Spears, stones thrown from a Sling (at which they are very expert) and Musketry (for each party have several Muskets) and continued pretty warmly for about half an hour or more. The Matavaians began then to give way and soon after one of their party being shot through the head with a Muskett Ball by one of the [Pare] people, gave way on all sides and took to their mountains next the Border of low land.[31]

Bligh put a stop to this minor war in which some of the *Matilda*'s men took part. The underlying causes of the conflict were not so easily settled.

Furthermore, it is sometimes assumed that chiefs, at this early period of trade, gained a monopoly over the market. Despite promises to Governor King of New South Wales, the most favored of Europeans' commercial and political allies, Pomare I, was not able to exercise a *rahui*, or interdiction on sales, to build up stocks of hogs in 1801;[32] and the following year his son limited a similar injunction to Mo'orea and failed to secure the export of hogs through his own agency at Matavai Bay.[33] The most experienced of the European traders in these years found the Matavai market temporarily exhausted and worked through his own brokers "all over the island," using his Matavai beach "factory" as a collecting point for shipment.[34] It was Turnbull, too, who witnessed the small amount of property accumulated by chiefs in the "Otaheitean treasury" at Matavai or on Mo'orea, where a high-ranking relative of the Pomares had no more than "five muskets, two pistols, three or four quart bottles of gun-powder, three or four pounds more folded up in some country cloth, ten gun-flints, a hammer, pincers, and a few nails of different sizes."[35] This was hardly enough to finance a new paramountcy, though it may have been enough in other cases to provide European auxiliaries with the means to advance a chief's fortunes.

This last aspect of the expanding market, European political brokerage, stemmed from commercial operations and from desertion. Of all the brokers Tahiti acquired in this way the most notorious were probably the sixteen mutineers and seamen of the *Bounty* who remained at Tahiti while Christian and the rest sailed for Pitcairn.[36] They were instrumental in assisting the tribal chiefs of Pare to assert their claims in the district of Pa'ea. One even became a "chief" himself in Taiarapu in 1790, before he was murdered by a fellow mutineer. But their stay was too short for lasting results, though the most talented of them left an account which rivals the best of the navigators' records.[37]

Lesser men such as James Connor, a seaman from the *Matilda*, integrated much more successfully into Tahitian society, where he carved out a career as a mercenary before his death on Borabora in 1804.[38] Similarly, Peter Haggerstein, a deserter from the *Daedalus*, married into the Tahitian nobility, acquired lands, and made an influential contribution to the status of his patron, Pomare I.[39] For a short period, Captain Bishop of the *Venus* and William House, master of the colonial brig *Norfolk*, made common cause with

Pomare II in 1802 in an inconclusive war, confirming the tendency of British naval officers and commercial visitors to side with a set of chiefs who might be held responsible for keeping order at Matavai and the northern anchorages.[40]

There were others (apart from the missionaries who were a special case); and they were brokers in a different way. Whole volumes were to be written on Polynesia as a source of new ideas in Europe. Much less is known about the impact of information received at Tahiti from Pacific islanders who had traveled abroad to England, Hawaii, New Zealand, and South America. Among the more intelligent of them was Hitihiti (Mahine), the Boraboran who accompanied Cook in 1773 to the South Pacific and Antarctica. Omai (Mai) of Huahine, who went to Europe with Furneaux, made, perhaps, a greater impact on London than on his homeland after his return in 1777. At least one of the four Tahitians taken to Lima in 1772 returned to enthrall his father with traveler's tales.[41] On the other hand, Reti, the chief of Hitia'a who impressed William Wales with his curiosity and his learning, clearly had limits to his understanding of the outside world and showed not the slightest interest in the fate of Aotourou, who had sailed with Bougainville.[42]

There is no way of knowing the changes to Tahitian concepts of their own place in the natural order, following the revelation of much wider horizons than their own cosmology contained. Possibly they fixed their attention on the immediate advantages, rather than speculation, though some European reactions must have given them pause for thought. Pomare I appears to have been eager to learn of the outside world and pressed Rodriguez for military information and a present of a suit of armor. But once the conversation turned to Tahitian sorcery, which Rodriguez "laughed . . . to scorn," mutual comprehension ended.[43] Most accounts of foreign lands and the ways of foreigners were received with amazement or frank disbelief.[44]

The missionaries fared little better in 1797, mainly because of the obvious difficulty posed by language. Once they began to overcome this obstacle, however, they made very poor progress in convincing Tahitians to accept a totally different set of ethical and cosmological beliefs. Even secular contemporaries, such as the trader John Turnbull, met with the same incredulity and resistance when closely questioned by Pomare II in 1803:

He asked me, upon the departure of the missionaries, whether it was all true they had preached. I replied in the affirmative; that it was strictly so according to my own belief, and that of all the wiser and better part of my countrymen. He demanded of me where Jehova lived; I pointed to the heavens. He said he did not believe it. His brother was, if possible, still worse. [Itia] was looking on, with a kind of haughty and disdainful indifference. It was all *[ha'avare]* or falsehood, and adding, they would not believe unless they could see; and observed, we could bring down the sun and the moon by means of our quadrant, why could we not bring down our Saviour by a similar operation?[45]

There was also in this intellectual exchange a good deal of Tahitian parochialism for an island which they declared to be "the finest part of the whole inhabitable globe" on the grounds that Europeans visited it so frequently.[46]

This view of their own environment, Turnbull saw, would be undermined not so much by the assertions of Europeans, or by the declaration that a European deity had universal significance, but by the experience of islanders abroad, especially at Hawaii, Sydney, Norfolk Island—places with small populations and, in the case of the northern Polynesian group, with a culture similar to their own.

We do not know what impact on Tahiti was made by seamen's accounts of Hawaii. Possibly the first Hawaiian to pass through Matavai Bay was "Toweraroo," who was returning on the *Discovery* to his own islands in 1792. Dressed in a scarlet coat and claiming to be a chief of Molokai, he attracted sufficient attention for Tahitians to persuade him to desert in order to repair firearms.[47] Pomare I returned him to Vancover with some reluctance. But other Hawaiians deserted from the *Nautilus* in 1798. By 1803, at least one Tahitian chief had been to Hawaii and returned to give a full account of Kamehameha's rise to power in 1795. At the same date the Hawaiian wife of the second mate of the *Margaret*, Turnbull's ship, arrived to set a new fashion in local styles of dress.[48]

From these few indications it whould seem that the commerce in ideas at Matavai was much less important, before about 1810, than commerce in provisions. Tahitians had undoubtedly gained an understanding of shipboard hierarchies—reminiscent of their own ranked society. They had heard much of European kings, especially King George; and they had learned of a Polynesian "king" who was experimenting with original and imported techniques of government.

But, in general, it would be safe to conclude that visitors to Matavai were valued for whatever could be assimilated into Tahitian culture, not for what might change it. Nails made good fishhooks. Firearms were feared and coveted. Europeans could sometimes be used to assist in local wars.

It is doubtful, moreover, whether Tahitians had been so completely won over to wearing European dress (as Bligh's reports suggested). The logs and journals of Bligh's officers do not depict Tahitians as "Ragamuffins"; and Tobin's drawings, which are accurate in other respects, do not show them wearing "Old Cloaths" either.[49] Turnbull, who came to Matavai seven years later, found Tahitians neatly dressed:

> Their drapery was composed chiefly of two pieces of cloth of the country fabric, one wrapped round the body, and another thrown gracefully over the shoulders, and descending to the middle of the leg. . . . The colours and quality of their dresses were various, probably to suit the taste of the wearers. . . . Their whole appearance was clean and comfortable.[50]

As with much else that was imported, articles of clothing enjoyed a brief and spectacular popularity before the wearers returned to their more traditional *maro* loincloth and the *tiputa*, or loose shirt. But for other artifacts demand was insatiable in a culture lacking in metals. Chisels were made into adzes; scissors and knives were eagerly adopted; muskets were prized. Sources of foodstuffs had probably not been diminished and may well have been increased as a result of the expanded market for produce.

On the debit side, Tahitians had also imported disease, which had begun to make serious inroads into the population of the group by the end of the eighteenth century. Both the Spaniards and Vancouver left minor epidemics behind them.[51] And coupled with this demographic change came religious and political wars of unprecedented violence.

TERRITORIAL POLITICS

The principal theme of Tahiti's political history from the earliest decades of European contact till well into the nineteenth century is the consolidation of titular and effective authority by the represen-

tatives of a family of chiefs from Pare-Arue districts. The sources
for this story are partly oral tradition and mainly contemporary
accounts.[52] But however the evidence is interpreted (and it is open
to various conclusions) there would seem to be nothing inevitable
about the survival and political advancement of the Pomare lineage (1767–1815). Their fortunes were discontinuous; and at times
they seem to have depended more on the weakness and disunity of
political rivals and on the assistance of internal and external allies
than on their own abilities as administrators or warriors. A rough
graph of their position as secular rulers would show, perhaps, a
fairly high peak shortly after 1767, when powerful rivals were in
decline and titles were accumulated by Tu (Pomare I). The presence of Cook assisted this process till about 1782, when the pretensions of the Pare-Arue paramountcy were deflated by a combination of rival tribes. Then, with the birth of Pomare II and the
acquisition of new titles and some military assistance from Europeans and Leeward Islanders, the family again asserted its social
and secular preeminence, reaching a high point in about 1792. Serious internal rivalries within the family and a growing resentment
of claims to tribute, services, and human sacrifices led to a decline
which military defeat turned into exile on Mo'orea by 1810. Thereafter a growing alliance with the missionaries who had shared the
political setbacks of the Pomares from 1797 brought about a restoration of titles and a new secular and religious status for Pomare
II which was consolidated from 1815.

Within this bare outline there are richer lineaments of ceremonial and the stark confusions of war. Tahiti by the latter half of the
eighteenth century, like the Leeward Islands and Mo'orea, contained a highly stratified society in which the place of the *ari'i*
nobility approximated that of a caste. The ritual validation of status before the gods and people at family, district, and tribal *marae*
was frequent and essential as a concomitant of political leadership.
No European accounts failed to mention religious practices so
deeply interwoven into the management of secular affairs. Later
missionaries found it impossible to make such a distinction, even
when the efficacy of traditional religious beliefs had been called in
question. Consequently, a prominent place was given to cult practices in the power politics of tribal society.

It was appropriate, therefore, that so much of Tahiti's political
history was recorded against the background of the establishment

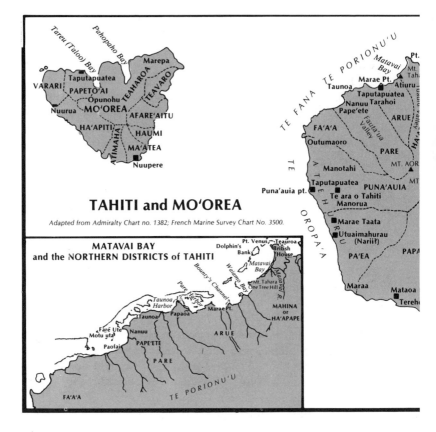

of the war god 'Oro. Like much else in the genealogies of the *ari'i* and their ceremonial regalia, the god derived from cult practices on Ra'iatea which were introduced in the first half of the eighteenth century to the western districts of Tahiti. He also took root in Borabora. With him came the powerful *'arioi* society (though its origins are not necessarily contemporaneous)—a sexually permissive corporation of entertainers and aristocrats organized into lodges under the patronage of the deity. With him there came, too, a limited amount of unique sacred regalia centered on the *maro ura* and the *maro tea* feathered girdles which a few representatives of the highest-ranking families in the Leeward and Windward groups had a right to wear in titled positions on tribal and national *marae* devoted to 'Oro. Among these were the Pomares.

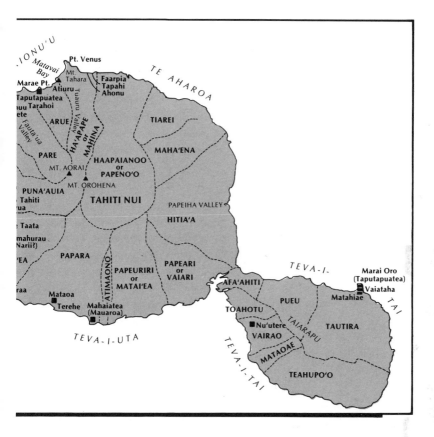

The Pomares, like other senior tribal chiefs in Tahiti, then, appear on the stage of recorded history both as secular leaders of a particular community—the Porionu'u of northwestern Tahiti—and as members of a much wider religious and aristocratic stratum with kin and ritual connections in other social and religious centers. The chance of European association with Matavai, on the border of their tribal domains, does not detract from this dual status as local "managers" and islandwide "paramounts," though one position was not without influence on the other.

At the outset, therefore, it is important to remember that the European tendency to ascribe rank in terms of territoriality—thus making Pare-Arue into a kind of "capital" district and the Porionu'u, a principal tribe—though it eventually came to be accepted as a working compromise in Tahitian politics by 1815, was not the only way of conceptualizing political advancement by the *ari'i*. Indeed, it is probable that it was not the most important way before notions of kingship became current on Tahiti toward the end of the eighteenth century.

Conversely, European association does not account for the Pomares' social or political position at the beginning of regular contact in the 1760s. The Spanish visitors, who might have been expected to have a totally different view of Tahitian politics because of their connections with the chiefs of Tautira, were left in no doubt about the current position of Tu Vaira'atoa (Pomare I).[53] He was the "Chief of principal rank," though not necessarily of unchallenged authority, in the island. Boenechea lost no time in touring the coast to meet this personage—"the *arii* Otu . . . a young man of twenty or twenty-two years, taller than ordinary in stature, well proportioned, swarthy in hue, and having an aquiline nose and black eyes."[54] He left Pomare in no doubt, too, that he was considered to hold sway over the other *ari'i* as a "dominion"—probably the first eurocentric notion to be introduced into the limited exchange of political ideas, and one which gave rise to "a long confabulation" among members of the Pomare family present.

And well it might. For the confusion between territorial authority, or control over tribal segments of the group's population, and *ari'i* privileges exercised in other tribal areas by reason of the chief's status was to last well into the nineteenth century.

Such privileges were not empty trappings of office. The demands for feast offerings and services levied on the tribes on whose lands the national *marae* were located were considerable.[55] Because of the geographical mobility of Tahitian nobility (and probably lesser ranks) in the Leeward and Windward groups, there must have been a constant appraisal of the limits to which ceremonial hospitality could be pushed and frequent tension generated by inadvertent slights to dignity or deliberate insults by overpressed junior chiefs and family headmen. The exercise of selective sacrificial by high-ranking chiefs added an extra dimension of uncertainty and resentment to the relationship between the *ari'i* and commoners.

Tahitian history, both in its recorded oral form and in European-derived versions, contains numerous examples of chiefs being humbled in their secular pretensions in the name of rival political alliances. In 1768 the paramount chiefs of the Teva-i-uta tribe, Amo and Purea, were crushed for attempting to advance their son's status by imposing a general *rahui* for his benefit and by building an enormous *marae* at Mahaiatea in Papara. This decline had the effect of enhancing Pomare's claims to ceremonial precedence, skillfully managed for him by his great-uncle, Tutaha. Indeed, by about 1773, after the death of other titled chiefs, Pomare "was universally acknowledged to be higher in rank-status than all other persons of Tahiti and Moʻorea."[56] But this did not entail unqualified acceptance of claims to services in all districts of Tahiti and Moʻorea, where there were tribes superior in strength to the Porionuʻu, though without perhaps such titled claimants or such good social and ritual connections with Raʻiatean aristocracy. Claims still had to be backed by force, and military force required coalition. The "succession war" at Moʻorea in 1774 which involved the Pomares did not immediately advance their secular claims very much in the neighboring island, but it did serve as a political bridgehead for later recognition of rank status there.

The presence of Cook probably assisted this minor development, though it did not protect Pomare's own district from a combined attack by the Atehuru and Faʻaʻa in 1782, as a way of cutting down the advantages that had accrued to a high-ranking but not very distinguished secular "manager" of tribal affairs. Shortly after that demise, Pomare I began, in Tahitian fashion, to transfer titles to his son—a lengthy process not completed before about 1791. During that period, the family's secular fortunes received some further assistance from Europeans which needs to be specified because it can be exaggerated.

Firstly, the *Bounty* mutineers may have staved off a possible attack on a convoy from Moʻorea carrying tribute to Pomare II in March 1790. In addition (and more certainly) they served as armorers in the continuation of the Moʻorean war which helped to advance the young Pomare's uncle, Mahau, though it is to be noted that Hitihiti, who had learned his business with Cook, made an important contribution to tactics and strategy in this campaign.

Secondly, in September 1790 a few mutineers joined in the expedition led by Ariʻipaea Vahine (sister of Pomare I) against Faʻaʻa in order to protect their schooner. A second action against Atehuru with assistance from Papara district enabled the Pomares to secure possession of important ceremonial regalia for their own *marae* at Tarahoi, where Wallis's pennant was added to the symbols surrounding the high office of the young *ari'i*, Pomare II.

Finally, the return of Bligh and the visit of Vancouver added to the prestige of the Pomare family and resulted in a certain amount of historical evidence that connections with Ra'iatea materially assisted the *ari'i* of Porionu'u, both through the 'Oro cult and through the presence of the important Ra'iatean chief and priest, Ha'amanemane.[57]

This support from the Leeward Islands for the Pomares at difficult periods of their history is well attested but not always easy to explain. Basically, it would appear to stem from the marriage of Tetupaia, daughter of Tamatoa III of Ra'iatea, with Teu, father of Pomare I (see Table 1). There were frequent *'arioi* tours (though this corporation was widely supported in both the Windward and the Leeward Islands); priests of the 'Oro cult renewed the ceremonial common to *marae* ceremonials throughout both groups; prominent *ari'i* such as Ari'ipaea Vahine, possibly Vehiatua of Taiarapu, and the Leeward chiefs exchanged residence and contracted alliances.

At first sight, however, the political history of the Leeward Islands (or the fragments we have from the late eighteenth century) illustrates the considerable difference between status claims and the secular performance of high-ranking chiefs. From the mid-eighteenth century there are examples of hegemony exercised by titleholders of Opoa on Ra'iatea over other *ari'i* on the island; of territorial unification of Huahine by a dynasty which controlled important marine resources at Ma'eva; and, finally, a complete disjunction between social rank and political power when the warrior chiefs of Borabora conquered Ra'iatea and Huahine. For a period in the 1770s, Puni of Borabora ruled Ra'iatea through deputies. After Puni's death in about 1786, another young warrior, Tapoa, rose to the leadership of the Fa'anui districts on Borabora and gave assistance to the Pomares, along with the Tamatoas who had regained a measure of their old secular authority by the end of the century.[58]

More important, the Pomares formed a family compact with a number of principal Leeward Islands *ari'i*—the Mai of Huahine, Tamatoas of Ra'iatea, and the Tapoas of Fa'anui on Borabora—

TABLE 1

The Pomare Lineage in the Hau Feti'i Main Descent Lines

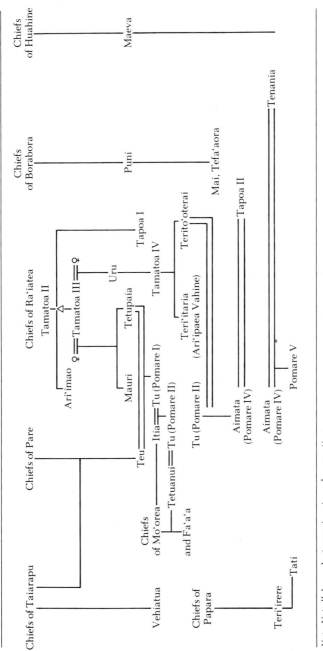

Note: Not all descendants are given in each generation.

Sources: Oliver (1974: figs. 25-1, 25-9); Newbury (1967b: app. III).

loosely termed the *hau feti'i* (family government), which lasted for two or three generations into the nineteenth century.[59] Already in 1792 this compact was sufficiently well established for Pomare II to be groomed for titles in both groups of islands by Ha'amane-mane (also called Mauri), who was styled by Vancouver's surgeon as paramount chief of Ra'iatea:

> So that his Territory is likely to fall soon by descent under the Government of the Otaheitean Family whose present extensive political views will no doubt also join two other islands by the Marriage of the Otaheitean King with the two Queens of Bolabola & Eimeo [Mo'orea] so that this young prince is likely in a short time to have the entire controul of the whole group of Islands, & indeed his father & the rest of the Chiefs frequently told us that his titles are greater than any King that ever reigned in Otaheite. He is stiled the *Earee rahie no maro oora* a title to which they seem to annex the same idea of greatness as we do to that of an Emperor's, by this it would seem that his elevation to the Government of the whole group of Islands is already considered as inevitable.[60]

And this, indeed, may well have represented the general political strategy and political ambition of the family, as seen in European terms. The boast of wider dominion was flattered by the attentions of visiting naval officers. Presents were given, salutes were fired, and every mark of respect was shown to the young Pomare, a lad of eleven or twelve years with "a fine open manly countenance."[61] According to another observer, there were only ten months to go before the final investiture, "when all the Chiefs and great people were to assemble at the Court at Oparre,"[62] though there were rumors that opposition was to be expected.

Much of the opposition to this program of titular consolidation in the following decade stemmed less from dynastic rivals than from those who opposed claims to lands and produce in other tribal districts. The language of local politics—which was complicated by the settlement of the missionaries from 1767—is full of suggestions of "kingship" and "rebellion," annexations, and schisms. The descriptions may not be entirely inaccurate. But opposition to the Pomares' ambitions, translated into "territorial" terms appropriate to eighteenth-century statecraft in Europe, requires qualification.

There are numerous early descriptions of territorial and political units on Tahiti, none of them entirely satisfactory, because of their assumption that titular overrule implied some kind of "possession" of the resource zones worked and exploited by the "subjects" of a chief. But beneath the tendency to introduce the language of feudalism there are certain constants which remained important till later in the nineteenth century. Firstly, Tahitians and Leeward Islanders retained the tribal nomenclature of the eighteenth century, even where there were demographic and boundary changes. But from the 1760s till the Tahitian-French war of 1842–1845, when tribal contingents still fought in units under their ancient names, there were six major tribes for Tahiti: Te Porionu'u, Te Aharoa, Teva-i-tai, Teva-i-uta, Te Oropa'a (or Atehuru), and Fa'a'a (Te Fana), plus one, or possibly two, in Mo'orea. These divisions were also preserved in the constitution of the Tahitian Assembly of the mid-nineteenth century.

The social and political structure of lesser units is far from clear. But, in general, kinship within extended families determined coresidence patterns in the scattered hamlets and houses around the shores and in the valleys of the two island groups. Territorial corporations of such families acknowledging a senior chief and possessing a common *marae*, assembly ground, and defensible boundaries made up some twenty to thirty "districts," or *mata'eina'a*, of varying size. These, too, with considerable changes in their demography and with some territorial amalgamations, survived in the nomenclature of administration in the nineteenth century. The early missionaries and other sources also employ a number of other "territorial" terms, sometimes denoting areas of cultivation, or sometimes work units and "divisions" under headmen and junior chiefs (such as *fenua, patu, pupu*). At least one missionary used the term *mata'eina'a* as a cognate for major tribal divisions;[63] and Captain Wilson of the *Duff* used it to refer to extended households. But for intermediary social units—that is, the followers of a chief, or chiefs, within a district—the term "company" (Douglas Oliver's "kin-congregations") may be appropriate. This would seem to be the sense of Teuira Henry's juxtaposition of the term *va'a* (literally a canoe) with *mata'eina'a*.[64] Later in the period of French administration, after a series of changes begun by the missionaries, the territorial unit, rather than the social unit under ranked chiefs, became the focus of local government.

But at the end of the eighteenth century, although boundaries were important, the district company, or companies, as groups of kin with retainers and servants, were the primary units exploiting land and maritime resources under the leadership of household heads ('iato'ai) and senior chiefs with titles at the district *marae*. Within these units coproprietors with rights in land were termed *ra'atira*, which distinguished them (in European eyes) from the "commonality," or *manahune*. It is hard to believe that the latter group was entirely excluded from property rights, though more or less constant warfare in the islands may well have given rise to dispossessed segments of society whose descendants had only marginal claims and who became part of proprietor households before reestablishing rights of their own. Demographic decline of the population as a whole later permitted many of this lower order to attain *ra'atira* status; and one could argue that a principal change brought about by the upheavals of the period 1792–1815 was a general leveling of social groups in terms of access to land and coproprietorship. Our sources of information are mainly from the missionaries, who were in some cases anxious to see a class of Tahitian "peasantry" develop to counterbalance the autocracy of chiefs. Where William Ellis in his *Researches* stresses class divisions in "ancient" Tahitian society, Ellis the missionary in the early 1820s (like Williams and Threlkeld) championed the cultivators of small holdings in the Leeward Islands.[65]

Consequently, some caution is needed in interpreting the evidence on land tenure for this period of rapid political and religious change. But one may agree with the missionary Hayward that there was no general "ownership" of territorial divisions by an *ari'i* and, moreover, that bilateral inheritance was already an important feature of proprietorship:

> The land is not common property. Certain plots belong to the King, Chiefs, Ratiras & natives generally which they consider exclusively as their own. There is scarcely an individual but has a claim to a piece of land in the district to which he belongs, & now there is scarcely a Bread fruit or Cocoa nut tree but has its proper owner. The Natives also have all their proper homes. If natives of two islands *marry*, they retain their respective property in each, and their children inherit it.[66]

Clearly, a subject as complex as land tenure was less simple than the missionaries imagined; but they had ample time to witness the general resistance to the attempts of the Pomares to extend their estates in the critical period when their titles were acquired in most of the major tribal *marae*. They came to notice, too, that the notion of "tribal lands" was extensive in denotation, including as resource zones those areas of shoreline and reef, at one extreme, and the upper mountain valleys, at the other, where district companies exercised rights.[67] They would probably have agreed with the perceptive William Wales who, as early as 1773, had noticed that produce, rather than soil or sea, was the guide to values set on particular zones: "and it appeared to me that the property of the Land was rather determined by the Trees which were planted on it than that of the Trees by the Land whereon they were planted, as in England."[68]

Chiefs of companies and tribal divisions had access to such produce of valley, littoral, and reef in two ways: either by inheriting family estates within their own *feti'i* or by receiving tribute from the coproprietors who worked the resource zones. Such entitlement was generally confirmed by the headship of the exploiting groups in the form of a chiefly title associated with company and tribal *marae*. There is some evidence that particular company and tribal lands were also associated, for the chief's benefit, with the *marae*, and that these lands could be delegated to subordinate chiefs and retained within the office of paramount chief. Such *fari'i hau* ("reception" lands) were to cause a good deal of trouble in the nineteenth century as the controlling rights of chiefs over land diminished.[69] But the main purpose of such *marae* lands (and the reason why their exploitation became controversial in the period of French rule) was to provide a source of tribute for ceremonial occasions.

Tribute, as an aristocratic lien by men of rank and the gods on the produce of lesser men, was well established as a form of deference, a placatory offering, and a mechanism for redistributing goods. In the case of the Pomares and other high-ranking chiefs tribute was a form of economic privilege for leadership before the gods, particularly 'Oro, resorted to with increasing frequency after 1792. First fruits, consecration offerings, *arioi* collections, and the highly political *tava'u* presentations at intertribal meetings to a paramount chief were assertions of an *ari'i*'s command of resources, as well as an essential accompaniment to religious rites, peacemaking, and economic exchanges.

It is possible, moreover, to interpret the tribute levies as an extension of a titleholder's political position, in resource terms, into other tribal zones. From this point of view much of the acquisition of titles to which Tahitian politics were devoted makes material sense, although it was not necessarily accompanied by extensions of "ownership" in terms of area. This hypothesis becomes clearer if the political position of the Pomares is examined at the period when most of their creative energy was absorbed in maneuvers over titles.

These maneuvers were complicated by the development of external trade at Matavai Bay and by the settlement of missionaries there in 1797. Neither of these two events, however, implied that the Pomares' fortunes were to be inevitably enhanced by new sources of wealth or by new allies; and the main chance (in Tahitian terms) was still considered to lie in the traditional acquisition of rights to *marae* lands, tribute, and other services by marriage, by ceremonial precedence under 'Oro, by alliances with other chiefs in Tahiti and the Leeward group, and, if necessary, by war.

The consecration of Pomare II as *ari'i rahi* would not appear to have been completed by the time the missionaries arrived, despite the assurances given to Vancouver and his men. While the titular position of Pomare I and his son was sound enough, the continuation of open commercial exchanges with visiting vessels at Matavai—the *Providence* in 1795, the *Betsy* in 1800, and the more numerous passages for pork made by ships from New South Wales in 1801–1802—widened the market to include a larger number of chiefs and *ra'atira*.[70] By 1804, the missionaries noted that muskets and other goods made their way directly into the hands of the "commonality" and that Pomare II had not succeeded in establishing a monopoly, despite his close association with foreign traders and government agents.[71]

The missionaries who had come in such large numbers, moreover, were a source of trouble and embarrassment. Eighteen men and five wives, all with rigid views on correct behavior, and all frightened by their isolation and their dependence on the chiefs of Matavai, were generously "given" a portion of the peninsula to settle on. They soon came to understand that this donation was not in perpetuity; but they also set about interfering with the arms traffic and the practices of infanticide and human sacrifice; and they tried to retrieve deserters for visiting captains.

At this point, in 1798, their interference would appear to have widened a breach between Pomare I and his son. The schism postponed the hope of a missionary–*ari'i* alliance; and eleven of the mission sailed with their wives to Port Jackson, leaving the remainder in a state of armed siege at the "Old British House" at Matavai. There they were well placed to observe a buildup of tribal tension when Pomare I transferred the headship of the district to a younger son and not to Pomare II, who went into alliance with Temari'i, chief of Papara, and with the ancient but sagacious Ha'amanemane. They attacked the Matavai companies near Point Venus in a short campaign which was fairly typical of the next thirteen years of warfare:

> Two men and a child only were found and these were instantly killed and conveyed next day by Haamanemane to the great Marae at Pare to be offered as the fruits of victory to Oro. The pigs and what little property were found became the prey of the victors, and the houses of the people were committed to the flames. Having expelled the people, Tu declared Pomare's power at an end, and his own absolute power was recognised by the people of Papara and Te Oropaa, who had accompanied the funeral procession [of Temari'i]. The district of Point Venus he divided with Haamanemane, and to secure his concurrence, gave him the eastern portion extending from the river to the valley of Ahonu.[72]

When 'Itia, Pomare's mother, objected to this division, Ha'amanemane rashly spoke too loudly against her; and with Pomare I's approval she had him murdered.

The Pomare family regained its political cohesion fairly quickly. Pomare I, as primary associate with Europeans, relinquished his secular authority to his son. Further missionary reinforcements arrived in 1801 on the *Royal Admiral*, but they remained in the position of observers, rather than active participants, in the power struggle evolving around the possession of the god 'Oro.[73]

That struggle would seem to have had as its main objectives access to the tribal *marae*, where 'Oro was ceremonially necessary to validate assumption of tribal titles, and, secondly, continued provision of tribute and human sacrifices as acknowledgment that Pomare II was *ari'i rahi* in substance as well as in name. The main stages, therefore, displayed a mixture of warfare to enforce or resist claims and more less continuous ceremonial which resulted in further demands on tribes hostile to Porionu'u and the Pomares. The Leeward Islands were included in this strategy of aggrandizement. Arms were sent to Ra'iatea in 1800, when Tamatoa was engaged in a war of his own, because Pomare II "felt that the fall of the present dynasty in that island would seriously affect his own position in Tahiti."[74]

Whatever their external alliances, the Pomares did not have things their own way. Consequently, there is a historical interplay, in the decade from 1800, of tribal raids and tribal consecration, hostility to the Pomares' claims, and exaltation of those claims. Politics in the Windward group have a curious chessboard quality in which the tribal *marae* and the arms market at Matavai were among the key squares, and priests, warriors, and occasionally Europeans made their moves to further or counter the ambitions of the principal pieces. Or as Douglas Oliver has expressed this mobility in other terms: "Locational centralization had not yet become the dominant strategy for aggrandizement; the ambitious individual extended his authority and influence not solely by increasing the sanctions behind specific statuses, or by eliminating rival statuses, but also by occupying *more statuses—including especially those having territorial bases elsewhere.*"[75]

Thus both the Leeward and Windward groups were drawn into the maneuvers of the Pomare *feti'i,* and Mo'orea and Ra'iatea became as important to the *ari'i rahi* as Pare or Pa'ea. For in 1802 the *pure ari'i,* or royal consecration ceremonial, was continued at Atehuru in the tribal *marae* and then at Tautira in Taiarapu. Resistance to this progress from the Oropa'a tribe of Pa'ea led to an attack on Pare and the allied tribal district of Fa'a'a (then under Pomare's brother) and to a combined operation against Pomare's forces by Oropa'a and Teva-i-uta in Tautira, where an important chief from Ra'iatea, Mateha, was killed. None of this skirmishing was conclusive, however, and the image of 'Oro was restored to Pa'ea *marae* after Pomare had made a savage counterattack on the Atehuru districts. At the same time there was an assertion of temporal control over family claims in Mo'orea by an expedition under Pomare's ally, Taute, chief of Maha'ena in the Te Aharoa districts. In July 1802, with the help of Captains Bishop and House and a party of nineteen seamen, a defeat was inflicted on the Oropa'a at Pa'ea, but an assault on their *pa,* or fort, several miles up the Orofera Valley, failed. 'Oro remained at the Pa'ea *marae* of 'Utu'aimahurau, and consecration ceremonies continued throughout much of 1803.

There had also been a significant extension of claims to status and access to the deity in terms of rights over land, if one report is to be believed. The trader Turnbull recorded that following the routing of the Oropa'a in July 1802, "Pomarre immediately dispossessed the principal chiefs of their lands, and divided them among his own friends. Edeah had a great part of these forfeited domains; and Innamotooa [Vahine Metua] the widow of Oripiah [Ari'ipaea] also experienced the royal munificence."[76]

Moreover, in May 1804, Pomare extended his operations to Mo'orea, taking 'Oro with him for a long visit of nineteen months. There, at *marae* Taputapuatea in Papetoai and *marae* Nu'urua in Varari district, he consolidated his lands and titles and installed as his representative the infant daughter of his mother 'Itea by her consort, Tenania of Huahine, with the title of Teri'ia'etua.

Some of this confident ambition may be attributed to the death of Pomare I in September 1803, which removed a more cautious political talent from the scene. The death of his brother Teari'inavahoroa, who had titles for Taiarapu, Papeno'o, and Fa'a'a, also left Pomare II and his mother free to reallocate lands in those important tribal districts.[77] When 'Oro was returned with great pomp to Tautira in January 1806, the royal progress moved into the final stages of the elevation of the *ari'i:*

> For some months thereafter, there took place an almost uninterrupted series of ceremonies which had the purpose of validating Pomare II's status of "King" of Tahiti—including the parallel supremacy of 'Oro, the god whose principal "seat" *(nohora'a)*—the *to'o*—was once again in Pomare II's physical possession. Before the *to'o* was transported to Tautira (in a canoe paddled mainly by Hawaiians left on the island by visiting ships) it was kept in Pomare II's own marae, Hetemahana, near Point Venus. At this new depository were enacted a "marae renewal" ceremony as well as the awesome *paiatua*, the refurbishing of 'Oro's image, and of other images with feathers from it—all accompanied by lavish expenditure of human offerings.[78]

The Pomare titles, according to the missionary historians, now included the tribal titles of Fa'a'a, Oropa'a, Taiarapu (Teva-i-tai),

Mo'orea, and, of course, Porionu'u. They do not appear to have included Teva-i-uta or Te Aharoa, though the latter set of companies was certainly allied with Porionu'u for much of this consecration period.[79] And the list of offerings and human sacrifices presented at the *pure ari'i* meetings, or at the *tava'u* in September 1806, included those from all tribal divisions. For the first time, too, the claim to allocate estates which had become part of the prerogatives of the *ari'i rahi* was extended to the deity (or exercised in his name) when a 20-mile strip of Taiarapu was deemed to be apportioned to 'Oro.

This emphasis on land allocation which Pomare II had engaged in at various times since his bid for power with Ha'amanemane in 1798 came to the fore again after a spectacular and treacherous attack by Pomare's forces on Oropa'a in May 1807, followed by the spoliation of the Teva tribes and the slaughter of several prominent chiefs. In October there was a division of conquered lands at a meeting at Pare, when even the missionaries were given a portion of the Oropa'a estates at Outumaoro.

From this pinnacle of titular and temporal authority, attained with a ruthlessness that stunned and exasperated Tahitians, Pomare declined rapidly the following year in 1808. The immediate cause lay in Matavai, the district most exposed to European contact, and formally a company of Te Aharoa tribe under the headship of the chief of Hitia'a, Taute. The defiance of the chiefs and *ra'atira* was made official in December, when

> a message was sent by the people of Teaharoa to the king importing that they reject the name of Poreonu, as including all the districts that extend from Faa to the isthmus; that Teaharoa shall be no longer considered as one with the districts of Pare &c; in short they refuse all subjection to Pomare's government, and declared themselves his enemies, so that war seems now to be inevitable.[80]

Ceremonial at the *marae* of the Pomares near Pape'ete did not help. On 21 December Pomare's war party was defeated by the Oropa'a. The bulk of the missionaries embarked first for Huahine and eventually for New South Wales. The Porionu'u districts were overrun and (as a symbol of rejection perhaps) a picture of King George given to Pomare was offered to 'Oro. More serious, the schooner *Venus* from Port Jackson was seized at Matavai, the mate killed, and the crew held prisoner. They were released, along with the vessel, when Captain Campbell accompanied Pomare on the *Hibernia* from Mo'orea in October 1809. But Pomare's party suffered a second major defeat at Maha'ena and retreated to Mo'orea following a truce in 1810.

✳ ✳ ✳ ✳ ✳

In his summary of the factors leading to the rise of the Pomares, Douglas Oliver has singled out for special emphasis the family's monopoly of trade, arms, and European assistance at Matavai, the extension of rank status through acquisition of tribal titles, and the validation of this status by the 'Oro cult.[81] For reasons discussed above, the first of these circumstances was less important than sometimes supposed; and certainly by the period 1800–1810 it is doubtful whether any chief had charge of the open market with Europeans. Much of the history of this market in pork and other produce indicates, on the contrary, that collection of staples and their export was in the hands of visiting trading captains and their agents, who were often Europeans. As yet, the politics of Tahiti were firmly rooted in traditional patterns of aggrandizement, though some of the techniques of European firepower were utilized by all sides and, indeed, may have helped change the tactics of Tahitian warfare from naval engagements to guerrilla-type raids. One may agree, however, with the general results of these methods. Calls on livestock, produce, and manpower for the endless ceremonies went beyond the tolerance of rival tribal leaders and, even in the companies of Pomare's own districts, beyond the willingness of *ra'atira* to oblige. A second innovation—seizure and redistribution of lands by Pomare II—was not unknown in Leeward Islands wars; whether it was entirely new at Tahiti or not, it provoked further resentment. Similarly, Pomare's cohorts of Hawaiians, *'arioi*, European deserters, and others were feared for their exactions. But they were also important for the creation of allies and offices under the *ari'i*; and they were expanded by contingents of freebooters and high-ranking kin from Mo'orea and the Leewards.

It is not difficult, therefore, to account for the opposition to the *ari'i rahi*. The leadership of this opposition is less obvious. Later writers tended to cite Opuhara, chief of Papara, as the guiding genius among opponents to the Pomares, but his policy is not readily apparent from contemporary records until after 1810. The problem was, perhaps, that most tribal chiefs and many of the ra'atira shared the premises on which the Pomares' rise to paramountcy was based, however much they resented the logic of their actions and opposed it in war. The missionaries soon perceived (for they had a vested interest in this area of social organization) that the Tahitian religious system was utilized by rivals in secular authority—or that "the present national religion is so blended with the civil concerns, or the privileges and authority of the chiefs, that they have no conception the one can stand without the other."[82] To a certain extent, therefore, territorial politics were caught up in a series of frenetic rituals which could only result in the elimination of the main antagonists.

This elimination had been accomplished by natural causes, as much as by warfare, from the turn of the century. At the most conservative estimate the population of Tahiti, Mo'orea, and the outliers had declined from about thirty-five thousand at the time of Wallis and Cook to something like nine or ten thousand for the two principal islands by 1800.[83] The Leeward group, possibly less exposed to imported diseases, numbered about five thousand in population by the same period of political crisis. Looking back later, after further changes in government and cult practices, the survivors among the chiefs inherited a diminished aristocracy and a demographically weakened society:

I observed [recorded a missionary] that the numerous old morais, far inland, up the valleys, and on the skirts of the mountains, were proofs that the inhabitants had formerly been very numerous. [Tati] said it was an undoubted proof: all the low lands were formerly fully inhabited, and in a good state of cultivation; but now the *fau [Hibiscus tiliaceus]* and other bushes and trees cover the land, and the remnant of the people inhabit merely the sea-side. This led him to mention a prophecy, or rather a threatening of the prophets, in former times. When there appeared a backwardness in the people to observe the injunctions of the gods, the prophet used to cry out, *"E tupu te fau, e toro te farero, e 'ore te ta'ata."* "The *fau* shall grow and overspread the land, and the branching coral the deep, but the race of man shall be extinct."[84]

That phrase will serve as an epitaph for eighteenth-century Tahiti. The market at Matavai opened the way for a devastating, if inadvertent, importation which afflicted, in varying degrees, much of the eastern Pacific. But the impact was not entirely fatal; nor was the initiative entirely taken from the hands of the *ta'ata fenua.*

CHAPTER 2

THE EVANGELICAL IMPACT

To the missionaries who left Huahine and Tahiti for Port Jackson on the *Hibernia* in October 1809 the conversion of Polynesia must have seemed a thankless and near hopeless task. They had failed and suffered losses in Tonga; they had been rejected in the Marquesas; and now their most serious effort in Tahiti had collapsed, as they thought, because of "the dissolution of Pomarre's government, and the total overthrow of his authority."[1]

There were also other reasons for their retreat to New South Wales. They lacked supplies and had been without information from the Missionary Society for six years. They lacked wives in conditions which tested the discipline of the most dedicated men. With difficulty two had been restrained from marrying Tahitians in 1797, but two others were "cut off" by their brethren for this and other evidence of impiety. Yet others—William Shelley, the Reverend James Elder, the Reverend John Youl, and Henry Bicknell—left to go into trade, to become settlers, or, eventually, to return to Tahiti once they had "changed their condition" by suitable marriages.[2]

Had they known it, help was already on the way in 1810, when Bicknell and his wife sailed from England for the colony with four "pious young women" whom the directors had thoughtfully recruited and sent out. They were snapped up by the brethren who reached New South Wales, in February 1810, and by James Hayward and Henry Nott, who braved the crisis but followed later.

Bicknell also brought with him reinforcement of a different kind and evidence that the pioneering years had not been entirely in vain—some hundreds of spelling books in Tahitian, first printed in

London.[3] For evangelists who believed that the path to a Calvinist-Methodist version of salvation lay through literacy and the "civilized arts," the printed word in a heathen vernacular was a step of the first importance. It led directly to the catechism and the Scriptures and, it was hoped, to an education in elementary industrial and commercial skills. Many of the missionaries themselves had experienced this combination of conversion and technical training in their own early careers. Some had been barely literate; and even the more educated among them had to master a wide variety of apprenticeships in agriculture, animal husbandry, carpentry, simple medicine, and midwifery. Like settlers in other parts of the Pacific, the Tahitian missionaries were jacks-of-all-trades; and, like colonists in Australia or New Zealand, many of them had an eye for opportunities to acquire land and develop produce markets.[4]

Literacy and mechanical competence, then, featured prominently among the "means for the conversion" labored at by the experienced band who ruminated on their position with the Reverend Samuel Marsden, chaplain to the colony and agent to the Tahitian mission on behalf of the society since 1805. They had even taught Pomare to read and write before they left, all the better to berate him and his island for not casting off its evil customs; and, to bring their point home, they argued: "Had Tahiti obeyed the word of the true God, Tahiti would not have rebelled, it would not have done evil to you its King."[5]

This was a political argument that may have carried some weight with Pomare in his years of trouble, though there is no sign in 1810 that he was ready to accept the remedy the missionaries proposed. In any case, the brethren in New South Wales were still bitter at their neglect by the society and only half-persuaded to reconsider their position by the arrival of Bicknell, spelling books, and spouses. Their main worry lay in the difficulty of backing up their work with supplies of clothing, foodstuffs, and other materials. From their experience the beginnings of literacy and preaching tours were not enough.

Marsden urged them to return.[6] Five of the missionaries—Henry, Scott, Wilson, Bicknell, and Davies—agreed to do so on conditions. These conditions were assured communications between Tahiti and Sydney to be arranged with the shipowners and merchants who were again investing in the successful pork trade and following the example of William Shelley, who had finished off a small schooner at Tahiti in 1807 and was soon to venture into the pearl and pearl shell trade. Marsden thought he had already shown that there were profits to be made and that the mission could be backed up by commerce; or as the directors phrased his advice more discreetly:

> Mr. Marsden is of opinion that the Otaheitan mission may be renewed with a probability of ultimate success, if a vessel of 150 or 200 tons were sent out from England with a suitable investment for Port Jackson and the islands of the South Seas; and which, by trading among them, and procuring their produce, would soon cover the whole expence of the equipment, and provide for the support of the mission, while it would secure the means of intercourse with the missionaries. The greater part of the missionaries now at Port Jackson have signified, by letters to the Directors, their readiness to resume the mission, if this plan can be adopted by the Society or by individuals, and a suitable opportunity should be presented by the restoration of tranquillity at Otaheite.[7]

For the directors this was a persuasive scheme. Whatever their failings to make good the problems of keeping a large body of men in the Pacific in times of uncertain shipping, the board of the society had spent a good deal already on the three expeditions sent out between 1797 and 1801. By 1812, in the sixteen years of its existence, the South Seas mission absorbed some £38,590—no less than 47 percent of total expenditure by the society on its missions in Africa, India, and other parts of the world.[8] Moreover, the average cost of the Pacific missionaries was about to rise from about £230 a year in 1813 to no less than £700 by 1815, mainly because of increased transport costs and the price of imported goods in New South Wales.

The missionaries themselves had ventured into trade from time to time, salting a few hogs and sending them for sale to the colony through Marsden or the ex-missionary Rowland Hassall.[9] But the board did not like it. Marriage brokerage and printing books were one thing; commercial speculation was something else, and Marsden's advice on this point was not followed. The initiative was to come from New South Wales, not London, when commerce combined with literacy to provide the "means of grace" for the final and most successful of the society's missionary investments in Tahiti.

REVELATION AND REVOLUTION

Between 1811 and 1813 some eight missionaries and their families ventured back to the Windward group to settle at Papeto'ai on Mo'orea. Most of them, like Nott, Davies, and Bicknell, were fairly accomplished in the language; and the first two had made astonishing progress, even before they left, in translating Old and New Testament histories, hymns, and simple catechisms. Davies had produced the spelling book, already in print, which began to set the principles of Tahitian orthography. Nott began his translation of the Gospel of St. Luke, printed at Mo'orea in 1818.

By then they had been reinforced by a further nine missionaries. Their total strength, concentrated on Mo'orea, was reckoned at no less than fifteen missionaries, including those on passage, in 1815.[10] If one takes into account that the average number of missionaries per station throughout the regions of the society's work was only two, Mo'orea must have been the most intensively evangelized community in the world; and per head of population, Tahitians, numbering only about nine thousand, were offered a ratio of teachers and preachers far exceeding many a London parish.

The "mass conversions" of 1815, then, are hardly surprising. Davies was able to take up where he left off by opening a school once more in September 1812 and collecting together some of the younger men and the servants of the missionaries as "Scholars." By June 1813 it was possible to gather together a congregation of some two hundred on Mo'orea; and a few of Davies' former pupils on both islands had begun to hold prayer meetings of their own. The missionaries most engaged in teaching and touring began to distinguish between the "learners" *(ha'api'i parau)* and the "prayers-to-God" *(Pure-Atua)* whose degree of open commitment had gone beyond tentative inquiry and exposed them to a certain amount of persecution. By July 1813 English and Tahitian services were held in an enlarged chapel at Papeto'ai, and the practice of writing down the names of those "making a profession" was adopted.[11]

From then on one detects an important change in the social composition of the "learners." By April 1814, the young men and boys in Davies' school were replaced by over eighty adults; and by the end of the year this number had grown to about two hundred. Many of these were chiefs and persons of some consequence for the future political history of the Leeward and Windward groups.

They included Utami of Taha'a, Teamo, chief of Matavai, Tama'ehu, a chief of Pare, Tamatoa, chief of Ra'iatea, and his brother Tahitoe, Paofai, chief of Tiarei, and his brother Hitoti, and a number of others who came up from Huahine and Borabora to assist Pomare. Pomare's second spouse, Teremoemoe, was numbered among the *Pure-Atua* in December 1814; and her sister, Pomare Vahine, who had arrived from the Leeward Islands, took a passing interest in the school.

But there were no baptisms; and the prime candidate for conversion, Pomare II, who had made his own personal application for this distinction as early as 1812, was not considered ready either morally or spiritually. For political reasons, therefore, until the senior *ari'i* allied to the mission cause had been reformed, the rest of the learners and prayers had to wait.

Yet Pomare's intellectual understanding of European and missionary habits of thought must have made considerable headway during these years of defeated hopes. His letters in the vernacular and in translation yield a good deal of information about his aims and his perception of his political situation. Taught to read and write by Jefferson and Davies in 1803 and 1804, he probably assisted with the compilation of the first missionary vocabulary which engaged Davies and Nott at that period.[12] By 1811 he was keeping a journal and may have done so "for a considerable time past," before the return of the missionaries.[13] Already at the beginning of the crisis he had written to the Missionary Society in terms which formulated a bargain: the banishment of 'Oro to Ra'iatea in return for cloth, muskets, and powder and "every thing necessary for writing—paper, ink, and pens, in abundance," English settlers, English customs, and instruction.[14]

It would be easy to dismiss this kind of overture as mere opportunism; and perhaps the full implications of "instruction" from such single-minded teachers were not appreciated. But there is also a certain war-weariness with the futility of ritual sacrifices, raid and counterraid, and a search for the answer to the predicament of Tahitian politics—namely, how to exercise power in a hierarchical and tribal society without continually alienating status rivals at one level and suppliers of produce and manpower at another. By 1810, Pomare had dropped some of the stilted phrasing and was writing in a fluent and idiomatic vernacular from Mo'orea to the absent brethren with local news about missionary property, his Leeward allies, Tahitian drunkenness, and a pearl trader's clash with Tuamotuans at Kaukura, ending with kindest regards to missionary children.[15] It is hard to discern the purblind devotee of 'Oro or the late scourge of the Oropa'a in any of this. By 1812 he could pen official and diplomatic letters to the missionaries which the directors felt were full of "the language of penitence and holy desires."[16] True, there was much in them concerning Jehovah, Christ, and the "Three-One," as well as an evident wish to be accepted as a Christian. William Henry, therefore, saw in him "one of the greatest miracles of grace ever exhibited on the stage of this world."[17] Henry's colleagues, who were closer to the realities of Pomare's drinking bouts and his homosexual entourage of male domestics, however, wrote other appraisals and recorded numerous "heartburnings" at his public and private conduct.[18] In the meantime, the sacrament of baptism was withheld. Hopes centered on Pomare encountered a facility of self-expression in matters spiritual and an unwillingness to conform in temporal behavior that misled the earnest readers of the society's *Reports* and gave rise to a good deal of disillusionment in later years. Pomare could not be molded into a perfect Polynesian Constantine.

But in one respect at least there was no deception. The earlier skepticism about the efficacy of 'Oro, already noted by Turnbull in 1802, had spread throughout Tahitian society to a greater or lesser degree by 1815.[19] In the face of death by disease, Tepa the god of healing proved ineffectual and was broken up in circumstances which suggest that fatalities of European origin were considered to be without remedy.[20] Some of the *marae* were already falling into disrepair. At others, ceremonies for 'Oro lacked the regalia and girdles once considered indispensable; and they lacked the presence of the *ari'i* Pomare from 1810. Missionary terminology gained currency; by 1813 there were those who termed all tutelar deities as "Satani," though they were not specifically rejected on that account.[21] Pomare's marriage to Teremoemoe in 1811 was politically important but dispensed with the ritual that normally accompanied such events. In March 1815, at a public *tava'u*, there was carefully staged rejection of traditional etiquette, and a blessing on the feast was given in the name of the new Atua. Visiting Leewards chiefs were urged to reconsider their own practices; and Davies is probably right in claiming that even on Tahiti, where traditionalists formed the core of Pomare's opponents, "the circumstances of the Island at that time had greatly damaged the system."[22] On Mo'orea, the same system was dealt a blow in February 1815 when the 'arioi priest of Papeto'ai, Pati'i, destroyed his gods.

But none of this new revelation entirely explains the restoration of Pomare's political paramountcy in 1815. It is likely that he perceived sufficient advantage in adopting the "god of Britain" and looked for real spiritual assistance from the missionaries in the van of the growing religious revolution. He even began to make his own list of "prayers-to-God" on Mo'orea, much in the manner of a politician collecting supporters in a safe constituency. But it should be remembered that the ari'i was far from being in exile from Tahiti. At various periods in 1811 he returned to Pare; and he was on Tahiti by invitation of the Porionu'u chiefs consistently between July 1812 and August 1814. Almost immediately afterward he inadvertently spent three months in the Leeward Islands, for the first time as far as is known, and made the most of the occasion by cementing the hau feti'i alliance and pledging his daughter in marriage with her cousin Tapoa of Huahine.[23] In May 1815 Pomare Vahine, his influential sister-in-law and daughter of Tamatoa, felt Tahiti safe enough to begin a tour there. In July she was obliged to withdraw in some haste to Mo'orea, under threat of attack by a combined force from Papara and the Porionu'u. Yet, in September, Pomare accepted invitations to return to settle refugees on their lands. He would appear to have taken a considerable expedition to Matavai and then marched round to Pa'ea in November. There his force was attacked by a coalition led by Papara and emerged victorious.

The Christian "conversion" of Tahiti in 1815, then, has tended to be interpreted in military terms. Indeed, the battle of Fei pi, as it came to be known, is rich in interpretations and short on facts. We cannot even be sure of the date—given as 12 November in missionary sources, a Sunday in December in Moerenhout, and May 1815 at one place in sources derived from Marau.[24] Remembering that the missionaries were one day in advance in their Tahitian calendar, Sunday 11 November would appear to be correct; the location was on the shore in the vicinity of marae Utu'aimahurau (or Nari'i) in Pa'ea.

None of the missionaries was present at this stirring event. The first post facto account is in their public letters and the version left by Davies in a letter of March 1816:

> In the beginning of November [1815] peace was apparently restored between the contending parties; and Pomare returned to Taheite to reinstate the fugitives in their different lands. He was accompanied not only by them, but by almost all the men who had renounced heathenism. At first, all things appeared to go on well; but suddenly hostilities recommenced, and the idolaters attempted, by a desperate effort, to support their tottering cause, their prophet assuring them of success. They came upon the King and his people on the Sabbath day, Nov. 12 *[sic]* at the time of morning prayer, expecting that, being so engaged, they would easily be thrown in to confusion. This we had anticipated as a probable occurrence, and had therefore warned our people against it; in consequence of which, they carried their arms with them wherever they went. Notwithstanding which, however, the sudden approach, and immediate attack of the Atahuruans and others threw them into considerable confusion, and some gave way; but they soon rallied again, as the Raiateans and the people of Eimeo had kept their ground. Several fell on both sides; but on the side of the idolaters, Upufara [Opuhara]a principal chief was killed. This event, as soon as it was known, turned the scale, and Pomare's party obtained a complete victory. But he treated the vanquished with great lenity and moderation, which had the happiest effect; for all exclaimed that the new religion must needs be good, because it produced such good effects; they declared also, that their gods were cruel and false and had deceived them, and sought their ruin; and therefore they were resolved to trust them no longer.
>
> On the evening of that day, when the confusion of the battle was over, the king and his people, with many of the idolaters, united in one large assembly, to worship the God of heaven and of earth, and to return him thanks for the events of the day.
>
> After this, Pomare, by universal consent, was re-established in his government of the whole of Taheite, and its dependencies, which he had lost by the general rebellion in November 1808.
>
> Since this affair, Pomare has continued at Taheite, making arrangements respecting the several districts—overthrowing all the vestiges of idolatry—destroying the gods, morais, &c. &c.—the chiefs now zealously assisting in their destruction.[25]

The oddest thing about this famous episode is that the missionaries took so long to report it, though Nott and Hayward were called over to Tahiti by Pomare in February 1816 and returned after a month's preaching to the new converts. It was Pomare himself who announced to the missionaries that the *ra'atira* of the island were being persuaded to build chapels and would become Christians, sending at the same time a collection of his family gods as an earnest of good faith.[26] By then Nott and Hayward had brought over the authorized version which was added to in detail in a public letter late the following year and copiously filled out in terms of a religious war by Ellis from his informant, Auna, in the 1820s.[27] Nowhere are we informed of the size of the host or the casualties—except for the most famous, Opuhara. Pomare, it would appear, did some fairly safe enfilading from seaward along with a few musketeers and a mysterious European from Ra'iatea named "Joe."

Moerenhout's account, while placing Opuhara at the center of events, is substantially the same as that of Ellis and interprets the battle in parallel terms of religious opposition between Christian and pagan.[28] Much later, Teva historians, who used a certain amount of oral tradition from within their own lineage, stressed the death of Tahitian "tradition" embodied in Opuhara, defender of the honor of the race, against the "usurper" Pomare, backed by the missionaries and other Europeans reputedly present at the battle itself.[29] It is possible to account for the vehemence of this version in terms of later Tahitian history, but not to accept some of its assertions which have no substantiation elsewhere.

One is left with the impression that the battle of *Fei pi*, which Ellis claimed to be "the most fateful day that had yet occurred in the history of Tahiti," has been much conflated by developments after 1815—the *annus mirabilis* of the "Tahitian kingdom." The missionaries did not rush in to consolidate this "victory," apart from a brief reconnaissance by two of their number. Indeed, it took them two or three years to move back permanently to the main island. There were reasons for this delay, connected with their shipbuilding enterprise. But in 1816 it is also probable that they interpreted Pomare's armed clash and restoration of authority in much the same way as they looked on the war between Taha'a under Fenuapeho and Ra'iatea under Tamatoa in the Leeward group, where "there were some old grounds of disagreement between the chiefs, yet religion was now made the handle on both sides."[30] For there, too, temporal control was asserted by the chiefs of Ra'iatea, Borabora, and Huahine in the name of the new faith once the news of events at Tahiti was received; and, as at Tahiti, the defeated Fenuapeho was treated leniently and his followers spared. But for the present the experienced missionaries on Mo'orea were content to await reinforcements before deciding how to turn these events to their advantage.

There are two other commentaries on the period: one by James Hayward, who was close to the changes he described, and the other by the Reverend James Elder, who had fallen out with the brethren but took a considered view of the reasons for their success.

Hayward reported in person to the directors in 1819 and was interviewed at length. Contrary to other interpretations of Pomare's elevated status in the "kingdom," he perceived that the *ari'i* had, in fact, lost his "despotic authority over the persons and property of the natives."[31] The sanctions available in the former religious system had disappeared; tribute of food and cloth was paid on a voluntary basis; and demands for services were less peremptory than in the past. Inevitably much of this change was ascribed to the influence of Christianity. But apart from causes, Hayward also noted that past aggrandizement by the *ari'i* in terms of land-controlling rights under tribal titles had been curtailed and probably rejected by the history of recent events. Pomare could give away no land but his own "without the consent of the parties to whom it belongs, and to whom he must apply for it, as a favour. . . . The political circumstances of the Chiefs & Ratiras have in no respect been affected by the introduction of Christianity. They are all profoundly attached to it. The disaffection (as well as that of the common people) which they formerly used to manifest against the King is manifested no longer."[32]

In other words, Pomare had not simply taken up where he left off in 1808. There had been a real shift of power away from the *ari'i rahi*, who had been tolerated back in Porionu'u from 1811, to the tribal chiefs and district companies that had survived the disease and continued intertribal wars.

This change in the relationship between *ari'i* and commoners was termed a "Revolution" by James Elder, who commented thoughtfully, in 1824, on the broader aspects of Pomare's return to "sovereignty":

> The accounts I have seen published respecting the change that has taken place at Otaheite, by the Missionaries & by the Deputation

ascribe the Change entirely to the preaching of the Gospel, they take no Notice of the Revolution that took place at the time Pomare was down from Otahite, to Emeo and the most of the Missionaries to Port Jackson about 1808. Yet to the Revolution is to be ascribed the greater part of the change that has ocurred. It is even doubtful if the new order of things might not have been wholly accomplished by the Revolution had the Gospel never been preached at all, nor never so much as made known to the Natives. But I am willing to believe there are some real Converts among them. . . . The Revolution was equally the finger of God, as if it had been wholly brought about by the preaching of the Gospel. The conversations of the Missionaries on Civil Government hastened the Revolution, and was the cause of their forming the present Government in existence at the Society Islands. They had often killed one Tyrant & got another in his room, with the continuance of Idolatry; and the bad & barbarous Customs, under which they had groaned for ages. When the free and equitable Government of England was made known to them, they quickly perceived all its advantages, and panted for one as nearly as possible to resemble it. The Chiefs were well aware of the Tendency of our Conversations, & address, to produce rebellion, and they would not have suffered us to remain among them, but that they considered, by the continuance of the Missionaries & Ships touching at the Island, from which they obtained firearms, & other property, they would keep down rebellion, and eventually compl[et]ely humble the discontented. On the other hand, the Chiefs thought if the Missionaries went away, Ships would not visit the Island, that they would get no more firearms, that War would be unavoidable & its consequences uncertain. Hence the Missionaries were safe from fear [and] evil. If the Revolution had not occurred, or the King been converted, no convert among the natives would have been tolerated.[33]

Having lost his paramountcy, continued Elder, Pomare was willing to be received back on terms:

The Otaheiteans had no objections to receive him back, if he would consent to the new order of things. Pomare & his mother were not deficient in the Methods of address, in conducting negotiations. The time was gone by for Pomare to command the Otaheiteans, he was now obseq[ui]ously willing on any conditions to obtain the favor of being "King" although with limited Power.[34]

And so, concluded Elder, tribute payments were consented to by family heads; infanticide and sacrifice were abolished; *tapu* avoid-

ances broke down; and the old gods, priests, and sorcery were rejected.

There is more than a grain of truth in this view that the "restoration" was the result of a political as well as religious compromise
on Tahiti. It fits the picture of the island in 1816 and the immediate first impressions of Davies and Hayward, who toured each district toward the end of the year.[35] The extension of Christian ritual
by the *Pure-Atua* was undeniable: no fewer than sixty-six "places of
worship" were visited by the missionaries, though Davies was careful to note a variety of responses within the outward conformity to
Pomare's orders for regular prayer meetings. Signs of recent devas-
tation were everywhere. At the old residence at Matavai, the
orange trees, lemons, and limes still flourished, but breadfruit trees
were dead, the land was overgrown, and the people were "thinly
scattered." Pomare, in residence there, was still paid tribute by the
district *ra'atira.*

But one of the abiding problems of Tahitian society was evident-
ly exercising the minds of the new converts. Many of the more interesting references in 1816 and 1817 to daily events in the missionary journals centered on the secular, as well as religious topics
raised at "Questioning Meetings" (as Ellis called them) on Mo'orea
or after sermons preached on Tahiti. Occasionally land tenure was
mentioned, as for example at Afare'aitu in November 1817:

A Ratira from Atahuru in Otaheite, complained of himself, that evil
dispositions were arising in his mind, on account of the conduct of
some strangers and neighbours. On being questioned by Brother
Davies what they had done, it appeared that the man had been in-
jured by their trespassing in an unwarrantable manner on his fishing-
ground. It is to be observed, that though the open ocean is free for all
that desire to fish, yet within the reefs every place is claimed as the
property of the adjacent coast. The Ratiras and land-owners, as well
as each sub-division of a district, have their respective fishing-ground;
and in former times, when strangers caught fish, they uniformly sent
some to the owners of the fishing-grounds; but this had been omitted
lately in several instances, the people pretending that since the old
religion and customs were abolished, therefore the customs relating
to the boundaries of land, fishing-grounds &c. were also done away.
Brother Davies spoke in strong terms against such pretensions, showing that the reception of the word of God had abolished nothing that

was good, just, and equitable; that it abolishes what is evil, and that alone, and if private property was respected formerly, it ought to be more so now.[36]

Clearly this injunction did not exhaust the subject. More "Questionings" took place in December 1817 on boundary marks. Davies cautiously referred the problem back to the ra‘atira to settle among themselves—or, failing this, to take it to Pomare. These insights into an area of delicate compromise and ready source of conflict suggest that land disputes were more widespread than the occasional examples cited and may have been exacerbated by the conflicts of tribal authority that marked the end of the eighteenth century. This interpretation would agree with Hayward's evidence in 1819 that coproprietors were eager to exercise exclusive rights to breadfruit, coconuts, and plantains following a time of troubles (though they attributed this to imitation of "the Law of Britain").[37] It agrees, too, with the somewhat piqued observation of William Ellis at Mo‘orea in 1817 that a strong sense of property values was present in exchanges: "They are a nation of *individuals*; and with the exception of the homage they pay to the King, and some other like expressions of respect to the great men of the district, they *act* as individuals, quite independent of each other. If, indeed, an application be made to the Chiefs, on any particular occasion, to unite in some project; such, for instance, as to put a place for public worship, a school house, or a dwelling house, the chiefs, as well as the people, will join together to do it; but in every thing else, each acts according to his own interest or inclination."[38]

One of the consequences of a developing (and perhaps usual) readiness to assert localized rights, as opposed to tribal claims, had already been displayed in the resistance to Pomare's pretensions—termed a "Revolution" by Elder. It was continued after 1815 into the 1820s in opposition to what William Crook called "the unjust ravages of the chiefs" (a phrase that is an echo of earlier missionary observations on social conflict in the period before 1815).

The natural consequences, however [continued Crook], are numerous litigations and disputes amongst the various claimants of the land. The one says "my father or grandfather was unjustly disinherited by the King, because he opposed his encroachments, or because he neglected some idolatrous right." The other replies "The land was given by the King to my father or grandfather, who had an acknowledged right to dispose of it at that time, and our family have had quiet possession of it ever since." We have taught them the nature of arbitration and have prevailed on some of our church members to settle their matters in that way, but the cases are so numerous that it will take a long time to settle them.[39]

In other words it is possible to trace a constant theme of difficulties over land rights which the accumulation of titles by Pomare had probably exacerbated by excessive claims to tribute and which wars and depopulation confused, leaving ways open to surviving *ra'atira* and the marginal *manahune* to consolidate new claims of their own to resource areas. The uncertainty surrounding tribal and family claims was not the least legacy of the period 1810–1815, when wars had continued between the Porionu'u, the Oropa'a, and the Teva of the peninsula. Quite possibly the missionaries were correct in their assertion that the purpose of Pomare's expedition in November 1815 was to settle such claims and arbitrate between contestants. Opposition to any such role by a former *ari'i rahi*, in whatever guise he may have come as neutral peacemaker at Pare or in Pa'ea on the border with Papara, is also understandable on the part of other *ari'i*.

But for the refugees in the valleys and mountains who had had enough of intertribal raids and who descended to the shoreline to construct their houses and make good their claims by occupation, the message of the *Pure-Atua* with its emphasis on peace and a new order and Pomare's stroke of statesmanship in not abusing his advantage after the battle of *Fei pi* must have been welcome. Pomare had no difficulty in persuading the *ra'atira* to join in the abolition of the outward symbols of a religious system that had not kept war and disease at bay and had outlived its usefulness. Perhaps the new *Atua* and his spokesmen could do better.

Pomare's conversion and political restoration, then, filled a need within Tahitian society for a new reference point, a source of leadership, and for a religious and political broker between Europeans and Tahitians. It was owing to his acumen (and perhaps that of his mother) that he correctly judged the situation in the districts in 1815; and it was from his close association with Europeans that he was able to offer guidance in a religious and political transformation of the old order. The military conflict with the old guard at Pa'ea was part of the risk taken to appeal to the chiefs and *ra'atira*, both as potential converts to a new deity and as proprietors with a stake in family land rights which were increasingly confused among victors and vanquished. But the battle itself did not usher in a "Christian era." That had already begun in Mo'orea among the "learners" and inquirers prior to 1815—and, indeed, with Pomare himself in terms which leave no doubt that his view of the new religion was, in the words of the missionary Charles Wilson, "clear and consistent; but we cannot expect him to overcome at once all of his prejudices."[40]

NEW INSTITUTIONS

During the last six years of Pomare's paramountcy important decisions were taken on the structure of island churches and island administration. The two were difficult to separate in theory and in practice. The missionary's rank was high in the hierarchy of chiefs and *ra'atira*, both as recipient of goods and services and as adviser for a multitude of minor technical innovations and social adjustments. For a time missionaries were the arbiters of "correct behavior," a source of enlightenment and printed books, the framers of rules. Above all, they determined the composition of church congregations by testing and admitting church members; and they set the standards of schooling for the new generation of Windward and Leeward Islanders who grew into the orderly and relatively peaceful society of the 1820s.

Some were more impressed than others by the destruction of the *marae* and the gods. One of the oldest of the missionaries, Henry Bicknell, who lived just long enough to see the fruits of two decades of hardship, was inspired to versify:

> Instead of plays and necromance
> Idolatry and ignorance
> Tis God they seek they read his word
> They sing his praise and serve the Lord . . .
> Instead of rioting and drunkenness
> Adultery and wantonness
> The change is great . . .
> The areoe society
> Changed for the missionary. . . .[41]

Tu-nui-ae-i-te-atua. Pomare II (ca. 1819). Engraving by
Hicks from an original drawing by William Ellis (1831).

But in practice this theme of substitution which filled pages of
official missionary publications ran into difficulties from the
moment of Pomare's triumph. Such a body as the "missionary
society" hardly existed locally. Never easily molded into a single
corporation and distant from their directors, the brethren who received Pomare's good news at Mo'orea were further divided by the
arrival of reinforcements. Much "arguing and disputing" ensued
over the location of the printing press which came with William
Ellis in February 1817; and Pomare's desire to see this source of instruction set up at Tahiti was disappointed.[42] For the time being it
remained on Mo'orea. The main body of newcomers—some six in

all with their families—added to the debate on strategy without satisfying the need for some elementary committee or council to make decisions. By early 1818 several missionaries took it upon themselves to move to Pape'ete and Matavai. The nearest approach to a concerted view of future policy was the agreement reached at the first annual May Meeting in that year to form new stations in the Leeward and Windward groups. In June, John Williams, John Orsmond, and Ellis moved with the Mission Press to Huahine and pioneered the churches on Borabora and Ra'iatea.

This diffusion of effort ran counter in many ways to Pomare's emphasis on the centralization of authority from his home district among the Porionu'u at Papaoa, halfway between Matavai and Pape'ete. The older *ari'i* practice of building on titles at tribal *marae* would appear to have changed in favor of recognition or appointment of trusted tribal chiefs and experiments with pantribal assemblies and offices. Largely at Pomare's initiative an Auxiliary Society was formed at the May Meeting on Mo'orea in 1818 for the purpose of collecting subscriptions of cotton, coconut oil, arrowroot, and hogs to be donated to the parent society in London.[43] Under the rules printed by Ellis for Te Societi Tahiti, tribal and district chiefs were listed as "patrons" and "governors" under Pomare; and for the rest of his career as "principal patron" or "president" *(peretetini)*, he supervised the Mo'orean and Tahitian branches, which acted as local cooperatives whose functions as subscribers for the cause of the Gospel were soon confused with Pomare's commercial ventures in produce exports. With the assistance of their missionaries the Leeward Islands chiefs formed produce cooperatives of their own.

Behind this direction of annual tribute there lay, too, a scheme for the codification of moral and administrative precepts which Pomare had discussed with some of the missionaries as early as October 1818. He was less anxious than they were to submit such a scheme to "public consultation" by chiefs and commoners; but he announced to the directors his intention of having a code of laws proclaimed at Papaoa, where "the Laws will be established, and a consultation will take place. The faulty parts will be corrected, and when it is very correct the people will return to their houses."[44] Framed mainly by Nott, translated by Pomare, and printed for distribution on the Mission Press, the *Ture no Tahiti* were accepted clause by clause at an assembly of chiefs and people at the royal chapel in Pare in May 1819. Consisting of nineteen sections, the whole code embodied the first written definition in Polynesia of penalties for theft, desertion, adultery, murder, bigamy, rebellion, and sedition. Fines, roadwork, cloth-making, and restitution of property covered most infractions. The death penalty was reserved for murder (including infanticide); and threats to the stability of the new paramountcy were defined exhaustively under "trouble-making." Several hundred 'iato'ai (household heads) and minor chiefs were listed and appointed judges to hear witnesses and apply the laws in thirty district courthouses.[45]

It is doubtful whether this early version of the code was ever enforced in detail, though much was made of it by supporters and detractors of the Missionary Society. In their confidential (as opposed to their public) report on Tahiti, the deputation of Daniel Tyerman and George Bennet, sent out from London in 1821, thought it a "dead letter."[46] The machinery of justice constructed from the heads of extended households may well have been too cumbersome to operate. Senior titled chiefs and Pomare himself had the main responsibility in the adjudication of the few cases recorded between 1819 and 1821. Two leaders of a small revolt were hanged in October 1819; two Tuamotuans and a man from Huahine were punished for sedition in October 1820; and in a more serious case in 1821 suspects were rounded up by Pomare's armed guard, and two were hanged and the others fined or set to work on the roads around Pape'ete.[47]

But an example had been given. Expanded versions of the code were proclaimed by Tamatoa for Ra'iatea, Borabora, and Maupiti in 1820 and for Huahine and Mai'ao by the chiefs Mai and Tefa'aora in 1822. As in the case of the Auxiliary Society, Pomare fashioned an institutional innovation as a support for his own authority; and the institution was diffused among autonomous churches and governments not under his immediate control.

Thus it is difficult to accept the term "missionary kingdom" without qualification until after 1821, the year of Pomare's death. Missionary individualism and close association with Tahitian and Leeward Islands chiefs ran counter to the formal centralization of authority, under the hau feti'i, pursued by Pomare. Nowhere was this clearer than in the spread of district churches and their patronage by allies, subordinates, and some rivals of the Pomare family. There were, too, constant causes of tension between many of the missionaries and Pomare arising from his personal conduct, his resentment of missionary participation in island trade, and his failure to set up a commercial monopoly.

Consequently, the "king's" royal baptism was delayed as long as the missionaries dared. Many refused to accept him as a serious candidate. But Henry Bicknell was broadminded enough to administer the sacrament at the royal chapel at Papaoa in May 1819.[48] Immediately afterward, other baptisms were performed at Papeto'ai and Matavai among candidates who had been more carefully instructed and selected for church membership.

Pomare, as far as we know, never took any of the other sacraments, though he attended public church services. His pride in his patronage of the mission was symbolized not by involvement in its rites but by the construction of his chapel—by far the largest building in the islands, some 700 feet long. Formed in the style of a *fare pota'a* with rounded ends and dedicated like the *marae* to a deity, it held an assembly of thousands and marked the apogee of the *ari'i*'s religious and secular career.

Compared with this grandiose structure most of the first district chapels, or *fare pure*, were neat and unpretentious buildings of plank and plaster. Not all district families were admitted as easily as Pomare into full church membership. In 1821 Davies, who settled in Papara, reviewed his selection procedure:

> The congregation at Papara is the largest in the islands, except the one I left at Huahine. The Church members are 44, and the baptised whom I have not accepted up till now as "testators" 284; but I intend accepting many of them soon as members of their Church. Apart from these, I have about 240 whom I call "candidates for Baptism" who are under discipline before they are baptised. . . . I have been here about five months and baptised 27 adults and 30 children.[49]

Cooperation with the chiefs of tribal divisions was an important condition for acquiring land and constructing a mission house and church. There seems to have been, too, some political strategy in the location of Davies in Papara, where Tati had been recognized by Pomare as head of his old enemies, the Teva. Similarly, Utami, formerly chief of Taha'a and an early convert, was set over

Puna'auia, central to the old tribal area of Atehuru, with the missionaries Darling and Bourne in charge. Hitoti and Paofai were delegated to rule over the Aharoa tribal division, and the latter was made secretary to the Auxiliary Society. In the peninsula, Veve, who was a relative of Pomare (and to Davies merely "a political Christian"), took the ancient title of Vehiatua and also came under Davies' guidance until William Crook moved to Taiarapu in 1823. Papeto'ai and Afare'aitu in Mo'orea were fairly closely administered with the assistance of Arahu, chief of Varari, who took the title of Ta'aroari'i. These districts were also the scene of missionary agriculture, shipbuilding, and the location of the Academy, a school for mission children run by Orsmond and later by Henry.

At the center of government, Henry Nott and William Crook settled near Pomare to give advice. Even there, royal authority was sometimes delegated to the chief of Porionu'u, Paiti (or Manaonao), an old servant of Pomare I and later president of the Auxiliary Society with the title of Ari'ipaea. In September 1820, after the birth of a son, Pomare handed him over to the Crook family for education and took a keen interest in the missionary school. In return, Crook came to depend on the royal largesse for supplies and acted as commercial broker in the precarious arrangements made with Pomare for part ownership of the vessel *Haweis*, the supply of sugar to George Bicknell's mill on Mo'orea, and the supply of medicines to the royal household.[50]

In all districts, therefore, the brethren were closely associated with *ari'i* and the heads of district companies for their daily subsistence and their material security. With some exaggeration the irascible Orsmond later summed up the long interdependence of missionaries and their patrons: "The greater the chief, the more he is feared, the more work is done. If he be good, the more the Missionary seem to prosper; if bad, the harder his times are. The Mission has ever been . . . the nursling of the Chiefs and Kings."[51]

But, in practice, there were limits to this incorporation of secular and religious leadership which were reached fairly soon in the sphere of commercial operations and agricultural development. Pomare had taken the closest interest in the 72-ton brig which the missionaries had under construction at Mo'orea from 1813. He requisitioned timber for her. He had referred to her always in proprietary terms as "our vessel." He was present at her launching at

Mo'orea in December 1817, when he startled spectators by smashing a bottle of red wine on her hull.[52] If she was not entirely his to command, he certainly had shares in her operation.

For their part, the missionaries and Marsden regarded the *Haweis* as a suitable substitute for the vessel the directors refused to send out to assure communications and enter into the pork and pearl shell trade with New South Wales. Marsden chartered the *Active* to transport two cargoes of pork and coconut oil as part of the Auxiliary Society contributions for 1818. The following year the *Haweis*, under the command of Captain John Nicholson and with a mixed Tahitian and European crew, made her first run to Port Jackson with "salted Pork and Cocoa Nut Oil which belonged to the Missionaries & was consigned on their account to Mr. Marsden."[53]

Pomare received nothing from this venture and determined to find other agents if he was to go on acting as principal on his own account and for the Auxiliary Society.[54] He persuaded the missionaries to give up their shares; and Samuel Henry, as son of a missionary and Pomare's agent, sailed the *Haweis* back to New South Wales with orders to have Pomare's rights recognized by Marsden and his deputy agent, the prominent Sydney merchant Robert Campbell. But with Marsden absent in New Zealand, and lacking experience in the ways of Sydney commerce, Henry unwisely rejected the terms laid down by the directors for allowing Pomare full ownership and provisioning the mission. He entered instead into a contract with the merchant Thomas Eagar in December 1820 for the advance of a vessel, trade goods, and casks for pork—all valued at £5,969, including commission, to be repaid in imports of island produce.[55]

Having sacrificed the *Haweis* (Campbell and Marsden disposed of her by auction),[56] Henry and Pomare quickly distributed the windfall cargo of cloth, cutlery, axes, saws, hardware, stationery, fishhooks, and looking glasses among chiefs and *ra'atira* "in a partial & disgraceful manner" to the exclusion of the missionaries.[57] Henry took Eagar's vessel, the *Governor Macquarie*, back to Sydney in June 1821 with one of the largest shipments of pork ever recorded—some 170,000 pounds obtained by a massive drive for domestic and wild pigs in February and March. Not till then were the missionaries permitted to resume barter trade and employ

Tahitian labor. There was precious little left over for Marsden's brig *Hope*, which arrived in April to take off the society's annual contributions.[58]

Worse, from the mission viewpoint, Pomare attempted to extend his control of available supplies to the Leeward Islands and ordered a prohibition of produce sales there. This was refused by Tamatoa with the backing of Williams and Threlkeld; and the chiefs of the group declared they "would not attend to the advice of Pomare to *rahui* the hogs, oil & arrow root for him and to sell nothing to the missionaries, they will have nothing to do with Pomarre's ship but will buy a ship of their own."[59] Pomare treated this defiance as a revolt against himself and his daughter Aimata— a position tacitly admitted by Ellis, who came over from Huahine to negotiate for "some degree of civil & religious liberty from the despotic, grasping & cruel hand" of the *ari'i rahi*.[60] Ellis also went to see Nott in order to frame his own laws for the island. This separation did not prevent Pomare from collecting another cargo in August 1821 for the *Westmoreland*, including stocks from the Leewards.

Meanwhile, in Sydney, Marsden had debts to clear on the Missionary Society account. He attempted to divert the *Governor Macquarie*'s cargo to a direct sale with the government commissary on the grounds that Pomare had been overcharged in Henry's contract with Eagar. Eagar seized ship and cargo; but in the subsequent court action which Marsden brought against him, the jury allowed him full value for vessel and goods but found for Marsden to the extent of £1,200. The *Governor Macquarie* returned to Tahiti and the Leeward Islands, in September 1821, for another shipment of produce which occasioned further remonstrances from Darling, Bourne, Williams, and Ellis against "monopoly." Eagar also promised Pomare that he was coming in person to collect the rest of his debts.

From this potentially dangerous situation of commercial rivalry and political tension between the Leeward and Windward groups, chiefs and missionaries were saved by a sudden decline in Pomare's health. Crook, who attended him along with Tati, Hitoti, and Utami, thought in the privacy of his journal that his removal from the scene might be "a public benefit."[61]

A second cause of strained relations was the course taken by early plans for developing agriculture. As with commercial ventures by the brethren these had their origins in the missionary practice of drawing bills on private traders. The practice got out of hand among the new missionaries who passed through Sydney in 1817 and 1818; and Marsden's chaotic system of accounts led him to snatch at schemes put up by Hassall, Eyre, and Smith, who had authorized him, on their own initiative, to spend £1,499 on current account.[62] They proposed to invest in sugar and cotton plantations which, they claimed, would benefit the society, "find employment for the natives and tend to promote their moral and religious improvements by correcting their natural idle habits and stimulating their industry."[63]

There were to be many similar proposals in Tahiti. The directors, too, had formed an agricultural committee for advice on development and sent out a West Indies planter, John Gyles, who was supported by Marsden and began work at Opunohu on Mo'orea in 1818. As with other experiments of this kind, shortage of labor immediately raised questions about the place of Tahitians in such schemes. Darling and George Bicknell, who pioneered the planting of cane sugar on the island, were obliged to pay 6 yards of cloth per day to have land cleared.[64] Gyles, who was familiar with a much lower supply price, antagonized Tahitians by attempting to treat them like West Indian laborers. Pomare, moreover, came out strongly against this mode of production on the grounds that "if the sugar concern prospered many persons of property would come and kill or make slaves of his people & take their lands from them."[65] It was a shrewd enough premonition. Privately the missionaries were inclined to agree, and they advised Gyles to withdraw, hoping they had learned enough to continue on their own. For his part, Marsden clung to a more orthodox view of economic development, prophesying that a Tahitian plantation economy would become to New South Wales "what the West Indies are to Europe."[66]

For the time being it was left to the sons of missionaries—Samuel Henry, Barff's boys on Huahine, and Bicknell's nephew, George—to take up cotton and cane growing. Bicknell and Henry proposed a contract for a monopoly of sugar manufacture at Mo'orea in the mill left by Gyles. Crook drew up papers for this arrangement, hoping to use the *Haweis* for transport, and stipulated a percentage for the mission from every ton produced. Henry also brought from New South Wales a Mr. Scott who began a tobacco plantation and undertook to manage Bicknell's sugar concern for a share of the profits.

But, again, the key to development was labor. Pomare refused to allow Tahitians or Mo'oreans to divert their energies from collecting and salting hogs in 1821 unless the sugar machinery was transported to Tahiti. And this Bicknell was obliged to do, settling on land given by the *ari'i* in Pare, where both Tahitian and mission-grown cane was crushed as a royal monopoly from August 1821. Thus, complained Davies, "the Sugar must be dear on account of the high demand of the natives for any work they may do. And not being disposed themselves to plant cane and turn it into Sugar."[67] By October 1821, this experience was about to be repeated with cotton-growing, when the missionary artisan, Armitage, surveyed Opunohu for a mill site. Pomare gave his approval reluctantly.[68]

Three months later he was dead; and his death released a variety of missionary commentaries on his character and passing. The Tyerman and Bennet deputation wrote a suitably touching account of his last hours. Nott stressed his long protection of the mission, while Williams and Threlkeld looked on his disappearance as a deliverance from his grasp. Others, too, had cause to praise or blame, according to their conception of the role they expected him to play in furthering their commercial or missionary interests. But it was William Crook who was probably closest to him in his last years and who confided to his journal his appreciation of the faults and merits of a man who

> possessed a very capacious mind compared with any of his people and therefore was overrated by others and overrated his own abilities. He was fond of despotic power and loved to have the persons and property of his people at his entire disposal. He supported the old practice that no woman should eat in any house that the king had honoured with his presence. He was naturally idle, seldom or never walked out except to bathe and seemed much more averse than his people to adopt European customs. His father planted many groves of coconut and breadfruit trees; the only thing of the kind he has done is on the isthmus [Taravao]. He inherited from his father a love of foreigners and was always the friend of Missionaries. He frequently evinced that he was under the influence of Antinomian notions and

seemed to steel his heart against convictions. He was much feared by
the people and was made very useful in bringing about the great
change that has taken place in the islands. And now that he is no
more among us, may God carry on his work to perfection by other instruments.[69]

Not all of Crook's colleagues would have agreed with this assessment. But they could hardly have denied the *ariʻi*'s inquiring mind
and ability to absorb technical information. Ellis had noted his desire to improve himself when he came to see the first sheets printed
at the Mission Press in 1817. The same year he had written to a
missionary in New South Wales requesting writing materials and
announcing his projected Tahitian dictionary (probably in cooperation with Davies and Nott). To Samuel Marsden he confessed his
ignorance in terms that suggest an awareness of how much the outside world had to offer. He continued to remedy his own lack of
knowledge. Captain Bellingshausen's officers, in 1820, found him
well supplied with books and maps; he had begun to study geome-
try in the busy years of lawmaking and commercial speculation; he
kept a close check on the accounts of the Auxiliary Society and continued to forward a small portion of contributions in the midst of
his other enterprises.

But his efforts at political centralization had not got him very
far, perhaps because the economic foundations of the "kingdom"
rested on levies of tribute rather than regular taxation. When these
levies were extended to the Leeward Islands, in the name of trade
with New South Wales, Pomare's status within the family oligarchy of chiefs in authority in both groups of islands was not strong
enough to withstand the autonomy of church and market advo-
cated by the missionaries. Yet, in other ways, he had assisted the
spread of missionary work. He had visited Tubuai and Raivavae in
the Austral group on a trading vessel, in 1819, settled differences
between their chiefs, and formally accepted their government, or
hau. He left a steward, or *faʻaterehau*, and encouraged acceptance
of teachers from Huahine and Tahiti who arrived after his death.
His close association with settlers and visitors from the Tuamotu
promoted contact with Kaukura and Anaʻa; and the latter island
sent chiefs to receive his magistrates and laws. But none of this
equaled his service to the mission by his settlement of Tahitian

tribal divisions in 1815, coupled with his intellectual rejection of one religious system and his acceptance of another.

Possibly he miscalculated some of the advantages to be had from patronage of a European mission. The laws were not intended simply to strengthen his hand, as the missionaries interpreted the new dispensation of 1819; or, as Orsmond put it: "The laws we have and are about to establish will provide more effectually for those in authority and then we doubt not they will provide more effectively for us."[70] Such a bargain was less a promotion of monarchy than a way of giving guidance to the chiefs and ra'atira on whose support the district churches depended. In any case Orsmond, like others of the mission, dismissed Pomare as "a known drunkard & a Sodomite." And when he conflicted with the missionaries on matters of trade and agriculture, the outward appearance of a Polynesian Christian "kingdom" bore little resemblance to the realities of a small and scattered society of churches and subtribal corporations whose demographic and economic survival in the Pacific was still uncertain.

Pomare, then, was no Kamehameha, nor a George Tupou. He had stature (he was about six feet two inches in height and heavily built); and he had a capacity to learn the politics of change at a time when Tahitians were under pressure from the outside and had exhausted the possibilities of their own system of religious leadership and tribal alliance. There were features of his father's policy which he developed and handed on to his successors—cultivation of a family compact with the Leeward Islands and friendship with British captains, the governors of New South Wales, and the directors of the Missionary Society. These policies had served him well and had taken him from the position of principal 'arioi and ari'i under 'Oro to become the island's principal merchant and paramount chief under the God of Britain in the space of two decades. He was not easily replaced.

CHURCHES AND CHIEFS

At Pomare's death nominal authority passed to Ari'ipaea Vahine and the chief of Porionu'u, Paiti: they acted as regents for the boy who had been born in 1820 and was now in the care of missionary families at Pare. In 1824 he was "crowned" Pomare III by Nott; and Davies (feeling slightly ridiculous) was "appointed by the chieftains of Tahiti and Eimeo to personify the king, as he is a baby, and answer questions in his name."[71] The association of missionaries and the paramount chief had never been more complete.

Great attention was paid to the education of the child, but much less to his health. He died of dysentery in 1827, after a good deal of public business had been conducted in his name; and his sister, Aimata, was appointed in his place at a meeting of chiefs held after the funeral. But this time there was a notable absence of official pomp; for Pomare IV, as she was styled, was only a girl of fifteen and an uncertain factor in the constitution that was being shaped by missionaries and chiefs.

The deputation had encountered her in 1821, at the age of nine or ten, "neatly clad in a blue-flowered frock, and . . . a straw bonnet," a healthy-looking child with ladies of honor dressed in English cottons.[72] As had been arranged in 1814, she was married in 1824 at Huahine to Tapoa II, a youth of sixteen, in European dress with salutes of musketry. Crook encountered her at Taiarapu the same year and found her "giddy and thoughtless."[73] She attended a Tahitian girls' school spasmodically, "but spends most of her time running about . . . and is ashamed to come to our house, except that she will sometimes hang about the back door when the people are taking up our food and get a little clandestinely." Her companions were reminiscent of eighteenth-century 'arioi—mostly "wild young men" who practiced tatooing, made cider from fermented mangoes, and slept and ate with the royal couple. After her accession thrust new responsibilities upon her, it was an open question whether all the chiefs would agree to pay her deference, though when the royal family visited Taiarapu, "the old chiefs, especially Veve," noted Crook, "make very much of them, present them with large heaps of food and large bundles of cloth and seem inclined to do away with the laws and set up many of the old customs again."[74]

There had, indeed, been a reaction against missionary strictures and prohibitions in the 1820s. Everywhere there was an unwillingness to believe that the laws were still in force after the death of Pomare. Church attendance declined, and there were unusual numbers of exclusions of erring members.[75] Even at Ra'iatea, where Williams cooperated closely with Tamatoa, it was found impossible to enforce the letter of the code against an adulterous ari'i

Teremoemoe (wife of Pomare II), Pomare (or Tapoa, spouse of Pomare IV),
Pomare Vahine, Otoore. Drawings by Jules Louis Lejeune, 1823.
Service Hydrographique de la Marine.

whose food and offerings were prepared by church deacons and members, regardless of new conventions.[76] More seriously, the missionaries reported outbreaks of heresy which threatened island government on Ra'iatea in 1824 and aimed at "destroying the whole of us including King & Chiefs."[77]

Examples of this rejection of the new order established in 1818 occurred regularly. In 1826 and 1827 two "apostate Christians," Teao and Hue, began a prophetic cult which disturbed the congregations of Pape'ete, Puna'auia, and Taiarapu. Labeled variously as "wild visionaries" and "antinomians," the *mamaia* prophets took their inspiration from the Scriptures they had been taught to read and from their own inner revelations and "inspirations." The worst outbreak was at Maupiti Island in 1827, where a deacon from Huahine named Ta'ua had won over two local deacons to his view (as revealed by the angel Gabriel) that the Mission Society was "a trick, that the law is a great grievance."[78] The chief of Maupiti, Ta'ero, lost control as anarchy reigned and banishment of the *popa'a* was preached.

It was the chiefs, as upholders of the codes, who managed to contain this mixture of apostasy and sedition. Tamatoa and Mahine of Ra'iatea and Huahine together with Mai and Tefa'aora of Borabora supported the missionary Platt, who formally "gave back" the laws to Ta'ero in 1829 and supervised the election of new deacons. Similarly, Utami at Puna'auia restored order to Darling's church and punished its rebels. *Mamaia* took some time to die out as a prophet cult. But the disaffection with the mission and the codes took other forms, leading the chiefs to act with increasing severity—so much so that Williams had to restrain Tamatoa's judges, who were eager to "cut off the ears" of prostitutes, and limited them to shaving heads instead.[79] At his station in Taiarapu Crook intervened with Vaira'atoa's judges when they passed a severe sentence for "fornication" by the sister of a chief who had married a man regarded as her nephew "according to their old customs."[80] Crook even went so far as to exclude the principal judge from the church.

Clearly there were risks in associating closely with chiefs and in controlling them. Church sanctions could not be exercised too frequently against men who were deacons as well as law officers and household heads; and Crook's decision to act as a court of appeal, "if judges, constables &c. act with savage cruelty, contrary to law in opposition to the advice of the missionary," raised other questions about the ultimate source of authority within the hierarchical alliance of chiefs, missionaries, judges, and church officials. As Crook saw the problem, there was a temporary power vacuum in 1827 on an island where leadership was weak "and Christianity has tended indirectly to lessen the power of the chiefs. It is true the missionaries have in a great measure succeeded to the power, but they being foreigners, and so much above the people, they cannot readily come into our ways."[81]

Thus the crisis through which the churches passed in the 1820s was as much a matter of differences of opinion between missionaries and chiefs as between their joint leadership and the dissent of apostates and backsliders within the congregations. The immediate remedy sought with the help of the deputation lay in the reform of Pomare's code of 1819. To some extent this process had begun already with the Huahine code of 1822, which defined penalties more closely and made provision for direct taxation, an exchequer, payment of judges, and trial by jury.[82] Ellis's example was taken up by Nott in 1823 and 1824. Tyerman and Bennet also approved and considered that his revisions with the chiefs

> tend to secure the liberty of the subject & private property against the encroachments of the Chiefs, yet they meet with considerable opposition from the Raatiras, or landed proprietors. They are willing to pay a tax for the support of the Royal family & to subscribe to the Missionary Society (for this Society is here National), but they are unwilling to support the Governors, as the principal Chiefs are now called— though by paying them a triffling tax, they might secure the best of their property against their claims to which they are now constantly exposed.[83]

The revised code of 1825 consisted of no fewer than forty-six clauses. Trial by jury was introduced at Tahiti and Mo'orea, but there was no obligation to pay small quantities of coconut oil, hogs, and arrowroot to the chiefs. Land disputes were referred to councils of coproprietors and chiefs. Most important (and in some ways the most durable provision of the code), a superior court, the To'ohitu (the "seven"), was instituted to hear appeals and serve as a political council during the minority of Pomare III and the early feckless rule of Pomare IV.

Nominally the To'ohitu consisted of the high chiefs of all the old divisions—the two Teva tribes, Aharoa, Porionu'u, Fa'a'a, and two from Mo'orea. In practice, the leading judges with political weight were Tati of Papara, Utami of Puna'auia, Tavini of Taiarapu, Paofai of Tiarei, and his brother Hitoti. A trial of strength with Pomare's entourage and the *hau feti'i* was not long in coming.

The issue was prostitution at Pape'ete by the bevy of young girls who surrounded the queen. "Many of these girls," confided Crook, "and it is confidently reported the queen herself, have been affected with the venereal. This had undoubtedly been the case with her mother and aunt."[84] In January 1828 the queen was obliged to surrender one of the delinquents who was found guilty by the judges. Backed up by Tamatoa and Tapoa II, the Porionu'u took offense and threatened war on the judges' districts "for breaking the queen's arm." Tati and Utami fully expected a fight; Paofai and Hitoti managed to soothe royal tempers.

At the same time, throughout 1828, the chiefs began to review such contentious issues as price-fixing, tribute, appeals, and revisions of the code at periodic meetings usually held at Pare. Such a council began to look like a rival government; and, until early 1829, it was far from clear whether Pomare would be bound by its decisions. For their part the chiefs and judges no longer accepted that "the queen's mouth is the Law."[85] Paofai and six of the Tahitian and Mo'orean judges extracted a promise from the young queen through her orator (the missionary Nott) that she would conform with the revised code. Her mother, Teremoemoe, and her aunt, Ari'ipaea Vahine, were openly reproved for their conduct at a grave and impressive ceremony. At the May Meeting of 1829 in the royal chapel the queen became president of the Auxiliary Society and Nott was made official counselor.

The *hau feti'i* passed through a further crisis before the chiefs won their point. Tamatoa's position was unsettled in Ra'iatea and Taha'a in 1830 by the disputed land rights of Boraboran chiefs. When the chief of Taha'a, Fenuapeho, was lost at sea, Tapoa, Pomare's spouse, was installed in his place and became leader of Tamatoa's enemies.[86] This breach effectively ended the royal marriage. Pomare returned from the Leeward Islands early in 1831 and was paid a form of tribute by Mo'orean chiefs and by her great-uncle, Vaira'atoa, chief of Taiarapu, which had been proscribed by missionaries and judges. The tributaries threw themselves under her protection at Pare, pursued by Tati, Utami, and Hitoti, who demanded a "judging." By March 1831 most of the island was assembled under arms at Pape'ete to settle the place of an *ari'i* in law. The queen and her supporters ranged themselves along the northern point of the harbor at Fare Ute and faced the crowds on the opposite shore, separated by half a mile of water. At this dramatic moment, Commander Sandilands of H.M.S. *Comet*, who had just arrived, hoisted his colors, fired a salute, and went ashore. Messengers were exchanged; deferential compliments were paid; and a token judgment of Vaira'atoa and two lesser chiefs was passed by Utami. The queen once more agreed to uphold the laws.

Her separation from Tapoa, however, became a matter of island politics. Her mother and aunt settled on her cousin Tenania, a youth of fourteen and grandson of Tamatoa, as a suitable replacement. Before Tenania's arrival from Ra'iatea, Tamatoa died and war broke out between his supporters and Tapoa, who lost a major battle in 1832. Pomare actively intervened to save what remained of the *hau feti'i* and sent Ari'ipaea Vahine and Utami to make peace between Tapoa and Tamatoa's son, Moe'ore. Tenania was then brought over to Tahiti, in November 1832, by Mahine, *ari'i* of Huahine, and the couple were "married by Archbishop Nott" (as one missionary wrote irreverently).[87] A few Mo'orean chiefs raised the point that the queen was not legally divorced and had probably broken the strict letter of the Tahitian code. There was a way out, however, "as her husband has been party in the late war at the Leeward Islands, and has been made the guilty person . . . this has been agreed to by the Chiefs, altho' it is not according to law, in order to obtain if possible an heir to the throne of Tahiti."[88]

Even this pressing reason of state was not allowed to prevail. The decision was denounced in Mo'orea and in Tautira. Pritchard and Darling tried to intervene. Some seven or eight hundred rebels clashed with the districts supporting the judges and the queen; some twenty were killed. The chiefs concerned were tried and banished for a time to Mai'ao.[89]

Thereafter Pomare settled down to her role as paramount chief while continuing to pursue the traditional family policy of strengthening her ties with the Leeward group. She produced six children with almost annual regularity between 1838 and 1847;

and two of these, Teari'imaevarua and Tamatoa, born in 1841 and 1842, were adopted by her first spouse, Tapoa II of Borabora, and by Moe'ore (Tamatoa) of Ra'iatea. She intervened in Borabora again in 1841 to make peace between Tapoa and Mai in a land dispute, arriving in person with a troop of about a hundred armed men and the Tahitian judge Paofai. Even more than her father she was drawn to the Tamatoa lineage. One of the earliest descriptions we have of her—as a woman of seventeen "of good figure and agreeable face, especially when smiling or in conversation"— comes from the period spent with the Ra'iatean *ari'i* and his court, who were dressed in European costume to meet the commander of a warship.[90] Ten years later, an American whaleman at Pape'ete described her in state procession with household guard, royal standard—red, white, red, in horizontal bars—the queen's consort and retinue, all attending church on the waterfront:

> The body of the church was occupied by the Queen and the military, and the galleries principally by women. . . . Queen Pomare is a good looking woman of a light olive complexion, with very dark expressive eyes and black hair. In person she is about the medium height, and is rather inclined to *embonpoint*, and as she stood up several times during the service, she rose with an air of dignity that was truly royal. She wore a white satin hat, flaring open and flattened upon the upper rim, after the Tahitian style, trimmed with broad satin ribbon and then surmounted by three white ostrich feathers. Her dress was of satin or figured silk, of a pink colour with slippers to correspond. The husband of the queen, *Pomare-tane* . . . sustains the relation of a Prince Albert to the government. He is a young man of about twenty one years of age, while her majesty is not far from thirty.[91]

But beneath this outward display of finery by a central executive there had been a further shift in authority to the district chiefs during the 1830s. They, no less than the missionaries, were alarmed by the spread of imported spirits and the riot and disorder that followed the growth of trade and foreign settlement. They supported Tati's plan for a temperance society in each district, passed a law to prohibit spirits sales in May 1834, and raided European stores around the port. Sabbath worship and school attendance were made compulsory. At Tautira, reported Orsmond, "you may see chiefs with ramrods, iron-wood clubs and other implements" keeping the congregations in order: "We are chief ridden, law ridden, and form ridden."[92]

Other missionaries also criticized the recourse to legislative acts to cover every kind of private and public behavior in the Leeward and Windward groups. Fines in produce and coin, road-making, cloth-making, temporary banishment to an outlying atoll, exclusion from the church—these were the usual punishments. For Europeans there were numerous regulations on desertion from ships, port fees and pilotage, and the powers of the *mutoi*, or port police. The last refinement in legislative proscription was a law framed at Huahine in 1837: "For the Foreigners on Board Ships Touching Here, Who Desire Bird Shooting, made in consequence of a woman having been killed by a bird Shooter."[93] None of this, warned a missionary who had experience of another field in Samoa, would solve the problems of social control "whenever laws are beyond the point to which the knowledge and moral feeling of the people has yet reached."[94]

But who was to judge this degree of understanding and acceptability or make the fine distinction between the business of Church and State which younger missionaries desired to see? The artisan Armitage also wrote a penetrating criticism of the South Sea missions on his return to London in 1836. But his condemnation of the results of European contact—meretricious goods, trade by missionaries, or the vanities of Tahitian Sunday dress—avoided the problem of corporate responsibility among the island's chiefs in a period of rapid economic change.[95] To Armitage, "the change that has taken place appears to be more of a Political change than of a Moral & spiritual one." Neither of these developments, however, touched on the difficulty of arriving at a working constitution in a society whose material advancement and exposure to new ideas could not be contained by the missionary contribution to government and social welfare.

Similarly, a high-minded newcomer to the field who arrived in 1839, Charles Stevens, made a blistering attack on Tahiti before he left the mission for good. He deplored the absence of a written constitution in conditions of privileged oppression by queen and chiefs. Court fines augmented the private purse; literacy was superficial; congregations were "unfaithful and corrupt"; the queen levied a tax on Pape'ete prostitutes, where (he was reliably informed by Pritchard) there were "19 applications for mercurial preparations to one of any other medicine" and venereal disease was "so general as not to be deemed disreputable."[96] The litany of deficiencies was long, amounting to an exaggerated but perceptive conclusion that in many respects the mission churches had been assimilated to Tahitian norms of behavior. Or as Stevens summed up his prescription for reform:

> When missionaries' children shall be better governed & their examples become less profligate & pernicious; when the Royal favor (as such) shall be no longer courted & the pride of rank no longer flattered, when secular encroachments upon matters purely religious shall meet with unanimous, prompt & candid resistance, when the missionary shall by some means be rescued from the degrading subjection of an unjust majority, or supported against popular revenge, when missionaries shall lay aside their divided pursuits, & the natives the suspicions which they have engendered, then & not till then shall we be authorized in expecting a prosperous mission.[97]

John Davies, who had grown older in Tahitian ways, would probably have answered these strictures in the same terms he used to conclude his *History*—namely, that the reception of the missionaries' message and the benefits of Western technology by islanders had been eclectic.[98] They had adopted what they wished to adopt and reached a level which could be favorably compared to other societies at a similar stage of development at other periods of history.

This somewhat bland defense, common enough to those who had settled fairly comfortably into island life, did not really meet the essence of Stevens' strictures, which for all their intolerant tone contained the important observation that little effort had been made to educate the sons of chiefs or church officers for positions of authority. An Institution for Native Teachers had been opened in 1829 with five pupils, increased to ten in the 1830s. A schoolmaster, Joseph Johnston, arrived in 1839 to take over, but he found it uphill work: "Of the 16 Scholars sent to Mr. Johnston from various parts of the island, 8 of whom were from 10 to 13 years of age, not one could read the Tahitian alphabet fluently."[99] Only six of these were the sons of chiefs, though some were sent in 1840 to a Normal School opened at Pape'ete for children of mixed parentage; and others followed Johnston to Papara, when he worked there in 1842 and 1843.

It was William Howe, who arrived in 1839, who put his finger on the more pressing reasons for a transfer of missionary authority to Tahitians themselves. He found he could no longer depend on the services of deacons and older members of his church at Afare'aitu on Mo'orea to row him across 16 miles of open water for meetings at Pape'ete. Rowers demanded payment; and between 1839 and 1842, he was drawing heavily on the Missionary Society for "boat expenses." Howe could see only one remedy: "It is really painful to contemplate the rapid increase of expenses which is taking place in this Mission; but there seems to be no possibility of avoiding it, but by raising up ministers from among themselves, for whose support the people must either provide, or remain without instruction."[100]

So it was that on the eve of Tahiti's greatest political crisis since conversion, economic reasons were added to the more general need for revision of missionary and ari'i responsibility for Church and State. To the tensions between chiefs and the Pomare royal house was added the decline in the effectiveness of the churches as teaching and reforming institutions. They had been hard hit by inflation.

In December 1842, therefore, the first candidate was selected for a new teachers' or "theological" institution set up and run by Howe at Mo'orea—this candidate was to be a "probationary student for the space of six months."[101] But the institution was soon embroiled in the troubles that followed French occupation, and two of its four students hastened to join "the Patriots" in 1844.[102] Those who remained wrote to the directors affirming their hopes of becoming ordained ministers. But Howe left Tahiti, temporarily, and the initiative was lost.

It was some compensation that the linguistic work on which the pioneers of the mission set such store came to fruition; and from 1838 it was possible to place a complete translation of the Tahitian Bible into the hands of the faithful. The first copies arrived in 1840 —a hundred for each station, where members flocked to buy them for a Chilean dollar each.

The missionaries, then, failed to resolve the problems of public order and social administration outside their control. They had provided the means, but they could not provide the methods by which Tahitians or Leeward Islanders were to set about adapting their social and political organization to meet the changes imported from the outside world. Their recognition that indigenous entrepreneurs were needed to exploit the rich sources of educational materials and manage the institutions they had created came late in the day—certainly too late to save them or the islands from the events of the 1840s.

In other ways they had foreseen that the process of "extending the frontiers of literate societies" (as a historian of Marquesan society has put it)[103] could be best entrusted to local recruits to the Christian faith. Davies' "Scholars" from Mo'orea had pioneered the process of evangelical expansion by the establishment of the first indigenous churches. They were poorly equipped to carry out this work. But by the early 1820s there were plenty of literate volunteers from the churches of Tahiti and Ra'iatea; and between 1821 and 1831 an astonishing number of over fifty Polynesian teachers were sent to the Cook Islands, the Austral Islands, Ana'a and Makatea in the Tuamotu, Tonga, and Fiji. Some at Aitutake and Rarotonga may be said to have founded the local Protestant churches. One, Tute Tehuiari'i, who was sent with his family to Hawaii in 1826, served as royal chaplain to Kamehameha III for thirty years. A few (like early Missionary Society men in Tonga) reverted to local customs. But most kept the faith and worked themselves into positions of trust and advantage among island governments.[104]

The Marquesas group absorbed no fewer than a dozen such teachers between 1825 and 1831; and, on the whole, the Marquesans rejected their message. Lacking the more stratified social classes of the Windward and Leeward Islands, the inhabitants of "mutually antagonistic valleys"[105] nevertheless had their own recognized divisions of rank and wealth: powerful priests and chiefs made incessant war and traded for muskets, powder, and allies. They suffered a disastrous decline in population from famine and disease between the 1790s and the 1840s, which left perhaps twenty thousand in the two main groups centered on Nukuhiva and Hiva Oa.[106] Contact with numerous deserters from visiting vessels and with missionaries was concentrated at Tahuata, around Vaitahu Bay, and at Taiohae and Taipivai at Nukuhiva. An expedition of American missionaries sounded out the chief, Iotete ("a large good natured man"), in 1833 and found him anxious to attract shipping and trade to Tahuata, which he was far from dominating.[107] The missionaries Darling, Stallworthy, and Rodgerson made an effort to extend their Tahitian churches there (1835–1838). They had some success in attracting small congregations, but they could not compete for attention with the European beach community which had been recruited into Iotete's war parties; nor could they advance the war he was making against Hiva Oa. At Nukuhiva, on the other hand, they were able to fix on Moana, the adopted son of Haape, a chief of Taiohae, because he had been abroad to Rarotonga (and probably to England). The missionary Thomson made him his protégé and brought him back to Nukuhiva in 1839, where he disappointed his mentor and "relapsed into the savage."[108] By then there were other missionary rivals in the field. Stallworthy witnessed the arrival of Catholics at Tahuata with a mixture of dismay at their potential and admiration for their stores and zeal.[109] The Marquesans saw them as yet another source of trade goods: "One man told me it was the property they wanted & not the instruction; another said they would listen to me with one ear, & to the Frenchman with the other."[110]

Outmanned and underfinanced, the London Missionary Society retreated from this outpost of doctrinal competition and general lawlessness. Having pioneered the frontier of literacy in the South Pacific, they were overextended on the periphery by the early 1840s. They were also in deep crisis on Tahiti, where they had first consolidated their base.

CHAPTER 3

THE MARKET
EXPANDED

By the third decade of the nineteenth century commercial exchanges between the islands of eastern Polynesia and the Pacific borderlands had developed some of the features of a specialized entrepôt trade. In place of barter there were produce brokers; South American currency facilitated transactions; and it was normal for a missionary to draw bills of much higher value on local traders and ships' captains than on other suppliers in New South Wales.[1] In 1839, the commander of the United States exploring expedition regarded Tahiti as a central place that "engrosses all the commerce" of neighboring archipelagoes.[2]

Commander Wilkes still anchored his vessels in Matavai Bay, as others had done before. Wallis or Cook would have recognized the hospitality; they would have been surprised by the decrease in theft and by the mission schools and churches. They might have been mildly astonished at the spectacle of local chiefs taking in the laundry of Wilkes' crews in return for payment in Chilean piastres and liberal provision of naval soap.[3] From the port pilot to the chief of Matavai there was a mercenary welcome for seamen.

It is not easy to set a value on entrepôt trade. But by the end of the 1830s, it may have amounted to £60,000 annually at Tahiti.[4] The export of Leeward and Windward Islands produce—coconut oil, sugar, and arrowroot—was worth between £5,000 and £8,000. In addition, there was a valuable export trade in pearls and pearl shell from the Tuamotu and Mangareva, valued somewhat vaguely between £5,000 and £10,000. There was a regular trade in provisions for visiting vessels and some export of currency and notes to other ports. In return, Tahiti imported stocks of European goods from Sydney, Valparaiso, stores from whalers—all worth about £15,000 at marked-up prices after landing. The rest of the trade balance was made up with some $60,000 worth of Chilean coin and notes.

The reasons for this modest expansion lay in broader changes in the exploitation of resources in the Pacific, The once-flourishing pork trade with New South Wales decreased in favor of commerce with Callao and Valparaiso, as merchants and small partnerships entered the Pacific from their base in Latin America. If there ever existed a "swing to the East" in British imperial and European trade between the late eighteenth and early nineteenth centuries, it may be held to have included a shift to Peru and Chile, as well as the ports of Northwest America.[5] Certainly, the long-term trend toward the development of the fisheries, including sealing, whaling, and pearl-diving, which derived from the search for alternatives to the North Atlantic and the East Indies, brought seamen round the Horn as easily as round the Cape of Good Hope. As British, American, and French merchants established themselves in Valparaiso, Lima, and Callao, the whalers of Bristol, Le Havre, and Salem sought out the sperm and right whales across the enormous grounds of the south and north Pacific. By the 1840s, in Commander Wilkes' analysis, the United States alone employed over six hundred vessels in this industry with a return of $5 million annually "by hard toil, exposure and danger."[6]

For respite from the long hunt, the islands of eastern Polynesia lay conveniently near the "offshore" ground and the coast of Peru, on the great belt of sperm whale and humpback whale migrations during the southern summer.[7] The Marquesas and Tahiti were preferred ports of call. From 1836, the American consuls at Pape'ete recorded some sixty to eighty entries of American whalers annually with transit cargoes worth between $1.6 and $2.6 million.[8] Wilkes (who exaggerates their numbers at Tahiti) thought they traded about $500 each in goods. Their logbooks are not very informative on this point, though their inventories of axes, flints, chisels, razors, and powder indicate why the Marquesas Islanders welcomed them; and their purchase of spirits and cattle at Pape'ete in large quantites amply demonstrates why missionaries and chiefs regarded them ambiguously as a source of income and trouble.[9] They were joined from 1831 by a dozen or so French whalers in New Zealand

waters and off the coasts of Chile and Peru, encouraged by government bounties and the reputation of Pacific ports.[10]

There were additional reasons for Tahiti's growing importance
in the days of sail. As the *Directory for the Navigation of the
Pacific Ocean* made clear, great circle routes between the main
ports, combined with prevailing winds and currents, gave advantages to entrepôt ports. In truth the exact crossroads of the Pacific
for vessels bound between Australia and Central America, or Can-
ton and the Horn, lay in about longitude 135° west and latitude
40° south, some 1,200 miles south of Tahiti, the Tuamotu, and the
Australs. But Tahiti was on the great circle route from the North
Cape of New Zealand to Panama, and near enough to the preferred
route from California to New South Wales. Moreover, for vessels
bound from the Horn and South American ports to Hawaii or the
North Pacific whaling grounds, the southeast trades and the Hum-
boldt Current encouraged a course toward Pitcairn and latitude
20° south, before standing north to Tahiti or the Marquesas, cross-
ing the equator and continuing on the northeast trades from about
latitude 10° north. From Hawaii it was usual (though not always
easy) to cross the equator at about the longitude of Tahiti, keeping
as much easting as current and trades would permit to as far south
as latitude 35°, before using westerlies toward the South American
coast. By contrast, despite the seeming ease of Mercator projection
distances, the track charts of sailing vessels from Sydney toward
Hawaii or San Francisco passed well west of Tahiti along the great
circle route past New Caledonia and Fiji. It required a long swing
south of New Zealand, or through the dangers of Cook Strait, to
link New South Wales traders with the market at Pape'ete.[11]

It was also from the South American ports and the Far Eastern
stations of Britain and France that naval vessels passed through
Polynesia with increasing frequency in the 1830s. Scientific exploration gradually merged into supervision, intervention, and a measure of European control. In some ways the standard was set by the
first American man-of-war to visit Tahiti in 1826, when her captain made a treaty of trade and friendship with the queen regent on
behalf of Pomare III; the missionaries made a move to secure a
measure of British protection; the Admiralty promised more regular inspections.[12] But it was Captain Robert Fitz-Roy who set a new
precedent in 1835, during the scientific voyage of the *Beagle*, by

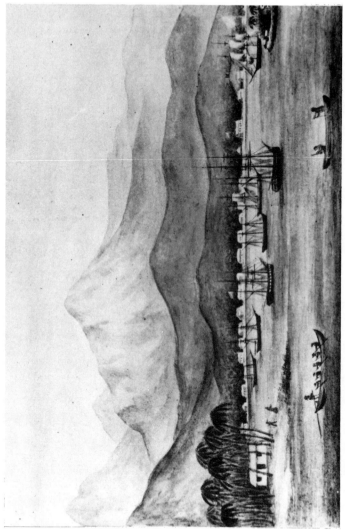

"The Harbour & Town of Papahitie. Island of Tahiti. Society Group. South Pacific."
Watercolor, 1839.

extracting a promissory note from Queen Pomare for 2,853 piastres for the plunder of a trader's vessel in the Tuamotu.[13] Apart from the question this raised concerning Pomare's jurisdiction in that group, the attention of naval officers commanding British vessels on the west coast of South America was drawn to similar cases concerning deserters, wrecks, and the politics of consular and naval influence by other powers.[14]

They were well schooled in gunboat diplomacy to protect British property at Lima, Rio, and Callao in the war between Chile and Peru in 1837. Their French counterparts in command at Valparaiso had positive orders from 1831 to promote French investment in trade by enforcing French consular treaties in the turbulent Latin American ports.[15] From 1836 they were also under orders to protect French whaling. In Paris, the minister of marine, de Rosamel, who was a former commander of the Pacific naval station, directed Dupetit-Thouars in the *Vénus* to survey the Pacific grounds as one of a series of new commercial, diplomatic, and scientific expeditions undertaken to promote French knowledge of the resources of the Pacific basin and to secure a share in their exploitation.[16]

In a sense, then, France, Britain, and the United States extended their consular and naval techniques from the American seaboard to the islands. The economic dependency of New Zealand, Hawaii, and Tahiti on outside markets to promote the development of the few staples they could provide in the conditions of European investment of the 1830s was matched by the political and humanitarian patronage of the Pacific naval powers. British missionaries and subimperial authorities in New South Wales, or the naval and consular officers of South America and Hawaii, were closely involved in this supervision. But only in one case—New Zealand— did investment of British capital, colonists, and rudimentary jurisdiction result in annexation. Elsewhere British government departments were content to work out solutions to the problems of island markets through the consular and naval brokers who served their purposes in other parts of the world. For most of the 1830s, France followed a similar policy. The United States, too, even in the 1840s, had little reason to transform patronage into empire. But from within the island markets there were other opportunists who were anxious to employ imperial means to further their own ends.

THE MIDDLEMEN

Against the broader background of European trade and settlement in the Pacific, small coteries of Europeans won themselves a place in island politics and commerce. Their entrepreneurial functions were unspecialized and overlapping: seamen became traders and occasionally merchants; nearly all traders sought to invest in land and ran small plantations or opened stores. Not all were successful. The consular records for Tahiti contain a lugubrious documentation of material distress caused by shipwreck, mutiny, desertion, illness, and death.[17] For every early name of a British settler recorded as leaving property, there are several scores of seamen registered as penniless flotsam from the Marquesas or the Tuamotu. The stratified communities of different nationalities were built on a broad and shifting ebb and flow of transients.

Commander Wilkes, therefore, divided European society in Tahiti into three categories—merchants, missionaries and their children, and the rest. In numbers they could hardly have been more than about seventy in the two main islands, perhaps a hundred if one includes the Leeward group in the count. But the title of merchant applied to very few. Edward Lucett and his partner, Colley, could be so called after they began to import on their own account as wholesalers from Sydney and Valparaiso.[18] Lucett also sailed his own vessel and possessed four properties in Tahiti. The hardworking Yorkshireman E. J. Hunter and his wife Suzannah Chapman could be included in this category. They had property at Ra'iatea and at Fare Ute, Pape'ete; daughters of theirs married Lucett and Colley, as well as five other prominent traders and officials.[19] Among the missionaries George Pritchard would certainly qualify, even before he became British counsul in 1837. So would Jacques Moerenhout, the Belgian who had begun to specialize in the pearl trade in 1828, became a planter, and imported his own cargoes from Chile and France. More doubtfully, one might include Alexander Salmon, who was on the scene by 1841 with a small amount of capital and a recommendation from the governor of New South Wales.

But capital and credit were in short supply; and before the registration of professions in the 1850s, it would be safer to conclude that most of the more successful residents were traders, making what they could from private ventures and investing in land and stores. Sons of missionaries were fairly prominent in this category, though one of the most experienced of them, Samuel Henry, had good cause to complain of the high risk and low returns from his commercial operations for the Pomare family.[20] Others, like Henry, were trading captains such as William Dunnett, Thomas Ebrill, Armand Mauruc, and Auguste Lucas, whose careers spanned the Pacific. They commanded vessels for other principals, taking a share for themselves, and they moved (in Ebrill's case) from the pork trade into the shell trade and finally into sandalwood or into the safe haven of a small sugar plantation. French settlers, though small in numbers, fell into the same pattern. But in their case they came through Valparaiso, and three of them—Auguste Lucas, François Rouge, and F. Desentis—had speculated in land in New Zealand before colonial laws made land sales more difficult in 1840.

Broadly speaking, then, the external connections of traders tended toward New South Wales for the British and toward Valparaiso for the French. Lucett also had land interests at Kororareka, where he formed a partnership with three settlers in 1841. Consuls Pritchard and C. B. Wilson kept in closer touch with the colonial secretary at Sydney on the daily business of shipping and deserters than they did with the Foreign Office in London. Moerenhout, as United States consul from 1836 and French consul from 1838, championed causes opposed by Pritchard and kept in close touch with Bordeaux houses at Valparaiso. His American successor, Samuel Blackler, who on any count dealt with more of his nationals in the whaling fleet than on shore, stood between this polarity of factions and quarreled with each in turn.

There were others who brought new talents to Pape'ete society in the 1830s—carpenters, shipwrights, even a doctor or two, who rubbed shoulders with tatooed seamen from the Marquesas, Hawaiians, and South Americans. The ex-president of Chile, General Freire, settled there. A Polish officer, Edmond Fergus, had served the mad designs of Baron Charles de Thierry when he passed through the group in 1835 and returned in 1840 to become a notable citizen. Herman Melville also came that way in 1842 as a mutineer from the whaler *Lucy Ann* and moved from the local jail to Mo'orea and back into the wider world. There were keepers of grog shops, billiard rooms, and eating houses along the small water-front. In 1842 a certain John Cain applied for a license to open the Franklin Hotel, which lasted till 1844. For, by the early 1840s, the port town boasted three consulates, two schools, churches, the queen's palace (an unpretentious bungalow), and a row of wooden houses and thatched *fare* among the groves of orange, lime, and breadfruit trees that ran down to the shore. There were two wharves and six schooners sailing under Tahitian colors. More were being laid down at Fare Ute and in Raʻiatea.

Missionaries were also traders. John Davies had once made a distinction on this point between barter for services and provisions and exchange for profit in which a number of his colleagues were engaged.[21] The distinction was a very fine one, especially in the years when the Auxiliary Societies still flourished as produce cooperatives. Indeed, these institutions can be counted as pioneers in the formation of a local market in the 1820s and an example of the ways in which shortage of credit in a tropical community was remedied by using a missionary agency in the islands and in New South Wales.

Following the example of Pomare II and Samuel Henry, John Williams purchased the schooner *Endeavour* through Marsden for the auxiliary on Raʻiatea in 1822.[22] The first cargo was sent to Port Jackson the same year, and Tamatoa and the chiefs agreed to defray the high cost of the vessel, insurance, and fitting out before ordering trade goods. All this credit had been obtained through the firm of Holehouse and Stokes and by bills on the Missionary Society "as a kind of loan to enable them to begin their mercantile pursuits."[23] Williams also traveled frequently to the colony in these years, and his salary of £55 per annum covered little of this extra expense. Instead, a private account was opened from the sale of produce, though this fund was kept separate from the account for Raʻiatean subscriptions to the society.[24] While the price of coconut oil remained high at £16 per ton and arrowroot at £56 per ton, it was not overoptimistic to hope to pay for Williams' expenses as business manager, as well to turn Raʻiatea into a hive of industry:

> Everything is succeeding beyond our most sanguine expectations—the Natives have prepared from 120 to 130 large plantations of Sugar & Tobacco. The learning to cure & manufacture Tobacco & to boil

Sugar is that which occupies my whole time as Mr. Scott the person I brought with me from the Colony not feeling himself comfortable leaves us by the return of the schooner—he has however brought the knowledge of three invaluable articles, the Boiling of Sugar, the Cure & Manufacture of Tobacco, & the Boiling of Salt 3 or 4 tons of which the Natives have made to enable them to send away their little Schooner with a full cargo. I have this day tried for the first time to make Sugar without any superintendence or instruction from Mr. Scott & am happy to say that I have succeeded in making good Sugar. You would be delighted to see the scenes of Industry our Island presents. Even the Women are employed with their little patches of Tobacco to purchase European clothing—the height of our ambition is to introduce these articles without expence to the Society. It is therefore agreed that a forth of the first crop be given up into the hands of Tamatoa the Chief to refund the money paid to Mr. Scott for his instructions.[25]

But in 1824 there was a sharp recession in the market for island produce in Sydney. The *Endeavour* had to be sold after making a loss of £1,800, and subsequent cargoes that year did not cover the cost of consignment.[26] On the other hand, there had been sufficient return from the venture to stimulate Ra'iatean imports of European goods and encourage "emulation among the Natives both in building and furnishing their houses" with "Chairs, Sofas with neatly turned legs and bedsteads of a superior kind," reported Williams.[27] The good news spread to the Austral Islands, and Rurutu sent a man to be instructed in boiling sugar and curing tobacco.[28]

The auxiliaries began to sell to local captains instead of consigning on their own account, as the price of oil fell to about £9 for a ton of 300 gallons. On Huahine, the missionary Barff disposed of some ten thousand bamboo pipes of oil in this way toward the end of 1824; and in 1825, at Puna'auia station on Tahiti, Darling planned "to fresh Model our Missionary Society in order to make it more effective" by allowing local sales.[29]

Missionaries' financial accounts for the period show that a number, like Barff, had fallen into debt, or "arrears," with the London Society because of payments made for casks forwarded for arrowroot "ventures" and other goods, and they requested permission to sell locally for a quicker turnover, fearing that enthusiasm would wane and subscriptions would be reduced. Pritchard, too, at Pape-

'ete began to sell directly to ships the small lots of his branch of the Tahitian auxiliary, forwarding the cash to London and requesting a receipt to show the subscribers.[30] There was, moreover, a loss of confidence in Sydney merchants; and in 1829 the missionaries, following instructions from the directors, took the important step of no longer making bills on individuals in New South Wales:

> We shall endeavour in future to sell all the Society's property for ready money (if we can) and forward the same to you. A box containing what money is now in hand accompanied by a letter from Paofai the Sec[retary] and translated by Mr. Nott who is on the spot will be forwarded by Capt. Emment of the Foxhound. There is some quantity of Cocoanut Oil now in hand at the different Stations which will be sold when opportunity offers and the proceeds forwarded to you. Oil and Arrowroot are now becoming articles of great trade in the Islands. We often have two and three Vessels purchasing at the same time, so that it is only those that love the Word of God that will subscribe their property to the Society. The greater part of the people prefer purchasing property with all the Oil they can make. This was not the case in the first years of the Society. Almost all the people gave, it being a kind of general thing which could not last.[31]

As the freewill contributions declined, other evidence of Tahitians' preference for the local produce market accumulated. Prices were deliberately raised by Tahitian price rings which demanded $10 and $12 for a hog previously sold for $4. Visiting traders blamed their conversion to Christianity. The missionaries blamed "a Lascar who . . . has fixed the prices of everything and is appointed salesman."[32] But it is also likely that the stocks of domestic and wild hogs had been depleted by the excessive exports of the first two decades of the century; and it was about this period that cattle were introduced from New South Wales and from Hawaii as an alternative source of meat, following the example of an importation donated by Sir Thomas Brisbane.

The use of currency to pay for goods and services spread very rapidly in the late 1820s and 1830s. Labor on the *Haweis* and on missionary agricultural enterprises had been paid in hardware and cloth till about 1825 or 1826. Thomas Blossom, the missionary mechanic who set up and ran a small cotton mill at Mo'orea, kept careful accounts of his wage bills.[33] Tahitian sawyers employed on construction were fairly cheap (only 111 yards of cloth costing about £12 were expended between 1823 and 1826). A few yards purchased a pig for a work group. One individual was paid for clearing guava weeds from the plantation with a teacup of gunpowder worth sixpence.

The enterprise failed. Spinning commenced in 1825; and when the first 50 yards of local cotton had been presented to Pomare III, the spinners went on strike—"not exactly for wages," wrote Blossom, "nor do we know what it was for. But they said they would not spin anymore at present."[34] The experiment was shifted to Afare'aitu, where Blossom paid cash wages and had more success with thirty to forty women and some of the children from the "Academy." But, as David Darling pointed out, their product could not compete with the imported variety, which could be purchased in larger quantities "than they would get for labouring at the Factory for Months and Months."[35] Nor would it purchase a bottle of spirits at the port, where, despite temperance laws, rum was sold at five bottles for a piastre.[36]

Tribute to the queen and chiefs, however, was still quantified in fixed amounts of produce laid down in 1830 at "2 bamboos of oil [one gallon] to the queen, and 2 to the governor. The second year, 4 fathoms of Tahitian cloth to the queen and 3 to the governor, from every family."[37] By 1834 the account of subscriptions to the Tahitian Auxiliary Society at the annual May Meeting amounted to 240 bamboos of oil and a cash sum of $88.50 (Chile). Leeward Islands accounts still continued to be reckoned in "bamboos" for most of the 1830s. But the Tahitian Society had changed over completely to subscriptions in *tara* by 1839, when $656 was presented at Papaoa.

The consequence of this development was serious for the missionaries. Rodgerson summed up their predicament in 1837:

> The natives are fond of dealing. Many of them have learnt the value of money and are eager to possess it, but their means of doing so are yet few. Hitherto we have bought nearly all our food with money. We can obtain 14 eggs for a quarter of a dollar, a fowl for the same. A pig weighing about 100 lbs. generally costs from 6 to 8 dollars. Occasionally we can buy eggs, fowls, fish &c. for knives, scissors, razors, files or cloth, but most natives prefer having money. This circumstance sometimes causes us considerable trouble as we are obliged to sell the articles which we obtain from home in order to get money before we can purchase the things we want.[38]

With the means of exchange came periodic shortages and steep price rises. It cost Rodgerson $7 a month to pay his servants. Cotton cloth valued at 6d. per yard in England was valued at an equivalent of 1/2d. to 1/4d. at Tahiti. All the missionaries reported an increase in their retail costs in 1840, when the price of hogs rose three or four times.[39] Flour cost $20 a barrel, and a barrel of potatoes $1.50. In 1842, Alfred Smee, a newly arrived missionary printer, found that his stock of goods imported for barter was useless at Tahiti: "The people like to receive money for everything they do or sell, and pay money for any thing they require. . . . The Tahitian Mission I fear is becoming a very expensive one."[40]

In many ways, then, the missionary example of trade and industry in the 1820s had been outdistanced by the economic opportunities open to converts by the 1840s. Contributions to help support the mission declined. Altogether only $1,974 was forwarded to England for the years 1838 to 1840 from the auxiliaries.[41] Salaries increased from a basic allowance of £30 to £50 with small supplements for wives and children. But inevitably the missionaries found it hard not to enter into the market in order to raise cash to live, and not merely to barter. The distinction made by Davies for the early 1830s was no longer an option by about 1837; "We are a set of trading Priests," confessed John Orsmond.[42]

There were different degrees of entry into the market; and if all Europeans with assets to trade were to some extent middlemen, there were those, like Pritchard, who specialized in business by becoming produce broker, merchant, and (more briefly) shipowner. He defended his economic functions fairly ably in 1834 in reply to a private letter from Ellis:

You are aware that I am stationed at Wilks' Harbour [Pape'ete], the place where most of the ships touching at Tahiti come to anchor. You are also aware that opportunities of obtaining supplies from England & from the Colony have not been frequent. The consequence is, we are obliged to purchase from ships such things as are necessary for our domestic purchases, & for barter with the natives. By such things . . . I mean suitable articles to give them as wages & with which to purchase from them hogs, fowls, arrowroot, oil &c. Living at the rendezvous for shipping, I have numerous applications from the brethren, even from Rarotonga to Taiarabu, to procure such articles as they think proper to order. It is not necessary to copy from my book lists of what I have procured for all the brethren. I will however enclose a copy of what I have lately purchased for two only, Messrs Henry and Platt.[43] From these lists you will be able to form some idea of the extent of my trading. In addition to this all the missionaries on Tahiti, not one excepted, send their oxen to me, that I may sell them to the shipping. While writing these lines, one has arrived from Mr. Nott and two from Mr. Davies.

I am not only charged with trading to an unwarranted extent, but with great keenness in trade. . . . If we purchase things from Ships, as we have of late been obliged to do, and give any prices that may be asked, each missionary will want his salary doubled. . . . I have no attachment to trading, but necessity has compelled me to trade so far as to provide for the various families in the mission. I speak the truth when I say that I had much rather be in my study than on board a ship trading. As it respects trading with the natives, I have occasionally bought arrowroot from them for cloth ribbands &c., part of which arrowroot I have exchanged for flour &c. on board a ship, & the other part I have sent to London to Mr. Roberts to sell & with the proceeds send out such articles as we needed. I have also hired the natives to make rope with the *purau* bark which I have exchanged with Captains for such property, as would otherwise have required hard cash to purchase. I have always encouraged the natives in industry, consequently I have devised various plans to get them to work. Such as are accustomed to carpenters' tools, I have employed in making cupboards, tables, bedsteads, boats & various other things for our family use. Others I have employed in putting up fences & planting potatoes. I have now a plantation of sugar cane, managed entirely by the natives. You will have the kindness to lay these things before the Directors. If they think such conduct is incompatible with my character as a Missionary, they have only to make me acquainted with their sentiments on the subject & I will immediately desist. They must however bear in mind, that if they prohibit me from trading altogether, they must appoint a domestic agent, who can render those services to the mission which I have been accustomed to do, or they must, which will be far better, devise some plan by which we can be favoured with our supplies, more frequently from England.[44]

But the directors shrank from either course; and the poles of Tahitian trade, in any case, were with Sydney and Valparaiso. Pritchard was allowed to continue in his role as merchant, planter, and retailer, moving to a higher social plane as British consul. He purchased a schooner, the *Olive Branch*, for $2,500 in 1837 and chartered her to the local mission for £60 a month to supply the outstations. He sold her at a loss.[45] Henceforth he turned his attention to his self-appointed duty of acting as political broker for the queen in her relations with the outside world without entirely giving up his mercantile and missionary functions. Undoubtedly the plurality of the offices and the threat of monopoly over the regulation of trade explain much of the hostility of his merchant and consular rival, Moerenhout. The market was hardly big enough for both of them.

The directors, however, enforced restrictions on the missionaries in other economic matters. Alexander Simpson, who had been producing 15 or 16 tons of sugar annually on his plantation at Mo'orea from 1835, was ordered to give it up, and he transferred it to George Bicknell. The venture had been shared with a Tahitian named Tepau'u (a son of Tati of Papara) and the port pilot at Afare'aitu, Toeropa, who had been in charge of sales to ships. It was typical of other advances by Tahitians in this area of production and marketing. Tati had gone into partnership with Moerenhout in 1832, when they sold about 18 tons of sugar. By 1840, there were some thirteen sugar mills on Tahiti, mostly run by Tahitians. Other new cash crops included European vegetables, coffee, and an imported variety of Tongan yams, the *uhi*, which Tahitians found to be more productive than the local species.[46]

There were other consequences of this economic change, more difficult to document. Enclosure of small lots of land around Pape'ete close to the main market was one.[47] Mostly these plots were used to raise and prepare produce for sale; but some in the port area were already the subject of litigation and dispute arising from "agreements" for sale or rental by Europeans. It is possible that other land tenure problems arose from the greater value attached to areas of the littoral suitable for cash crops and from the continual and unresolved difficulty of trespass by pigs and cattle. In 1837 Darling thought that:

> The principal thing [which] occupies the Chiefs, Governors and Judges at present is the differences that take place about land which belongs to families that are now extinct, or nearly so; they find [it] very difficult to decide who is the proper person to inherit such land as many often put in equal claims for it; sometimes the difference arises from the divisions of different lands.[48]

On Borabora such a dispute had nearly led to war in 1841 and had to be settled by the intervention of Tahitian judges. The compact settlements once favored by missionaries in the Leeward group, moreover, had begun to break up by the early 1840s as *ra'atira* took a closer interest in cultivating cash crops on scattered lots of family lands. There was also the point, explained by Ra'ia-teans to the missionary Charter, that the increase of cattle on the island required they protect their crops: "Do not the Missionaries' sons live sabbath after sabbath on their land at Opoa, & why should we not do so too?"[49] Charter could not persuade them to re-medy their falling church attendance, nor to give up their "worldly conversations . . . upon subjects relating to their land, property &c." which occupied them in the evenings.[50]

Another sign of change was the entry of chiefs into the retail trade on Borabora, possibly the only instance of this kind in Tahiti or the Leeward Islands:

> There are now two small stores belonging to Foreigners on this island. One of which is kept by Tapoa the other by Faaite a principal chief. The people having got their money for oil, proceed to these places, and as far as the firms afford, procure such articles as they want. The articles sold by Tapoa are the property of Mr. Bridge who resides at Tahiti. Those in the possession of Faaite belong to Captain Hunter of Raiatea. There is only one foreigner residing on this island who is also endeavouring to set up a small trading establishment. The assortment kept at these stores is very imperfect and the prices ex-ceedingly high; so that it will be a disadvantage to many when we commence paying in money alone.[51]

Such arrangements between Europeans and Leeward Islanders and Tahitians were a rich source of litigation. The To'ohitu and lesser judges had trouble enough reaching decisions over indige-nous land cases at a time of modest economic development. When European concepts of property and legal redress for debt were added to the techniques of production and exchange, the chief's au-thority over the terms of trade and order in the marketplace was extended into poorly understood areas of European cooperation and settlement.

For, in common with other Pacific communities, Tahiti and the Leeward Islands faced two kinds of adjustment. The formal consti-tution of island society had been modified internally in the direc-tion of institutionalizing authority among a combination of titled and lesser chiefs, judges, and missionary advisers. External contacts between the local market and New South Wales and Chile brought in casual and permanent settlers. The answer of the chiefs to the problems of illicit traffic in spirits and the lawlessness of deserters was to use the new institutions of Tahitian government to pass prohibitory laws. An economic and religious middleman such as Pritchard took it upon himself to tutor Tahitians in techniques of control by demonstrating, for example, the use of leg-irons for runaway sailors—because "in such cases . . . the Natives are as so many overgrown children."[52]

But clearly there were limits to this kind of instructive paternalism in settling relations with foreigners who had recourse to consular or naval patrons of their own. Consequently, those who administered the districts and the island churches were called on to negotiate in wider terms of reference than the rules laid down in the codes of laws or the port regulations encompassed. Increasing contact with the outside world called for continuous adjustments of the techniques of control and of imported alien ideas on property, compensation, residence, and, ultimately, the sovereignty and independence of the islands.

Tahitians were not given very much time to make these adjustments. One interpretation of their history in the 1830s, therefore, is to stress the accumulation of precedents in naval and consular arbitration in order to account for French occupation. In a sense this development is a logical consequence of the development of trade. For in 1839 and 1840 there was a sudden increase in the number of merchant sailing vessels entering Pape'ete. Some twenty-four British brigs and schooners and twenty British whalers imported and exported cargoes valued at about £40,000.[53] Six American merchantmen imported goods from Valparaiso. One French brig and three French whalers entered. More ominously, British, American, and French men-of-war anchored at Pape'ete at an average of three or four a year from 1836 to 1841.

The interests these naval visitors came to protect were hardly in proportion to the amount of consular and station correspondence which accumulated around cases of shipwreck, desertion, the return of Pitcairn Islanders, or the admission of would-be settlers. There is a monotonous regularity in the dispatches of the British, American, and French consuls whenever Pritchard, Moerenhout, or Blackler deplored the incapacity of the Tahitian government of queen and chiefs to deal with external problems. Pritchard, therefore, encouraged the view that British patronage could be counted on, though overtures for formal protection in 1822, 1832, and 1838 produced little more than a vague promise of "moral" support. The queen, moreover, had paid some stiff fines in 1831 and 1836–1837—some 4,650 piastres in all—for losses sustained by British traders. But, for reasons of his own, Pritchard promoted the vision of Tahiti as a great center for British trade—the "New West Indies" of the Pacific; and his fear of foreign rivals led him in 1840 to make a visit to London to plead the cause of British intervention.

By then, too, Consul Moerenhout who had written with sympathy and insight on local history in 1836 committed a different view of Tahitians to paper in dispatches five years later. He stressed the "sense of inferiority" among the chiefs, who were only too willing, he thought, "to place in foreign hands the reins of government" and allow themselves to be run by foreign advisers.[54]

From the American consulate Samuel Blackler, who had experienced at first hand the rough justice of the Tahitian police, wrote an empassioned series of complaints to the State Department, urging the establishment of a naval station to end the "total inefficiency and duplicity of the Tahitian Government."[55]

It is fairly easy to make this kind of interpretation from the consular records. Things at Pape'ete sometimes got out of hand. There was nothing new in this: in 1823 Crook noted in his journal a case of "great drunkenness" on board an American vessel involving Paraita, treasurer of the Auxiliary Society, which resulted in a brawl, a trial, and an acquittal.[56] It was a scene many times repeated, for there is an undercurrent of violence beneath the calm scenic beauty of the port in these years. Consul Moerenhout barely escaped with his life from a murderous attack by a South American in 1838 and his wife did not survive. There was a particularly serious riot in 1841, during the visit of a Spanish vessel, which led to a trial before Utami and a mixed jury of Tahitians and Europeans and ended in convictions for assault. But law enforcement by the *mutoi* was often indiscriminatory and provoked resistance to raids, fines, and confiscations.

The police could be reinforced and reformed; and a serious effort was made to do both in 1842. But the evidence of the consuls touched deeper issues and assumed that only external intervention

Paraita, Regent. *Illustration*, 22 January 1848.

could settle them. This assumption should be tested, however, against another body of evidence (so far little used) which was assembled by the judges and officials most involved in cases arising from European settlement.[57]

Surviving correspondence in the Tahitian vernacular shows that a fairly consistent effort was made from about 1836 by the queen's representatives to come to grips with the unpredictable ways of the *popaʻa*. By the end of the decade, some of these officials—Uata, the queen's paternal guardian and her *Papaʻi parau*, or secretary, and Paraita, her orator—issued summonses, collected taxes, investigated land transfers, and conducted a careful correspondence with Consul Pritchard and Acting Consul Wilson. There is no indication that they, or the Toʻohitu, were being directed from the consulate or the mission house, though missionaries did occasionally collect evidence in particular cases. Periodically other officials, Rotea and Atea, who acted as scribes to the To'ohitu, sent reports to Pomare or to her consort Ari'ifa'aite, especially when they were in the Leeward Islands (1840–1841); and these sources suggest, too, that the court and the judges were developing a bureaucratic technique by keeping records of fines and extradition charges and had more than a superficial understanding of the importance of precedents.[58]

There emerged fairly late in the history of independent Tahitian government a concept of formal regulations (te parau taroa) as a body of law or executive instructions, separate from the code, issued by chiefs and judges.[59] There also emerged a willingness to learn from previous errors and reform the code, particularly as it applied to Europeans. The assembly of chiefs and judges was revived in 1842 and met at Papaoa chapel in April to consider the problems of foreign contact. A revised code was approved; and although more important events soon overtook the reformers, it provided a basis for the early legislation of the French protectorate.[60]

But precepts were one thing and the Tahitian courts and district administration something else. Redress for theft, damage to property, or loss of stock could be infuriatingly slow, even when missionaries or their sons were plaintiffs. Wilson listed some seven outstanding failures to carry out decisions of courts and laid them before the 1842 assembly.[61] A petition from French and British settlers ran to five pages of detailed grievances.[62] A French version by Mauruc and Fergus listed special complaints;[63] and extended versions of this cahier de doléances were sent to Captains Du Bouzet and Dupetit-Thouars when they arrived to investigate the position of their nationals in the last months of Tahitian independence.[64]

Nearly all of these cases were occasioned by insecurity of land tenure. There was a constant confusion of usehold rights, granted by a Tahitian, with freehold or leasehold rights in the European sense. Tahitians were as unwilling as they always had been to part with estate in perpetuity or to forgo a share of the improved value arising from plantations or buildings. Already, by 1842, some of them had begun to accept rents in cash for family properties around Pape'ete and at Fare Ute. Not even the lands of the consulates or the mission houses were considered as alienated irrevocably. "So powerful is this repugnance to the admission of foreigners to any of the privileges arising from the possession of land," noted

Wilkes, "that those who are attempting to cultivate sugar etc., hold their leases by so uncertain a tenure as to prevent them making any permanent improvement."[65] The case of a French settler, Lefèvre, is reasonably typical:

> A relation of my wife made me a present of land on which I made a sugar plantation; later this relation wanted one of my foals and wished to buy it. I told her that since she had given me some of the land I would give her the foal as payment. . . . But some time later she wished to take back her land and her husband and his friends continually break down my fence.[66]

Lefèvre had at least arrived early enough to marry a Tahitian. This method of acquiring land rights as a member of a *feti'i* was formally ended in Tahitian law in about 1838 on the advice of the missionaries, and marriages with Tahitians were forbidden until 1841. Acquisition by sale was also forbidden in the revised code of 1842. In the Tahitian records which found their way into the British consulate, there are only one or two registered land grants; but there are at least a dozen cases of disputed "ownership."[67]

There were other contentious areas of jurisdiction. In a case of compensation arising at Huahine over the brig *Hannah* in 1842, local judges were unable to enforce their decision on a European. Wilson took the unusual step of referring the dispute to the governor of New South Wales.[68] Enforcement of the prohibition laws regularly produced confiscations of rum and brandy from retailers, "who despite this," reported Captain Du Bouzet, "and growing rich on this illicit trade—the most profitable in the land—claimed that they were ruined and persecuted because they were French."[69] In this protest they were unanimously joined by those whom Consul Wilson called "the Lower Class of British Subjects" (after they had abused him for not protecting them).[70] Finally, since about 1832 a number of laws had been passed to extract fines from deserting seamen and prevent their residence at Tahiti. It was arguable that such measures and the right of extradition were within the interests, if not the competence, of the Tahitian government to enforce. When they applied, at the request of Pritchard and a few of the missionaries, to Roman Catholic priests, their purpose was more than questionable. The well-tried middlemen who had introduced their version of Christian laws and institutions to Polynesia were attempting to secure a monopoly.

THE CATHOLIC CHALLENGE

The advent of Catholic missionaries to Tahiti in 1836 had been feared for some time. Protestant stations in eastern Polynesia were vulnerable to penetration by rival denominations; and there was evidence that priests were the harbingers of foreign naval and consular intervention. The French government had supported the commercial and religious settlement led by Jean Rives at Hawaii in 1825.[71] The London Missionary Society and the American missionaries closed ranks to form a common front against this "invasion," which was soon exaggerated by rumor throughout the Pacific.[72] Little came of the expedition in terms of trade, and the missionaries of the Sacred Hearts Congregation who reached Hawaii in 1827 were increasingly isolated. Fathers Bachelot and Short were expelled in 1831 (although some lay brothers were allowed to remain). An Irish father, Arsenius Walsh, was ordered out in 1836.

But this reaction could not prevent the establishment of a Sacred Hearts mission at Valparaiso and the creation of a Catholic sphere of influence in eastern Oceania in 1833 under Bishop Rouchouze. French Catholicism followed the lead of French trade; and on the advice of a French captain, Rouchouze dispatched Fathers Caret, Laval, Liausu, and Brother Murphy to the Mangareva or Gambier group, southeast of the Tuamotu, in 1843.[73] He personally visited the new bridgehead with reinforcements in May 1835 and helped to decide the political balance between the tribal chiefs who supported or opposed the mission. Within a year, both the chief priest, Matua, and his nephew, the *akariki* Maputeoa, were won over. The symbols of the old religious system, already undermined by a few teachers from Tahiti, were renounced; and the baptism and conversion of the group's small population of about two thousand began in earnest. In a short space of time the foundations were laid for a Catholic theocracy which transformed the economic and political structure of Mangareva.

The increasing influence of Valparaiso was watched with misgivings in Tahiti.[74] The missionaries jointly prospected the Marquesas Islands with an American expedition in 1833 and made a more determined effort to secure a foothold. In Tahiti, district congregations were warned in the early 1830s of the dangers of Catholicism (equated by some with the *mamaia* and other mystical aberrations). Above all, the example of political support, as in Hawaii, was stressed. As the chiefs and the Toʻohitu took upon themselves the enforcement of new laws to secure church attendance, prohibit spirits sales, fine deserters, and control landings under the port regulations, the danger of factionalism among the more ambitious of Tahitian leaders was foreseen.[75]

There is no evidence that missionary misgivings made much impression on Tahitians, though the chiefs may have felt, like Governor Kuakini of Hawaii, that British Protestants had prior claims to their loyalties.[76] It is more likely (to judge from subsequent behavior) that they were curious to see the anathematized preachers of a foreign cult—providing their movements and influence did not pose any real threat.

They were soon given an opportunity when Rouchouze sent Brother Murphy to spy out the field at Tahiti and Hawaii on the *Peruvian* in 1835. He was not allowed to land.[77] The following year, Rouchouze sent Fathers Caret and Laval, who, with a French carpenter named Vincent, disembarked at Tautira and took shelter with Moerenhout. Pomare accepted payment of a landing fee, but an assembly of chiefs and judges under Pritchard's guidance decided to end their residence. On 12 November they were embarked on the schooner *Eliza* by the *mutoi*, who, as Moerenhout reported, "tore up the roof of my house, forcibly introduced several men into it, broke the lock of the door and dragged away the poor defenceless priests to the outside; they then carried them away on their backs—one seizing a leg—another an arm and in this manner hurried them the whole length of the beach."[78] To cover their decision the chiefs passed new port regulations in 1836 making all landings subject to the discretion of the Tahitian government.

A lengthy correspondence ensued between Pritchard, who based the sectarian prohibition on the letter of local laws, and Moerenhout, who invoked the "Laws of Nations" and challenged the position of the mission in external relations. He suggested toleration in religious affairs. Pritchard's reply was unequivocal: "For Roman Catholics and Protestant Missionaries to labour together in peace and harmony in a small field like this, or in the Sandwich Islands, is just as likely as it is for light to have fellowship with darkness, or Christ and Belial to dwell together in concord."[79]

The dispute began to divide Tahitians also. The extreme attitude

Tahitians Coming from Church. Lithograph from an original drawing by Max Radiguet, 1843.

of Pritchard and some of the missionaries was emphasized again in 1838, when Dupetit-Thouars arrived from Valparaiso at the end of August with orders from Admiral Rosamel to extract reparations for the eviction of Caret, Laval, and Vincent. Under threat of bombardment by the *Vénus*, Pritchard acted for Pomare and paid an indemnity of 125 gold ounces (equivalent to $2,000 Peruvian). The queen apologized. A borrowed French flag was saluted with gunpowder donated by the *Vénus*. Pomare was lectured on the rights of French nationals by Dupetit-Thouars and by Dumont d'Urville, who arrived with the *Astrolabe* and *Zélée* in September. Moerenhout was appointed French consul (though he continued to act for the United States till 1839);[80] and a most-favored-nation treaty secured French rights of residence.

But this impressive display of force did not secure the right of priests to preach "their peculiar doctrines," which were proscribed by an assembly at Papara in November 1838, less than two months after the French warships left.[81] Present were Captain Elliot of H.M.S. *Fly*, Pritchard, Moerenhout, Darling, Orsmond, Wilson, Rodgerson, Pomare, and most of the principal chiefs and judges. Darling read out the terms of the new law "Concerning the Propagation of tenets inconsistent with the true Gospel":

> Let Tahiti and all the Islands of the Kingdom of Pomare Vahine the first stand unique under that Gospel which the Missionaries from Britain have propagated ever since the year 1797, that is these forty years past.
>
> When Foreigners come from other countries to this, on their landing let this law be put into their hands that they may know, if such persons persist in teaching tenets which are inconsistent with that true Gospel which has been of old propagated on Tahiti. If they build houses for worship, if they congregate followers in uncultivated places that they might teach them all kinds of strange doctrines.
>
> If they trouble the usual modes of worship, and propagate strange Customs for the sake of accusing[82] that do not comport with the written word of the God of truth, such person has become guilty of breaking this law, and will be judged and awarded.[83]
>
> This shall be his award. He will be sent to his own land and shall not reside on Tahiti.
>
> If any Tahitian shall propagate Doctrines inconsistent with the Gospel of truth, such as are called Mamaia because they are doctrines inconsistent with those which have been taught by the Missionaries

from Britain, and with what is found in the written word of God, that person has violated the Law. If he be a person of rank or a common man, it is the same, he has broken the law, and will be judged and awarded. He will be sent to his native land to accomplish the sentence of the law in; if it be public road, fifty fathoms; if any other work such as it is found in the Laws.

If he persist in refusing to do it, he will be judged, and new work imposed on him.[84]

Pomare and the chiefs approved, with the exception of Hitoti. Moerenhout pointed out that France would not accept the law and that England would have to support it. Captain Elliot was not to be trapped and preached a few remarks about toleration. For the rest, Tati and Darling spoke in favor of the measure; Paofai and Orsmond were for treating Catholics kindly, but opposed their teaching; Rodgerson preferred to abstain. Elliot then called for a show of hands and argued that Tahitians alone should vote. After several more hours of discussion, the law was passed "unanimously." The law against foreign marriages was also reaffirmed, though there was a small concession, reported Rodgerson: "Those females who shall be found pregnant by foreigners will be allowed to marry them."[85]

Condemned by Lord Palmerston and abolished in 1839, when Laplace arrived on the *Artémise* and added a new clause to Dupetit-Thouars' treaty, the doctrinal legislation of 1838 marked the bankruptcy of Tahitian and missionary efforts to seek refuge in the institutions they had created. It did not immediately benefit the Catholic missionaries, who had diverted their efforts to the Marquesas in 1838. But in 1841, Father Caret arrived from Ua Pou and plunged into a dispute—not about religion, but about a donation of land made in the usual conditions of doubtful legality by a British settler, William Archibald, and opposed by Moerenhout. The Catholic mission had breached the ramparts of Protestantism under cover of the French navy. It had still to build a rival church in Bethel.

There were signs that the factionalism feared by the British missionaries had been encouraged by the obvious strength of French visitors. Chiefs had accepted presents from Laplace. Worse, complained Stevens, Paofai, secretary to the Auxiliary Society, was in correspondence with Bishop Rouchouze and had been sent "a pair of valuable silver spectacles. If anything is done or undone that displeases these chiefs, they do not hesitate to threaten the brethren with receiving the Catholics."[86]

It was in this atmosphere of uncertainty and mistrust that Moerenhout was able to work for the destruction of Pritchard's influence with Pomare's government. The British consul left for London in February 1841. A difficult case of law enforcement arising from waterfront brawls led some of the senior chiefs—Paraita, Tati, Hitoti, and Paete—to request assistance from French naval officers in a document drawn up by the French consul.[87] It is not certain that all the chiefs understood the document, which rumor soon inflated into a full "treaty"; but whether or not they signed "as it were in the Dark," as one of them later confessed, their loss of faith in the advice of missionaries was confirmed.[88] Three of them were prepared to act in a similar fashion when Dupetit-Thouars returned in 1842 to take advantage of the situation the Catholic question had helped to create.

Meanwhile, throughout 1841 and 1842, first Captain Ebrill and then C. B. Wilson struggled to fill Pritchard's place as British intermediary between the Tahitian judges and chiefs and the settlers. Two complicated land cases arose and required the establishment of rules governing Tahitian customary tenure as well as the rights of two Europeans—Henry and Hamilton, who had consequential claims. Four judges, Rotea, Paete, Paofai, Poroi, handled the matter competently enough. But Hamilton's claim was disputed by an 'iato'ai of Pare, Paraita, who brought his considerable political influence to bear on the Tahitian court.[89] He also acted as "regent" during Pomare's absences, though this function was shared with Uata and Paete. The case dragged on, together with others concerning a grant by Teremoemoe to Captain Cotton and the potentially serious land lease contested by the Catholic mission. The latter case was taken up by Captain Du Bouzet, who arrived at Pape'ete on the *Aube* in May 1842. He persuaded the judges to recognize part of the lease as valid, though he was uneasy about arbitrating on behalf of the mission's landlord, William Archibald, a British subject.[90]

This development confirmed Wilson's suspicions, already conveyed to the British consul at Valparaiso, that the French were "aiming to have a dependency here."[91] In London, Pritchard took up the same theme with the Foreign Office in March 1842, when the news of Moerenhout's "treaty" of 1841 reached him.

But there is no evidence that Du Bouzet, or any other French officer, had orders at this stage to do more than see the rights of nationals respected. These rights, Du Bouzet perceived, were not easy to determine in a society of mixed ethnic origins and changing values. On the whole, he was little impressed by the bickerings of French and British settlers. He noticed, however, that there were men in the Tahitian government such as Paraita, Hitoti, Paofai, and Utami who were the mainstays of the courts and the code.[92] He also had to reckon with a new talent, Mare, the queen's *auvaha*, or orator, in May 1842—"a very clever man with a mental grasp beyond the rest and to whom they generally turn at difficult times."[93] Du Bouzet got into debate with him on the issue of the laws, currency, and land as they concerned settlers; and he emerged deeply impressed with his adversary's skill and with a better understanding of Tahitian concepts of temporary and inalienable rights. For Tahitians, he warned, would not suffer their relatives to be dispossessed by individual contracts between single coproprietors and Europeans, particularly at a period when land was an obvious source of crops and income. On the settler side, he predicted that refusals to abide by the rules of property, marriage, and trade, as the missionaries and Tahitians framed and interpreted them, would lead to acts of violence.

CHAPTER 4

OCCUPATION AND RESISTANCE

THE SEIZURE of the Marquesas and Tahiti in 1842 by France was a minor episode in nineteenth-century imperial expansion. It has been well described from the point of view of European diplomacy, international rivalry, and the actions of consular and naval agents. The expulsion of Consul Pritchard, the petitions and remonstrances of missionary pressure groups in England, and the patriotic reactions of the French press in 1843 all have their place in the history of Anglo-French relations. Both governments were exposed to the criticisms of "patriots with a telescope twenty-four thousand miles long of which prejudice is the fieldglass and that speck called Tahiti is the object of vision."[1] Both governments were persuaded to compromise in the context of broader interests. Guizot was prepared to compensate the consul; the British Foreign Office was prepared to remove him. Overzealous officers were called to heel.

It is not hard to agree with Guizot that in Europe the discussion of events at Tahiti took on, "in the eyes of the public, an importance out of all proportion with the truth of the matter and the interests of the country."[2] Certainly neither country was about to go to war.

But there was a war precipitated by French actions. It has virtually no place in the history books and is hardly remembered today in the islands. The conflict that broke out in 1844 and lasted till 1847 was, arguably, of more immediate importance to Tahitians and Leeward Islanders than the diplomatic correspondence that had a bearing on their status at a different level. It also revealed much about the internal political and social tensions set up by the previous decades of institutional change; and the resolution of the conflict had an important bearing on the ways in which France was to administer the group.

Consequently, it is possible to interpret the end of Tahitian independence in 1842 in two complementary, but distinct, ways. From one point of view, it was the outcome of increasing scientific, commercial, and strategic interest on the part of France in the South Pacific—an adjunct to a more important involvement in Latin America. There was a "pattern of rivalry"[3] between France, Britain, and the United States which has overtones of eighteenth-century conflicts and which lasted well into the new century in places as far apart as the Falkland Islands, New Zealand, Hawaii, and New South Wales. And if it appears to later historians that British or American preponderance in the seaboard lands of the Pacific basin was bound to settle the issues of jurisdiction and political control still open in the 1830s or 1840s in the islands, it was by no means so self-evident to contemporary observers. Governor Gipps had been worried by Dupetit-Thouars' treaty-making at Tahiti in 1838; the pamphleteer John Dunmore-Lang discerned a political threat in the presence of French whalers in New Zealand waters; and nervous missionaries in New Zealand recorded their "apprehensions" of foreign designs.[4] Hawaii, too, was a source of minor imperial neurosis, encouraged by the movements of men-of-war and the unacknowledged status of the kingdom as an independent polity. One extension of this theme is to stress the political capital made by France out of a Tahitian "religious dispute" which was tidied away by 1847 in a diplomatic agreement.[5]

Another view emphasizes the autochthonous development of island "kingdoms" and the ways in which internal schisms in Tahitian government (to follow W. P. Morrell's perceptive analysis) led to chiefs becoming the "instruments" of the French consul.[6] J.-P. Faivre, on the other hand, while developing this approach through French records, has concluded that French occupation was the *"coup de grâce"* for a Polynesian culture already in decline but given a chance to recover under French rule.[7]

Tahitian historians who might be expected to take a considered view of the reasons for French occupation have tended to take refuge in the period before 1842—or pass as quickly as possible over the whole uncomfortable episode in terms which reflect contemporary European sources.[8] Their ancestors who were closely involved in these events, however, both appreciated "great power" influence and were well versed in the extension of such influence into local politics. Queen Pomare and Leeward Islands chiefs used the petition as a diplomatic weapon, outlining their version of recent historical events with a well-developed sense of the uses to which history may be put in pleading a cause. From among the stoutest opponents of French rule in 1846 there came an "Appeal" to Britain and America which stressed the divisive results of European contact and the immediate causes of the war in some detail.[9] Its authors saw the protectorate flag as a "land-plundering flag." And there is something to be said for a historical view that conjoins the strategic acquisition of island property by an imperial naval power with the local theme of difficulties over the exploitation of a natural resource. For, while European rivalries and missionary antagonisms have their place in Tahiti's crisis, the immediate cause of contention, as in other Pacific societies, lay in land tenure.

The theme is closely connected, moreover, with rivalries between the Pomare family and other island chiefs in the 1830s. Increasingly, judges and district officials were drawn into land tenure disputes and intervened to settle the problem of evaluating "donations" to Europeans. They were also at odds with the *ari'i* Teremoemoe and her daughter, Pomare, because they had assumed proprietory rights over an important block (called Vaititarara) on the Pape'ete waterfront and made parts of it over to the British consul and, later in 1843, to the British navy.[10] The eldest son of Tati had fallen out with his father over land rights inherited by his aristocratic wife, Marama Ari'imanihinihini (Atiau Vahine), but retained under Tati's stewardship.[11] Part of the reason for Pomare's protracted absence in the Leeward group had been to settle land disputes arising between her ex-spouse, Tapoa, and Mai, chief of Borabora. Pomare herself had made several attempts to assume the land titles of families that had died out, but she had been opposed by the To'ohitu.[12] Some of the internal crisis, then, stemmed from a clash of status rivalries and uncertainties among Tahitians over changes in the value of Tahitian estate.

But while land problems can be discerned in local history, it is less easy to explain the timing of French occupation and why France thought it necessary to supplement the naval protection of French nationals, commerce, and whaling in the 1830s with possession of island bases. Toward the end of that decade Captain Laplace, who had taken an active part in securing written guarantees at Tahiti during the visit of the *Artémise*, came nearest to summing up the results and limitations of this form of diplomacy. Naval protection, he recognized, would become more difficult "as the white race, by settling every land washed by the Pacific Ocean," was assisted more formally by the British and American governments:

> Thus it is necessary, in order to carry out this role with success, to understand well the influence the present state of these countries will have upon their future, the methods used by the English to establish a kind of supremacy there, [and] lastly, the way to be taken by France, not to make conquests there, but to prevent her rival's plans for settlement until these Southern lands have undergone the great revolution which must give birth in that hemisphere to a new race, a new policy and new interests.[13]

This view of competitive coexistence agreed well enough in 1839 with attitudes inside the Ministry of Marine and the Department of Colonies up till 1842. By then, the minister, Duperré, and the director of colonies, Saint-Hilaire, would have been prepared to take a more positive line about acquiring islands posts. But Guizot and the Quai d'Orsay were less enthusiastic, fearing counterclaims from the United States, Britain, or the Australian colonies. Thus the spoiling action envisaged by Laplace represented something of a compromise between two departmental approaches to the need to underwrite French interests; and the appearance of a consistent policy of aggrandizement in the Pacific during the government of Louis-Philippe is misleading. For a brief period only did France seek to acquire bases in the Indian Ocean, the south Philippines, the Marquesas, Senegal, and Gabon—"grandiose designs . . . with mediocre results"—which Guizot cut back when they had just begun.[14]

Among these bases projected in 1839 were the Marquesas Islands, which Dupetit-Thouars had singled out for special attention. They had been thoroughly surveyed by him and Dumont d'Urville. He was on good terms with the chief, Iotete of Tahuata. He had installed three missionaries—Borgella, Desvault, and Nil Laval—and they kept him informed about their reinforcements in

1839 and local conditions of trade.[15] The group, therefore, concluded Dupetit-Thouars in a report of 22 August 1839, would make an excellent penal colony (unless New Zealand was considered to be a better one).[16] The Marquesans would make good sailors and good customers "as they progress in civilization." From this center it would be possible "to expand by means of religious conversion and commerce" as the British did. A second report in November 1839 stressed this use of official and unofficial agents in imitation of the relationship he believed to exist between Protestant missions and the British Admiralty.[17] At the same period, Dupetit-Thouars submitted his lengthy analysis of Pacific whaling, its problems of maritime discipline, and the distribution of the richest whaling grounds.[18] This was sound practical advice on the exploitation of a natural resource, especially on the west coast of South America and the east coast of New Zealand. Again the need for a permanent base for these two whaling grounds pointed to the Marquesas.*

But for the moment these valuable reports were filed away during the uncertainty over French efforts to colonize Akaroa in New Zealand in 1840. From the beginning, plans had been vitiated by a refusal to risk diplomatic complications with Great Britain. French interests were small—four mission stations organized by Bishop Pompallier and a score or so of French whalers in 1839. The Ministry of Marine agreed early that year to send a vessel to the area to protect these interests and to support by loan of a transport the Bordeaux-Nantes Company, floated to settle some 30,000 acres claimed by a French whaleman on the Akaroa Peninsula.[19] It was never part of the plan to forestall the British or commit France to a military settlement and claims to the three islands. The flag was to be hoisted at Akaroa only; and land was to be purchased for France only through the agency of the company. Captain Lavaud was ordered to supervise the settlement, discipline whalers, and collect flax seeds and sugarcane *[sic]*.[20] He sailed on the *Aube* and remained for nearly three years in New Zealand waters, preceding the colonists but arriving a month after British possession of the South Island and six months after the Treaty of Waitangi. The

---

* His report was not as thorough as Wilkes' survey of whaling or the scientific location of the sperm whale grounds by Lt. M. F. Maury, USN. All three reports were printed in Findlay (1851:II, 1335–1342).

French colonists landed at Akaroa in August 1840. The outcome was hardship, litigation, and the eventual liquidation of the company.

The following year, plans for the Marquesas were revived. Dupetit-Thouars was promoted to the position of rear admiral and commander of the Pacific naval station at Valparaiso with orders to obtain treaties from the Marquesans and expend up to 6,000 francs for presents.[21] The motives were straightforward enough: "Our trade and above all our whalers require a port of call and protection in the Pacific."

There was, as yet, no thought of taking other posts as well. Indeed, the first reports from the French consulate opened at Sydney in 1841 indicated that the basis for Duperré's optimism about the expansion of French exports might well be unfounded because of local duties and regulations.[22] From the Valparaiso consul came discouraging news of a decline in the number of French whalers entering the Pacific, though French trade with Central America and the west coast of South America had risen in value by 1840 to nearly 53 million francs and some 180 French vessels. Still there were those in the Ministry of Marine who took notice of the detailed suggestions of the French trader Auguste Lucas, smarting from loss of land in New Zealand, that France should forestall Britain in Tahiti.[23] It may even be that Duperré agreed with the Bordeaux captain's assessment of the "colonizing spirit of England—a universal expansiveness which gives her a massive preponderance in the marketing of all goods in Europe." But, if so, he was not moved to enlarge Dupetit-Thouars' instructions to cover adjacent islands. In January 1842, Admiral Buglet at Valparaiso had given assurances to Pomare that Louis-Philippe's government "neither wished to conquer her territory, nor wished to take it under protection."[24] Duperré confirmed this policy in a dispatch to Dupetit-Thouars in November 1842.

Dupetit-Thouars may also have had a wider vision of his task when he found himself in command of seven warships, 1,800 men, and two companies of marine infantry after leaving Brest on the *Reine Blanche* in December 1841. He was a thoroughly competent seaman who had served, like a number of his contemporaries, in the Algiers expedition. He had made his mark in Pacific exploration, hydrography, and naval diplomacy. There is a certain stiffness and formality about his relations with foreigners, though he was not a humorless man; and he was no more overbearing than Dumont d'Urville or any number of British captains in the Pacific. He had cooperated with Belcher at Hawaii, though he was punctilious on points of national honor—a characteristic also shared with British officers. One detects in his reports on the Marquesas a capacity for wishful thinking and an envy of the British position in the Pacific which led him to exaggerate the value of the group, its demography, and its resources.

He was soon disabused. The *Reine Blanche* and her transports left Valparaiso in April 1842 in great secrecy (though a British consular officer at Santiago correctly guessed their business and destination). At Tahuata, in May, Dupetit-Thouars' old friend Iotete, on the advice of the missionaries and fearing perhaps reprisals for the pillage of an American whaler, signed away the independence of the whole southeastern group over which he had little authority. A similar ceremony took place at Hiva Oa and Nukuhiva, where Moana and five chiefs signed away the northwest islands and sold Hakapehi Bay for 1,800 francs, flour, seed, and a red coat with colonel's epaulets. The group was to be administered provisionally as a squadron of "stationary ships" under Captains Halley and Collet, who were to fortify themselves on Tahuata and Nukuhiva with two hundred men each. French traders and whalers were to be supplied, and the good offices of the Catholic missionaries were to be used in relations with the Marquesans.[25]

But already before he left the Marquesas for Tahiti, Dupetit-Thouars encountered problems not allowed for in his instructions or his previous experience. At Tahuata, Iotete's son was held hostage when his tribe refused to labor for the garrison; supplies for barter ran short; crops failed.[26] At Nukuhiva, the admiral found artillery and a fort insufficient for his new responsibilities:

> It is no longer enough; King Te Moana and his chiefs, having recognised the authority of H. M. Louis-Philippe, come to me today in order that I should settle their differences, not only with the men of the garrison, but also between themselves and between them and foreigners; they demand that I should regulate pilot, anchorage and watering fees, residence on the island etc. etc.; they even want me to fix the price of goods which up till now they have exchanged for muskets and war powder.[27]

The dream of a cheap port of call faded. In his reports written at sea, when the *Reine Blanche* sailed for Tahiti, Dupetit-Thouars reflected on the difficulties of administering his unruly and immobile "squadron" without the means to control trade in spirits or arms or to halt the devastating depopulation which he had earlier minimized. After his departure, relations with Iotete deteriorated, and an attempt to take him prisoner resulted in the death of Captain Halley, land sequestration, and the promotion of a Catholic convert, Maheono, to the position of "king" of Tahuata.[28] One officer even planned to turn the Marquesans into tributaries paying produce and livestock to the garrison.[29] The group, in short, could only be developed by making a greater investment in men and money than two isolated garrisons. This conviction (which would have been confirmed by the disaster at Tahuata) was doubtless still in the admiral's mind when he anchored at Pape'ete at the end of August 1842.

There his official business was really little more than to investigate charges brought by the Catholic mission against Consul Moerenhout, who had been overcautious in supporting claims to leasehold. To this relatively minor issue was added a whole series of complaints by the handful of French settlers about seizure of contraband spirits, prohibition of land sales, and the conduct of the *mutoi*.[30] Worse, rumor had it that Pritchard might return from England with a treaty to nullify the usefulness of the Marquesas post. Together with Moerenhout the admiral proceeded to use the grievances of nationals in order to cover any threat to the tenuous French hold on Tahuata and Nukuhiva and prevent a Tahitian "Waitangi" or another Akaroa retreat.

As Pomare was absent at Mo'orea awaiting the birth of a child,* Paraita, Tati, Utami, and Hitoti were invited to dine on board the *Reine Blanche* on the seventh, and a meeting of Dupetit-Thouars and the chiefs was announced for the eighth to settle outstanding public business. The night before, the four chiefs returned ashore to Moerenhout's residence, where the terms for a request for French protection were drawn up, roughly translated into Tahitian, and signed by them.[31] At the same time the British and American consuls were warned that hostilities might break out. The following

---

* Tamatoa, born 23 September 1842.

day, this maneuver was reinforced by the issue of a fearsome proclamation which contained all the complaints of French settlers.
Many of these, the admiral himself admitted in his covering report,
were simply the "grudges of drink-dealers . . . ever at odds with the
laws of the land." But the Catholic priests, he thought, and at least
one of the French residents had been unjustly treated in their land
cases. There was enough to serve his purpose. Violence, pillage,
and brutal usage at the hands of the *mutoi* were listed in tones of af-
fronted patriotism. A bond of $10,000 or provisional occupation of
the island within forty-eight hours was demanded, or hostilities
would commence. A loophole was left for Moerenhout's negotiations: the admiral offered to consider any proposal likely to
"gratify the just indignation" of France.[32]

Pomare did not receive this formal "Declaration," only a copy
of the protectorate request to which it seemingly gave rise and
which was taken to Mo'orea on the morning of 8 September. There
are several extant versions of this document, most of them translated from Moerenhout's original in French and published in official papers. There is also another, less-known version, translated
into English by Samuel Wilson (son of the missionary and brother
to the British acting consul); and this reads like a translation of the
Tahitian text, which has not survived:

> To the Admiral Du Petit-Thouars.
>
> Because we cannot govern our government in the present circum-
> stances so as to harmonise with Foreign Governments; and lest our
> land and our government and our liberty become another's, we
> whose names are written underneath—the Queen and the high Chiefs
> of Tahiti write to you asking that the King of the French may pro-
> tect us.
>
> Here are the conditions of this agreement.
>
> 1. That the name of the Queen and the government of the Queen and
>   the government of the high Chiefs and their authority may remain
>   upon them and upon their people.
> 2. All laws and regulations in the government established shall be
>   made in the name of the Queen and her name signed underneath.
> 3. The Queen and all the people shall keep possession of their lands.
>   Land disputes are to be left to themselves. Foreigners shall not in-
>   terfere with them.
> 4. The people shall be left to regard God according to their own
>   desire.

5. The Churches of the British Missionaries now existing, shall be left unmolested and the British Missionaries still discharge their functions.

It is the same with all other people, they shall not be molested in their thought towards God.

Upon these conditions, if agreeable, do the Queen and the high Chiefs ask the King of the French for protection. All affairs relative to foreign Governments and concerning Foreigners resident at Tahiti shall be with the French Government and the person put in authority by said Government with the advice of her authorities—such as Port Regulations Etc. Etc. And do all the functions to establish harmony and peace.[33]

	Signed PARAITA	Speaker to the Queen
Signed Pomare	UTAMI	
	HITOTI	
	TATI	

Translated by me
     SAML. WILSON

(Interpreter and Translator)

This copy is undated and was forwarded to the State Department by the U.S. consul, Blackler, with an explanation that the chiefs had signed before Pomare. It would also seem to have been prepared in some haste: there is no mention in Article 3 of native land courts. Conversely, in the official French version "Foreigners" (which might be held to include the French) are not specifically excluded from a say in the district courts. Paraita is designated by his correct Tahitian title and not the function of "Regent" bestowed on him by Moerenhout and Dupetit-Thouars. Finally, the position of Pomare's signature, usually first in other versions, suggests, too, that it is a more faithful record of the order in which the signatures were obtained.

There is some evidence that Pomare held out but was persuaded by Alexander Salmon (or Ari'itaimai Tane as he appears in one version of the protectorate request), by the missionary Simpson, and by Judge Tairapa, one of the To'ohitu. It was rushed back to Tahiti before the ultimatum expired. On the basis of this request, a "Proclamation" (which Pomare did not see) was drawn up in her name and signed by Paraita.[34]

This document made a theoretical distinction between French external sovereignty and Tahitian "possession of the soil." It was a fairly novel piece of imperial constitution-making at this date. The administration by French officers and the queen was to share jurisdiction and authority between the courts already provided for in the Marquesas under naval regulations and the institutions and laws of Tahiti. In practice, it was to be a makeshift of rule by a tri-umvirate consisting of Moerenhout, as French commissioner, two naval officers, and the Tahitian chiefs and judges. A mixed jury was appointed to hear land cases. Property was declared inviolable as a check to the *mutoi*; the old code remained in force as a check to the settlers who were now required to furnish certificates of nationality and pay trading licenses; and, finally, a clause of the proclamation prohibited interference by other Europeans—as a check to the missionaries. The Tahitian flag of red, white, and red horizontal bands was quartered with the tricolor. When the *Reine Blanche* departed a few days later, the temporary acting commissioner had six marines at his disposal, no funds, and a warning from Dupetit-Thouars that France might not ratify the experiment.

The reaction of Europeans was not unfavorable; and even the missionaries accepted the new order. Only the Catholics complained because the whole group had not been annexed. Several important court cases were heard under Tahitian laws, and the judges' decisions were confirmed by Moerenhout's provisional government.

But by the end of the year, the enforcement of licenses alienated traders and retailers "who saw the domination of France harder than that of the missionaries."[35] Reform of the *mutoi* by Moerenhout produced a set of recruits whose exactions were even more outrageous than before. Worse, Pomare (now safely delivered of her child) was encouraged to have second thoughts when Admiral Sir Thomas Thompson brought the *Talbot* into Pape'ete harbor in January 1843, saluted the queen's flag, and refused to recognize the provisional government. At an assembly convened by Darling and Simpson the element of *force majeure* was cited as an argument to invalidate Dupetit-Thouars' actions. Tati and Utami made contrite disavowals of their part in the affair, blaming Moerenhout for the conspiracy. The queen retired to Puna'auia as conflict between the chiefs threatened and tearful letters were sent to Victoria and to the British station at Valparaiso to undo what had been done.

This delayed reaction was aggravated by the return of Pritchard in February 1843 and by the blatant opinions of Captain Toup Nicolas, who transported the consul from Sydney. For, in New South Wales, reported the French consul to Guizot, the public cared little for the Marquesas but strongly resented the loss of Tahiti to France.[36] Some of this resentment would appear to have strengthened Nicolas' own view that Pomare and the chiefs should not be abandoned "into the hands of a Power which they so much dread and so heartily detest."[37] Neither he nor Pritchard was prepared by orders or by temperament to cooperate with an administration they judged to be established by a "foul crime of Treason."[38] The consul refused to supply jurors; as a trader he tried to introduce copper coinage and encouraged the queen to establish a market monopoly at Pape'ete; as an ex-missionary he mounted the pulpit to preach against the provisional government and all its works. In this he was backed by Nicolas, who interfered with land cases and ordered British subjects to boycott the courts. Orders from the Admiralty, through Valparaiso, arrived too late to remedy his example; but his information, which was a good deal more detailed than Pritchard's, earned the consul a reprimand and explicit instructions which arrived in January 1844 to "abstain from every act or word which might be misconstrued into an intention to give offence."[39] Again the dispatch was too late.

French commanders who called at Pape'ete in 1843 could not remove the impression that Britain would guarantee Tahitian independence and that the last word had not been said. Nor could they prevent Pomare from flying a personal house flag quartered with a crown, despite Moerenhout's protests. It had been given by a British officer: it symbolized the ultimate frustration of the provisional government; and it served as a pretext for outright annexation when Dupetit-Thouars returned in November 1843.

GOVERNOR BRUAT'S WAR

Notice of the Marquesas annexation, which was made official at the end of 1842, roused little comment. Captain Armand-Joseph Bruat was selected to command the new post in February 1843, and stores and munitions were collected at Brest and Toulon for an early departure. But his final instructions were delayed, and he did not sail till May, two months after the first versions of Dupetit-Thouars' initiative, complete with rumors of the exodus of English missionaries, reached the French press. When British mission circles took up the cry against "the imposition of Popery by the arms of France," in April 1843, Guizot hastened to give assurances that Protestants would not be hindered in their work.[40] For the Foreign Office had made it clear that the British government had no objections to the protectorate, providing it was not a precedent for further expansion, particularly in the Hawaiian Islands. The Foreign Secretary Lord Aberdeen was embarrassed to learn of an equally unauthorized protectorate arranged in that group by Lord George Paulet in February 1843 and reported to London in June. This was formally disavowed, and France and England agreed to consider Hawaii as an independent state.

Dupetit-Thouars staked his career on a ratification and wrote from Valparaiso in November, offering his services as governor and hinting that perhaps Hawaii should be considered as well.[41] An undated minute by Admiral Roussin, minister of marine, defended him on the grounds that Pritchard might well have acted first.[42] The Council of State accepted the protectorate, but not his offer to rule it, on 7 April 1843. The Ministry of Marine was now left with the problem of arranging an administration for two very different possessions.

Bruat was given draconian powers under a royal ordinance of 28 April 1843 to govern the Marquesas in much the same way as French generals were expected to keep order in Algeria.[43] No alteration was made to these powers when Roussin formulated his instructions to act as commissioner as well at Tahiti.[44] What was good enough for a soldier settlement of the Algerian type with its military tribunals and land appropriations was thought to be more than adequate for the kingdom of the Pomares. In fact, Admiral Roussin and his successor, Baron de Mackau, were fairly skeptical at this stage about the formal distinction between the two possessions and set little store by the agreements of 1842:

> The convention made between Admiral Du Petit-Thouars and Queen Pomare will have to serve as the basis of our Protectorate; the powers that are attributed to us there are badly defined. You should nevertheless observe in the form of all your acts the ostensible character of

our authority, without, however, compromising the good of the administration and our political interests by too many scruples. You will understand that such an imperfect limitation to our power cannot be an insurmountable barrier to our influence and action. If you compare the Protectorate exercised by England over the Ionian Islands with that granted us over the Society Islands, already you will see how much the latter is restricted.[45]

The parallel with the first British protectorate of 1815 was an apt one. Governor Sir Thomas Maitland's "Primary Council" was not unlike a French administrative council of officials and a few settlers, and Maitland's description of the Ionian Assembly—"so exceptionally fond of points totally in detail and of making use of fine words"—might well have applied to Tahitian assemblies in the 1850s.[46]

But Bruat was also ordered to create "a political and judicial hierarchy" from the chiefs and judges and to sanction their offices. Pomare was to be stipended from the governor's funds or from port revenues at the rate of 25,000 francs a year (or slightly less than half the governor's own salary of 60,000 francs).

For France was prepared to pay for the politics of influence in the Pacific. It was well established that colonization in the English sense was not the objective to be pursued: "With the well-being of all classes in France, large emigration is not possible," Bruat was informed.[47] In a similar vein, the Chamber of Deputies was told by Guizot, in June 1843, that the aim of commercial protection could be achieved with small posts—"the smallest possible, costing as little as possible."[48] Both the budget commission and the chamber responded fairly generously to support the new annexed and protected islands, voting no less than 4.5 million francs.

Indeed, it was overgenerous. When the new minister of marine, de Mackau, entered office in July 1843, he found a deficit of nearly 3 million francs in the naval accounts.[49] The policy of paying premiums for colonial posts to secure a territorial insurance against future developments, such as the Panama Canal or investment in French whaling, suddenly looked less attractive when the ministry had to run 207 ships of the line on a budget for 164.

It is arguable that at this point in 1843 the long traditional association between the French navy and French Catholic missions took on a more positive character. The congregations became not merely pioneers of civilization, entitled to transport on government vessels and treaties in their name as French nationals, but also guardians of the French flag on island outposts that the state was unwilling to finance. This change in policy was first outlined to Bruat as "a question of accepting in principle the type of sovereignty which a treaty signed by chiefs confers on us" at Wallis, Tonga, or Mangareva—and then "to gradually join the whole of the Polynesian group to the French Establishments, missionary influence will be our principal means of success."[50]

The result was a vague protectorate over the Wallis group, at the request of Bishop Pompallier, under a flag with mission insignia. In 1843, Dupetit-Thouars was ordered to provide transport for Bishop Douarre to New Caledonia and, typically enough, went further and arranged protectorate treaties (though the flag was withdrawn in 1846). A similar missionary role was arranged for the Sacred Hearts Congregation at Mangareva in 1844. Thereafter, this small-scale imperialism through the missions was made even more informal. Bruat and Admiral Hamelin at Valparaiso were ordered to give them moral support but not to invest the mission stations with protectorate flags in the name of France.[51]

For a brief period only, then, did the combination of Church and State militant take the form so long feared by Protestant missionaries. Meanwhile Bruat had sailed from France with only 200,000 francs at his disposal for general expenses. It was little enough to found the new centers for maritime strength in eastern Polynesia; and although the rest of the budget was paid in due course, financial shortages dogged his early governorship.

Calling first at the Marquesas in October 1843, Bruat quickly assessed the worth of Dupetit-Thouars' posts and confirmed the appointment of their commanders. Nukuhiva, he saw, would never become a kind of "admiral's flagship" (envisaged in his first official ordinance).[52] His attention, moreover, was immediately turned to Tahiti. Dupetit-Thouars, once he learned from Bruat that the protectorate had been ratified, took advantage of his superior rank to take this news to Queen Pomare, arriving at Pape'ete on 1 November. Bruat arrived four days later at the climax of a new crisis.

Faced with the intransigence of Pritchard and the refusal of Pomare to abandon her personal house flag, the admiral hoisted the tricolor on 6 November. Salutes and drums drowned out a brave attempt by Mare, the queen's orator, to deliver a verbal protest. Pritchard struck his consular flag and took the queen into the consulate at news of the annexation. On 8 November Bruat began his governorship installed in her house with full, if unratified, powers over both groups of islands, four ships of the line, and over a thousand men—"labourers, artificers, troops . . . and the officers necessary for a civil establishment."[53] There Dupetit-Thouars left him two days later to make what he could out of a situation created very largely by the admiral's impetuosity.

Nothing on the scale of the French occupation had ever been seen in Tahiti. Bruat was intelligent enough to realize that the power at his command required restraint if the peace of the island and his new career were to survive. He was heavily dependent for advice on Moerenhout as director of Native Affairs and on Tati and Paraita among the senior chiefs; and this tended to isolate him from sources of information sympathetic to the queen. She could not be entirely dispensed with because the annexation might not be approved in Paris. On the other hand, Bruat believed her to be completely under the influence of the Protestant mission; and when she was transferred from Pritchard's care to H.M.S. *Basilisk* at the end of December, there was an additional risk of a dispute with British naval officers. For all his forces on the board, the most important piece eluded his grasp. Bruat turned in January 1844 to exploiting the political advantage to be gained by associating lesser chiefs with his big battalions and confirmed a number of them in lands and titles, beginning with Paraita, who was reappointed to the position of "regent."[54]

Pomare countered this move by urging the population to remain calm until Britain came to the rescue. Her letters were intercepted; some of her officials were arrested and interned on the frigate *Embuscade*; and Bruat threatened to seize her lands. He also proscribed a number of chiefs who had taken part in a "rebel" assembly at Papara. The threat, in the words of Orsmond, "was a most unpolitic measure at this time on Tahiti . . . it raised frightful apprehensions—created insurmountable aversions to the French, and induced all to assemble in arms against them."[55] An attempt to capture the chiefs who had taken part in the Papara assembly failed. Bruat sent the frigate with a second vessel to secure the peninsula of Taiarapu by building a fort on the Taravao isthmus. Work was begun on blockhouses behind Pape'ete, and defenses were completed on Motu Uta, the islet in the harbor. All of this entailed expropriation of *ari'i* lands. The occupation of other lands for barracks and camps at either end of the town, on the whole of the waterfront at Fare Ute, and on the site of St. Amélie village along the River Tipae behind the town continued throughout 1844 into 1845, when the protectorate was restored and new regulations were passed.[56] European properties were not exempt (though few of them were freehold). The Franklin Hotel was among the first to disappear. The grog shop of Victor Chancerel, who had retailed for Moerenhout, was not spared either.

The situation quickly deteriorated when Bruat went to inspect the post under construction on Pomare's lands at Taravao, leaving Pape'ete under the command of Captain Foucher d'Aubigny. Suspected movements of Tahitians on the hills overlooking the blockhouses caused the nervous commandant to declare a state of emergency and arrest Pritchard on 3 March as a likely cause of trouble. After five days of incarceration in one of the blockhouses, the consul was transferred to a British warship and deported to Valparaiso into the notoriety of an international incident. But, by then, Bruat had a general insurrection on his hands.

Armed opposition to the French, from 13 March 1844, centered first on Pare-Arue, on the eastern division of Te Aharoa, and in districts adjacent to the Taravao forts, which were attacked on the twentieth. A naval bombardment of houses and plantations along the eastern coast in Hitia'a followed, but Bruat was obliged to keep most of his forces at Pape'ete because of the vulnerability of the town. The leaders of the rebellion at this stage were drawn mainly from among Pomare's close relatives and from chiefs who were their district delegates. Mo'orea and the Teva were in a state of growing excitement but unaffected by the military maneuvers. Te Aharoa tribal chiefs provided generalship and coordinated contingents from other districts who supported the Pomares or whose disaffection was caused by the more immediate issue of land sequestration.

This leadership fell at first on Fanaue, who held titles in Maha'ena and Vairao districts. He concentrated some four thousand men on the shore opposite Maha'ena pass and planted the Tahitian flag on one of the small hills overlooking the beach (about where the coast road reaches Putaiamo village). There, on 17 April, Bruat stormed his trenches after a naval bombardment, killing some seventy-nine insurgents at a cost of thirty-six marine infantry. The bulk of the Tahitian forces retreated into the fastness of the Papeno'o Valley with an outpost at Ha'apape. Bruat withdrew to Pape-'ete with a sincere respect for his enemy and a new appreciation of the difficult political and military problems he faced. His immediate action was to release the officials and chiefs still on the *Embuscade* and await reinforcements while countering British missionary and naval influence.

For their part the Tahitians remained divided between the small pro-French party created by Moerenhout and the anti-French chiefs and officials alienated from the new government. After Maha'ena, the mass of the population in the districts actively supported the fighting men in the Tahitian camps at Papeno'o, Puna'aru, and Fauta'ua, deep in the easily fortified mountain valleys in the center of the main island. Mo'orea was officially kept out of the war by the influence of Judge Tairapa, from July 1844, but contingents from that island and from all districts fought in the camps under their district chiefs. Where these were not present, they elected new ones to their titles. Fanaue was demoted for his mistaken tactics, and effective generalship passed to Utami and Mai'o, an ambitious *ra'atira* and subchief of Pa'ea, within the Puna'auia camps. Pitomai, a delegate of Atiau Vahine, and Fareahu, a To'ohitu judge, led the camp at Papeno'o. A few leaders surrendered in 1844 and 1845 and were confirmed by Bruat in the titles of districts whose chiefs were still among the rebels (see Table 2). Some prominent families were divided when, for example, Tati's son Ori, chief of Papeno'o, fought in all battles against the French, while his brother, Faitohia, was appointed by Bruat over the hostile district of Tautira. Conversely, from within the hard core of the *hau feti'i* which had most to lose from annexation, the queen's uncle, Vaira'atoa, was persuaded to join the French by the two collaborators, Alexander Salmon and his wife Ari'ioehau (Ari'itaimai) in 1845, and Bruat appointed him as chief over Pare-Arue. But Ari'itaimai's mother, the redoubtable Atiau who had married the eldest son of Tati, did not surrender till December 1845.[57]

Broadly speaking, then, the Tahitian resistance comprised most of the population, though there was less positive support, as the war dragged on, for the Pomare family than a deep-seated aversion to a European presence which occupied lands and arbitrarily imprisoned Tahitians.

Bruat was convinced that their camps were as much centers of English hostility, as Tahitian opposition, to the French. In fact, the missionaries were far from unanimous in their views, though they were an obvious target for suspicion, just as they were blamed by Tahitians when Britain did not intervene. Four despaired and left. Others, like Darling, clung to the hope that they would be "delivered" by the British navy and supplied the rebel camps with "the means of Grace" but little else. Davies, Orsmond, and Henry, to varying degrees, were willing to cooperate with the new rulers, fearing that distortions in the British press and patriotic rallies in support of Pritchard would only hinder their work. Bruat thought the missionaries would have acted much the same under British rule, "which would not have failed to limit their ambitions."[58] Nothing damned them more in his eyes than the Missionary Society's dismissal of Orsmond for "acts of hospitality and friendship" to his men and for refusing to assist "the oppressed islanders."[59] Bruat made him government pastor at Pape'ete, but came to weary of such an eccentric collaborator. He remained justifiably suspicious of more intransigent opponents such as Thomson and Rodgerson on Tahiti or more subtle detractors such as Charles Barff at Ra'iatea.

A greater source of anxiety was the presence of British men-of-war—no fewer than a dozen between 1843 and 1846. Some of their commanders openly voiced their disappointment at the turn of events, though by January 1844 the British government's policy was known, and they were ordered to recognize the protectorate and salute its flag early in 1845. It was on the suggestion of Captain Hope, H.M.S. *Basilisk*, that Pomare was transported to the Leeward Islands in July 1844; and it was Hope who refused to acknowledge the protectorate throughout that year of tension at the port. The tension was not relieved by the visit of Consul General Miller from Hawaii to rebel districts in October 1844 to deliver letters from Pomare (though he got on well enough with Bruat, who permitted him to go to the war camp at Papeno'o). The chiefs took heart from his attentions, and one—Ari'inoho of Pa'ea—was tried

TABLE 2
Titles and Chiefs: 1818–1845

Division and District	Chief (titles in italics)	Appointment
Porionu'u		
Pare-Arue	*Ari'ipaea* Vahine*	Also titles *Teri'itaria* and *ari'i* Huahine; sister of Teremoemoe.
	Ari'ipaea (Haumure)†	Son of *Vaira'atoa*; nephew of Pomare I.‡
Te Aharoa		
Ha'apape (Mahina)	*Tari'iri'i*	Peueue (delegate of Teremoemoe). Moe† (May 1845).
Papeno'o	Ori†	Son of Tati and successor to his wife's mother in district titles.
Tiarei	*Manua*	Hitoti† died 1846; succeeded by son of sister of Paofai, a minor
	Hitoti†	(Hitoti iti, 1835–1901).
Maha'ena	*Ro'ura*	
	Fanaue*	
	Ro'ura Vahine†	Daughter or sister of Fanaue.
Hitia'a	*Teri'itua**	Exiled by Pomare IV (1835) and pardoned (1839). Daughter of sister of Tapoa II, Huahine.
	Tuavira†	1849; son of Pomare IV.
Teva-i-tai		
Afa'ahiti	*Moearu*	Mairi Taui, delegate for Ari'iaue, son of Pomare IV.
Pueu, Nuhi	*Tetuanui maraeta'ata*	*Maraeta'ata* Tane;* brother of Utami.
	Maraeta'ata Vahine†	
Tautira	*Vehiatua*	
	Fa'aitohia†	Eldest son of Tati.
Teahupo'o	*Vehiatua*	
	Peueue*	Rebel confirmed in titles by Bruat in 1845.
Mataoae, Toahotu	*Moeteraui*	
	Puna*	
	Toahere†	A member of Paraita's family adopted by Puna.
Vairao	*Vairora*	
	Fanaue*	Replaced by Bruat.
	Huruino†	Son of Fanaue's delegate.
Teva-i-uta		
Papeari	Atiau Vahine*	
	Pitomai	Delegate of Atiau Vahine, promoted by Bruat.

TABLE 2 (continued)

Division and District	Chief (titles in italics)	Appointment
Papeuriri	*Fare'ahu**	Remained a To'ohitu.
	Rava'ai†	Brother of wife of Paraita, nominated by Bruat 1844.
Atimaono	*Teari'ifa'atau**†	Sister of Haumure *(Ari'ipaea)*† and his delegate.
Papara	Tati*†	
Oropa'a		
Pa'ea	*To'ofa*	
	Maro*	Deposed by Bruat.
	Pohearu*	
	Ruarei†	Appointed 1846; related to Tati.
Puna'auia	*Pohuetea**	
	Utami*	Adopted son of *Pohuetea* titleholder.
	Pohuetea†	Son of Utami's adoptive "father"; deposed by judges and Bruat.
	Aifenua Vahine†	Sister of *Pohuetea.*
Te Fana		
Fa'a'a	*Tepau**	
	Atiau Vahine*†	Had married eldest son of Tati (Tuati).
Mo'orea		
Afare'aitu	Hapoto*†	
Hauai	*Ta'ero**†	
Ma'atea	Pe'e*	
	Pe'e†	Nephew of predecessor and a To'ohitu.
Ha'apiti	*Marama**	
Teavaro	Atiau Vahine	
	Marama†	Delegate of Atiau.
Papeto'ai	*Manea**†	Under Judge Tairapa.
Moru'u	Te'auta'aia*†	
Varari	*Vaira'atoa**	
	Mahine*†	

* Appointed under Pomare II.
† Appointed under Bruat.
‡ Sources conflict as to whether this Vaira'atoa is a brother of Pomare I or Pomare II. I think the latter more likely—that is, that he is Teri'inavaharoa, who died in 1805.

Sources: Henry (1928); ANSOM A 52/9, Bruat, "Mémoire adressé au capitaine de vaisseau Lavaud," May 1847; Cottez (1955:434–460); Teissier (1978:1–139).

by Bruat's To'ohitu and exiled to Makatea for consorting with him.[60] The warship *Talbot* saluted the new flag of the protectorate, however, on 10 October before taking Miller back to Hawaii.

The formal restoration of the protectorate constitution was delayed till January 1845; for, by then, it was possible for Bruat to assemble a respectable number of judges and chiefs and draw up a list of district and court authorities paid from local revenues. But it was a political stalemate so long as the bulk of the chiefs remained in opposition. Pomare, who had been advised to remain at Ra'iatea by Miller, showed no sign of trusting whatever terms the governor proposed.

Bruat, therefore, decided to end her exile by taking over the Leeward group—a plan he had kept in mind ever since his arrival. He was worried, too, by the movement of Captain Lord George Paulet (remembered for his initiative at Hawaii) to the group on the *Carysfort* in July 1844.[61] By early 1845, with the permission of the Ministry of Marine, Bruat raised the protectorate flag at each of the three main islands. It was promptly torn down at Ra'iatea and Huahine, but at Borabora a small number of partisans under the chief, Mai (an old rival of Tapoa), were encouraged by Commander Pradier of the *Phaeton* in June 1845. Ra'iatea was declared to be in a state of blockade.

In Paris, however, Guizot had decided by June 1845 to agree to British requests, inspired by the missionaries, that there should be no extension of the protectorate until it was known whether Pomare had any "sovereign" rights in the Leeward Islands. An international investigation began which uncovered a good deal of interesting material on the *hau feti'i* and their historic claims throughout the period of the Pomare's ascendency, but which was bound to be influenced by the opposing purposes of the investigators.[62] Moerenhout and Bruat played up Pomare's status as *ari'i rahi*; Miller and the missionaries played it down and emphasized the "independence" cultivated since the 1820s. Discussion of *ari'i* privileges in terms of territorial "sovereignty," in any case, begged important questions about the consent of lesser chiefs and *ra'atira*; and their attitudes to the French were clear enough. As the investigation continued and the blockade of Ra'iatea became a farce, Bruat feared for the general position of his government both at Tahiti and in the Leewards, where "a public enquiry, so far from leading to the discovery of the truth, would only stir up the means of dislodging us."[63]

His fears were justified. Admiral Seymour, during his visit to Ra'iatea on the enormous eighty-gun *Collingwood* which he had brought to investigate the terms of an indemnity for Pritchard, had declared all French enactments there null and void.[64] He actively discouraged the impression that England would fight, but the resistors took heart from the sight of his first-rate battleship (the first seen in the islands). French allies on Borabora were expelled. In January 1846 Captain Bonard, who had a reputation as a fire-eater in Tahiti, unwisely exceeded his orders at Huahine. He was routed by Queen Teri'itaria (Ari'ipaea Vahine) and her mixed force of islanders and Europeans with the loss of eighteen men killed and forty-three wounded. The evacuation of Borabora followed at once, and the blockade of Ra'iatea was raised.

News of this defeat "spread like wildfire through the camps" in Tahiti.[65] In March, the rebels attacked Ha'apape from the Papeno'o Valley. Bruat made a landing at Puna'auia beach in April and was repulsed. With fresh reinforcements from France and some hundred Tahitian and Boraboran recruits he made another costly attack up the Puna'auia Valley in May.

But the war camps were short of supplies and munitions and suffered from disease. Every month they held out emphasized the political point that Bruat had already learned and taken to heart— there could be no peaceful administration without a measure of cooperation. They could not secure a French defeat, and probably not a French evacuation, though the cost of the campaign to France was among their most important weapons.

What could not be won by frontal attack from either side was decided by stealth in a brilliant operation described by the missionary Thomson:

About the beginning of Decr. [1846] a native of Rapa in the Fautaua camp immediately behind Papeete and which opens a passage through the interior to the other two camps discovered a path up the face of the cliff by which a position might be gained that would command the camp. He deserted from the natives, came to Papeete, and volunteered to lead the troops for a stipulated reward, I believe 200 dollars. Shortly afterwards all the troops marched up the valley [Papeno'o]. The great body placed themselves in front of the regular advance to the native camp, as if about to storm it. All in the camp were on the alert to defend their road; a large number were however absent on a foraging expedition. In the meantime the native of Rapa with about 30 French natives and 40 soldiers were scaling the cliff at a little distance, the Rapa man ascending by the path which he had discovered, and lowering a rope pulled up and fixed a rope ladder by which the troops gained the summit about 1,000 feet high and prepared to fire upon the camp a little below them. The natives seeing that resistance was now in vain laid down their arms and were marched in as prisoners of war together less than 100. The carrying of this position opened a passage to the other two camps.[66]

Papeno'o and Puna'auia surrendered to Bruat in a dignified ceremonial which respected the persons and titles of chiefs while making sure that some five hundred muskets and four cannon were handed over. Pomare still delayed in the Leeward Islands, despite numerous overtures and diplomatic missions, torn between the promise of status and income under the protectorate and pressure from Tamatoa and Tapoa to keep intact the aristocratic independence of the *hau feti'i* whose Leeward Islands, at least, had been recognized and neutralized by France and Britain.* Naval visitors found her well settled on Tamatoa's lands at Ra'iatea but unable to take a considered view of her situation and the military and diplomatic activity caused by her prolonged absence.[67] She remained proud and fickle. Bruat might well have dispensed with her altogether. Possibly sensing this, she finally made up her mind; and with due pomp she was met at Mo'orea and conveyed to Tahiti, where a formal submission was signed on 7 February 1847 in which Pomare confessed that "my mind was darkened and I listened more to foreign words."[68]

GOVERNOR LAVAUD'S PEACE

It had been a costly little war which helped to expand foreign trade more than French trade and reduced the importance attached to the Marquesas in favor of Tahiti. Altogether, the administration had achieved precisely the opposite results of official policies proclaimed in 1842 and 1843. The financial largesse of Bruat's first

---

* Notice of the agreement to regard the Leeward Islands as independent was conveyed to Bruat at the end of 1846, but official diplomatic recognition did not come till the Declaration of London (19 June 1847).

budget had been reduced to just over 2 million francs in 1844; it was reduced still further in 1846, though military expenditure on the accounts of the Pacific naval station at Valparaiso continued to mount.

Bruat had the greatest difficulty in transforming ministerial estimates, sanctioned nearly a year away by sea mail, into provisions and specie. Not all local drafts issued by the administration were honored in Paris; trading houses at Pape'ete and Valparaiso demanded coin in payment for official contracts and made a good profit supplying South American dollars at a heavy discount.[69] Troops were not paid, works were delayed, and in July 1844 there were only three months' rations left, as the administration lived from hand to mouth and depended on British traders, such as Lucett, or on naval stores. There was some peculation, discovered only much later by a commission of inquiry. A short-lived municipal bank collected trading and retail licenses between 1844 and 1846 but could not hope to cover local expenses. Its records show, however, that the business community of Pape'ete expanded rapidly to take advantage of the military market, and at the end of the war in 1847 some 180 licenses were issued. Inflation was rampant. By the time Lavaud arrived, in May 1847, there was a monumental deficit resulting from excessive issue of drafts locally on the Ministry of Marine and from shortage of cash.*

The hoped-for share of Pacific commerce was disappointing. For the five years between 1845 and 1850 French vessels (including warships) accounted for only 20 percent of tonnage at Pape'ete,[70] compared with American, British, and other shipping. Even local schooner traffic and whalers amounted to more than entries under national register. The settlement of French troops and artisans on expropriated plots of land at St. Amélie in the 1840s produced indifferent results. Most drifted away, leaving their cottages and peasant gardens in the valley behind the town, for commerce, cattle-raising, and quicker returns from wage labor. Their example was common to the small wave of fortune hunters that came in the wake of the occupation (and flowed out again to California in 1849). Tahitians also profited in 1847, when there was a rise in

---

* Local currency at this date was based on denominations of the Peruvian piastre, rated at 5 francs 25 centimes. Bruat tried to stabilize the rate at 5 francs, but it often rose as high as 5 francs 40.

wages for all kinds of labor.[71] Everywhere, at the end of the war, family heads were busy putting their lands in order by "erecting houses to secure possession of them" and to profit from the demand for cash crops.[72] Payment for services by a spendthrift administration, both high and low in Tahitian society, soon vanquished "all their pretended hatred of the French."[73]

This new concentration of resources at the main port left the Marquesas defenseless during the war and their commandants powerless to check a trade in muskets organized by the small community of freebooters living on Hiva Oa. At Nukuhiva, a chief massacred five of the garrison in 1845 and was summarily executed. Little was gained by paying Moana or Maheono 3,000 francs a year each, though a French warship assisted the former to reduce the Taipi tribe by bombardment in 1847. But Lavaud disapproved of the practice of subsidizing warrior chiefs, and he did not believe that attempts to build up the status of Moana would serve the French cause in conditions of penury. The post at Vaitahu was omitted completely from the 1847 budget; and Nukuhiva's share of total revenue amounted to only a fraction of the money spent on Tahiti. The Ministry of Marine decided to abandon the group in 1848, and it was left to Lavaud to hand over Nukuhiva to the gentle care of the Catholic mission.

The withdrawal was recognition of the shift in emphasis away from the argument from naval strategy made by Dupetit-Thouars to the practical politics of conquest undertaken by Bruat. It was part of the legacy of the war.

Bruat's second legacy to his successor was a refinement of the institutions that had been adapted to his need for local supporters. The war had emphasized that Tahitians were more than capable of making a concerted political demonstration but were also amenable to overrule—providing certain guidelines were accepted concerning revenues, lands, and titles. Bruat took the view that the political structure of the islands, consisting of queen, chiefs, and courts, was to be preserved intact. He was doubtful whether the queen exercised much authority over the more influential guardians of the code of laws, but he singled out the custom of keeping district headships in the hands of families approved by local district companies and ra'atira as one to be carefully observed. He drew up for his successor's guidance a detailed analysis of all offices, institutions, and personalities. Possibly Alexander Salmon and Orsmond assisted him in writing his *mémoire*, completed in 1847. On any count it is a remarkable document, full of insights into chieftainship, chiefs, and foreign residents and the equal of any intelligence report.[74]

In addition to this emphasis on rule through district chiefs, Bruat's practice of consulting French allies during the war promoted the Tahitian Assembly, which had been revived in 1842. He used it in 1844 and 1845 to sanction regulations on land registration and other measures; through it he collected evidence about the Pomares' relationship with Leeward Islands chiefs; and from it he drew candidates appointed as judges and chiefs. In making such appointments, he promised to take into account "the rights, the pretensions, and the political influence of every important family in order to be able to favour partisans without contravening the customs of the land."[75] The assembly was to be used to represent these partisans, just as the Toʻohitu was expanded to include old enemies and new allies "in a proportion which assured to our friends a majority in this tribunal."[76] He also began to pay for lands rented from Salmon, Pomare, and other Tahitians from 1845.

Thus Lavaud was left with the means to rule indirectly after Bruat had confirmed chiefs in office and paid them small stipends. In all, on the two islands, there were only nine chiefs whose titles were reallocated by Bruat, and six of the new appointments were from the families of deposed chiefs. There were some rewards for members of the French party, but Peueue, a former rebel, emerged as paramount over the Taiarapu Peninsula, just as Tati and Paraita were paramount over the western Teva and the Porionuʻu. In three other districts, Bruat sanctioned new chieftaincies filled by the choice of the *raʻatira*. At Papenoʻo, this entailed the pardon of a leading rebel—Ori. Atiau Vahine and the rebel Pitomai were also left in office.

Paradoxically, therefore, there was less open resentment in Tahiti in 1847 than in the Leeward Islands, where the memory of the bombardment of Fare on Huahine died hard. Conceivably, too, the centralizing process begun under the missionaries had been carried a stage further by the formal incorporation of the Tuamotu and the Austral island of Tubuai into the protectorate. The chiefs of Anaʻa and Makatea had come to do homage to the queen, after her return, and were given protectorate flags. The chiefs of Tubuai came to fight on the French side, and the *ari'i* of the island, Tamatoa, was stipended for his wounds and his services.

Lavaud, then, who had been appointed to clear up the financial mess of Bruat's administration, found that the peace had been well prepared for him. He was a sound choice with experience in the Pacific, an unpretentious officer who was also a Freemason. His task, as he saw it, was retrenchment and a formal definition of the place of Pomare in the revised constitution.

The financial question was largely decided for him by the parsimony of the ministry. Pomare's position was less easy to prescribe. In August 1847, he drew up a convention to clarify the rather vague promises extracted from her by Bruat, and the queen was persuaded to sign it by Alexander Salmon.[77] By its terms, the payment of chiefs and the abolition of the old tribute system were confirmed; and, secondly, the governor refused to admit the paramountcy of any chief over others. The assembly was to be elected annually by the district *ra'atira* to discuss enactments arising in the governor's council or proposed by the assembly itself. Parallel to this legislative body, the Tahitian judiciary, headed by the To'ohitu was to be appointed by the queen and governor. Appointment of the *mutoi* was left to the chiefs. Above all, although civil courts had been set up by Bruat in 1845, land cases not involving Europeans were left to Tahitian jurisdiction.

This fairly liberal measure would have rendered the 1842 treaty and proclamation obsolete—which was what Lavaud hoped. But it should be remembered that Bruat's special powers decreed for the Marquesas had been applied to Tahiti and Mo'orea by two governor's decrees in 1845, and criminal jurisdiction fell under Bruat's courts-martial.[78] These powers gave a considerable reserve of authority to the French commissioner as partner in the joint executive. Moreover, the convention assumed a maximum of goodwill between Pomare and European administrators and restraint from interference in the "internal organisation of the Society Islands."[79] It did not touch on important questions such as use of district lands and other privileges within the province of titleholders. Finally, neither the minister of marine, Arago, nor Guizot was prepared to submit this constitutional novelty to the chamber in the last days of Louis-Philippe's reign or in the first troubled months of the republic. Guizot thought the convention had merits, recognizing that Tahiti was unique as a territory where "all the details of political and administrative organisation should, above all, be determined by local circumstances."[80] But the most he would approve was the proclamation of the convention as an internal measure between queen and governor "susceptible to later modifications." The minister of marine, with a more doctrinaire approach to colonial questions, saw that the assembly and the convention might become the means for "gallicizing" Tahitians and wrote to Lavaud in this sense:

> By means of the active influence which you are able to exert over the Queen and the Chiefs, by the confidence you inspire in them, you will quickly accustom them to seeing you participate more and more in the internal administration. Thus the Protectorate will become an institution more apparent than real under which sovereign rule will be progressively established.[81]

For no governor was ever legally bound to observe the convention's terms, though Lavaud proclaimed it to the assembly in 1848. The protectorate constitution consisted, then, of the treaty of 1842, Bruat's decrees and precedents, his draconian powers in the area of criminal jurisdiction, and Lavaud's definition of the Franco-Tahitian executive. The Tahitians had made their case for keeping as much of their customs and control of their lands intact as European settlement would allow. The French, as Arago prescribed, would make theirs.

But, for the moment, there was no rush to assimilate the protectorate to the pattern of a French colony. Bruat and Lavaud revised and extended the Tahitian Code of Laws as the basis of local jurisdiction for their Polynesian charges.[82] Of the thirty-one laws, fifteen were radically changed or abolished. Regulation of imports fell under French administration, and the retailing of fermented liquors (except beer and wines) to Tahitians was still prohibited. Agreement about local distilling proved more difficult (Tahitians in the 1845 assembly complained they were too poor to buy imported beverages), and a law permitting preparation of orange toddy was passed. Bruat rescinded the law after disorders.

More important, Bruat made the transfer of land to Europeans subject to a governor's decree, and he allowed counterclaims to be decided by district judges and the To'ohitu.[83] Europeans were prohibited from attending Tahitian land courts. On the other hand, the belief of the missionaries that islanders should be encouraged to cultivate land was supported by Lavaud and retained in the revised code. Similarly, the principle of compulsory education and the law against breaking the Sabbath were upheld in the governor's council after they had been revoked by the 1845 assembly (though the Sabbath law was allowed to lapse in the revision of 1848). Among other changes, a legal distinction was drawn between mayhem and slander, which the old code had included in the same law; the scale of fines for damage to property was increased; marriage between Tahitians and Europeans had to be registered in French law. Some of the code's stringency about adultery was removed: charges, henceforth, could only be brought against offenders by parents or relations, and not by Europeans, "except where a bad and shameful action has been committed in public."[84]

The tribute system was replaced by a civil list for the queen. Taxation in kind was abolished for road work, commutable at the rate of 2 francs a day, as laid down in the 1848 code. A percentage of district collections was to be paid to the *mutoi* and judges; chiefs were to receive between 200 and 300 francs (£8 to £12) annually from the queen's revenues. Missionary Society contributions were ended. The 1848 assembly was pleased to support the suggestion of Lavaud that all church properties—schools, houses, and chapels—be registered as "inalienable national property."[85] These, it was made clear, were to be administered by district congregations and not by general services demanded from all district families. "There is a strong disposition," wrote the missionary Howe, "to make the religion of Tahiti national, and in fact it is that or nearly so already, and every step taken in reference to us by the governor will tend to complete it."[86]

A census was held in 1848 which gave a total of 9,454 Polynesians for the two main islands, with perhaps 500 or 600 Europeans (including troops and officials).[87] There were estimated to be some 12,000 Marquesans and perhaps 8,000 or 9,000 islanders in the Tuamotu and on Tubuai. Pape'ete, as the capital of this scattered territory of about 30,000 inhabitants, had suddenly grown to over a thousand citizens. Military and naval engineers had already begun to plan its water supply and shape it into a colonial town. At the beginning of 1848, with the agreement of the missionaries, the local calendar was changed and Tahiti ceased to be a day in advance of the rest of the world.

CHAPTER 5

CHURCHES AND STATE

TAHITI had become French in name; but Tahitians remained deeply influenced by the work of the London Missionary Society. And although the political guidance of the British missionaries had failed to protect the islanders from other aliens and loss of independence, the structure of district administration and the content of elementary education and religious observance were durable legacies.

The first governors had to come to terms with these facts. Lavaud found in his census of 1848 that about half the adults of Tahiti and Mo'orea could read, write, and count, and most of the rest could read.[1] He paid due respect to the pioneers of literacy but thought they had not gone far enough: "Because like most missionaries they preached church doctrines as incontrovertible and established truths, when they should have concentrated on reforming the customs of the population and driving home to them principles of morality."[2] Doubtless the missionaries would not have made this anticlerical distinction; and they had, in any case, left a large place for open discussion of the eternal problem of applying ethical norms to personal and public behavior. For guidance, they had prepared a body of published texts; for leadership, they had begun to form a body of church deacons and a few ministers with whom responsibility for the churches lay.

We know little about these early Tahitian and Ra'iatean pastors. The delicate task of forming them fell on William Howe, who had foreseen the need for them in 1842. John Barff also ran the "Theological Institution" at Mo'orea, and he later set up one of his own at Raʻiatea and Tahaʻa. Howe revived the pastoral school when he returned to Papeʻete in 1847, and he associated it with the Mission Press, which turned out a surprising number of new works in Tahitian. These included a short history of the world, an abridged *Pilgrim's Progress*, the adventures of Aladdin with his lamp, and some introductions to mathematics and accountancy.[3] But theological commentaries and the revised Tahitian Bible were the principal fare of converts and the mainstay of the *tuaroʻi*, or textual debates, that had already become part of the pattern of Protestant church life.

In the rural districts the churches remained the focus of local government, giving social and religious guidance and providing a source of secular control. In his analysis of district authorities, Bruat also listed pastors and deacons, where they functioned. The church at Pare had expelled one for being pro-French; another at Taiarapu was suspected of running powder and arms. In three districts he observed that Tahitian pastors were also judges; and in 1847 deacons in Taiarapu had a say in the nomination of a new judge to the Toʻohitu. Later administrators also noticed this close correlation of temporal and religious offices.[4] The effective chief of Faʻaʻa in 1859 was not Mahearu Vahine but her husband, who was pastor, judge, and teacher. Mahaʻena district was run by Roura Vahine's husband, who was a pastor and teacher from Raʻiatea. When a chief of the subdistrict of Avirua in Tautira could not get official permission to form a recognized district of his own in 1859, he simply formed a separate church which acted as a new administrative unit.*

Consequently, Bruat and Lavaud gave a good deal of thought to eliminating the influence of British missionaries while retaining the structure and personnel of the institutions they had implanted in Tahitian society. Bruat was persuaded that the church had its uses as a means of social reform—"a powerful instrument for good in our hands, and therefore a great financial saving."[5] The school and the chapel were not to be touched. At the most, thought Bruat, the

---

* For the place of parish churches and their leadership, see Vernier (1948) and Levy (1975). The description of Rapa society in the work by Hanson (1973: 136–139) would apply to Tahiti and other communities over a longer period. But the history of the indigenous churches in French Polynesia has yet to be written, and until one is, much of this chapter must be regarded as a tentative outline of a central theme.

Sisters of St. Joseph de Cluny who had come as a teaching and nursing order to Pape'ete in 1844 might be used to instruct the daughters of the Tahitian nobility; and the administration might win over some of the future leaders of Tahitian society by sending sons of chiefs to be educated in France in order to form a nucleus of trained officials (and opponents of the Missionary Society) from among Tahitians themselves.

Seven such candidates were sent to France in 1847.[6] The first reports on their progress were not encouraging: one died, and others succumbed to the temptations of Paris. But two, Ta'ataari'i and Tari'iri'i (Vaira'atoa), were later prominent in district administration.

Another solution to the problem of British missionary influence was to ask for French Protestant teachers to supervise the queen's children, entrusted temporarily to Thomson and then to a sergeant of marines. Lavaud could not persuade Pomare to accept a Catholic teacher (though she later allowed her youngest child, Teri'itua Tuavira, chief of Hitia'a, to be sent to France for a Catholic education). With some insight he recognized that ministerial reluctance to sanction such a policy would hinder progress in advancing French interests because "resistance to the introduction of French ministers to Tahiti will not help our priests to be accepted, and will delay for a long time the amalgamation which would come about, if ministers of their own religion could teach the French language to the islanders."[7]

But this advice was not accepted in Paris for the moment, and Lavaud's successor, Commandant Bonard, pronounced in favor of using Catholic missionaries as the chosen instruments for Tahitian cultural advancement. The Catholic mission, however, was not very well placed to accept this role in the early 1850s. The priests of the Sacred Hearts Congregation had made no progress during the war; and the destruction of Caret's house and chapel by fire left them without a church. Father Heurtel settled at Pape'ete as mission superior in 1847, and Bishop "Tepano" Jaussen (d'Axieri) established a school and church at Point Venus in 1849. But between 1841 and 1854, the congregation register for Tahiti shows only 143 baptisms, and significant advances into the Protestant districts were not made before some vigorous pioneer work by Father Collette from 1855.[8]

ETARETIA TAHITI

Bonard favored the Catholic cause by applying direct pressure on remaining members of the Missionary Society. They were forbidden to preach without an invitation from the district congregations and permission from the director of Native Affairs. Following the "nationalization" of church properties in 1848, two district electoral laws were passed by the Tahitian Assembly in 1851 and 1852, bringing the selection of pastors before all district *ra'atira*. This legislation, in Bonard's view, would end the influence of the LMS and weaken "the Secret Society of *ta'ata Etaretia* (people of the Church)."[9] Eligibility of candidates for the offices of deacon or pastor was made as wide as possible; and if an agent of the LMS was elected, this appointment was still subject to ratification by the administration. William Howe earned Bonard's displeasure by preaching against the anniversary festivities for the 1848 republic and was threatened with imprisonment. Ministers of the Tahitian churches were forbidden to have any relations with a foreign power.[10] By 1855, deaths and official discouragement had depleted the society's ranks, leaving only Howe to fight a rearguard action till 1863. He got himself into deeper trouble by publishing a defamatory anti-Catholic tract, *Tatara ra'a* (A Refutation), in 1853 which circulated for two years before it was suppressed.[11]

A new administrator, Governor de la Richerie, determined to put a stop to this kind of internal strife between the missions. He took up Lavaud's suggestion for French ministers as a way of keeping Bishop Jaussen in check while removing the last reminder of a British presence. The perpetuation of religious tensions, argued La Richerie, resulted from "the continuation of English influence by the notion, taken to its extreme, that all that is not Catholic is English"; and, he continued, "I do not perceive anywhere the progress to conversion to Catholicism of a population so long devoted to the Protestant faith. This faith has, moreover, been given a regular and legal organisation in 1851 and 1852 by Governor Bonard, an organisation which it would be difficult to overthrow today."[12]

Bonard would probably have been pained to hear this paradoxical judgment on his anti-Protestant policy. But this policy was largely reversed when, in May 1860, a bill and a petition for

French pastors were examined by the Tahitian Assembly.[13] There was to be no official head of the Tahitian churches; their only ministers were to be Frenchmen or subjects of the protectorate; the French government was asked to send two members of the Paris Evangelical Mission to be provided for out of local revenues and given houses and land by the local population. The bill and petition were approved by 126 votes to 18.

On the face of this, it looked as though Howe would have to retire from his post at Pape'ete, and that pastoral visits by the two British missionaries still in the Leeward Islands would have to cease. But neither Howe nor the British consul, Miller, was inclined to press the matter. Howe had been allowed to come and go as he liked by La Richerie; and he had been in touch himself through the LMS with the Paris Mission. As he explained to the directors in London, the clause excluding all but French and Tahitian ministers "was to crush a statement which has been industriously sustained by a certain party (the Bishop), namely that Protestantism is necessarily opposed to France and is purely English."[14]

The petition was well timed, for La Richerie had just fallen out with Monsignor Jaussen over the quality of the schools run by Catholic missionaries; and from the administration's point of view it was an excellent opportunity to obtain French teachers without wounding the religious pride of the Tahitians.[15] Advised and persuaded by Howe and the LMS, the Société des Missions Évangéliques (SMÉ) agreed. In 1863 Thomas Arbousset, who had spent twenty-five years in South Africa, and his son-in-law, François Atger, arrived as ministers of the Reformed Church of France.

Arbousset did not stay long, and his considerable authority in the mission field severely tested the structure built up by Howe within the framework of local laws. Welcomed by Howe and Pastor Daniela, the queen's chaplain, he took over the parish of Pare, by election, and moved into Daniela's house. Instructions were issued in Tahitian, written by Arbousset and translated by Howe, to be read in the district churches.[16] He toured in style, and at the end of 1864 he established an annual pastoral conference at which Atger, four Tahitian ministers, and Arbousset examined the morals and knowledge of those who had been elected to district appointments. The work of some thirty Tahitian pastors and forty-nine deacons came under scrutiny, and the business of twenty-eight protectorate parishes was reported in detail for the first time in the history of the local churches. There were seventeen immediate excommunications of church officers. In 1865, the aging French missionary departed, leaving the stamp of his disapproval on the condition of the Protestant schools and much practical advice on fund-raising to draw some of the district congregations out of their apathy toward education. Atger thought him "more of a bishop than Bishop d'Axieri himself."[17]

But the strictures were necessary. If the Etaretia (or Ekalesia) were strong in district administration, their educational facilities were no longer adequate to meet the new requirements of Tahitian society. They had 2,639 communicant members and 1,270 pupils in elementary schools, but few of these advanced very far beyond the level of proficiency noted by Lavaud in 1848. Attendance was irregular, and the deacons were hardly paid at all for teaching from primers in the vernacular. At Pape'ete, by contrast, the Sisters of St. Joseph de Cluny were joined in 1860 by the teaching order of the Brothers of Ploermel. Four years later they had 119 pupils and were the only serious secondary institutions outside the Protestant pastoral college at Ra'iatea. Under La Richerie, the sisters began a second school at Taiohae in the Marquesas and were allotted funds for twelve bursars when their portion of the local budget was raised to 14,000 francs a year in 1861. The teaching brothers, with a staff of four led by Pierre Ropert, received 9,200 francs from the same source. The Sacred Hearts Congregation was able to take over former Protestant schools in five districts without much difficulty, in the early 1860s, and received a small allowance of 240 francs a year for each of them.

It was not till 1866 that the SMÉ was able to compete when Pastor Charles Viénot opened a Protestant boarding school at Pape'ete and ran the Mission Press. He was joined by Pastor F. Vernier and his family in 1867, and the serious business of reviving the churches and the schools began:

> The desire to learn French is more and more evident among the Natives. Our establishment in Papeete has only served to encourage their minds in this direction. We have thus started to light a fire which will soon devour us. For lack of Protestant institutions which do not appear, the priests are accepted as a substitute, and they display a zeal and action which are universally praised.[18]

For a French Protestant church with a strong sense of cohesion under persecution, it was intolerable to allow parish schools and churches to fall into the hands of pastors and teachers who could be elected by a majority of adults in a district who might not all be Protestants. Tahitian pastors could be disciplined, but they could continue to administer the sacraments. Worse, in an extreme case on Ana'a in the Tuamotu, the bizarre electoral politics of church appointments resulted in the selection of a Catholic priest as Protestant minister for a "Protestant" district congregation in a numerical minority.[19] Taking the view that the election of a pastor was a religious act, Atger and Vernier argued that church administration and discipline had to be separated from electoral regulations on the choice of chiefs in local government.

To set their own house in order, they persevered with Arbousset's pastoral conferences, chastising the fallen, refusing the sacraments to congregations whose children attended Catholic schools, and refusing to consecrate Tahitian pastors who were chiefs or members of the To'ohitu. A code of "ecclesiastical discipline" was drawn up with the help of the LMS missionary Green; and a hierarchy of standing committees and subcommittees began to challenge rulings by the Native Affairs department on decisions taken by chiefs in matters of church organization.

In reply, the administration circularized Tahitian district councils to be on their guard against "illegal interference" from the Protestant mission. "We understood," wrote Viénot, "that we were on the brink of a serious crisis from which would come either a liberated or a totally disorganised Tahitian Church."[20] A project for a Tahitian synod was rejected by the administration on the grounds that it would become the only institution to install or depose church leaders, contrary to the electoral law of 1852. The French missionaries pointed out that Bonard's law was really intended to diminish the influence of the LMS and was very close to the French Revolution's civil constitution of the clergy in imposing on the religious community "the candidate elected by an unbelieving or indifferent majority."[21]

In 1876, therefore, the French pastors printed their church regulations and held their synod illegally. Two excommunications took place; and other Tahitian pastors looked to the French administration to protect their offices. But Commandant Michaux temporized; and in 1879 the provisional constitution of the Tahitian churches was rescinded by the Ministry of Marine. A new constitution was drawn up in Paris by a representative of the SMÉ together with Guizot and the minister, Jauréguiberry (also a Protestant); and this was approved at Papeʻete by the local administration in the certain knowledge that French Protestant support for the annexation of 1880 could be relied on.[22]

Although there were further revisions of the new constitution of the Tahitian churches, the main point had been accepted. The Etaretia Tahiti was to have a hierarchical structure of officeholders, and the local politics of this acceptance occupied the Protestant pastors between 1879 and 1884. Europeans now had the authority to remove Tahitian ministers and deacons from their posts, and this power was extended by courtesy to the visiting LMS missionary, Green.[23] At the same time, the independence of the churches from government control was reaffirmed. Their leadership was appointed to a tier of parish councils, three regional councils for Tahiti and Moʻorea, and elected to a central council of district delegates and European pastors. The French administration was given a token representation; but, in the event of disputes, the final decision lay with a commission which included members of the Central Council, Tahitian officials, and judges of the Toʻohitu, under the director of Native Affairs. The constitution was promulgated for a second time in 1884, as a colonial decree, and accompanied by the code of church discipline which had been perfected by Vernier and Green.[24]

The old autonomy and laxity of the district churches on the two main islands were considerably reduced, though they still went their own ways, apart from occasional pastoral visits, in the Leeward group, the Tuamotu, and in the Austral Islands. It would also be accurate to describe Tahitian Protestantism as a single Tahitian church from 1879 onward, though the "national" character of the religion learned from British missionaries had been apparent over a much longer period of time. There was, however, a much stricter European control of church affairs through the annual conferences than there had ever been in the May Meetings. Advice and exhortation had been replaced by a written constitution and a touch of Calvin's *Institutes*.

This cohesion and centralized direction also placed the Protestant pastors in a better position to make their voices heard, amid those from other interest groups, in the political institutions of the territory after the annexation in 1880. They took their campaign against the sale of spirits and for a larger share of the education budget into the Colonial Council and the General Council. They repeated, as an article of faith in the midst of pressures for Tahitian "assimilation" to European culture, the policy of the SMÉ, laid down in 1865, which stressed the need for "missionary tutelage" of a society "insufficiently developed from a religious and intellectual point of view."[25] This sense of patronage permeated the framework of the Etaretia and placed the very small number of French pastors in a position of influence not enjoyed since the 1820s by the pioneers of the LMS. It was no accident that the territory's elected representative to the Conseil Supérieur des Colonies in Paris was for many years an authority on the French Protestant Reformation (but who knew little about Tahiti); or that district congregations functioned as electoral constituencies in local government politics. The significance of the change was not lost upon the Catholic bishop of Tahiti, who complained in 1884: "They have taken to themselves the secular authority of the districts, not in an open (and therefore unpolitic) manner, but in such a practical way that in the districts no action is taken, except on the initiative and advice of the Protestant Synod."[26]

Thus by the 1880s, when the constitution of the territory as a whole had been developed in the direction of closer supervision from Pape'ete and from Paris over a larger number of islands, the old battle lines between Catholic and Protestant still ran through the rural communities, while the general staff on both sides maneuvered with civilian officials at the center. Gains and losses were measured in terms of the statistics of baptism, school enrollments, marriages, and church attendance. Separate cemeteries held the casualties, to keep them apart in death as in life.

Yet the propaganda war was more measured in tone, tempered perhaps by colonial laws on libel, and also by an awareness, as the century moved to its end, that both sects labored for a common cause amid the official indifference, and even hostility, of much of the European population. Bishop Jaussen joined the toilers on the frontier of literacy and made a notable contribution to the Tahitian vernacular by publishing the first Catholic catechism in Tahitian in 1851 and a major grammar and French-Tahitian dictionary in 1861. One of the earliest elementary textbooks for teaching French to Tahitians was published by a Catholic missionary in 1884 for use in the Tuamotu.[27]

There were other, more subtle changes in their respective positions as the dispensers of French culture. The French Protestants consolidated their hold on Tahiti at a period of increasing anticlericalism in France; and on them fell some of patriotic favor enjoyed by Catholics in the 1830s and 1840s. The SMÉ won a measure of support from the republican ministries of successive French governments for their francophile and educational role overseas, while the Sacred Hearts Congregation went through a long period of legislative erosion of their religious and educational work.

CATHOLICS AND MORMONS

For much of the period after 1860 there was still a great material contrast in the resources of the Catholic and Protestant missions; and this difference had a bearing on the part they played in promoting agricultural or industrial training in the territory. The early British missionaries had stressed the mechanical arts in their own efforts to survive and even prosper in the Pacific. Catholic priests took this interest in development much further.

Tahiti had a complement of one bishop, eight priests, and a dozen or so teaching brothers and sisters for a Catholic population which had grown to about a thousand souls by 1880. The Marquesas stations expanded under their own bishop from four priests to nine priests and five brothers and sisters for a population of less than seven thousand by that date. There were usually between four and six priests in the Tuamotu and at Mangareva. Very little use seems to have been made of catechists at this period, and Bishop Jaussen appealed constantly for reinforcements from Europe in order to make tactical advances in fields untouched by Catholics—the Leeward Islands, the Cook Islands, and the Austral group.

When these were not forthcoming, both Jaussen and his successor, Bishop Verdier, concentrated on fortifying existing strongholds in the style of the Jesuits in Paraguay or the congregation's mission at Valparaiso. They accumulated extensive properties in Tahiti, the Marquesas, and at Mangareva; and they financed a program of agricultural and industrial development with local artisans which surpassed anything attempted by the administration.

Jaussen reported that it cost him about 390,000 francs (a sum equal to about one-half of Tahiti's official budget) to run his stations centered on Pape'ete in the 1850s and including Tahiti, Mo'orea, and the Tuamotu.[28] Bishop Dordillon's system of accounting is less easy to follow, but it is clear that he, too, had little difficulty in raising money in Valparaiso or in France to pay for the Marquesan posts and the mission's agricultural experiments there. Both Jaussen and Dordillon, moreover, acquired lands in their own names in the Papeno'o Valley and in the Marquesas, which created difficulties over death duties when the question of succession was raised.

The amount of construction work undertaken by the two bishops and their priests was prodigious. On the island of Hiva Oa with a population of about 2,500 Marquesans there were sixteen churches and ten other mission buildings by 1879. Every island in the Mangareva group and some in the Tuamotu boasted stone presbyteries and chapels. At Pape'ete Jaussen planned a "cathedral" in 1850, in the belief that "a fine monument and exterior decoration are the best means of winning over our Kanakas, or rather Maoris"; he estimated that it would cost between 150,000 and 200,000 francs.[29] When, eventually, it was built on a reduced scale (because of faulty foundations—attributed by Jaussen to the malice of the governor of the day), the artisans were Mangarevans. Bishop Dordillon reported that the construction of four stone churches and two in timber in 1877 cost just over 100,000 francs. Hatikia church, conceivably the most beautiful in the Marquesas, cost $20,000 in 1879.

Clearly such investments were meant to endure and provide training in new skills for the population. The highest concentration of stonemasonry was at Mangareva, where a cathedral 160 feet by 60 feet was already standing in 1841 at Rikitea, followed by convents, churches, and presbyteries in a mixture of Doric, Ionic, and Corinthian styles, with occasional adaptations of decorative motif to include marine shells, mother-of-pearl, and carved coral blocks.[30] There was a stone tower where the *akariki*, Maputeoa, might take his pleasure. His palace (never completed) was flanked by medieval watchtowers. The point of Aukena Island, facing the harbor of Mangareva, is still dominated by a huge stone belvedere.

All this architectural exuberance had a social as well as a financial cost. In small societies whose productivity was so finely balanced between food surpluses and food shortages, as in the Marquesas and Mangareva, it is arguable that major alterations—to patterns of subsistence, to the allocation of labor between agriculture, fishing, and manufactures, and to the environment itself —aggravated the effects of imported diseases. In the Marquesas, warfare was an additional, and perhaps decisive, factor after the introduction of the musket. The statistics of births and deaths available for Mangareva, insofar as they are accurate, indicate a more gradual decline from the 1840s, marked by severe periods of mortality as a result of epidemics. In thirty years between 1838 and 1871, Mangareva lost about one-third of its population of two thousand, and the decline became more severe between that period and the end of the century.[31]

A great deal of Mangarevan labor was diverted into spinning, weaving, building, and ceremonial. Trees and vegetation were cut down at vulnerable areas of the shoreline. Quarries and lime kilns were constructed. Imported foodstuffs and manioc replaced taro and breadfruit, though potatoes, sugarcane, and new varieties of vegetables and fruits were also introduced. Sheep and goats may have added to the problem of soil erosion.

Contemporary accounts of these changes either extolled the virtues of missionary hegemony in encouraging industry or attacked its monopoly of services and production. Although the missions in Mangareva and the Marquesas did not make the kind of profits attributed to them by anticlerical critics (and rival traders), nevertheless their ventures into pearl shell, pearls, cattle, and cotton, and the high level of imported materials and foodstuffs, equal the turnover of fairly respectable cooperatives and minor commercial firms. The fact that returns from the sale of exports, such as they were, were plowed back into island enterprise and into much of the ceremonial and architectural ostentation that characterized the Catholic mission did nothing to lessen the suspicion that priests were making a good living out of their masons, teams of divers, copra harvesters, and cotton spinners.

An examination of some of the records of these enterprises suggests, however, that their profitability was often well below the investment in capital and instruction required to start them in conditions of poor communications and uncertain demand in the 1850s and 1860s. The sale of pearls and pearl shell constituted one of the more immediate sources of income for the Mangareva mission and the royal lineage in whose name the trade was organized. Diving teams were recruited by the mission and toured the Tuamotu when local lagoons became difficult to work. The shell was sold to visiting traders, and the returns in the form of manufactures and foodstuffs, tools, and livestock were distributed among the converts to expand the work of the mission.[32] In selling pearls for the *akariki* the missionaries acted as agents, and one venture at least resulted in a loss in 1846 when the employee of a Valparaiso firm "disappeared" with 2,319 piastres worth of the finest exports. Thereafter the mission and Maputeoa sold pearls through the Société de l'Océanie in Le Havre. Much more was gained from the steady tonnage of Mangareva shell which went directly to Valparaiso or was sold in transshipment at Pape'ete through local firms.

One of the more ambitious of mission enterprises, cotton-growing in the Marquesas, was encouraged initially by Governor La Richerie and by the high prices offered in the early 1860s.[33] Responsibility for management fell on the Catholic missionaries on Hiva Oa, who persuaded Marquesans to produce 1,550 kilos of baled cotton, which fetched a good price of 18,600 francs at Pape'ete in 1865. By the end of the 1860s, Father Dominique Fournon had under his supervision about a dozen valleys on the island in a system of cultivation and production which paid the Marquesan useholders as cash-cropping farmers for their daily labor. As prices for cotton fell, the mission (in Fournon's name) incurred debts of up to 10,000 piastres at Valparaiso, though this was covered for a while by income from other sources—"either from coconuts or from cattle"—which subsidized Marquesans for producing an unremunerative crop on their own lands.[34] Indeed, profit was a secondary consideration in Fournon's view of the enterprise, which he enthusiastically built up as a means of "drawing the natives to the mission through the advantages which work brings to them." For this reason, large-scale plantations employing only wage laborers were avoided, and Marquesan smallholdings re mained the basic units of production:

> The Kanakas like this system because they can work them when they wish and as much as they wish to. That is why the missionaries are required to go and look at their work often in order to assess it and pay for it in goods. It is the same with cotton harvesting. We have to pay for crop-gathering nearly every day, after the cotton has been weighed. Each must be given what he wants, if the cotton is to be picked with care. Often they request beef, fish, tobacco for a part of

the working day. You can understand how many aspects there are to this employment, and that it is even unworthy of a missionary according to our European ideas, though it may not look that way to the Kanakas.[35]

In the absence of detailed accounts of prices paid to growers and to the "manager" of this producers' cooperative, it is difficult to say who was exploiting whom. Fournon's dedication to his elementary scheme for planting and marketing was no proof against a fall in the market or against attacks from critics of the economic role of the mission. Bishop Dordillon in 1879 concluded that "cotton growing uses up more than it produces"; and complying with orders from the head of the congregation to reduce targets open to criticism by the French administration, he instructed Fournon to cease commercial operations.[36] At the same time he sold off the mission's herd of cattle at Taiohae Bay. The collapse of the cotton enterprise immediately put at risk the loyalties of some seven or eight hundred converts on Hiva Oa. The island society reverted from agriculture to warfare, and in 1880 a naval expedition from Tahiti was mounted to restore order and confiscate muskets, powder, and shot.[37]

There are few examples of encouragement of agriculture by missions at this period. Bishop Jaussen did little with his cattle or land at Papeno'o or with the vanilla plantation owned by the mission at Papara. All this became a source of embarrassment and a political liability.[38] Perhaps it should not have been. A later age engrossed in problems of underdevelopment has seen vastly greater sums pass in the form of grants and loans to doubtful schemes for tropical agriculture and the employment of expensive expertise by state corporations. In the mid-nineteenth century, a missionary cooperative that preserved land for cash-cropping farmers was a rare and enlightened initiative when plantations worked by landless laborers were the preferred mode of production.

There was one other set of missionaries who felt that conversion to Christianity was something more than a matter of literacy and social conformity to alien patterns of behavior. When Mormon disciples of Joseph Smith—Rogers, Pratt, and Grouard—landed at Tahiti in 1844 they attempted to apply their frontier skills to local development in the same way that LMS "mechanics" had done earlier. They were mistrusted as much by the LMS, however, as by

Bruat's military administration, as a potential cause of dissent. But at Tubuai in the Austral group, at the periphery of French control, Pratt won over a small community of foreign seamen, local deacons, and chiefs. Together they founded the first church of Jesus Christ of the Latter-Day Saints (Kanitos) in the Pacific.[39]

Their approach to conversion was facilitated by the linguistic work of Tahitian teachers. But they also brought to their task a directness and simplicity which deplored local morals while enabling them to enter into the life of the society they had come to reform. Grouard married at Ana'a, and he built missionary craft—three in all, the last being a schooner of 80 tons laid down at Tubuai. We do not know exactly what doctrines these pioneers taught: probably, as their historian conjectures, a heady mixture of promises of imminent change, practical ethics, belief in the gift of healing, baptism by total immersion, and the autonomous administration of the church by lay officers.[40] They also emphasized the export of cash crops and independence from other commercial or administrative intermediaries. At Tubuai in 1845 Pratt could boast: "You see the reins of government are within the church. . . . I am prime minister of the island."[41]

Pratt returned to America and brought back with him a small band of missionaries and their wives. Three returned almost immediately, four moved to the Tuamotu in 1850, and two went back to Tubuai. One of the more militant Mormons, James Brown, a veteran of the Mexican War, built up his own version of local government on Ana'a by appointing converts to run the districts under the American flag, which was hoisted as a symbol of loyalty to the church and resistance to the French. In October 1851, Brown was arrested for this subversion, imprisoned at Pape'ete, but allowed to leave for Raivavae and the United States. His departure and that of most of his colleagues removed effective leadership by Americans, but it did not end the Ana'a Mormon churches.

For, when the first Catholic missionaries landed on Ana'a the same year, they encountered hostility to their doctrines and a more general antipathy to French appointments of chiefs and judges with Tahitian *mutoi:*

> We found ourselves up against a sect of twenty years' standing, enthusiastic, unscrupulous and which the Paumotuans for want of the truth

looked on as the support for their nationality against the Protectorate. Many times by allusion to the Tahitian war the missionaries were publicly and openly treated as assassins. Those who seemed to be attached to us were treated as *Piri-Farani* (joined with the French).[42]

Pratt and Grouard had been prevented from extending their pattern of anti-French and anti-Catholic Mormonism by the strict application of the Tahitian laws of 1851 and 1852 on district church ministries. But their legacy of institutional organization, economic self-sufficiency, and militancy, especially in the Tekotika district on Ana'a atoll, could not be easily uprooted by the pro-Catholic minority left as chiefs under Gendarme Viry in 1852. The gendarme's close association with the Catholic missionaries Fouqué and Loubat led to a tragedy in November 1852 when Mormons from Tekotika murdered Viry and attacked the two priests, who barely escaped with their lives. The rebels' posts were captured by Tahitian auxiliaries after an expedition had been sent from Pape'ete. But it was not till 1855 that the foundations of the first Catholic church in the Tuamotu were laid in stone, by government order, on the ruins of the Mormon chapel at Ana'a.

The episode was, perhaps, exceptional (though other combinations of Protestantism and resistance to French rule appeared in the Leeward Islands). The Ana'a revolt against both Catholicism and French officials made a deep impression at Tahiti, where Bishop Jaussen wove the story into a general treatise supporting his claims to special consideration for his missionaries by the administration.[43] Commissioner Page circulated rumors that Catholics had brought the trouble on themselves by making forced baptisms (though none of the evidence lends itself to this interpretation). The execution of four of the Ana'a Mormons and sentences to hard labor of thirty or forty others satisfied neither the Department of Colonies nor the Protestant community in Tahiti, where the case was looked on as a Catholic provocation.[44]

It also illustrated how far a small but determined sect could penetrate the conventional alignment of secular and religious authority in the outer islands by offering a novel brand of salvation and material progress. It was not the last time that islanders looked beyond the "majority" missions for assistance from other quarters.

In 1853, for example, a chief from Fatuhiva, Matanui, was sent by his tribe to Hawaii to recruit missionary teachers. He returned with two Hawaiians, the Reverends Kekela and Kauvealoha, two teachers, an American minister of the Sandwich Islands mission, and James Bicknell, carpenter and nephew of a missionary. This massive reinforcement to Matanui's position on his island can also be regarded as a counter to the installation of French administration and Catholic missionaries on Nukuhiva and Tahuata.[45] When a Catholic priest disembarked in association with a French naval officer at Matanui's valley to restore the balance, opportunities for religious-political factions increased. Adherence seems to have been decided not by doctrinal debate but by the amount of property available to the "converts." When the material support of the Hawaiian mission vessel *Morning Star* was reduced, the position of the Hawaiians became precarious. Bicknell withdrew in 1865, taking seventeen Marquesans with him—some of whom eventually returned. An American missionary, Titus Coan, toured the group in 1867, but he was more impressed by the limited progress of the Catholics than by the failing venture from Hawaii sponsored by Matanui.

In the isolated Austral Islands there were similar instances of external recruitment of teachers and deacons to local churches. A visiting missionary wrote that the people of Rurutu desired a "foreign" pastor, rather than one of their own number, "for the sake of the respectability they imagine his residence confers upon their island."[46] At Rimatara, the churches imported Rarotongan missionaries in 1857, and some were still there as pastors of the local congregations in the 1870s.[47] Tubuai seems to have remained staunchly Mormon throughout the period, though occasional French or British missionaries noted that the term, in fact, embraced a wide variety of imported beliefs and church practices with Bible studies and church collections as the principal activities.

In the Leeward Islands, which were stoutly Protestant and anti-French till the end of the century, the monopoly of the churches by one religious sect, closely involved in island government, led to frequent schisms. Pastors and deacons were also judges. The influence of the few European missionaries of the LMS was very limited outside the pastoral school at Ra'iatea.[48] The association of Tamatoa, *ari'i* of Ra'iatea, with a particular faction of the church in 1865 divided his officials, his district chiefs, and his judiciary, who were also grouped around the churches of Taha'a and at Uturoa and Opoa. This situation had arisen, explained a missionary, because his predecessors had encouraged the formation of church settlements on the two islands of Ra'iatea and Taha'a, but these had since been subdivided as the population returned to agricultural lands in other parts of the islands:

> This plan involved the necessity of setting apart certain days for the procuring of food. The principal plantations lay in the neighbourhood of Opoa on the east side of the island, and at Tevaitoa on the west. As time rolled on the church was formed and deacons selected. Some finding it difficult to go to their lands and get back again before the Sabbath proposed to build a small place of worship near their food land, intending to go to the settlement every Ordinance Sabbath. At length Mr. Chisholm thought it better to ordain two Native pastors, the one Napario for Opoa, and the other Huana for Tevaitoa, as help to him and teachers in the schools. The latter individual fell into sin shortly after his ordination. The former soon became troublesome and showed his covetous spirit by early desiring to keep for himself the whole amount which the church subscribed annually towards the Society. Upon Mr. Platt's remonstrances with him on this subject he insulted him and charged both him and Mr. Morris with wishing to get the people's money for themselves.[49]

Tamatoa's secretary, two chiefs, and several judges sided with the dissident deacon at Opoa and formed a new (or old) district round the breakaway church. Although supported by the churches at Uturoa and Taha'a, Tamatoa was deposed when Napario was deprived of his deaconship (though in 1867 he was restored and the church at Opoa was brought back into the fold).[50] There was a similar schism on Huahine in 1876, arising from more complex disputes between the queen, chiefs, and ra'atira over contributions to pay for church construction.[51]

Beneath many of these instances of enlistment of outsiders and internal tensions, one detects a real desire for material support, for guidance in the wise investment of collections, and for improvement in the living standards of church members. There is a measure of truth in the observation of a trading captain, in 1888, that even in the solidly Catholic islands of the Tuamotu, "if a Muslim missionary were to arrive tomorrow, he would convert all the inhabitants at a cost of fifty francs a head."[52] Catholic priests were not unaware of this material basis to religious welfare. It was also a theme taken up by the Mormons when they returned to Tahiti for a reconnaissance in 1874:

> With a world of wealth in the form of pearls, mother of pearl, marine shells and coral, beach-le-mar [sic], fungus, cotton, coffee, sugar, coconut-oil, and the finest tropical fruits in the world, they are poor, because they are compelled to take in exchange for them the pittance allowed them by their commercial masters. Nothing could be easier than the formation of a joint stock, or co-operative organisation, by the California Saints and these brethren unitedly. This, in due time, would make the mission self-sustaining, would bring some revenue into the tithing fund, and would make the parties wealthy.[53]

These commercial and religious visionaries had been surprised to find a small Mormon community still functioning at Tiona (Zion), near Pape'ete, under the charge of an East Indian, David Brown. Some of this spirit of Californian enterprise on a Pacific frontier was also present in the Mormon William Nelson, who arrived in 1878, and in Thomas W. Smith, who followed him to the Tuamotu and Tahiti a little later. Both were struck by the relative poverty of islanders in the outliers; and both thought that a producers' cooperative among members of the Mormon Church would be a means of saving souls and improving meager resources.

But who was to run it? Nelson disappeared from sight in the islands; Smith thought he had "gone native" before returning to the United States. Smith himself concentrated on building up local branches of the Kanitos (Saints)—there were thirty or forty, he claimed, by 1885—and he supervised the construction of a new church at Tarona (Sharon), in Papaoa, Tahiti, where the elders had got into debt. He mistrusted the influence of Brown ("not a white man"); and while he praised the steadfastness and abilities of the Tahitian elders, he thought them "rather too anxious for office and power."[54] By the middle of the year he had come to the conclusion that a cooperative would not work because the Tahitians and Tuamotuans "are too childlike in their mental make up for a work of that kind. I have seen enough of their character to enable me to judge that they could not carry out a company enterprise."[55] And so the plan was dropped, though the Mormons later used the well-tried method of keeping open communications and transporting trade goods by running a mission boat of their own. She was the *Evanelia*, purchased in 1892 for $90,000, one of a long line of missionary vessels and numerous small whalers built by the island churches. On her first venture into the pearl shell trade in 1895 she was lost at Rangiroa.

Moreover, like the French Protestants, the Mormons fell back on training auxiliaries but kept control through a centralized and closely supervised church organization with voluntary contributions and a system of annual conferences. They were tolerated uneasily by the French administration, which saw in them an American advance guard in a territory that was already open to "Anglo-Saxon" influences.

Ever since the Tahitian war and the Anaʻa revolt, relations between the administration and the churches had been ambiguous. The simplicities of Franco-Catholic or Anglo-Protestant polarities certainly existed in the minds of some British missionaries and some Catholic bishops and priests. The tricolor and the Mass were firmly associated, too, in the minds of Mangarevans and possibly some Marquesans and Tuamotuans. But churches in the islands were also parallel administrations and, occasionally, trading corporations. The French administration had, indeed, preferred to leave some of its islands in the hands of Catholic missionaries for a time in the 1840s and 1850s. Administrators at Papeʻete came to resent such rival authority. Not all governors were pro-Catholic; and even before the anticlericals of the Third Republic reached the Pacific, there was a series of conflicts between the congregation and the representatives of the state.

These clashes arose as much from conflicts of jurisdiction as from the mission's disapproval of the morals of administrators. When La Roncière challenged Father Laval's autonomous theocracy at Mangareva by sending officials and levying fines in the mid-1860s, the priests were obliged to defend Rouru convent as stoutly as their administrative independence.[56] By 1880, incidents had multiplied at Tahiti, too. Government House was less imposing than the immense edifice inhabited by the bishop of French Oceania in the "quartier de la Mission," but it was more powerful. Father Laval was recalled from Mangareva to spend his days at Papeʻete. Attacks in the press left their legacy of stereotypes and exaggeration well into the period of open republican hostility to the congregations. As the mission's provincial (and future bishop in the Marquesas) recognized, the tensions dating from Jaussen's episcopacy derived mainly from the administrative functions assumed by priests in island societies:

> It would be difficult to prove that Father Laval had not busied himself overmuch in the administration of the group, to the extent even of assuming the title of "minister," despite the prohibition of Mgr. d'Axieri; it would be difficult to prove that as a minister and all-powerful, he had nothing to do with the punishments, the fines, whether real or exaggerated.

Moreover, to keep at bay the agents of a "Voltairian" government at Pape'ete, continued Father Martin, Laval and his colleagues had been driven to deny the validity of the French protectorate over Mangareva; and this could be construed as a lack of patriotism in a missionary society which was already suspect because of the number of Dutch and German priests in its ranks in the late 1870s. And finally, concluded Martin, "we have against us . . . the purchase of numerous lands and a large amount of livestock."[57]

Such temporal encumbrances could be got rid of. Monsignor Verdier, who valued mission property at about 900,000 francs in 1885, sold off much of it or gave it away to Tahitians who already occupied small lots of Catholic land.[58] Other lands in the Tuamotu were handed over to district councils and were registered. By 1898, there was little of Jaussen's property left to declare, and many of the Marquesas estates were regarded as colonial domain. A "Catholic corporation" was set up in 1913 to take over legal proprietorship of other lands, and a formal concession was made by Governor Rivet in 1931 to save what was left from confiscation.

The Catholic mission, in short, was all but destroyed as a temporal power in parts of the outer islands, and even its schools were closed on Nukuhiva and Tahuata for a period between 1919 and 1924.

The Protestant French and Tahitian Church was also a parallel administration, formally constituted by 1884, but less vulnerable to attacks from administrators. Its congregations were poor. In the area of education, therefore, the Etaretia found it difficult to match the constitutional status won through the efforts of Pastors Vernier and Viénot. At the end of the 1870s, the financial assistance given from the local budget to Catholic schools and the Catholic mission amounted to 74,540 francs. Two French pastors, twenty-three deacons, and forty-nine teachers received 11,860 francs. The proportion of Protestant pupils to pupils in Catholic schools (who were not all Catholics) was approximately two thousand to some five hundred. It is arguable that most of the latter were taught to a higher standard. A little more came to the Protestants from collections (in devalued Chilean piastres), amounting to about 10,000 francs from all island groups. Tahitian elementary teachers were paid 10 francs a month, compared with 2 or 3 francs per day for laborers in the 1880s or the 60 to 100 francs per month paid to domestics.[59]

They fared even worse after 1880. On the whole, both Catholics and Protestants had a smaller portion of the budget to quarrel over, as the colonial subsidy for all schools decreased from 116,849 francs in 1885 to an annual average of 70,000 francs in the 1890s. In 1901, the first government school for training teachers was opened at Pape'ete.

By the end of the century, the earlier belief that the missions would be the principal agencies for the spread of French culture had foundered—either for lack of trained teachers or because the missions themselves had been forced to compromise with the central place held by the Tahitian vernacular as the language of commerce, district administration, and religious experience. The Tahitian Bible, commentaries, and hymnbooks still held their own as the principal, and often unique, texts for instruction. Catholic attempts to overcome this influence and Viénot's school at Pape'ete spread little French into the rural areas or the outer islands. The Mormons, on the other hand, after noting that Tahitian was the lingua franca of the Tuamotu, made no effort to use anything else and produced their mission newspapers in the vernacular as well.[60] They may even have agreed with the French Protestant view that, despite local regulations requiring classes in French, it was preferable to work through the Tahitian dialect and preserve some of its qualities:

> To remain in contact with this people, to prepare the youth to play a social and religious role, to preserve above all its originality and personality, it was necessary to make broad and justifiable concessions

to the Tahitian language. Mission work in a native country which did not understand that fact would inevitably fail of its own accord, at the same time as it would add to the destruction of the spirit of those whom it claimed to enlighten.[61]

On the other hand, radical republicans such as Governor Petit thought, by the end of the century, that religious institutions were irrelevant and that religion among the islanders was unsophisticated and therefore unessential. Even such statistics as he collected suggested otherwise:

District	Protestants	Pastors: Tahitian (European)	Catholics	Priests (Catechists)	Mormons	Kanitos
Tahiti and Mo'orea	1300	4	2430	16	8	1550
Tuamotu	100		3025		860	
Marquesas	?		3549	8		
Mangareva	?		1520			
Australs	2043	(35)	26		98	
Leewards	4600*	39				
Total	8043	78	10,550	24	966	1550

* ANSOM A 160/23, Petit to Ministry of Colonies, 15 March 1903. Petit's statistics include children and Europeans. French Protestant returns give a total of 4,378 church members (adults).

Faced with this list of denominational converts, Petit suggested government schools and compulsory display of the Declaration of the Rights of Man in classrooms.

The missions had learned, however, that the churches had replaced some of the social structure of localized kinship groups. Catholic festivals, the annual Protestant *me* (May) and New Year's celebrations, the round of meetings, classes, and communions—all provided occasions for corporate action, rivalries, and reconciliations in small communities whose administrative leaders played little part in local government. The dependence of the Protestant churches on indigenous pastors, deacons, and elders was fundamental; and from their ranks came the teachers and social organizers unprovided for by French administration. There were signs that Catholic missionaries, such as Verdier, had also begun to understand the importance of forming a corps of married catechists by 1885 to keep alive the work of priests in the more distant parishes of the Tuamotu. From the Leeward Islands to the Australs and Rapa, one of the main diversions for Protestants, noted Pastor Brun, was the Thursday Bible lesson and analytical commentary— a linguistic and didactic exercise which has lasted in the remoter communities of the territory till the present day.[62] It was a Mormon, Burton, who recognized that the structure of the churches also provided occasions for public assembly not given by the administration: "There is a very important social service rendered to the isolated native by the conference which is generally overlooked, that is they furnish a meeting-place for relatives and friends from different islands . . . and they enjoy each other's society in a variety of services which elevate them in social life."[63]

Inevitably there were political overtones in some of these occasions in the Leeward Islands, and the Pape'ete administration was obliged to remove Pastor Brunel from Ra'iatea when he championed the local churches too enthusiastically and opposed the immoralities of Fourteenth of July celebrations.[64] Inspector Revel in 1914 considered that all effective authority still lay in the hands of local pastors, and not till 1916 was a Catholic mission post tolerated there.

But elsewhere the activities of the parishes were fairly easily supervised by the French administration. The churches offered an alternative to a prosaic administrative conformity on the main islands. On the more distant atolls they were often the principal social and political institutions and an avenue to the outside world.

CHAPTER 6

THE SEARCH FOR STAPLES

TAHITI'S MARKET had been stimulated by traders, whalemen, and missionaries and by French military and civil expenditure. For the remainder of the nineteenth century, the economic development of the central island and its dependencies was based on a narrow range of marine and agricultural cash crops. With little or no hinterland, Pape'ete performed the function of capital and entrepôt port. The lack of specialization which had been a feature of the 1830s and 1840s was still evident in the activities of seamen-traders and occasional planters, but the network of island agencies and the cost of business licenses and communications increased the amount of capital required to enter the market as a full-time occupation. There were fewer beachcombers and more substantial merchants.

With the exception of cotton, the staples of trade remained much the same as before 1842. There was a greater variety of European manufactures and an accumulation of hardwares, ships' chandlery, cordage, and other stores necessary for shipwrights at a colonial naval base in the age of sail. In early contemporary photographs, Fare Ute has the appearance of a small, but well-stocked, shipyard. For the port now served a wider area of eastern Polynesia; and the market for produce and imported goods reached into the atolls of the Tuamotu, to the distant Austral Islands, and into the valleys of the Marquesas group. With the widespread use of South American currency and some encouragement of shell divers and copra and cotton growers throughout the territory and in the independent Leeward Islands, commercial direction of the terms of cash-crop and barter trade from Tahiti was fairly soon established.

It should be recognized that the quantification of this development in contemporary records is subject to reservations. French statistics of Tahiti's trade values, as gross imports and exports, are a function of a steady increase in customs declarations at the main port of entry (see Table 3).[1] These include large quantities of administration materials for public works in the early 1850s, and they are inflated by the reduplication in returns of values in transit. They are also an incomplete guide to total exports of produce from the territory, because the Leeward Islands are not included, prior to the 1890s, and a certain (and unknown) amount of trade took place directly between some of the outer islands—Mangareva, Ana'a, the Marquesas ports—and other ports of the Pacific without passing through Pape'ete.

Nevertheless, the crude statistics suggest that the commercial life of Tahiti underwent two periods of expansion: first as a result of French occupation and second, at the turn of the century, as a result of improved communications in the Pacific basin and larger investments by restructured companies in certain of the tropical staples.* Beneath this broad generalization, there are indications of more subtle changes which had a direct bearing on the material existence of the islanders and the European community which settled as planters and traders.

The separate ventures undertaken by captains are less typical of the period from the 1860s. Many of the smaller licensed traders had their origins in the traditional enterprise of seaman-trader, and many still owned and sailed their own craft. But the trend in local business was toward small partnerships of shore-based entrepreneurs—Hort Brothers, Clark and Keane, Chapman and Turner, Foster and Adams—or into agency and commission work for an overseas firm or a local principal. Thus a number of adventurers who made a profit out of running supplies for Bruat's bountiful administration, such as Jean Laharrague, or later arrivals such as the schooner captain Victor Raoulx, stayed on to become agents for their firm at Valparaiso or at Bordeaux. Others were employed by one of the Tahiti merchants who invested in the expanding trade of the Tuamotu dominated by John Brander, William Hort, and Étienne Amiot, who had begun as a commission agent for the French merchant house of Ballande.

The local merchants were mostly foreigners and they supplied

---

* This later development is discussed in Chapter 9.

TABLE 3

Total Trade Values: 1840–1915

(Quinquennial averages, in thousands of francs)

Period	Tahiti, Mo'orea and Dependencies	Period	French Polynesia
1840–1845	2,024	1881–1885	8,374
1846–1850	3,946	1886–1890	6,229
1851–1855	5,328	1891–1895	5,920
1856–1860	4,149	1896–1900	6,442
1861–1865	3,995	1901–1905	7,936
1865–1870	6,016	1906–1910	8,359
1871–1875	6,422	1911–1915	16,449
1876–1880	5,868		

Sources: TBCP 8, Annual Reports; ANSOM J and K; Annuaire, 1863, 1885, 1917.

an essential demand in island trade at any period—the extension of credit in the form of money and merchandise and the bulking of produce for export. There were only nine firms paying merchants' licenses in the early 1860s. Two decades later, there were a score of them. Only three of these date back to the early protectorate; and one, Brander's firm, had become a registered company in the 1880s (Darsie and Co.) alongside three other companies, two American and one German. The fate of the small firms that disappeared is instructive. Apart from one or two who died, leaving little estate, the principals William Keane, William Hort, Thomas Stratfort Adams, John Hart—all prominent merchants and planters in the 1860s and 1870s—sold their interests to larger concerns founded about the period of annexation. Their assets were acquired by the successors of Brander and by the Société Commerciale de l'Océanie (SCO). Jean Laharrague survived as a family firm run by three brothers and financed from abroad. Victor Raoulx and Louis Martin (also a captain and founder of one of the oldest French firms in Tahiti) owed much of their success to specialization in French merchandise, and they were supported by much larger enterprises in France and at San Francisco. They also invested in land.

The general pattern, then, as elsewhere in tropical commerce, was toward amalgamations, incorporations, and closer association with metropolitan and foreign merchant houses and produce brokerages. A few firms made a living from construction and transport in Tahiti—Adolphe Poroi was one. And Alexander Salmon, who associated with John Brander and was one of the most successful businessmen in the territory, experimented with copra, coffee, and livestock without depending on interisland trade.

But for most of the small entrepreneurs island trade was the lifeblood of their existence—an endless search for profitable cargoes among the atolls, a kind of treasure hunt for the cheapest source of pearl shell, coconut oil, copra, and cotton. For a few there was a hope of finding pearls. Most aspired to become landed proprietors; and among the many who did in the 1850s and 1860s, there were some who attempted to develop trade by plantation agriculture. Cash crops from smallholders and divers, and plantation cultures with their heavier investment in land and labor, were two modes of production which provided returns in the shape of marketable staples: both for a period fired the imagination of the administration; and both had implications for island societies and their limited endowment of natural resources.

THE TRADERS

The key to island trading was shipping. John Brander, who brought a considerable amount of capital with him to Tahiti in 1851, concentrated on seeking out sources of supply and owned as many as eight vessels sailing under the protectorate flag. Other merchants owned more than one vessel (rarely more than three), but most of the wholesalers advanced merchandise on a commission basis and accepted produce from traders in return. There was an overlap in these two functions: William Hort sometimes ventured forth on his vessel, *Good Return*, to trade on his own account; and at other times he sent her to the islands or to San Francisco with a paid master; John Hart made voyages of his own on his schooner *Aorai*. These men, like their predecessors, were in a transition stage between maritime prospecting and founding a firm.

The number of local craft expanded rapidly in the 1850s. There were ten schooners and brigs of over 60 tons operated by trading captains (the largest was Brothers' *Esperance* of 300 tons); and there were some thirty to forty schooners of about 40 tons average. Nearly all sailed under the protectorate flag. Eleven had Tahitian, Ra'iatea, or Tuamotuan captains.[2] One other, the *Maria i te aopu*, had a French captain, Daniel, but was owned by the Catholic mission and the regent of Mangareva, Maria Eutokia. There were others sailing under the independent flags of the Leeward Islands.

The largest schooners, brigs, and occasional barques entering the port of Pape'ete were nearly all engaged in the Valparaiso, Sydney, and San Francisco trades. The value of imports and exports with the North American port equaled those between Pape'ete and Chile by 1863, though this combined trade was well below the value of trade with Britain and the British colonies. The same year a regular sailing line every two months was established with San Francisco; and by the early 1880s, America had surpassed every other country in the territory's trade values and exchanged about one-third of Tahiti's imports and exports.[3]

The smaller cabotage craft were constructed locally or, more usually, at Auckland, Sydney, Hobart, or in California. Marquesans in at least one instance fitted out their own schooner in the 1850s (she was found by the French brig *Railleur* after a gale had blown her to Rangiroa in the Tuamotu).[4] The four or five protectorate captains regularly engaged in the Tuamotu trade—Aumeran, Bellais, Amiot, Cébert, and Hort—were joined in the 1860s by Tuamotuans. They had earned cash by diving and operating the small fleet of whaleboats and canoes used to accompany the diving teams and to collect coconut oil and other produce at the atolls.

> Since then, commerce has expanded, and the natives of some islands, with a better understanding of their own interests, have had a dozen pretty, decked whale-boats *(chaloupes)* built at Pape'ete, from two to ten tons; and with these they come themselves to offer their produce to Tahiti merchants. In this way they avoid being at the mercy of the first trader who arrives and taking without a choice whatever the middlemen give them in the islands.[5]

But this initiative by islanders was a temporary feature of the Tuamotu trade. By the 1870s, transport of produce was firmly in the hands of European traders and merchants—possibly because the increases in port fees and licenses at Pape'ete deterred the Tuamotuan "separate" traders, but more likely because they rarely cleared their craft of debt.

The scene of this modest commercial expansion, moreover, was barely under the control of the French administration and was an easy market for a variety of commercial extortions. The eighty or so islands of the Tuamotu were remote and isolated. Only about one-third of them were inhabited by a population estimated at some eight thousand concentrated on the largest atolls—Rangiroa, Fakarava, Makemo, Kaukura, Raroia, Hao, Hikueru, Amanu, and Ana'a. The most distant, Timoe in the Mangareva group, lay nearly a thousand nautical miles from Tahiti. The nearest, Kaukura, Ana'a, and the high island of Makatea, were within about 125 to 200 miles. Some twenty-four had entrances suitable for the passage of schooners of moderate draft, while three or four (Rangiroa, Arutua, Makemo, and Raroia) could take vessels of the largest tonnages into the lagoon.

Pearls and pearl shell had been sought there since the beginning of the century. A high price of 40 piastres a ton in the 1830s and 1840s had brought Moerenhout and Mauruc and a number of others to the group; and the mission at Mangareva had followed up with its own divers. The price had fallen to about 25 piastres a ton in 1845.[6] But it recovered quickly at Pape'ete, after the end of the war, and rose to over 500 francs (100 piastres) and more in the late 1850s and 1860s.[7] It was to rise still further to levels of 1,500 and 2,000 francs f.o.b. in the early 1880s. In these market conditions there was something of a "shell rush" which acted as a stimulus to other forms of trading.

Shell diving was exhausting work, and it became more dangerous as accessible banks were overexploited. A good diver could work in depths of 50 to 60 feet, but more usually in about 30, and bring up some forty shells a day. Good-sized shells were about 6 inches in diameter; but already in the 1860s divers were reducing the future of the lagoons by taking smaller sizes of as little as 3 inches.[8] In poor weather, the daily total per man might be only twelve or fifteen shells.

The local price paid to a diver depended on his circumstances. If he could afford to wait, he collected a hoard and held out for a price of about 5 francs for fifty average-sized shells, or 15 francs per 150 kilos if sold by weight. But these are notional values. More often, the diver already had advances from a trader; and one report of the early 1860s estimated that "almost all the natives of the western sector of the Tuamotu archipelago are in debt to the merchants of Tahiti. Some, in order to pay off their debts, will even have to work for several years. In 1861 the amount owing by Tuamotu natives reached about a hundred thousand francs. The district of Putuhara alone on Anaa island owed some fifteen thousand francs."[9]

As the total export value of shell at Pape'ete in these years was just under 200,000 francs a year, the extension of credit amounted to roughly half the value of a season's diving operations. It could, of course, be covered in other ways; and the expansion of the coconut oil trade at the same period represented both a second source of profit for merchants and another form of ready income for islanders. By 1854, it was estimated that Ana'a alone exported 130 tons of oil worth 150,000 francs (or about 100 francs per head of population).[10] Only Takaroa, Takapoto, and Niau seem to have followed this example. The value of the estimate, in any case, was equal to the Pape'ete market price for the late 1850s (2 francs 50 per gallon) and certainly not the price paid to Tuamotuans. What they received in return in the way of goods was marked up by at least 50 percent of the wholesale value of merchandise landed at Pape'ete.[11]

Nevertheless, there was a speedy transformation in the style of living on Ana'a following this development. By 1856, noted a missionary, all the men were "decked out in trousers, shirts, silk scarves, and many even in coats, and of course the children who would run naked in the village, if we were not there, also have their best clothes."[12] The market expanded quickly to other islands of the group. Twenty years later, Thomas Brassy visited Hao and saw islanders who lit their cigarettes with Swedish matches and whose wives were clad in the cotton prints of Alsace, Switzerland, and Manchester, while "their food was cooked in an iron pot made at Wolverhampton."[13]

By then, too, the administration had begun to take an interest in the long monopoly enjoyed by Brander and by Hort in the Tuamotu trade. In 1867, the French resident at Ana'a tried to enforce a fixed price of 50 centimes per liter for coconut oil.[14] The web of commercial debt, explained Resident Carrey, enmeshed chiefs, judges, and *mutoi* and had been extended to encompass the land rights of families. At Ana'a, "where the presence of the resident required a certain display of justice, the merchant did not acquire land without getting a signature from a member of the family that the property has been held against full payment of all individual debts. If the Kanaka refused a bottle of spirits soon overcame his scruples."[15] The *mutoi* had been prevailed on to reserve stands of coconut trees for payment of debts. Boats on which half the debt had been paid off were frequently reclaimed. The monopoly was broken when Carrey allowed William Stewart to use the administration schooner, *Rusé*, to transport his goods to Ana'a, raise the price paid for cash crops, and undercut by 30 percent the price of imported merchandise. A sack of flour fell quickly from 60 to 32 francs, and a cotton wrap *(pareu)* from 7 francs 50 to 5 francs. For a few weeks Stewart was able to purchase all the oil the islanders could supply.

For the first time, too, the administration attempted to regulate shell diving by closing the lagoon at Ana'a for three years. The governor visited the group in 1873, and the selective prohibition of diving was applied to five other atolls and to the specified shell beds of ten more. This may have helped certain lagoons to recover, though it is open to doubt whether the legislation was strictly enforced, and the fine of between 50 and 100 francs was hardly a deterrent. By the early 1880s, only thirty-five islands of the archipelago were producing shell, and fewer than ten of these produced any pearls.[16] The notional price per kilo paid to divers had risen to 1 franc and 1 franc 50, compared with the Pape'ete market price of 2 francs. High demand prices continued to encourage exports. When direct shipments of shell to Valparaiso and elsewhere were prohibited by cabotage regulations in 1880, between 4,000 and 5,000 tons annually began to pass through the capital.

Traders began to export copra instead of coconut oil from about 1872 in response to changes in the vegetable oil industry in Europe. This development had important consequences for the wide range of island producers in the Tuamotu and elsewhere. In general, they had been obliged to sell their product as they extracted it, for want of suitable techniques of storage and preservation. The marketing of sun-dried copra, on the other hand, could best be done from accumulated stocks and in bulk. Island schooners and whaleboats with their shallow draft and broad beam were well adapted to accept small, but heavy, cargoes.

The initial market price for copra at Pape'ete was fairly high at 300 to 350 francs per ton (though producers in the Tuamotu received only 25 centimes per kilo).[17] An improvement in local trade values in the 1870s can be attributed almost entirely to the collection of copra for export at Pape'ete. There was a temporary fall in price to as low as 170 francs per ton during the trade depression of the early 1880s. But the territory was soon exporting between

John Brander's House at Ha'apape.

2,000 and 3,000 tons of copra annually—less than Samoa, and only half as much as Tonga, which had comparable populations.[18]

Two other new staples appeared early in the protectorate period. From 1850, several million oranges were exported annually to San Francisco and Australia, rising to a peak value of over 100,000 francs in the late 1870s, before a blight on local trees and competition from California ruined the trade. Vanilla, which had been introduced to Tahiti in 1848, began to appear in the export statistics at the very high price of 51 francs a kilo in 1864. The price remained high till about 1879, when there was a dramatic fall to 16 francs per kilo and a slower price decline in conditions of expanding production before the end of the century.

Finally there was cotton, which was planted in Tahiti, Mo'orea, the Marquesas, and the Leeward Islands in the 1860s in order to profit from the demand occasioned by the American Civil War. By

1880, baled cotton and cotton seed accounted for over half the value of exports, and this staple remained relatively important well into the 1890s.[19] For small producers, the return of 2 francs to 2 francs 50 per kilo was sufficient from a crop which demanded little labor for the smallholdings that were typical of island agriculture.

Traders, then, had been encouraged by the demand for easily bulked cash crops and by a relative absence of taxes and controls. The Leeward Islands were included in the local market system, both as a source of produce and cheaply constructed vessels and as a port of refuge when the Pape'ete administration began to extract a greater percentage of revenues from the trading community from the late 1860s. With a population of no more than three or four thousand Polynesians and some fifty Europeans, Ra'iatea, Huahine, and Borabora provided produce valued at 300,000 francs in 1879—nearly as much as the protectorate. During the cotton boom of the 1860s about 100 acres of Huahine and Ra'iatea were given over by smallholders to the valuable staple and produced 40,000 pounds of baled cotton a year.[20] In the 1870s, there was a change to copra as the main source of income. Tahiti traders with shipping interests began to transfer from the protectorate flag to one of the Leewards flags to escape shipping dues on heavier tonnages. The German consul at Tahiti invested in the group and shifted the assets of the local branch of the SCO to Ra'iatea in 1877.

On the other hand, the Austral group benefited little from the traders' flexibility. Tubuai enjoyed a brief period as a free port of entry before a resident was sent to collect shipping taxes in 1874. Rurutu and Rimatara depended on the largesse of mission vessels and had little to exchange. The distant island of Rapa with a population of only 150 came to the attention of the English Panama Company and was visited in 1867, when poor-quality lignite coal was discovered. A resident was appointed for fifteen months, and the island was claimed by France in 1882. But apart from participation in the Tuamotu shell-diving trade and a thriving trade in taro for a period, the Rapa islanders were tenuously linked to the market developing at the center of the territory.

That market turned over a great variety of items. A sample of a month's entries at Pape'ete in January 1866 gives six schooners under the protectorate flag, one British vessel (owned by Brander), and a Ra'iatean schooner (owned by J. D. Blackett). Between them these vessels imported 15 tons of coconut oil, 2 tons of shell, some 5.7 tons of cotton, 770 pounds of coffee, 5 tons of arrowroot, and a miscellany of pigs, fowl, dried fish, fine mats, tobacco, nets, lime juice, and *tamanu* wood.[21] Exports were made up of flour, calico, perfumes, fishing gear, staves, beans, biscuits, and empty casks. Long-distance trade with San Francisco for six months in 1871 was carried by eight schooners, four brigs, and two barques. Cargoes to the American port included cotton, oranges, coconuts, vanilla, coffee, sugar, molasses, the edible sea slug, and guava jelly, valued at $137,727.[22]

The entrepôt trade gradually extended to the Cook Islands as well as the main groups of the territory. Its essential feature, so far as traders were concerned, was the opportunities it allowed for establishing agencies to obtain a lien over local produce. But two other points stand out in the consular returns and in declarations recorded by the administration. First, there was a rising percentage of South Sea island produce in total export values—from about 30 percent in the early 1850s to 70 and 80 percent by the end of the 1870s. This increase reflected, in part, the development of cabotage and the use made of Pape'ete for transshipment after the establishment of regular sailing lines in 1863. It was assisted, to a lesser degree, by a decline in freight rates which made the connection with San Francisco commercially advantageous. By 1865, the charge per ton was 10 francs cheaper to the United States than to Sydney or Valparaiso.[23] And any of these routes were cheaper than the rate of 150 francs per ton to France. It was a differential which Tahiti traders had to reckon with throughout the century, and one which helps to explain the very small percentage of metropolitan French trade in the commerce of the territory. Secondly, there was an absolute rise in the value of staples, particularly pearl shell and cotton. Production of the latter crop, moreover, and the change from coconut oil to copra, attracted investment, much of it from merchants, into plantations.

THE PLANTERS

Encouragement of agriculture featured prominently among the projects of early governors, as it had among the missionaries. But the problem of reconciling different conceptions of land tenure remained. Plans for development—"to stimulate the native" (in

Governor Bonard's phrase)—were, therefore, in constant tension with the autonomy allowed by the protectorate agreements to Tahitian control over land alienation. At one level, then, such plans were simply a continuation of the spirit of the code of laws, which had much to say about the need to work and the dignity of labor. But at another level they derived from the conviction of commissioners, such as La Richerie, that Tahiti would not progress economically or politically until the population had been made to renounce all that was "irregular" in local customs.[24] Material prosperity and a redefinition of the constitutional status of Tahiti and Mo'orea were seen to be linked to social change. Tahitians were to give up "the communal life where there is no fixed domicile, no proper name, no individual property, in the French sense of the word."[25]

The reorganization of Tahitian land tenure in the "French sense" of forming a society of peasant proprietors entailed enclosure and definition of family usehold rights. The consequences of the opening series of moves, which took the form of regulations, surveys, commissions, and court hearings, were far-reaching.* The more immediate results probably benefited some of the chiefs.

In 1850, Bonard decreed that 30 hectares of every district were to be fenced off and compulsory labor was to be used to grow cash crops for sale.[26] His successor, Du Bouzet, found that labor had been diverted by many of the chiefs onto chieftaincy, or *fari'ihau*, lands which supplied surpluses for district feasts but did little to help provision Pape'ete or visiting ships.[27] On the other hand, Commissioner Saisset, in 1859, observed on his tour of Tahiti that the chiefs and *ra'atira* of four districts had persevered with sugar plantations fairly successfully, but the market price had fallen to a level where other districts were discouraged.[28] Three in particular—Tiarei, Vairao, and Mataoae—had abandoned cultivation for quick returns from the orange trade. In others, Europeans were engaged in planting sugar and coffee and raising cattle. There was a small cotton plantation run by the trader Andrew Gibson at Papeuriri.

The early evidence, then, suggests that Tahitians were not averse to agricultural production but were sensitive to price changes and

---

* The legal aspects of land tenure are considered in Chapter 8.

eager to see immediate returns from investment of time and labor. Du Bouzet suspended the compulsory enclosure and cultivation law (which had been extended to Ana'a in the Tuamotu), and he turned his attention to the problem of unrestricted cattle grazing. The Tahitian Assembly petitioned for total abolition but could not agree who was to put up fences. The assembly of 1866 abolished open grazing in the six western and northwestern districts of Tahiti, where planters were permitted to kill wandering stock. An immediate result was wholesale slaughter of cattle by anyone who could complain of trespass and a subsequent dependency on Hawaii for supplies of fresh meat. The problem, thereafter, was subsumed under the more general question of land registration.

So far as sale of land to Europeans was concerned, leases and deeds required French permission and a delay of a year to hear counterclaims.[29] Thereafter the lease or deed was looked on as proof of possession. In the event of disputes between Tahitians and Europeans, the case was heard before a French magistrate who was to take into account French laws and the views of the district *ra'atira*.

In 1851 the administration introduced the concept of public lands and left the way open for further expropriations of the kind that had led to the Tahitian war. But, in practice, great caution was exercised, and little more than the coast road and property already acquired at Pape'ete and Taravao were registered in this way. Elsewhere schools, the houses of Tahitian officials, and church lands were registered as district, or communal, property inalienable to the administration or to private persons.

The key to Bonard's plan to stimulate agriculture was thought to lie in an extension of this procedure into Tahitian tenure. In 1852 he set up a registration commission consisting of Darling (son of a missionary and official interpreter), a member of the To'ohitu, and the chiefs, judges, and *ra'atira* of each district visited.[30] An initial distinction was made between *fari'ihau* lands, linked with the office of chief, and the lands of coproprietors—"the little breadfruit lands of each man" which were to be described in a district register *(puta tomite)* for the cost of a few francs. Disputed lots were to be decided by the To'ohitu.

Only nine districts were surveyed between 1853 and 1860. According to the first register for Puna'auia, just over four hundred names were written down for 778 blocks of land. In some cases, notably those of Queen Pomare and the chief, Teri'itua, up to six or seven blocks were inscribed for the same person in different parts of the district. Usually the head of a household seems to have registered, but nowhere is there a complete list of useholders. No plans accompanied the written descriptions. As disputes and complications arose almost at once, no fewer than seven separate registers were required for each district to keep track of inheritance, sales and donations, reconciliations *(fa'atiti'aifaro)*, transfers, and the estates of chiefs.[31]

A Committee for Agriculture and Commerce set up by La Richerie attempted to speed up the process by sponsoring a decree in 1862 which required the compulsory registration of all lands within a year, on pain of a fine of 50 francs. But no commission was appointed to supervise such an ambitious undertaking, and by 1863 the territory's surveyor conceded defeat. Tahitians did not come forward to declare their rights in territorial terms, and there were no surveying instruments to measure such claims.[32] Fortunately, little was done beyond checking some of the registrations of the 1850s, or nearly the whole of Tahiti would have been in debt to the courts. Further efforts were made in 1866 and 1868 to inscribe family lands, and a new commission of chiefs, judges, and *ra'atira* went on tour to record claims which were to be published in the *Messager de Tahiti* as a preliminary to absolute title. This mammoth task was never completed either, and the main result was a mass of counterclaims and litigation which began to weigh on the To'ohitu and inhibit the transfer of lands to Europeans from 1866.

Whatever else they gave rise to, the early commissions demonstrate that cash crop production was already well established in Tahitian land use and the amount of land transferred to Europeans was fairly small. In addition, two agricultural surveys made in 1866 (see Table 4) and 1877 indicate that the average size of lots, including many held by Europeans, was about 2 hectares, excluding land occupied by coconut stands and land with breadfruit and orange trees.[33] Other cash crops were thinly, but evenly, spread throughout both islands. Cultivable land was not scarce.

Conclusions based on the incomplete data of this period of the protectorate should not be pressed too far, particularly as the

TABLE 4
Agricultural Survey of Districts: 1866

District	Planters		Labor
	Polynesian	European	
Pape'ete (Fauta'ua)	6	21	30
Ha'amuta (Pirae)			
Puna'auia, Pa'ea	103	7	5
Papara, Papeuriri,			
Papeari	4	28	12
Fa'a'a	3	20	2
Vairao, Teahupo'o	1	3	0
Tautira	2	1	0
Hitia'a, Maha'ena,			
Tairei, Papeno'o	8	3	0
Ha'apape, Papaoa	1	1	0
Total (16 districts)	128	84	49
Total area cultivated	285.2 ha	203.7 ha	

Note: Atimaono plantation had a total of 400 hectares under cultivation; 916 Chinese and 323 Pacific islanders were employed there.

Sources: Rapport fait à M. le Commandant commissaire impérial par la Commission d'inspection des cultures, Pape'ete, 1866; TBCP 8, Miller to FO, 19 November 1866.

"surveyors" left out estimates of Tahitian sources of produce from certain major staples and, of course, from lagoon, reef, and off-shore fishing. Absent, too, is any account of a major European enterprise in cotton-growing, which had begun to produce significantly by 1866.

But the returns indicated that among smaller European and Tahitian holdings there was only a marginal difference in size for lands producing cotton, sugarcane, coffee, taro, fruit, and vegetables and supporting some sheep and cattle. Excluding Atimaono plantation, the largest European area under cultivation was 18 hectares planted by Labbé near Pape'ete. Chiefs also featured as planters in Puna'auia, Pa'ea, Teahupo'o, and Papeuriri. There were three Hawaiians, one Tongan, and one Ra'iatean cultivating smallholdings. The pastor, Maheanu'u a Mai, and Alexander Salmon had some 18 hectares from Pomare planted between them at Fa'a'a. The president of the To'ohitu, Paofai, had a small cotton and maize plantation near Pape'ete and employed four Tahitians. In general, the labor listed consisted of immigrant Cook Islanders paid between 2 francs and 2 francs 50 a day before the massive introduction of Chinese and others.[34] It is also to be noted that hardly any of the Europeans were completely dependent on agriculture.

Listed among them were fifteen traders and merchants and an assortment of shipowners, doctors, officials, captains, carpenters, and members of the Catholic mission. Only four were inscribed as "planters."[35]

It is against this background of indeterminate land tenure reform and amateur experimentation with cash crops that the investment in cotton in the 1860s is to be viewed. The sudden rise in prices for South Sea Island cotton from 1861 stimulated land speculation and the produce market, and a number of measures were taken by Governors Gaultier de la Richerie and La Roncière to circumvent Tahitian resistance to the transfer of property. In 1863, a system of subsidies for areas brought under cultivation and the free distribution of seeds was financed by the administration. In the same year the Agricultural Bank was created with powers to buy and lease lands and to make small loans up to 2,000 francs at 5 percent interest.

The bank (never separate from the administration treasury) was a useful cover for all kinds of operations: it could use settlers' savings; it could issue paper currency *(bons de caisse)*; and it could expropriate land. Its first purchases on behalf of the administration were made without reference to the land surveys already completed and without ministerial approval.

In January 1863, 117 hectares were bought by La Richerie in Puna'auia, though only a third of this was reported to Paris.[36] The average price per hectare was 47 francs 50. The Ministry of Marine suspected that pressure had been brought to bear on the useholders. The president of the bank protested that the sales had been regularly made, but evidence of deeds is lacking.[37]

Clearly, a much larger investment was required than the bank could provide by using administration revenues. It was left to William Stewart, a Scottish adventurer who had traded in Spain and Australia, to conjure up the required capital on the strength of a visit to Tahiti in 1862. He leased some 385 hectares in Teahupo'o to begin with, and he offered La Richerie's administration 50,000 francs for the right to purchase more lands (which he later claimed amounted to 12,000 acres).[38] The governor's Administrative Council considered this offer in 1862 and decided the choice was to be left to individual Tahitian proprietors, if they could be found. At least three officials were opposed to any kind of sale, but five others

sided with La Richerie, who surmised that all Tahitian lands would
pass to Europeans anyway "for a few casks of rum or gin."[39] Back
in England, in 1863 Stewart persuaded his brother-in-law, Auguste
Soarès, to launch the Polynesian Plantation Company Ltd. with a
capital of £100,000. A determined man "with a long black beard
and black hair . . . and with a black piercing eye," Stewart then set
about making his capital and influence work.[40]

The area in which Stewart was supposed to make his purchases
was the rich plain behind the coast at Atimaono, Papara, and
Mataiea. He was promised that the imports and exports of the new
enterprise would be free of customs; and he was given to understand that the administration would overcome any difficulties
arising from Tahitian land tenure. The Ministry of Marine, however, instructed La Richerie, at the date of Stewart's return to
Tahiti in 1864, that the administration had no right to expropriate
so large an area for a private company.[41] But in London, Soarès
was already in the process of changing its name to the Tahiti Cotton and Coffee Plantation Company, and Stewart, as its accredited
manager, had begun to acquire more land.

In March 1864, Governor Gaultier de la Richerie toured the
three districts to persuade chiefs to sell, though great care was
taken to give an appearance of neutrality by the publication of a
back-dated letter to the district councils stressing that they were
"completely free" to do business with Stewart.[42] By the end of
1865, the company was legally in possession of about 3,400 hectares extending over the Atimaono plain. Not all the leases and
deeds are extant; but it would appear that one of the principal deal-
ers was Pomare, who disposed of some thirty-three blocks without
consulting the councils concerned. A legatee of the estate and historian of the company who saw its papers recorded that the first
survey of Atimaono made in 1868 gave the property an exaggerated frontage of 3½ miles on the seaward side and a depth of
some 7 miles inland—a superficial area of 6,800 hectares.[43] But
when the plantation was sold in 1875, the area for which there
were valid titles amounted to only 3,800 hectares. Shorn of its pre-
tension, then, Stewart's enterprise had roughly doubled the amount
of land held by Europeans in Tahiti and Mo'orea.

But Atimaono plantation had not yet solved two problems—
labor and transport to overseas markets. Tahitians refused to work

for the wages offered by Stewart. Local merchants and shipowners were quickly alienated when their richest and most influential representative, Brander, was denied privileges similar to Stewart's. Brander also resented his intrusion in the Tuamotu trade. Consul Miller, as official spokesman for the British community, fell out with Stewart over allegations of "pressure of the government on the natives."[44]

Once again Stewart turned to official patronage. An effort had already been made to remedy Tahiti's labor shortages by importing Cook Islanders and ninety-eight inhabitants of Tongareva (Penrhyn Island), in 1862, on the government schooner *Latouche-Tréville*. They were allocated to planters at 20 francs a head under two-year contracts, though nothing was said of repatriation.[45] Permission was given to Stewart to introduce up to a thousand Chinese coolies, recruited through the French consul at Hong Kong, on seven-year contracts, and up to five hundred Pacific islanders for indentures of three years. Wages were fixed at 78 centimes a day (for a month of twenty-six working days). The working day was twelve hours, and the scale of rations was laid down at 8 ounces of fish or meat and 4 pounds of fruit or vegetables per day.[46] All immigrants were to be repatriated at the expense of the company.

Stewart introduced 993 Chinese in three cargoes and employed most of the thousand Gilbert Islanders, Cook Islanders, Tongarevans, and New Hebrides laborers who were imported between 1862 and 1872. By 1868 the work force on the Terre Eugénie estate (as Stewart named his plantation) numbered 1,297 immigrants under thirty European mechanics and overseers. Land was cleared and planted, roads were built, and the site housed a score of stripping machines, two hydraulic presses, a maize mill, a sugar mill, and a small foundry. Around the landing place between the coast road and the sea at Araiteva, the Chinese occupied a shanty town of several hectares, gambled their wages, and awaited the end of their long contracts. A small fishing industry was organized at Taravao to supply the plantation. Two schooners were purchased to transport bales to Pape'ete. To keep order, La Richerie posted gendarmes and a handful of marines to the district. On the hill behind the estate Stewart built a palatial mansion in Jamaican style and named it Montcalm.

It was the largest enterprise of its kind in French Polynesia.

"Montcalm," Atimaono Plantation.

From its foundation till the peak of production in 1868, about 4.5 million francs were expended by the company.[47] Profitability is more difficult to estimate. Cotton prices fell sharply on the London market from 4 shillings per pound to a shilling and less in 1872. One observer who was not dependent on official reports, which tended to exaggerate the success of the enterprise, thought that the company had earned nearly 5 million francs from sales of cotton and maize by the end of 1868. This income may have covered the investment and running expenses, but it would have left little for shareholders.[48]

As prices fell, Stewart became vulnerable to the attacks of his enemies. The death of three Chinese and the public execution of a fourth fed rumors about labor conditions at Terre Eugénie.[49] Despite glowing reports by an investigating commission of officials and traders set up by La Roncière (and which Miller refused to join), the reputation of the comapny was further damaged by the murder of one of its captains engaged in blackbirding on the *Moaroa* in the Gilbert Islands and by the investigation of this traffic in French territorial waters by naval officers.[50] Shipping for Stewart's exports became more difficult to find. La Roncière loaned the company government vessels when Brander and Hort, who possessed the best local schooners, refused facilities to their rival. Finally, at Pape'ete, magistrates of the local judiciary who were at odds with La Roncière over financial and constitutional reforms found a way to bring about the downfall of planter and governor together.

When William Stewart quarreled with his brother, James, over the management and sale of one of their stores in 1868, a lawsuit followed. William was ordered by the court to pay 25,000 francs within twenty-four hours with the plantation as security.[51] Governor La Roncière came to the rescue with money from the Agricultural Bank. James fled to San Francisco before news was received from Auckland that his brother was solvent and could have met his fraudulent demands.[52] William Stewart escaped prison, but the management of the plantation never recovered. A new accountant arrived in 1873, and the books were found to be in such disorder that William was declared a bankrupt. He died in September, leaving debts in San Francisco and Tahiti amounting to £13,000, the correspondence of a persecuted mind, and the stuff that legends are made of. The plantation drifted into liquidation and was auctioned off to a syndicate of planters, traders, and businessmen in 1875.

The fall of Terre Eugénie did not end small-scale plantation production, but it made the administrators of the 1870s cautious about sponsoring investment at the mercy of overseas markets, uncertain labor supplies, and the envy of those who specialized in the growing entrepôt trade in cash crops. Only in the Marquesas were there a few belated attempts to transfer concessions to Europeans. Twenty-eight deeds of sale on Nukuhiva were registered for eighteen planters, but the areas were relatively small. At Mo'orea, lands expropriated in 1867 for plantations were given back to the original owners.

The number of settlers, however, continued to increase, and the pattern of smallholdings remained typical of agricultural production. No more than 250 of the Chinese and Pacific islanders were still working as laborers in the late 1870s. The rest had been repatriated or had become hawkers and retailers around the port. Some settled in the Leeward Islands. A few of the Polynesian immigrants ran plantations of their own on land rented from Europeans for a share of the produce. The system of labor recruitment, which encountered severe criticism after the passing of the Pacific Islanders' Protection Act of 1872, was suspended by the Ministry of Marine—already made nervous by the activities of Peruvian vessels in the Tuamotu and by the *Moaroa* scandal. In these conditions, the cotton harvest often remained unpicked and fell to the ground—"the shroud of our agricultural riches," complained the Agricultural Committee.[53]

A partial survey of production in 1877 for Tahiti and Mo'orea indicates that the number of planters had doubled to about 196 since the survey of 1866.[54] The area of smallholdings given over to cultivation of cotton, sugar, coffee, maize, vegetables, oranges, and grass for grazing amounted to about 6,000 hectares, and this area did not increase by much for the remainder of the century. In addition, there were estimated to be about 2,300 hectares of land occupied by coconut stands in the early 1880s. These were improved and expanded during the following four decades to become a mainstay of the territory's economy.

Those who improved these plantations followed the lead of merchants like Brander, who laid out his property in Ha'apape, near

Point Venus, in coconut palms and fruit trees. But his income was made from trade, and his firm transacted about 57 percent of total invoice values at Pape'ete in 1868.[55] When he died in 1877, he left a business and estate valued at 6 million francs. Lesser men— Amiot, Gibson, Wilkins, Hort—also looked on plantations as secondary to their main interest, which was a quick turnover in produce and merchandise.

Their success in this field tended to concentrate both financial wealth and social status among the English-speaking section of Tahiti's community of mixed nationalities. In a sense, both Stewart and La Roncière were transient outsiders; and their offense was to challenge the coterie of Anglo-Tahitian businessmen who dominated the commerical life of Pape'ete in the middle decades of the century. Financial failure did not necessarily lead to ostracism. (Hort went bankrupt in 1869 and was set on his feet again by Brander and Salmon.)[56] But they could not forgive the special patronage given by governors to a newcomer.

There was, too, resentment at inroads into Tahitian land tenure. Equally important to their standing and of special importance for the political relationship between Tahitians and the French was the close association of English-speaking settlers and the *ari'i* nobility. Salmon and Brander, by their marriages, founded a dynasty which inherited money, lands, and titles. Their descendants formed an elite which attracted foreign consuls, traders, and planters into its ranks. Later, Henry Adams, the aristocratic American historian, became a special client and the literary spokesman of the Teva lineage. Less happily, the Salmon branch of this lineage consolidated its own relationship with the Pomares by the marriage of Marau Salmon and Prince Ari'iaue (Pomare V) in 1875. There had been, however, considerable disquiet at the cavalier way in which Queen Pomare had disposed of district lands in the 1860s; and tensions over land remained a source of friction between Salmon and Pomare heirs well into the next century.

From the Salmon–Ari'ioehau genealogy (see Table 5) the process by which European and Tahitian notables combined money with rank is clear enough. The first generation of Salmon descendants incorporated John Brander and the American consul, Dorence Atwater. They inherited the Papara chieftaincy and its titles; they went into business with the SCO through Nari'i Salmon; and they could lay claim to part of the Pomares' inheritance through the marriage of Marau. German consular and trading interests, as well as Leeward Islands titles, were associated with the second-generation descendants of Brander and Titaua. It is hard to find a French name in the genealogy till the third generation.[57] It was a social and economic ascendancy which French administrators frequently kept in mind.

A second cause for tension between the mercantile community and the administration was the mounting cost of running the port. The slipway, wharves, and sheds deteriorated rapidly and were frequently repaired. A visiting French naval officer was astonished to find an arsenal and stores on Fare Ute crammed with coastal beacons, ships' cradles, and thousands of meters of sailcloth and cordage, but none of it available for commercial shipping.[58] Eventually, the slipway had to be leased to Brander to put in order and operate as a concession.

Moreover, at this period assistance from France for the local budget declined to less than 200,000 francs a year from 1870, though military and naval expenditure continued to be paid for. The immediate consequence was increased duties and taxes on trade. Commandant Du Bouzet had set up a committee in 1857 (expanded later into the Committee for Agriculture and Commerce) to enlist merchants' and traders' support. They fixed a charge of no more than 1 percent ad valorem on imports in transit and drew up a low scale of duties on specific items for a five-year period.

From this modest beginning there evolved a complex political and fiscal cooperation between settlers and officials. By the mid-1860s, about one-third of revenues came from imposts on trade. The temptation to expand this source was irresistible but had to be balanced by concessions in the form of public works for the small municipality; and whenever this uneasy bargain was broken, there was invariably a financial crisis at Pape'ete.

The earliest example of such a crisis occurred when La Roncière overestimated the willingness of foreign and French settlers to pay for the cost of constitutional reforms. In 1865 he swept away the old customs tariffs and the traders' committee that fixed their scale. He imposed, instead, a monthly contribution on every trader and merchant in proportion to the estimated value of his imports for the year.[59] The smaller importers were hard put to find their

TABLE 5
Anglo-Tahitian Descent Lines

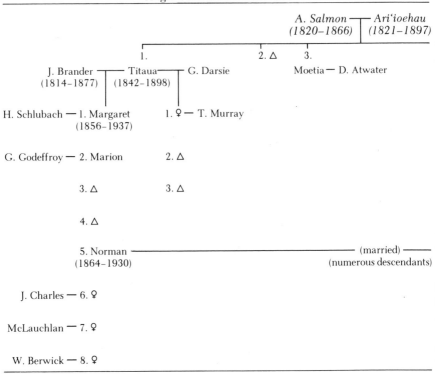

Sources: O'Reilly (1975:66–67); Salmon (1964:200).

monthly fees before cargoes had come to hand. Applications for postponement of payments multiplied. A number of minor financial scandals such as a deficit left by a departing treasury-paymaster increased the fiscal burden; and as it became clear that La Roncière planned new taxes and a magnanimous sacrifice of the metropolitan subsidy, the regime collapsed in an official coup d'état by the governor's subordinates.*

After this temporary bankruptcy in 1870, when French treasury drafts had to be imported to meet the administration's debts, a system of proportional licenses was established. The ad valorem duty

---

* The political aspects of this coup are discussed in Chapter 7.

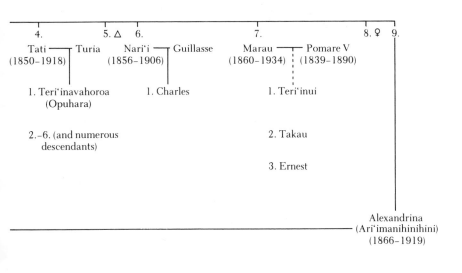

4.		5. △ 6.		7.		8. ♀ 9.
Tati ——┬ Turia		Nari'i ——┬ Guillasse		Marau ——┬ Pomare V		
(1850–1918)		(1856–1906)		(1860–1934) ┊ (1839–1890)		
1. Teri'inavahoroa		1. Charles		1. Teri'inui		
(Opuhara)						
2.–6. (and numerous				2. Takau		
descendants)						
				3. Ernest		

Alexandrina
(Ari'imanihinihini)
(1866–1919)

(or *octroi de mer*) was restored at a new level of 9 percent, plus 25 percent of the local market price for selected items.[60] Once again, this huge impost depended on traders' cooperation. The scale of market prices at Pape'ete was not easy to ascertain when goods of different origins paid different freight charges; and collection of information from reluctant importers soon involved work for more clerks than the administration possessed. The market-tax method was abolished, in 1875, for a single duty fixed at 12 percent plus a surcharge on luxury items.

This simple tax and the increased trade of the 1870s were immediately beneficial to the administration. Indirect trade revenues doubled between 1871 and 1879, amounting to half the budget of a million francs. The next most important source of revenue—business licenses—brought in about 200,000 francs a year. The bulk of expenditure—some 700,000 francs—was now spent on roads, a new wharf, an improved water supply at the port, a hospital, and increased salaries and wages.

Merchants and traders began to demand a larger voice in deciding the allocation of expenditure. In 1877, some thirty-four firms (nearly the entire commercial community in Tahiti), headed by the SCO, petitioned the Ministry of Marine and Colonies for a "liberal constitution." They complained, with some exaggeration, that traders and merchants contributed nine times the metropolitan subsidy and, more accurately, that a European settler paid 270 francs a year in taxes, on average, while Tahitians paid next to nothing.[61]

Commandant Planche allowed them representation on a general commission for tax reform which deliberated through twenty-six sessions in 1879. But by then there were more important constitutional proposals in the air and the existence of the protectorate itself had been called in question.

CHAPTER 7

QUEEN POMARE'S PROTECTORATE

In 1850, Tahiti could still be described by a visitor as more of "a military outpost than a commercial colony": the island was under nightly curfew and the population had only recently been disarmed.[1] Twenty years later, another foreign observer found French rule there "a mild and equitable sway": independent churches were at the center of district life and Pape'ete was fast becoming the trading capital of eastern Polynesia.[2] Someone closer to the scene—the sharp-tongued critic Dora Hort—judged that the protectorate had become "a palpable misnomer" administered by "young ensigns and middies in whom was vested an amount of authority which they rarely failed to abuse."[3]

It is true the authority of governors and their subordinates still rested, in part, on the Marquesas ordinance of 1843, sanctioned again by a decree of 1860. But legal texts and the trappings of office were not everything. The forces they commanded had shrunk, after 1850, to one or two vessels and some three hundred men, while the area under their nominal control had expanded from the Marquesas, Tahiti, and Mo'orea to the Tuamotu, Tubuai, Mangareva, and, for a period between 1853 and 1860, to New Caledonia. They came and went in fairly quick succession—some fifteen of them between 1850 and 1879; and on the whole they were left to find their own way through the mass of legislation, both French and Tahitian, that had appeared in the local gazette, the *Messager de Tahiti*, since the occupation.

That paper, moreover, was published both in French and Tahitian, reflecting the dualism of a hybrid administration in the most unusual of French territories. The rapid turnover of governors and naval commissioners, therefore, left a good deal of initiative with minor subordinates—secretaries with a knowledge of the vernacular, Tahitians, and settlers. The queen relied less on her partner in the joint administration than on a network of relatives within the Salmon-Brander families and among the chiefs and deacons of the districts. She also cultivated her contacts with the Leeward Islands *ari'i*. Occasionally, she appealed over the heads of local officials to a former governor or to the emperor or the French president whenever she sensed that the formal distinction between "internal" and "external" affairs had been ignored and her interests were threatened.

Those interests, like those of chiefs and Tahitian notables, centered on salaries, status, and land. On the first, there was little room for argument, so long as the queen's Civil List had to be supplemented from the French budget. The second derived from titles and family alliances; and it was sustained and flattered to some extent by the attentions of admirals and officers, by presents and the formal protocol of visits and audiences, balls and banquets, that passed the time in a tropical backwater. It was also connected with the estates held as family possessions and as a mark of chieftainship.

The politics of intrigue surrounding titles and succession to titles and appointments to the To'ohitu and to the offices of the churches were the lifeblood of local administration among Tahitians, missionaries, and settlers. They were instinctively countered by French officials anxious to reduce the area of Tahitian autonomy, foreign influence, and British missionary tradition. But to achieve this end it was necessary to reinterpret the framework of the protectorate, as constructed by Bruat and Lavaud, in order to exercise authority in district affairs as well as among settlers in Pape'ete—"the left and right hand of a people who can only develop by agriculture and maritime trade," as one of the more ambitious of the naval governors put it.[4]

Superficially, then, governors* appeared powerful and the queen weak. In practice, their powers were circumscribed both in Paris and at Pape'ete. So long as the administration felt bound by the protectorate agreements, there was little inducement for

---

* Strictly speaking they were posted as naval commandants and commissioners after 1858. The functions of colonial governor were formally revived in 1881.

France to provide greater subsidies or to underwrite an investment which was not supported by the Department of Colonies in the Ministry of Marine. Any attempt to change the constitution, it was thought, would meet with objections from Britain or the Australian colonies. The minister of marine, Ducos, could see no way to carry out proposals made by Governors Bonard, Page, and Du Bouzet for assisted immigration and development.[5] His successor, Chasseloup-Laubat, was content to aim at financial self-sufficiency for the post and allow for cultural and economic improvement "within the fairly narrow limits of what is possible."[6]

So governors were left to manage as best they could with eight administrative departments, thirty senior officials, a chief magistrate, a company of marines, some engineers, a small steamer, and a schooner. Their immediate subordinate and head of the secretariat took the title of *ordonnateur* (director) in 1855, in keeping with practice in older colonies. But in Tahiti this financial watchdog was sometimes head of the judiciary as well; and in 1863, *Ordonnateur* Trastour found himself chief magistrate of the Criminal Court, president of the Appeal Court, paymaster general, president of the Committee for Education, and a member of the governor's Administrative Council. The last body included two French settlers. A number of other settlers—Labbé, Brander, Salmon, Langomazino, Drollet, Adams—were called on to fill positions as magistrates in the wide variety of courts and committees which carried out the small amount of public business by the letter of colonial laws. On the whole, Tahitians were not included in this area of settler administration (though Maheanu'u, as vice-president of the To'ohitu, sat on La Richerie's consultative council in the early 1860s).

Tahitian administration centered on the queen, the To'ohitu, and a separate treasury set up in 1859 in the charge of minor officials directly responsible to the queen and governor. Expenditure rapidly got out of hand until, by 1864, the queen, chiefs, judges, *mutoi*, pastors, teachers, district councils, and royal boatmen cost 183,799 francs. Less than half of this expense was covered by district revenues.[7] The rest had to be found from within the main budget for administration. In theory, Tahitian households were supposed to pay a general head tax of 10 francs from 1863 and parents a fee of 50 centimes a month for each child at school, but little of this revenue was ever collected. Male Tahitians were liable for work on churches, district lands, and roads and could commute their labor at the rate of 4 francs per week. But there were no complete civil registers, and tax revenues hardly amounted to more than 80,000 francs in the 1850s and 1860s. In 1875 tax collection was taken out of the hands of chiefs and organized by the gendarmerie. Revenue from this source rose to 150,000 francs a year shortly before annexation in 1880. When at the end of 1876 the Native Affairs department was reorganized, the Tahitian treasury came under its director and was absorbed into the general budget.

But for a period of nearly thirty years, Tahitian district finances escaped the vigilance of the *ordonnateur* and depended on the largesse of governors of the day to meet the extra cost of household cavalry, guards, servants, a doctor and tutor to the royal children, interpreters, and ladies-in-waiting.[8] A palace begun in 1862 went through several architects, many budgetary improvisations, and several thousands of francs. It was not completed during the queen's lifetime.

Often unaware of their predecessors' expenditure, governors appear to have been generous. The queen was paid about 37,000 francs, including expenses, and she was allowed another 40,000 to 50,000 francs for the lease of lands. Chiefs' stipends increased to 600 francs (£24) a year in the 1870s; a few were paid as much as 720 francs, while others divided their stipend with a "representative" or sometimes with the head *ra'atira* of a district council. Pomare does not seem to have used her income for personal benefit. Rather, it was spread as widely as possible through her entourage and family in the form of presents and allowances. She went on tour frequently, visiting the districts and the Leeward Islands; and possibly she was more comfortable in this progress than in the titular partnership at Pape'ete.

Her interest in district affairs was more than ceremonial. In thirteen of the *mata'eina'a* of Tahiti and Mo'orea she held titles and rights to lands (sometimes *marae* lands). In the early 1850s, the To'ohitu formally recognized Pomare's claims to other estates once held by Vaira'atoa, Ari'ipaea, and Teremoemoe as *fatu* (overlords) but more usually conferred in trust on local chiefs and stewards.[9] Her policy in the Leeward group was to consolidate and expand other family titles by intermarriage between her children

Queen Pomare IV. Photograph by Mrs. S. Hoare,
Pape'ete (ca. 1875).

and titled chiefs. She also took care to supervise the findings of the
district land courts and the Tahitian Appeal Court, whose members had become the guardians of all aspects of Tahitian land
tenure.

For, following Bonard's attempts at land registration, the rise in
produce prices, and the stipending of chiefs, district headships
became coveted but complex roles. In 1855, the Tahitian Assembly
approved a law setting up district councils consisting of the chief,
district judge, senior *mutoi*, and two *ra'atira* elected by district
landowners. The function of councils was to oversee local district
properties, supervise celebrations, act as a preliminary court for

minor police matters, and serve as a land court and commission to register claims, sales, and other transfers of title.

Most of the early hearings of these councils arose from disputes between families over lands held in a variety of ways—by descent or inheritance within a company; by *'aitau*, prescription, or right of possession; and by *pupu*, or donation. Acts describing and registering land blocks became common in the western districts from the 1850s; but the naming of useholders as "proprietors" immediately called in question the priorities of single claimants. A wide variety of hearings arose from the entitlement of groups of useholders to access to a resource area; and there was litigation about the boundaries or limits of family usehold. A further difficulty was that the *puta tomite* (council registers) recognized at least eight or nine zones between mountainsides *(tua mou'a)* and the coral reef *(a'au)*, each with its distinctive terminology, over which claims to different kinds of natural produce could be exercised by individuals and groups of individuals. But the most important zone was agricultural land, *fenua*, divided into enclosures between valley floor and tidal shoreline, although there were other hotly contested sites for fruits and timbers in the valleys and valuable fishing holes *(apoa'a 'ia)* in the lagoon.[10]

In this legal and ecological confusion chiefs and judges had to walk carefully. On the one hand were requirements to arbitrate and record decisions approved by the assembly and the judges; on the other were the claims of district families to which they were frequently parties. At stake were the patrimony of district companies, sources of revenue from cash crops, and their own positions as titled stipendaries of the administration. Chieftainship itself with its right to use *fari'ihau* lands was part of the contest. The practice of approving succession to office by district elections, subject to confirmation by queen and governor, was rich in possibilities for conflict.

In 1854, for example, the district chieftainships of Papara and Papeari fell vacant along with two on Mo'orea which had been held by representatives of Atiau Vahine.[11] At Papara there was little difficulty: elections were arranged, and Ari'itaimai, daughter of Atiau and granddaughter of Tati, was chosen and approved. At Papeari some eighty of the *ra'atira* met in the house of the former chief and chose one of three of his lineal descendants. At Teaharoa on Mo'orea the former chief's nephew was chosen; and in the district of Moru'u it was decided by the *ra'atira* that the chief had left no suitable relatives. A list, headed by the most senior male members of respected families, was sent to Commandant Page. Page chose the first one on the list and approved the elections. Pomare, however, refused to sanction the elections at Papeari and on Mo'orea, claiming that the candidates were not relatives of Atiau Vahine, and she presented herself as the inheritor of titles in Moru'u.[12]

The administration hesitated. (A new governor succeeded Page in November 1854.) At stake were the lands which went with the Marama title in Mo'orea and Tahiti and which were worked by district labor for the chief's benefit. According to Alexander Salmon, spouse of Ari'itaimai, the lands at Papeari should have reverted to Atiau's family (and therefore to his wife). Page replied that Bruat's confirmation of headships had made no mention of land rights belonging to absent chiefs.[13] But he could not make up his mind how much of Atiau's land was *fari'ihau* and whether it went with a district title to a new incumbent. Equally important, he did not want relatives of the Salmon family with English connections to acquire more rights or to unsettle chiefs who were eager to possess *fari'ihau* as a bequest of the administration, now that tribute had been abolished. Accordingly, he published the new nominations without Pomare's consent, and his successor upheld this decision.[14]

The case did not end there. Salmon took the matter to Paris and petitioned the emperor.[15] But it did little good: the right of senior *ari'i* to appoint their own representatives and control district lands as their patrimony was lost. Districts became administrative divisions, rather than divisions of interrelated families. By the end of the 1870s, nine of the thirty-one districts recognized before 1850 had been subsumed into larger units and shared a single council. In twelve of the districts of Tahiti and Mo'orea, the chiefs and council chairmen appointed by commandants had no traceable family connections with previous titleholders. In nine others there was a titled chief descended from the highest-ranking family and approved by the *ra'atira*, but this chief did not preside over the council. At Pare, the director of Native Affairs acted as president from 1877.

There had also been some notable depositions of chiefs. The most notorious was that of Ari'itaimai, who was summarily dismissed in

1867 from the chieftainship of Papara and replaced by the council president.[16] She protested to La Roncière and received a reply from the director of Native Affairs, Frédéric Bonet, who charged her with maladministration of a district which had a reputation for cattle theft and drunkenness. At the same time he rejected her claim to any authority over the district of Ha'apiti (formerly under Atiau) on Mo'orea: "And on this matter the imperial commissioner orders me to tell you categorically that as the daughter and as the wife of a foreigner you have in fact no right to exercise authority or to hold any title in the territory."[17] This insulting letter ended Ari'itaimai's career in administration, though it did not end her influence or that of other members of her family. It may well account for some of her resentment of the Pomares' status in later years.

Pomare herself was better placed to defend her interests, though under Bonard and successive governors she found cause to complain to "friend Lavaud" that her authority over chieftaincy nominations had waned and that under the *hau Tamaru* (protectorate) other Tahitians carried more weight.[18] For their part, the governors resented her entourage of foreign friends and her policy of entrenching relatives to conserve estates associated with titles. Some also took the view (cultivated perhaps by Papara chiefs) that she had risen to her position at the expense of older families and could not retain it without the "consecration" given by French overrule.[19] Others simply disapproved of the amount of district resources expended on feasting to celebrate her tours. All were deeply distrustful of a court which still had considerable standing with foreign powers and foreign visitors. Gaultier de la Richerie summed up the dilemma of an administration in partnership with the queen. On the one hand she could not be prevented from appointing her own informal counselors if autonomous authority "in the European sense of the word" was allowed in some measure to the Tahitian executive. On the other hand, such a clique of merchants, occasional LMS missionaries, consuls, and naval visitors, he feared, could easily become "an engine to breach our authority."[20]

The way out of this dilemma was to seek support, at first, in other institutions of Tahitian government. The Tahitian Assembly which had met under Bruat and Lavaud to reform legislation became, under Bonard, an instrument for countering the maneuvers of the queen. From 1851 till 1866, the assembly met almost every year at Pape'ete in the old Protestant chapel or in the new *fare apo'ora'a* (Assembly House). Its members consisted of some thirty-eight chiefs, judges, and elected delegates *(iriti ture)* or lawgivers.[21] In 1853 there was a delegation of twenty-five chiefs from the Tuamotu.

Their business—revising the code and giving acceptable form to commandants' decrees—was usually prepared in the Administrative Council before being presented to the assembly by a Tahitian spokesman in the pay of the administration. The clause of the 1848 convention giving the assembly's proposals force of law if passed in three sessions was never applied in practice. Instead, Bonard dressed up this first Polynesian parliament in a motley of European procedures with standing orders, a ballot for votes, and numerous amendments. Deputies welcomed a motion making members "inviolable" after the *mutoi* had taken action against one of their colleagues. They welcomed, too, time set aside for petitions from the districts. But these got a mixed reception. Those from the Tuamotu went unheard; some proposing payment of delegates were enthusiastically passed and accepted by the administration; others which were unpopular repetitions of laws already discarded from the code were torn up and thrown out of the Assembly House windows. Sessions were entertaining but lengthy. The tendency was for all the chiefs to talk till agreement was reached, and the ballot was regarded as a tiresome interruption. Too often there were more black or white balls in the voting urns than there were voters. Members were expelled for disorderly behavior; and the 1858 session began with the suspension of President Tairapa for inebriation.

Commandant Saisset was not in favor of their meeting at all. La Roncière held only one session of the assembly during his governorship; and after 1866 it was not called together again, except as a brief formality to proclaim Pomare V king in 1877. With its passing there remained only a corpus of Tahitian laws as a basis for the legal and administrative functions of the district councils, the To'ohitu, the chiefs, and the queen's court.

LA RONCIÈRE'S "TAHITIAN KINGDOM"

By the mid-1860s the increased cost of Tahitian participation in local government and the promise of a change to a successful plantation economy encouraged a new governor—La Roncière—to introduce a series of reforms designed to adapt the protectorate to the legal system of other French colonies while making the settlers pay for a local budget shorn of its subsidy from Paris. These ambitious changes were dressed up as a plan for improving the status and influence of the Tahitian executive.

The author of this unlikely constitution came to Tahiti with a background which included a notorious sentence for "attempted rape" in 1835. He had, however, redeemed himself during his subsequent career as a colonial inspector in Algeria and in the administration of minor French posts in India and St. Pierre and Miquelon. He began at Pape'ete by following an anticlerical policy and appointed a series of officials hostile to the mission at Mangareva. There is little to suggest his abilities were any worse than many of his predecessors; and he may not have been entirely wrong in some of his judgments on local administration.

In 1865, he persuaded Pomare to sanction a measure (previously urged by Bonard and Page) which extended French laws to Tahitians in all matters except land tenure cases. He wrote sensibly enough in favor of appointing professional magistrates to replace the series of untrained amateurs who presided over local courts. In 1868 a decree was signed by Napoleon III which incorporated the 1865 legislation without change and provided for a properly constituted police court, civil court, and superior tribunal for civil and criminal cases.[22] An imperial magistrate, or attorney general, was designated to supervise the local judiciary. In the Marquesas and the Tuamotu officials were given powers of justices of the peace. Land cases were to be left to the district courts and the To'ohitu; and provision was made for Tahitian assessors when Tahitians appeared before a European judge.

The first attorney general, Alexandre Holozet, arrived in 1869. By then La Roncière was at loggerheads with all his senior officials and the commercial community at Pape'ete. The struggle arose from his patronage of William Stewart; and it was exacerbated in 1868 by his reversal of judicial decisions made by his *ordonnateur*, Boyer, and the magistrate, Langomazino, in the civil action between Stewart and his brother. Boyer and Langomazino were removed from office by the governor—an act which a commission of inquiry in Paris later condemned as "an abuse of authority."[23]

Although this would have been sufficient to ensure his recall, more fuel was added to the fires of local opposition when it was learned that he planned to give a greater share of executive authority to Pomare. Boyer, Langomazino, and Holozet led the Papeʻete settlers in their outcry against three ordinances issued in May 1869.[24] The queen was given an advisory council of Tahitians and Europeans and complete control of all Tahitian revenues. The council was also to have jurisdiction over settlers—a right surrendered to Dupetit-Thouars in 1842. There was to be a general council of Europeans elected to advise French administrators. In short, La Roncière began to undo some of the innovations of French rule while endowing the territory with a representative institution more usual in annexed colonies. There was to be a complete distinction between French and Tahitian administrations, yet settlers were to be in a measure responsible to both executives.

The great weakness of this scheme was its failure to specify how the expenses of internal administration—roads, hospitals, education, for example—were to be shared by different budgets with unequal sources of revenue. Nor was it made clear who was to pay for the new judiciary which administered to both Tahitians and Europeans. It was unlikely that the settlers would accept increased taxes on trade; yet these were immediately necessary, since La Roncière proposed, in a bid for ministerial approval, that the metropolitan subsidy to the local budget should be ended.

It was a strange mixture of impractical fantasy and genuine appreciation of the anomalies of the Tahitian constitution. But nothing was said of the Tahitian Assembly. Certain clauses of the ordinances signed by Pomare were never published in the official gazette; and by these La Roncière's trusted friend Louis Jacolliot, who had arrived from French India as a magistrate, was to be made president of the Toʻohitu with the power to appoint judges to the Tahitian courts.[25] Finally, La Roncière himself believed that the creation of the "Tahitian Kingdom" would not impair in the slightest the overriding authority of the French governors. "If I have created an authority for the queen, an administration," he confided to the Ministry of Marine, "both are more than ever dependent on the Imperial Commissioner as representative of the Emperor; nothing can be done without him."[26]

Opposition in Tahiti was speedily dealt with. Boyer and the attorney general, Holozet, were arrested in May 1869—allegedly for plotting to ship La Roncière to New South Wales. When Commandant De Jouslard arrived early in June with orders to put an end to the "Kingdom," he learned that Boyer and Holozet were on their way to San Francisco. There they were turned back by instructions to the French consul from Paris. At the end of June, La Roncière was writing (with a touch of hysteria) to the Ministry of Marine that his cherished reforms had been undone by his successor. Complete order was not restored, however, till the end of 1869, when the commander of the Pacific naval squadron arrived with a wordy letter from Napoleon III demanding French control over white settlers.[27] Pomare, "in terms calculated to save appearances," revoked her three ordinances.[28] La Roncière was recalled and retired.

The storm blew over after raging briefly in other colonies, where partisans of settler representation printed lurid accounts of the affair as a caution to autocratic governors. But in Tahiti the cry had been partly against an excess of liberalism for which the settlers would have to pay and against the power of the executive over the judiciary. Although the word "assimilation" was not yet part of the vocabulary of French expansion, practice in some ways preceded the doctrine, and judges such as Holozet and Langomazino were strongly attracted to the idea of legal conformity for all the inhabitants of the territory, as a solution to the "inconsistencies" of successive administrations.[29]

High on the list of anomalies which offended professional lawyers was the continued jurisdiction by Tahitian courts in land tenure disputes. If some of the political aspects of land tenure had been quietened by the payment of elected and approved chiefs, the economic and juridical aspects took up all the time of the To'ohitu and a good deal of space in the *Messager* in the years of La Roncière's governorship. From 1865, they sat as a court of appeal, usually under a French magistrate, though the assembly, in 1866, managed to keep French judges out of hearings at a district level. But in a muddled clause (which may or may not have been read to the assembly in its published form) the way was left open for Tahitian land cases to be decided before French tribunals, or for the To'ohitu to apply relevant sections of French civil law.[30]

Thus the demarcation between French and Tahitian jurisdiction as enshrined in the 1842 agreement became vaguer. With some truth Pomare complained to the commandant in 1870: "Little by little the competence of Tahitian courts has been reduced, first in sales, then in donations, boundaries, delimitations, divisions, and now more recently even the investigation of genealogies and the recognition of inheritance rights have been appealed before French tribunals."[31]

There was, indeed, a high concentration of land appeals in the period after 1865. Over the next five years the To'ohitu handled nearly four hundred such cases. An analysis of those for 1869 and 1870 suggests some of the main problems that had arisen from registration and district jurisdiction.

Of the 147 cases heard in these two years, the highest proportion was from Pare, Puna'auia, and Fa'a'a, districts of relatively dense European settlement and rising land values. There were only thirty-two other cases from other districts of Tahiti; and some of the eastern districts are not mentioned at all. There were nineteen from the Tuamotu (Ana'a and Fakarava) and five from Tubuai and Ra'ivavae.

Over half the appeals were concerned with outright proprietorship between Tahitians of different families; 20 percent were disputes about inheritance by Tahitians claiming a common ancestor; and the remainder were about boundary demarcations.[32] A large number of cases were dismissed by the To'ohitu because the appellant lodged his appeal five years after the publication of a claim by the defendant or for other technicalities unappreciated by Tahitians. The registration of one or several blocks in the name of one member of a group of coproprietors (their exact relationship is not specified) resulted in disputes with absentee claimants who said they were also proprietors. Such appellants usually argued that the useholders had been tolerated by their ancestors at some time in the past. This description of usufructory rights acquired by Tahitians always brought forth an exhortation (one imagines from the presiding French judge) urging written evidence to supplement registration. In the absence of such documents, other proofs were admitted, such as the burial of ancestors, the placing of boundary stones consecrated at a family *marae*, or the planting of trees. On the other hand, the court occasionally ruled that such usehold had to have been tolerated for at least thirty years. Otherwise the lineal descendants of the original coproprietors were judged to have a more valid claim. It was not always easy for de facto useholders who enjoyed planting and harvesting privileges to demonstrate that a formal donation had been made, more particularly as the Tahitian law of 1855 required the testimony of at least three *ra'atira* who had witnessed the ceremony before a claim could be considered for registration. But such claims were upheld.

Apart from "donations," real or spurious, the second important business of the court was concerned with exclusive claims to land arising by inheritance from a parent or grandparent. The law of 1855 was not very explicit in its definition of lineal descendants and expressed no preference for patrilineal or matrilineal kin. The judges were to examine the genealogies of all parties, though the clause tried to narrow these down to "near relatives descending from the same stock" among whom disputed land would have to be fractioned in equal shares.[33] Most of these claims arose from single-name registration. There is no evidence that such "owners" attempted to sell land (though there must have been a temptation in these years of plantation investment). Possibly the counterclaims were made as a safeguard against such speculation. Two things are clear: bilateral inheritance was admitted and was common; and the technique of multiple fractions was resorted to to avoid dispossession of coowners. Land owned in the name of a female proprietor, however, reverted to her mother's family rather than to her husband's, where there were no children.[34] A surprisingly large number of women appeared before the To'ohitu (which may reflect a preference for male claimants in the district courts). But it is also clear that they were able to transmit property rights, thus increasing the scattered and multiple claims.

Other criteria were occasionally drawn from the Napoleonic Code, though this was not promulgated in full at Tahiti till after annexation. An adopted son took precedence over his mother, where they were the sole inheritors of a father's lands.[35] A Tahitian woman married to a European was obliged, at his death, to conduct her case in Tahitian courts. The code had a bearing, too, on rights in marine zones.

The many demarcation disputes indicated that survey was the weakest feature of registration. In such cases from the Tuamotu there was a complication arising from rights to shell-diving, lagoon fishing, and reef fishing. For, according to Article 538 of the Civil Code, these areas were part of the public estate and inalienable, and at least six decisions of the To'ohitu at this period refused to extend boundary claims beyond the shore.

While the courts labored to preserve as much of Tahitian jurisdiction as possible, some official minds questioned the need for them at all. When, in 1875, a Tahitian appealed in a boundary dispute with another Tahitian to a French superior tribunal, the magistrate gave a decision in his favor on the grounds that French laws had become the laws of the land. This was more than a legal quibble: it was a political question of the first importance. If the last strongholds of Tahitian competence were demolished, what was left to justify a dual administration?

The debate came to a head in 1876 during the hearing of an inheritance case for five blocks of land in the district of Haumi, Mo'orea. The lands had already been divided among the claimants the year before by the district council and the To'ohitu. One of the parties appealed to the Court of First Instance and was awarded a larger share in a judgment based on the Napoleonic Code. The case then came before the governor's Administrative Council to decide which of the two legal systems was to prevail. The matter of family ownership was not in doubt; and a large section of the council, in opposition to the attorney general, thought that at this point the Tahitian judiciary had done its work. French laws were to decide subsidiary questions of divisions and boundaries.[36] When his officials could not agree, Governor Gilbert-Pierre ruled that the case could not be heard in French courts and sent it back to the Haumi district council. The Ministry of Marine and Colonies upheld this ruling; for the time being the district courts and the To'ohitu were to be preserved.

Thus trends which La Roncière's "Kingdom" legislation had either sought to halt or accelerate were brought to offical attention in Paris and stimulated reflection on the future of the territory. The minister, Admiral de Genouilly, was of two minds. He thought the protectorate was "an admitted fiction." But he objected to setting up a new Tahitian executive—a measure "which will profit no-one and will not meet the obligations which our position in Tahiti imposes on us."[37] Only Admiral Cloué, as commander of the French Pacific squadron, was bold enough to state the logic of the reversal of La Roncière's scheme. The queen, he observed, had become a figurehead; and the assembly merely served to rubber stamp legislation. France would do well, he concluded, to annex before Pomare died and the reign of her son, Ari'iaue, became a time of troubles.[38]

But for the moment that time had not come, and the queen survived. She never relaxed her efforts to have her position acknowledged by something more than a stipend and a palace under construction. She clung to the remnants of her Advisory Council, and she protested to Marshal MacMahon against the amalgamation of the Tahitian and general budgets. She objected so vigorously to *Ordonnateur* La Barbe acting as temporary commandant in 1876 that Rear Admiral Serre of the Pacific squadron was obliged to take over the administration till a new governor arrived.

She was still a factor to be reckoned with in local politics, but her own dynastic maneuvers were less successful. Of her six children by Ari'ifa'aite, three had died by 1855. A fourth son born in 1839 took the title of Ari'iaue. A daughter, Teari'imaevarua, was adopted by Tapoa, *ari'i* of Borabora, who bestowed on her the title of the chiefs of Fa'anui.[39] She was "crowned" by Platt in 1860, but married a chief of Fa'a'a and played little part in Leeward Islands politics. A fifth son, Tamatoa, was made paramount of Ra'iatea in 1857. Her sixth child, Teri'itapunui, became a respected chief of Mahina district, and the last, Teri'itua (Prince Joinville), died in 1875.

Her own choice of successor was Ari'iaue. He had been married to an *ari'i* of the royal house on Huahine in 1857, but divorced her in 1861. Pomare arranged a political match for him with her favorite among the Salmon-Brander family by pledging him to Joanna Marau Ta'aroa a Tepau Salmon in 1875. Educated in Sydney, Marau was only fourteen at the time, while Ari'iaue was thirty-four. Pastor Green was one of the celebrants and saw the union as part of the redeployment of Protestant forces during the sensitive negotiations taking place about the Tahitian Synod.[40] The British consul also gave the match his blessing, because it united the Tahitian royal house with the most prominent Anglo-Tahitians. No one had much good to say for the heir apparent, who had lived a dissolute existence through the 1860s. There may have been an understanding that Pomare was to abdicate in favor of Ari'iaue and his new spouse. If so, it did not survive the disastrous marriage and the first drunken excesses of the prince in the bridal chamber.[41] Nor was the marriage viewed very favorably in Paris, where the Department of Colonies kept a close watch on the queen's health and that of her son, who was reported to be suffering from syphilis, tuberculosis, and bouts of pneumonia.[42]

By the date of this confidential report it was clear that Pomare would not resign. She bore her sixty years remarkably well. Two

Mormon missionaries in 1874 found her careworn "but still straight as an arrow, and retaining all her faculties in perfection."[43] She attended the fashionable round of balls and enjoyed cheating admirals and ensigns at cards. On 11 September 1877, the missionary Green reported that she was too unwell to attend a soiree on the frigate of Rear Admiral Serre, who had taken charge of the administration at her request.[44] On the seventeenth she died of a heart attack at the age of sixty-four. When Green and Serre went through her papers, they found nothing of political interest and only "immense notes" on the Scriptures. To his society Green wrote: "For many years past she has found herself more at home in religious meetings than in the discharge of her regal duties; in fact she has frequently absented herself from Papeete for weeks together with some Sisters from the church at Papeete and her domestic Chaplain (a student of ours at Tahaa) and visiting the several districts of this Island or that of Moorea employed herself with the female members of the Church by holding meetings for mutual edification."[45]

The titles of this pious old *ari'i* were transferred to her son at a formal session of the Tahitian Assembly on 24 September. She had, in a sense, personified her territory (in much the same way as the British monarch she admired personified her times), and her passing left the way clear for political change. The initiative for this change came from Serre, who was careful to surround the new *ari'i* with a small council approved by chiefs and judges. He even persuaded "Queen" Marau to rejoin her spouse briefly; but Pomare soon returned to his mistress and refused to recognize Marau's first child (or indeed any of her children) as his own. This left the king's niece Teri'vaetua and her cousin, Prince Teri'ihinoiatua, in line of succession. Serre's replacement, Commandant Planche, considered them too closely associated with the British, American, and German communities at Pape'ete and dissolved the Advisory Council, leaving the question of a Tahitian executive open and reserving greater freedom of action for the French. To Planche, Pomare possessed little more than ceremonial value: "We will make of him and his family whatever we wish."[46]

ANNEXATION

French colonial experience in other parts of the world was also brought to bear on Tahiti. Two colonial inspectors, Jore and Le

Clos, made their rounds in 1874 and carried out a fairly searching examination of the central administration. They did not visit the outer islands.

They declared the administrative services to be inefficient, unwieldy, and, in some cases, redundant.[47] Financially, they considered the territory sound enough to take over more charges from the state, providing the Tahitian budget was not kept separate from the general budget. But the weight of their criticism was directed at the Native Affairs department, whose finances were beyond the control of the *ordonnateur*—and this, they argued, had delayed assimilation and allowed "ancient Kanaka customs" to impede a steady progress toward that "position of order, clarity, regularity, and economy" dear to the heart of French colonial accountants.[48]

Jore was not quite so doctrinaire. He recognized that district administration had been maintained as part of the protectorate constitution, though he thought that the Native Affairs department had "oppressed" the population with corvées and taxes.

Neither inspector suggested annexation as a solution, but Governor Michaux was ordered to set up a commission to revise the functions of the Administrative Council. Once they had begun their task in 1876, its members eagerly extended their terms of reference to proposals for a new constitution based largely on a decree framed for New Caledonia. They planned a representative council and easier conditions of land transfer; but they stopped short of recommending full colonial status for Tahiti. Their proposals, Michaux hoped, would steer a middle course between deference to the position of the queen, chiefs, and judges, on the one hand, and the "legitimate aspirations" of the settlers, on the other.[49] Both communities would be represented in a council by two Tahitians and three Frenchmen chosen by the governor.

After Pomare's death, Commandant Planche set his officials and an expanded commission to work revising these plans for reform. From their labors there emerged, in 1878, proposals for control of the Native Affairs department by a director of the interior, a partly elected Administrative Council, and retention of the governor's full powers under the 1843 ordinance—particularly over the local press, in which there could be no discussion of the constitution. As Planche saw the situation, "to call in question our very presence in the islands could not be interpreted by a court as a journalistic offence, but that would be, however, a piece of journalism that the government cannot tolerate at any price."[50]

None of this constitution-making touched the organization of the territory as a whole. Yet it was in neighboring groups that much of the political future of Tahiti was decided; for it was there that French authority was most in need of support. The Marquesas, which had been abandoned to the care of the Catholic mission, had decreased in population to about six thousand by the 1870s. The authority of the chiefs, wrote a French official on Nukuhiva, "is suspect and disobeyed from the moment it is used to counter the population's habits of rape and drunkenness, either by expelling the chiefs or by killing them."[51] Customs were collected from 1873 on, but fines demanded by the resident, as justice of the peace, were ignored. Outside of Nukuhiva and Tahuata the population was openly hostile, and Hiva Oa revolted after the termination of the mission's agricultural experiments.

In the Tuamotu a resident and two gendarmes had helped to bring Ana'a under the same system of administration as Tahiti. They shifted to Fakarava in 1879 and began to collect port dues. Governor Planche appointed a police commissioner to Tubuai and Ra'ivavae in the same year. Protectorate laws were enforced at Mangareva after the departure of Father Laval, but there was no resident to rule the group's six or seven hundred inhabitants till 1880.

The Leeward Islands some 80 miles northwest of Tahiti gave the administration most anxiety. The politics of the small chiefdoms were deeply influenced by an improved market for cash crops and by the deteriorating authority of the missionaries and the *ari'i*. In 1852 and 1853 Teri'itaria of Huahine and Tamatoa of Ra'iatea, who had both adopted children of Pomare as successors, were forced to abdicate when they abused "the old practice in which chiefs indulged of taking food from the plantations of their subjects whenever they chose to."[52] A separate British consulate was set up at Ra'iatea between 1852 and 1854, and Consuls Nicolas, Chisholm, Wodehouse, and Ross interfered constantly, threatening fines and floggings for overzealous island judges who convicted British traders. When intimidation failed, sections of the population were bribed into appealing to outside governments; and to the consuls, at least, it seemed clear that sooner or later the independence guaranteed by the Anglo-French Convention of 1847 would have to be sacrificed for a stable administration. Such a possibility, thought Consul Miller, would probably move the French at Tahiti to act first.[53]

The two most likely protectors of European interests were America and Germany. Occasions for intervention were provided all too easily by the social and political tensions between the *ari'i* of the old *hau feti'i* and the church pastors and landowners who resented tribute and were profiting from European trade and the price controls enforced by local laws and courts.[54] In 1858, a chauvinistic American consul took advantage of a dispute between the *ra'atira* and Tamatoa V to arrange for the cession of Ra'iatea to the United States. Tamatoa banished the rebels who supported this move, but the State Department ordered a warship to investigate. When the U.S.S. *Vandalia* brought back the exiles (including two Americans) at the end of 1858, a skirmish occurred at Taha'a and the chiefs of the "American party" were defeated.[55]

The schism which had arisen because of Tamatoa's overbearing conduct now spread to the Ra'iatean churches when pastors at Opoa and Vaitoare refused to hand over their collections to European missionaries. The opposition grew, and Tamatoa and the missionaries, Green and Vivian, were expelled by the chiefs and pastors of Taha'a in 1865. Tamatoa wrote to Consul Miller at Tahiti to assist him "powerfully," since his coronation in 1857 had been an occasion for presents from England.[56] But Miller recognized that British patronage of Pomare's children was no longer possible and that the influence of the LMS had waned in a society where church and district leaders were fully aware of the bounds set on the pretensions of the *ari'i* in Tahiti. Tamatoa's paramountcy was broken, and he was banished permanently in 1871 in favor of the *ari'i* Tahitoe.

Similarly, Teri'itaria, daughter of Tamatoa IV and queen of Huahine, was forced out of office in 1852 after French, British, and American agents had collected compensation on behalf of Brander, who had a trading post on the island. The *ari'i* Teururai (Ari'imate) was set in her place with a government of ten headmen, magistrates, and constables. But when this paramount chief attempted to expel Chinese immigrants from the island in 1868, his position was quickly ended at a simple ceremony and all his titles were transferred to his wife, Ari'imate Vahine.[57] His offense in assisting French officials to recapture refugees from Atimaono had disrupted production on some of the chiefs' plantations. There was, too, a fear that an extradition agreement with Tahiti in some way sacrificed the independence of the island to the French.

Only on Borabora was there a measure of stable government under Tapoa. Peace deteriorated when he adopted Pomare's daughter, Teari'imaevarua, who was consecrated "queen" by Platt in 1860. She may have reigned, but she did not rule; and effective control passed to Tapoa II, who had been to France and who later acted as regent for the daughter of Tamatoa V.[58] Typically enough, trouble broke out over the lease of the Scilly Atoll (Fenua Ura) by the *ari'i* to the trader Brothers in 1876, which was contested by a Pape'ete firm that held a separate lease from the chiefs of Maupiti. Fighting took place between Borabora and Maupiti and Brothers was expelled from the group.

There were other breaches of the peace arising from assessment of labor for house and ship construction in monetary terms. Chiefs also contracted debts on behalf of their communities who were unwilling to make repayment. Revenues from increased port traffic accumulated in the hands of chiefs who were then refused traditional services except for payment. Everywhere economic change compromised the prerogatives of titleholders.

In these conditions, the Leeward Islands were a risky but profitable field for investment for firms seeking to avoid the rising scale of duties at Tahiti in the 1870s. They were given a lead by the SCO, which entered local commerce by taking over the firm of Wilkens and Co. at Pape'ete in 1876. Its local directors were Adrien Sieffert, Herman Meuel, and Gustave Godeffroy, who was also German consul from 1877 and married into the Brander family.[59] All three had private interests in land and trade in the Leeward group.

The business of the company was far from flourishing at the end of the 1870s, partly because of losses sustained during a hurricane. But by shifting its headquarters to Ra'iatea, the SCO diminished Pape'ete revenue from customs by a sizable proportion, and it posed a threat to the political neutrality of the group.[60] Godeffroy would have been prepared to see some form of German control by protection or annexation. His views were not shared by Captain Von Verner, who commanded the *Ariadne*—the first German warship to visit Tahiti in 1878. The presence of the vessel was sufficient, however, to confirm the suspicions of Planche when she proceeded to the Leeward Islands with Godeffroy on board; and a French gunboat was dispatched to follow her movements. With the help of his wife, Marion Brander, the consul assured the chiefs of Huahine, Borabora, and Ra'iatea of the Germans' peaceful intentions. There was no political response from the chiefs; and Godeffroy's proposal to transfer his consulate to Ra'iatea, alongside the SCO, was not approved in Berlin. The most that was allowed was a second visit by a warship, the *Bismarck*, in May 1879, when some of the chiefs of Huahine were persuaded to sign a treaty of friendship which was flatly refused at Ra'iatea and Borabora.

Even this document appears to have been innocuous enough: no more was requested than security for the lives and property of German subjects who, it was agreed, were not to sell spirits. Deserters were to be surrendered; no German subjects were to be expelled unless the German consul attended the Huahine court passing sentence.[61] There is no evidence Germany had designs on the group, though there were regular requests from the SCO and its consul-director in the Pacific for naval visits.[62] The importance of the episode, in French eyes, was the fiscal and diplomatic loophole left to a third European government.[63]

In Paris, the head of the Colonial Department, Michaux, reminded Admiral Jauréguiberry of the criticisms of the colonial inspectors and the projects for constitutional reform after the death of Pomare. He agreed with the views of Rear Admiral Serre that the Tahitian share of administration would either have to be increased or abolished. It could not be left to absorb revenue provided by Pape'ete merchants. But he could not take another "Tahitian Kingdom" seriously.[64]

Jauréguiberry, for his part, was concerned not only with the clarification of an anomalous protectorate treaty, but also with German commercial activities in the Pacific, particularly where he thought they threatened the independence of the Leeward Islands.[65] The growth of foreign commerce so near to Tahiti imposed on France "the necessity of affirming without delay supremacy in this area" and, at the same time, ending a protectorate in which Pomare V was unworthy "in his character, conduct and lack of administrative ability" to continue as partner in a joint administration.[66] On 9 September 1879 Planche was ordered to proceed with annexation.[67] Thus, for administrative, commercial, and diplomatic reasons, the formal end to the protectorate and the independence of the Leeward Islands was decided. Much amateur and professional negotiation was required.

Planche bungled his task badly. He overestimated his influence with Pomare and the chiefs, and a petition for annexation received only three signatures.[68] One of the reasons for this setback was the unwillingness of French Protestant ministers at Tahiti to persuade deacons and chiefs to agree so long as Planche refused to sanction a new constitution for the Protestant Synod. This difficulty was removed late in 1879, when a dispatch from Jauréguiberry ordered the constitution of the Tahitian churches to be published before the arrival of Planche's successor, Commissioner Isidore Chessé.[69] By February 1880, the French mission was ready to assist Chessé, not only in Tahiti but also in the Leeward Islands, where the German threat to trade was associated in the minds of pastors with the growing proportion of German priests in the Catholic mission.[70]

Chessé moved first to Ra'iatea, where he organized a request for protection from some of the chiefs and hoisted a protectorate flag on 9 April 1880. He had persuaded part of the population that Germany was seeking a permanent colony in the group. But only at Ra'iatea was this believed; and in Borabora and Huahine similar overtures to save the islands from a German peril were rejected. At Tahiti, Consul Miller protested at the maneuver, which he saw would be used "as the basis of some ulterior proposal from the French to the British Government for the latter to consent to set aside the Convention of 1847."[71]

By the end of the year, Chessé knew that his actions had been disavowed by the Ministry of Foreign Affairs after protests from commercial groups in Hamburg and Berlin. The British Foreign Office was less interested, at this stage, and was prepared to allow the extension of the protectorate in return for French diplomatic concessions in West Africa.[72] The protectorate flag of Tahiti, therefore, remained provisionally over Ra'iatea; and the date for final ratification of Chessé's measures was repeatedly postponed during eight years of tedious diplomacy.

He had more success at Tahiti. Pomare was persuaded to sign a proclamation donating "Tahiti and dependencies" to France with "all the guarantees of property and liberty" for Tahitians.[73] This was formally accepted by Chessé on 29 June 1880. There was some surprise when this transfer of sovereignty was announced, and Consul Miller declined to take part in "the consecration of this new state of things" (just as his father had refused to acknowledge the protectorate in 1845).[74] Pastor Vernier reported the news to his society in Paris and congratulated himself on his "little part in our recent peaceful conquests."[75] For the first time the consulate and the Protestant church held discordant views on the political future of the island.

In January 1881 it was learned in Tahiti that the French Parliament had ratified the annexation, and both the terms of Pomare's abdication and the state law ratifying the cession were published.[76] The king was pensioned off with 60,000 francs a year. In return he ceded Tahiti and all its undefined "dependencies," providing that "all little matters" of jurisdiction were left to the district councils and all "matters relative to lands" were left to Tahitian courts. Neither of these conditions feature in the text of the law passed by the French Parliament, though. In one sweeping gesture, French nationality was extended to all Pomare's former subjects in Tahiti, Mo'orea, and the Tuamotu, and foreign settlers were encouraged to apply for French naturalization.

Early in 1881 Chessé completed his work by visiting and annexing the Mangareva group and the distant island of Rapa. French Polynesia now included four annexed archipelagoes: Tahiti and Mo'orea, the Marquesas, the Tuamotu, and Rapa; and there were two protectorates at Ra'iatea and in part of the Austral Islands. It still remained to settle the Leewards question which had precipitated the annexation; to give the new colony a constitution; and to devise a pattern of regional administration which would cope with so many scattered responsibilities.

CHAPTER 8

THE POLITICS
OF ASSIMILATION

TAHITI and its dependencies were fully incorporated into the French Empire at a period of expansion in Africa and Asia and at a time of debate on the value of new possessions for the metropolis. Three major factors were at work to encourage revision of past administrative and economic policies. The first derived from a greater appreciation in France of the extent and diversity of overseas possessions in the 1880s—an enlightenment fostered by geographical and commercial societies, encouraged by patriotic and chauvinistic interest groups with a stake in colonies, and popularized by the Colonial Exhibition of 1889. By then the generation of local French republicans at Tahiti who had welcomed the annexation also had a favorable press in Paris. Articles and books by Varigny, Vignon, and Deschanel publicized the strategic and economic advantages of French Pacific territories.[1] There was a strong anticlerical element in the latter's account of Mangareva and a fashionable acceptance of predictions of the value of Rapa and the Austral group when a canal through Panama was projected. In 1889, the administration at Tahiti also published the first of a long series of reports and speculation on the consequences of cutting the isthmus.[2] The same year, the first tourist *Guide de Tahiti* was on sale in Paris. For the sentimental there was Midshipman Viaud's exquisite dreamworld of *Rarahu* and the *Mariage de Loti*. For the reformers there was Henri Mager's book, *Cahiers coloniaux de 1889*, which expounded the views of settlers who desired closer links with France and which even printed a letter by "un vieux Tahitian" who argued for the end of special treatment in law for France's Polynesian citizens.[3]

Such publicity was a reflection of Tahiti's own press, which burgeoned like some tropical plant into no fewer than thirteen newspapers, periodicals, and short-lived reviews. Several changed their name to escape press laws, but not their polemical style. Nearly all were owned, edited, and printed by local lawyers, merchants, and part-time politicians, such as Léonce Brault, Gaston Cognet, Germain Coulon, the intelligent ex-communard Albert Cohen, and a strident and deluded critic, Eugène Brunschwig. Behind the republican patriots and defenders of lost causes stood a solidly respectable business community headed by Victor Raoulx, François Cardella, Paul Martiny, and other Frenchmen who sought to replace foreigners who had dominated local trade from its beginnings.

"Assimilation" was a word they employed frequently in their writings and debates, though they were far from agreeing on all its implications. In Tahiti the term had at least three meanings, two of which were not new to the territory.[4] Legal assimilation of the population to the obligations of French civil and criminal codes had been tried in various degrees since 1842, culminating in the appointment of French magistrates but stopping short of complete jurisdiction over land tenure. With some truth, one of the local partisans for the completion of this process claimed that the legislation of 1866 which had ended the Tahitian code of laws "gave to France the key of Tahiti"; Chessé, by arranging the annexation, "had only to open the door."[5] Secondly, economic assimilation, or the extension of metropolitan tariffs to island trade, was to make its appearance as republican dogma in French Polynesia in 1892. Lastly, in a vaguer sense, assimilation implied the extension of the French language, customs, and values through education—a policy which various administrators had tried to promote by using Catholic or Protestant missions.

But the term meant much more than this in metropolitan thinking about the place of distant island posts in the French Empire. The second major influence on French Pacific policy derived from the place of French local government institutions in colonial administration. Colonial commissions led by delegates from Martinique and Guadeloupe had tried, in the late 1870s, to adapt the French Constitution of 1875 for promulgation overseas. The search for simple formulas failed in the face of regional differences and a principle preserved in French imperial rule since 1815—

namely, that individual territories had a right to separate legislation to meet their particular problems. But if this failure checked the spread of conformity, it still left intact the model to be followed. The system of general councils and communes applied overseas in various ways since 1854 was, therefore, "assimilationist" not in the sense that these institutions worked everywhere in the same way passing the same laws, but in the sense that the system promoted the ultimate political control of colonies by the French government.

Indeed, a few colonies participated directly in this metropolitan organization of the French Empire by representation in the French Parliament. For others, there was the Conseil Supérieur des Colonies, a purely consultative body in which French Polynesia had a voice from 1886. Such centralization set limits to local aspirations for autonomy. For, overseas, a governor's administrative council was a miniature council of state. Autonomy for a representative institution such as a general council, in French colonies or in French departments, meant no more than a limited say in the management of a budget and the right to voice opinions on other matters.

This centralization, moreover, was facilitated by a third development of importance in the last quarter of the nineteenth century —better communications. In 1881, Tahiti received news of the ratification of annexation via the New York–San Francisco telegraph only a month after the measure had been passed by the French Parliament (though it took a month or more for these tidings to percolate through to outlying archipelagoes). From 1883, the Ministry of Marine and Colonies began to appoint officials who were civilians, rather than naval officers, although the French naval tradition remained strong in local administration and retired officers continued to be used in a number of capacities. With the evolution of a Ministry of Colonies by 1894, telegraphic orders came from ministers and undersecretaries who were less concerned with naval stations than with ordering civil servants trained in the newly founded Colonial School in Paris. By the end of the century, the senior cadres of Tahitian administration were solidly civilian, subject to the reports of a professional inspectorate, and loyal to the methods and precedents of an expanding imperial bureaucracy directed by a civilian department of state.

Tahiti, then, became the capital of a colonial territory at a time of experimentation when French colonial expertise moved toward its zenith. It was a time of optimism and confidence before the arteries of empire had begun to harden into the formal centralization demanded later by short-lived ministries in Paris—and before the crushing exigencies of the First World War shattered plans for economic development. Whatever the dogmas of later colonial theoreticians, compromises with the structural and social inheritance from the territory's immediate past had to be made.

THE GENERAL COUNCIL

In the first place, republican fervor to assimilate local government to a French pattern was forced to take into account that the overwhelming proportion of the electorate was not European and most of the settlers were not French. Ability to use the French language was, of course, a qualification for candidates and a method of screening out both Polynesian and foreign contestants from the political arena. Nevertheless, there was always a danger that a Tahitian electorate might be attracted to representatives whose views were opposed to the majority of French settlers. This fear accounts for much of the intensity of local politics during the period 1880–1903; it accounts, too, for the reactionary policies of the French community, which paradoxically prided itself, by contrast with the administration and the churches, on a "progressive" attitude toward government in the islands.

The new colony, in any case, had to wait five years for a constitution that would test the ability of settlers to manage their own affairs. In the meantime, there was some reshuffling of local officials and some experimentation in electoral representation. A director of the Interior replaced the *ordonnateur*. A Secretariat, an Office of Colonial Administration, and an Office of Finance and Provisions took over the work of the old Native Affairs department and were grouped in the Department of the Interior. All this cost twice as much to run; and it was abolished in 1898 for a fully staffed General Secretariat which employed colonial clerks *(commis)* whose standards few Tahitians could reach.

Responsible to the governor were five officials—the director of the Interior, the attorney general, a head of Naval Administration, a medical superintendent, and a treasury-paymaster. By a decree of 1885, they formed with two nominated settlers a Privy Council which the governor was obliged to consult and which discussed all local legislation.[6] The governor could suspend his officials, but he could not redefine their functions or dismiss them; nor could he interfere with judgments made in local courts. His power to spend was similarly curtailed: all expenditure in excess of 5,000 francs had to be justified to the ministry before authorization; he could sell property owned by the state, but again not in excess of 5,000 francs. His powers of expropriation were left conveniently vague, but the Privy Council had to be consulted.

Governors of Tahiti during the period before the First World War were many—twenty-four in thirty-six years, including some who were subordinate officials acting temporarily. Few, except perhaps Lacascade, Petit, Fawtier, and Julien, made much of a mark, either in the Pacific or in other territories. None were long enough in Tahiti to gain more than a superficial knowledge of the islands, and few had sufficient influence in Paris to promote the development of the colony by investment or immigration. "The governors," wrote Paul Gauguin, "the select of the administration, shine like stars with all their glitter on their arrival; like shooting-stars they come and shoot off to another latitude."[7] Much as before annexation they found themselves in the hands of local politicians.

The forum for politicians was the General Council of eighteen elected members. Four came from Pape'ete, six from Tahiti and Mo'orea, four from the Tuamotu, two from the Marquesas, and two from Mangareva and the Austral Islands.[8] The powers of the council, as defined in 1885, were clear but limited: the governor was required to accept their views on the revision of electoral lists, purchase of property by the administration, transactions with private companies, charities, pensions, and all taxation to meet expenditure, except customs and wharf dues. In all other matters the council was permitted a voice, but in the matter of the budget this voice was muted by the peculiarities of French colonial practice. The annual accounts and the budget, as presented by the director of the Interior (the only link with the administration) included everything except metropolitan subsidies and salaries of senior officials. The influence of the council was limited to optional expenditure, as distinct from obligatory expenditure which the governor could approve if the council refused to pass it. Optional expenditure was difficult, but not impossible, to change in Privy Council once the General Council had voted the budget. It was also the least important section of the budget.

There was one other concession: the council might correspond with the ministry over the governor's head or set up an investigating committee with the right to examine relevant documents from local departments. It appointed its own permanent commission to examine accounts and function as an interim committee between annual sessions.

Elections were held for a temporary Colonial Council (1880–1882) and for a General Council in 1883 and 1884. The proceedings of the first body were never published and it accomplished little. But the electorate gained experience. By 1885, there were 2,200 male electors on the rolls in Tahiti and Mo'orea, though only about two-thirds of these voted. Only about 8 percent were European settlers, and the strains of unaccustomed democracy produced electoral anomalies.[9] The district chief or the *mutoi* usually advised electors how to vote. In 1883, three districts sent in returns which tallied exactly with their rolls, and one of these inscribed the same candidate on all its voting cards. In the district of Fa'a'a, where 112 male electors made six votes each with a possible maximum of 672 returns (in a system of proportional representation), some 692 votes were recorded.[10] Bribes were commonplace, and the influence of French officials was used to favor some of the candidates.

From the outset this Lilliputian electorate, which was divided at first into two electoral colleges, threw up two main parties—the French (Catholic) Republicans, elected by Pape'ete merchants and traders, and Tahitian and French Protestants, elected by the districts. This pattern was maintained after 1884, when the General Council was elected from a single list. The change in procedure was an attempt on the part of Governor Morau to respect the principle of equality between Tahitian and French European citizens. In his ordinance which dissolved the council of 1883, he pointed out that the selection of the same number of candidates from separate lists by 344 European electors and 2,188 Polynesian electors took no account of the numerical difference between the populations.[11]

All that was logical enough. But nothing was done to represent the outer islands as yet; and the elections to the General Council of

1884 were marked by the same cleavage between rural and urban electorates. Petty infringements of voting rules, unverified electoral lists, and hot exchanges between rival newspapers—the pro-Catholic *Messager de Tahiti*, run by Cardella, Martiny, and Raoulx, and the pro-Protestant *Océanie Française*, edited by Cohen and Auguste Goupil—set the stage for the minor dramas of the next two decades. Both parties were united only on two points: the powers of the council were inadequate; and the rest of the territory had to be enfranchised. The reply of Paris to the first was the new constitution of 1885; the second was never popular with the administration, which delayed it as long as possible.

But until 1890, when a Municipal Council was created, the General Council was the main representative body in the colony with a voice in government. Its members, on the whole, represented the main island, and they duplicated the business of a plethora of minor bodies—the Chamber of Commerce, the Agricultural Committee, the Works Commission, the Council for Hygiene and Public Health, the Council for Public Education, and the Committee for the Agricultural Bank.

The council's victories over the administration were few. With great difficulty they obtained the right to elect the chairman of the bank, formerly a guarded preserve of the director of the Interior.[12] Through the same bank the council was responsible for buying land for Pape'ete's first public hospital and for preserving the palace and grounds of Pomare V as a historic monument in 1900, when a German trader, Gaspard Coppenrath, purchased this edifice. They prevented the French government from sending shiploads of hardened criminals to the colony. They were successful in voting an end to the Interior department in 1898, and in so doing they exchanged the director (the only official present at their debates) for a secretary general—an administrative nonentity at this time in French colonies. Finally, through the reports of various committees, the council kept up a steady criticism of schools, public works, immigration, and the police, and they debated the important questions of Chinese settlement and the sale of spirits to Tahitian-French citizens, topics which they were too divided to settle.

Most of these matters were secondary, however, to the main business of scrutinizing indirect taxes and the optional expenses of the budget. Their inability to determine the use of all revenues was compensated for by procrastination over voting sums which they had the power to deny, notably the allocation of subsidies to the Protestant and Catholic missions. The majority of members campaigned, too, against the election of a Protestant for several terms as the colony's delegate to the Conseil Supérieur in Paris, and they refused to acknowledge Franck Puaux as the successful candidate. By the end of the 1880s, relations with the administration had deteriorated to the level of a series of personal feuds between the council's president, Cardella, and Acting Governor D'Ingremard. It was a time of "anonymous posters and insults in the press," complained the unfortunate administrator in 1889: "The sessions of the General Council are a pretext for tumultuous meetings where the mob comes to demonstrate against the head of the Colony and everything connected with the administration; and the dissolution which has always been urgently requested by the Governor's Council begins to look like the only remedy for the situation."[13]

The following year the noisy cabal was reinforced by members of the newly elected Municipal Council. Both bodies, which had settlers in common, fell out over the allocation of revenues from the budget for the Pape'ete municipality. The sum itself was never more than 200,000 francs, but the ability of the General Council to reduce it resulted in a three-cornered dispute with the members for Pape'ete, the members elected for the districts, and the administration over the town's share of trading licenses and import duties. In 1890, it was agreed that one-third of these revenues was to be paid into the municipal chest; but, thereafter, the proportion was reduced till, in 1900, the Governor's Council requested Mayor Cardella to take legal action against the General Council for its parsimony.[14] Nothing came of the case. The municipality never had complete control over roads and port facilities, and it had the building of only one school to its credit. Even less than the General Council did it benefit the colony, so long as it was denied adequate funds.

Toward the end of the 1890s, party lines in the council began to change. The pro-Catholic majority split their united front, and a series of anticlerical governors altered the electoral procedure in ways which gave a greater voice to the districts of Tahiti and Mo'orea. In 1894, Cardella and his friends broke away from other candidates put up by the French settlers and campaigned on their own. Bishop Verdier tried to persuade both factions to join forces on a single electoral list, but Cardella refused and carried his disagreement with the bishop so far as to vote against the annual subsidy to the Catholic mission.[15]

The second mistake of the Catholic majority was to carry their attack on Governor Gallet's administration too far in 1898. Gallet's proposals for a new property tax and increased subsidies to steamer lines calling at Tahiti were persistently (and shortsightedly) blocked. The governor complained angrily to Paris that ever since the creation of a General Council, "the business of the territory has been in the hands of the present backward majority whose clandestine leader is the head of the Catholic mission."[16] To end this opposition he reduced the seats in the council to eleven in August 1899 and, in so doing, ended elected representation from the Tuamotu. Pape'ete was given only four seats, compared with seven for the rest of Tahiti and Mo'orea.

There was rejoicing in the Protestant camp led by Pastor Viénot and allied with Auguste Goupil, while Bishop Verdier lodged a complaint with the French Ministry for Foreign Affairs. After new elections, the hard core of Cardella's supporters was reduced to four and the council included two Tahitians, Tati Salmon and Temari'i a Temari'i (though others had been elected before 1885).

But the council's days were numbered. It was consistently bypassed in matters relating to the budget, as governors wrote into the obligatory expenses items members refused to vote. In 1898 the more vociferous section of the settlers, tiring of the mere formalities of office, petitioned for an end to "overseas tutelage" of Tahiti from Paris and demanded no less than complete financial and administrative autonomy for the colony, even at the price of paying for all metropolitan subsidies.[17] The point of frustration had been reached where the assembly preferred radical change, even dissolution, to ineffectiveness. In 1900, moreover, the colony was called on to pay for its police, treasury, courts, churches, and all charges of internal administration still borne by France. In return, the metropolitan subsidy was raised to 2,000 francs a year—much less than the cost of the new burdens. As the minister for colonies, Decrais, interpreted the Financial Law of 13 April 1900, only administrators were competent to estimate and propose the budgets of colonial departments.[18] The General Council, continued Decrais, had been instituted to advise and confirm, but not to administer.

This interpretation left the council redundant. Without consultation or ceremony it was abolished by Governor Petit, on orders from Paris, in 1903.[19] In its place the Administrative Council was revived, consisting of officials from the governor's council, two nominated Europeans, the mayor of Pape'ete, and administrators from the Leeward, Tuamotu, Marquesas, and Austral groups—if they could get to Pape'ete.

The experiment in representation at the center had its influence on the district chiefs. There was a tendency to inflate their functions without giving them any financial responsibility; and the fact that chiefs and ra'atira were also electors and church members brought Pape'ete politics into the rural constituencies. Indeed, the question had been raised shortly after annexation whether districts might provide fully elected councils for all local government purposes. But the director of colonies, Michaux, thought that the incorporation of kinship institutions into the pattern of French local government was not to be taken too literally. Tahitians had "parliamentary habits," wrote Michaux, but the numerical superiority of the population gave them "in conditions of complete equality a pre-eminence which is perhaps not consistent with good policy and with the legitimate influence which we must continue to exert. On the other hand, municipal institutions which are desirable in all countries where interests are concentrated could not be set up, without taking into account different nationalities and the chiefs' prerogatives maintained in the Act of cession."[20]

This dilemma in assimilation was less precisely perceived in Tahiti. There were French settlers who knew exactly what should be done. Goupil in the Océanie Française conducted a campaign which forced Pomare V to give up his privilege of court domestics provided by the districts in turn, and he waged war on the continued existence of the To'ohitu and the district land courts.[21] In this campaign he was supported by Governor Morau, who thought that Polynesians could not fail to desire republican institutions, as they were already swept along "by the ideas which steep our modern society and which are the direct consequence of a law of nature which calls us ever forward."[22]

But this evolutionist thinking did not get far in practice. The district councils could not be made into "municipal" bodies while they had no members who understood French legislation. Goupil wished to call the chiefs "mayors," but this innovation overlooked the sources of authority in the districts. Conflicts between a French-appointed president of a council and the district pastor or a gendarme were not uncommon. In 1884, for example, while Goupil, Morau, and others were talking assimilation in Pape'ete, the district chief of Papeto'ai, backed by the French resident of Mo'orea, was at loggerheads with the parish church council, backed by Pastor Vernier, over the use of labor for public works during the three months required to organize New Year festivals.[23] To make the chief a "mayor" would not have solved a conflict which arose from a system of parallel administration and a close dependency of chiefs on administration patronage. In Paris a wiser counsel prevailed, and the colony's delegate, Puaux, advised the Ministry of Marine to make a presentation of tricolor sashes to the chiefs, but none of the other attributes of French mayors.[24]

The idea of full municipal councils was dropped in favor of elected municipal "commissions" consisting of a president (chief or administrator), three councillors with a vote, and five advisory members. The first elections took place in 1887. The results were approved only in nine districts, and they were annulled in thirteen others for irregularities—participation of candidates in the voting, falsified returns, or canvasing by Protestant pastors.[25] On the whole, the new system did not result in any great changes in the composition of district councils. The distinction between titular and advisory members was fictional. No funds were allocated by the General Council (where ideas on assimilation did not extend to district finance). Even Goupil, the partisan of municipalities, was forced to admit in the Privy Council that the extension of full citizenship to Tahitians meant the end of cheap district labor: "The truth is that all communal buildings which were once raised by corvées are now in ruins and disappear gradually without being replaced, because the natives are not simple enough to pay taxes in work which they need not, and which Europeans do not, pay."[26]

This comment and other evidence from church records suggest that district administration had passed from a stage of voluntary services, unless for pastors, and had not yet reached the stage of regular taxes in money and payments for work. Labor taxes were not restored till 1898 (possibly illegally), when a road tax commutable into a week's work was reintroduced. Otherwise the Tahitian was asked to pay a head tax of 20 francs, a dog tax, or fines in cash like a European. From time to time he was threatened with a tax on uncultivated land to stimulate agriculture, but this was never applied. Wherever Governor Gallet toured in 1901, he was petitioned by the chiefs and the district councils for a return to the old system of district taxes which could all be paid in workdays (and could, therefore, be met with a minimum of effort).[27] The system was restored in 1905, and the head tax was halved.

The only feature of district administration which was strengthened by the experiment with "commissions" was the power of the governor to approve or suspend district chiefs. Between 1885 and 1906, in the twenty-two administrative districts of Tahiti and Mo'orea, there were changes of "president" everywhere, usually two or three times, with the exception of Papara. Party politics at the center had much to do with this instability. When a new chief (a Catholic related to Victor Raoulx) was elected at Afare'aitu in 1895, the anticlerical Papinaud selected the candidate with the second-largest number of votes on the grounds that immigrant Polynesians had taken part in the vote (which they usually did) and that the chief had just been deposed for mismanagement anyway. In addition, campaigning for district votes intensified after the Cardella party blocked the payment of district pastors and deacons in 1887. "These events," wrote a Tahitian member of the General Council, "have given food for thought to many people who have a large influence with the people and who had kept outside the electoral struggle in order not to mix religious and parochial interests."[28] Annual electioneering by pastors, priests, and traders became an entertaining feature of district life. It reached a peak in 1899 when the Catholic votes from the Tuamotu were lost. Then Cardella carried the contest a stage further by trying to influence district council elections. Broadsheets were distributed promising to avoid taxes, preserve land rights, and maintain the Protestant faith.[29] Governor Gallet countered this extension of municipal politics into district administration by decreeing that chiefs could be appointed, whether elected or not, from outside senior district families if necessary. Six of the district chiefs who had assisted the propaganda of the Cardella party were replaced at once, and three others, including Prince Teri'ihinoiatua of Pare-Arue, were made to withdraw their signatures from a petition protesting against lack of representation from the outer islands. New presidents were appointed from outside the former chiefs' families for Pa'ea, Teahupo'o, Maha'ena, Tiarei, Afa'ahiti, and Papeno'o.

After this coup there was not much left for the chiefs to do unless they were equipped with a better education than most of them possessed to keep district land registers and take an active part in agriculture and public works. A few managed this transition from prescribed to elected and appointed status and kept pace with the requirements of a cash economy. Tati Salmon ran Papara and Atimaono districts from 1885 and sat on the General Council. He was in the forefront of Tahitians who became deeply involved in commercial and agricultural speculation in the conditions of easy credit prevailing in the 1880s and 1890s. At Puna'auia, the chief Teri'iero'o a Teri'iero'o followed his father in office after schooling with the Ploermel Brothers and work as a clerk and in district education. He began a career of long service, supervising roadbuilding, encouraging vanilla plantations, and administering island churches as a member of the conseil supérieur of the Tahitian Synod.[30]

There were similar examples on Mo'orea, where Winifred Marama Brander ran Ha'apiti district and went into the local schooner trade and Pai a Ani was both chief and planter at Papeto'ai. Sonorous Tahitian titles still sound through the lists of chiefs and council presidents in the pages of the *Annuaires*, but their connection with previous titleholders is open to doubt. Few are descended even from the chiefs who approved Pomare V's cession to France. The Vehiatua title would seem to have disappeared from Taiarapu with the last incumbent, Teri'irere, who had fought in Bruat's war and in New Caledonia and who died a Chevalier de la Légion d'Honneur in 1889. The Pomares were still represented by Prince Hinoi, who is listed as chief of Afa'ahiti, Hitia'a, and Mahina in the late 1890s, along with Isbella Shaw, his mother, who had been wife of Teri'itua (Joinville) and mistress of Pomare V. By 1906 his functions had been limited to Arue district, and he died without issue in 1916.

Where chiefs declined in authority, the gendarmes expanded into district administration. By 1900, their posts at Pape'ete and Taravao had about twenty men with Tahitian constables to keep order. Justices of the peace on circuit dealt with minor police matters, and civil and police courts at Pape'ete dealt with more serious cases and appeals. But day-to-day sanctions were exercised by the gendarme and *mutoi* in matters of stock trespass, vagrancy, obstruction, and disturbances caused by drunkenness. For the rest, the churches with their pastors, deacons, priests, and elders were authority enough.

LAND AND TERRITORY

Assimilation was also considered to mean the acceleration of land registration in Tahiti and Mo'orea and the extension of this system throughout the colony. If (as the *Océanie Française* argued) tribute payments to chiefs had gone and the hierarchies of the old social order had been leveled down to *ra'atira*, then landusers could be defined as landowners and the claims of families to unoccupied land could be dismissed.[31] For the present, it was admitted, the Tahitian courts could not be abolished, but the sanctions of the legislation of 1852 and 1866 against those who failed to register or lodge counterclaims were to be revived for application.

Other opinions went even further. According to a legal decision made in a French Appeal Court in 1882, the Tahitian assessor in land cases was held to be redundant, since Tahitians were now "Frenchmen on the same footing as other Frenchman."[32] It was inadmissible, therefore, that a Tahitian who had his land registered under French law could still be required by a district council and the To'ohitu to renounce his claims because a relative could prove direct lineal descent from the original occupying family. Yet this continued to happen; and in 1887 a nephew of Paraita had been forced to hand back registered land to descendants of Paraita's widow who had made him a "donation."[33]

There was, too, still an argument about *fari'ihau* land, looked on by Governor Morau in 1884 as "a kind of communal property" used to keep up the social and economic status of chiefs appointed by the administration.[34] But other members of the governor's council contended that recently installed chiefs might lose this privilege if descendants of former titleholders chose to take them before a Tahitian court. *Fari'ihau* blocks had been enlarged in the 1870s by sections of *ra'atira* holdings for schools, chapels, and meeting-houses. The Tahitian members of the council pointed out that these civic donations would never have been made if it had been foreseen that land rights would be vested in chiefs from outside senior district families. It was recognized, too, that *fari'ihau* could only be alienated (as some chiefs had tried to do) with the permission of the Tahitian Assembly, and this body was defunct.

To meet these problems, a plan was put forward by Frédéric Bonet, who served in a number of political and administrative capacities and had a thorough knowledge of Tahitian and land tenure. It was debated by the Colonial Council and the administration in 1887.[35] The essential feature of Bonet's proposals was to continue registration and to recognize unclaimed land as district or "communal" domain. A decree of 1887 outlined the method, which assumed the Land Department had taken possession of all territory and would assign blocks to claimants after undisputed declaration or after disputes had been settled.[36] Unclaimed lands were to form a *faufa'a mata'eina'a*, or district "patrimony"—presumably available for transfer by lease or sale. A delay of a year from the date of promulgation was allowed for declaration of claims. A suggestion in the Colonial Council that such declarations might be made in the name of families of useholders was rejected in the governor's council, where Goupil argued that this would perpetuate "joint ownership"—an anathema to assimilationists. A short period was allowed for counterclaims—no more than a month in Tahiti and six months in the outer islands. After this period of grace, a property certificate was to be granted.

The main objection to this legislation was that it neglected the most elementary provision for a cadastral survey, and it set an impossible deadline for Tahitians and others to cope with the technicalities of registration at Pape'ete. When the limitary date of December 1888 passed by, the administration had either to accept the responsibility for enforcing the legal fiction and dispossess over half the useholders of the territory or fix a longer period for claims to be lodged. A further three years were allowed in 1895, when it was discovered that no registration forms had been sent to the outer islands. But in its essentials the decree of 1887 was left unchanged till the 1920s.

It was soon clear, too, that the administration was incapable of handling the bulk of claims and counterclaims. By May 1892, the *Journal Officiel* had published 4,656 claims, mostly for Tahiti and Mo'orea. In addition, there were more than 8,000 other claims waiting in the Pape'ete Land Office. Three years later a committee of the General Council reported that little progress had been made:

> The constitution of territorial property, the goal aimed at, is not being realised in the face of the apathy or ignorance of the natives who in general believe they have finished when they have filled in their declarations. However, the task should not have been undertaken everywhere at the same time. It involves, as it operates, an enormous movement of records and constitutes bulky archives which encumber the [Land Office] and make the slightest research excessively laborious, thus adding to the delays which hinder the delivery of property titles; and in addition those titles are little in demand by the parties concerned.[37]

By 1913, the total number of published claims had risen to 21,386 for the whole of the territory. But by then their usefulness as a basis for protection or for transfer of land rights had been thoroughly tested and found wanting.

Before the registration of land could be carried out or completed, the outer islands of the colony had to come under French control. Even on Tahiti and Mo'orea, where occupation was longest, passive opposition to interference with land tenure, as well as fear of dispossession, were strong, at a period when rising values for cash crops increased speculation in plantation lands. Worse, much of the "bulky archives" disappeared when Fare Ute was flooded in 1906. The tendency of Tahitians to look on claim forms as titles undermined the whole purpose of the operation; and even where certificates were issued by the Land Office, there were few plans. Such plans as were made were paid for by Europeans and the Euro-Polynesian families who had begun to emerge from the period of economic change during the protectorate as the successors to the *ari'i*.

For the bulk of the population of Tahiti and Mo'orea, perhaps one-third of land under some form of cultivation had been registered over the half century since Bonard's legislation. About another third was still in a chaos of litigation, compounded by Bonet's stimulus to the production of doubtful paper "titles" from

1887. The rest was unsurveyed and unregistered.[38] In the absence of controls over land-using groups by chiefs or by administrators, the way was left open for continuous wrangles which were alien to French law and which the Tahitian courts prolonged with eloquent satisfaction. A case concerning the lands of the *Vehiatua* titlehold-er of Taiarapu who had died in 1889 went on for nearly twenty years. In the Leeward Islands, complained a local newspaper in 1914, claims extended to all resources—"the sea, the mountains, the fish and clouds."[39]

Moreover, French control did not result in complete registers of population in Tahiti and Mo'orea, where indifference to the for-malities of marriage, adoption, and inheritance speedily confused the records that existed after two or three generations. Changes of name did not help. It was not sufficient to keep records at Pape'ete: they had to be revised at district level, and the district councils could not, or would not, do this.

Finally, the French administration never succeeded in grouping the population into villages (though this was tried in the 1870s). Bi-lateral inheritance and scattered lots encouraged mobility between districts and islands. Land transfers by sale, donation, and lease were not common, but they were not unknown between Tahitians. Except where Europeans entered into these transactions, adminis-trators' "control" of usehold was limited to property speculation under French law in settled areas around Pape'ete or in special re-source zones such as Makatea and the Tuamotu lagoons. Else-where, cousers were mobile, elusive, and mostly unrecorded.

The universality of application assumed in legislation, then, had to be modified by the limits imposed on the authority of adminis-trators in their capacity as rulemakers and social engineers. These limits were even more evident in the outlying dependencies of Tahiti. The constitution of 1885 was silent about the organization of half the population of the territory, and Bonet's land decree was passed before the Leeward Islands became French possessions.

While the abrogation of the Anglo-French Convention of 1847 hung in the balance, the protection of Ra'iatea was no more than provisional. French naval officers visited the island to settle Euro-pean complaints and induce a few French allies to accept natural-ization. When the unpopular *ari'i* Tamatoa was forced by his sub-jects to abdicate, a chief of Taha'a was appointed in his place and "the whole of the Government (save one governor Teraupo'o) were enrolled as Frenchmen and nearly the whole of the people banded together as one man to resist them."[40] Two villages of the island were bombarded in November 1887.

On receiving news of the Declaration of Paris in March 1888, which removed the last diplomatic obstacles, Governor Lacascade annexed each of the three islands. At Huahine there was some defiance and the old flag was hoisted, "the ceremony being of a partly religious character and partly of an opposition display," reported a British missionary.[41] Chiefs and judges continued to govern according to the island code of laws under Queen Teha'apapa. In 1895, she was pensioned off and a resident administrator was installed.

At Borabora, Queen Teri'imaevarua kept the island neutral. A vice-resident took charge between 1895 and 1897, but he fell out with the chiefs over land, taxes, and control of traders. He was replaced by a gendarme who reduced the Borabora *mutoi* from thirty to nine and the island's judges to one. But local laws remained in force.

At Ra'iatea, the division between the bulk of the chiefs and the people, led by Teraupo'o, was not so easily healed. In theory, Tamatoa was replaced by a daughter of Tahitoe as "Queen of Avera"; but real authority had passed to the rebel chief, who carried the Ra'iatean pastors with him. Pastor Brunel, who was a witness of these events, took over the island's school in 1894, made frequent visits to the camp of the "teraupistes," and gained a sympathetic insight into their control of trade, taxes, and the paramount chief.[42] The British consul at Tahiti visited the island to make it clear that no British help could be expected.[43] Governor Gallet was obliged to send an expedition in 1897 after the rebels had enforced a blockade of the island's main port at Uturoa. Some two hundred prisoners were taken, and most were exiled on Ua Huka in the Marquesas till 1901. The leaders of the rebellion, including Teraupo'o and his brother, Hupe, were sent to New Caledonia till 1905.

Not much is known about this minor example of resistance or its leaders. There were hardly more than 359 Ra'iateans under arms, while the French had about a hundred supporters at Uturoa. Teraupo'o has left some correspondence with the British consul which only shows that he expected British intervention and had a passionate belief in the power of the Protestant religion to save the political independence of the group. The exiles in the Marquesas were reported by a Catholic missionary to be "fanatical Protestants" who set about converting local Marquesans, gave displays of fire-walking, and composed *pehe paripari* (laments) on their fate.[44] The principal casualties, by the end of the 1890s, were not among the rebels but in the ranks of the *ari'i*, whose position was made untenable by their own subjects or by French officials.

But Teraupo'o was something more than a disaffected Ra'iatean whose resentment had been caused by a kick from a French captain "dans la partie la moins noble de son individu."[45] The story may even have been true. It does not, however, explain the antipathy of other Leeward Islanders to French rule, their attachment to autonomous church institutions (which continued to make large collections during the resistance), and their casual demotion of "chiefs" attracted by French inducements. Above all, they would also appear to have resented French port duties and diversion of revenues at a period when the Leeward Islands trade was flourishing. They may also have feared land alienation.

In this aspect of resistance they were joined by Germans in the group, one of whom, the planter and trader G. Neuffer, was an adopted son of Teraupo'o and supplied arms and funds.[46] But one of the issues at stake between Teraupo'o and pro-French chiefs at Uturoa was disputed land, and this dispute was exacerbated by the unwise insistence of officials that Ra'iateans should live in villages rather than on their scattered plantations of cotton, vanilla, coconuts, and maize.[47]

Fortunately, perhaps, French administrators in the Leeward Islands learned to consolidate their rule with a fairly light hand to avoid further unrest. Land commissions of Ra'iatean judges were appointed to extend the 1887 land legislation to the group in 1898; but the French magistrate, Bracconi, who followed up their work strongly opposed efforts to apply the French Civil Code.[48] All preliminary claims, in any case, had to be revised; and the administrator's Appeal Court labored in the wake of the commissions with little information on the registers to guide it and harangued by "incessant exchanges between members of the court and amateur barristers."[49] Fresh appeals were lodged with unwearying regularity, as rights over fruit trees, taro patches, and coconut plantations were pedantically transformed into rights over territory on a piece of paper in fractions and divisions which bore little relationship to the seasonal complexities of usehold and proprietorship and which, all too often, served as a pretext for further disputes.

There was, in addition, a great deal of confusion over "town lots" (originally set aside by chiefs to allow the population to congregate at villages). Speculation for such lands around the port was rife. Many Tahitians who had enjoyed temporary rights of residence in Ra'iatea bought up their old sites. One such case which came before an administrator in 1904 involved the properties of a trader, a Ra'iatean family, and the very grounds of the administrator's office.

But, on the whole, the local codes were respected, as revised in 1898 to make provision for compulsory land registration; and while these were still applied, the initiative in determining the pace of registration lay with island judges, and the pace was very slow.

For different reasons, land registration made little progress in the Marquesas either. The French administration there consisted of no more than a resident assisted by three or four minor officials and a brigade of ten gendarmes. Penalties for distilling spirits were paid by sale of a few sacks of copra, and imprisonment was, in the words of a resident, "a kind of honorary distinction."[50] French civil laws on marriage, births, and deaths were ignored. In 1893, Resident Tautain, who had been in the group for six years, advised that the French should withdraw.[51] In another report he noted that in the 1880s there had still existed a traditional respect for certain families and chiefs among the valley tribes which might have assisted a form of administration based on a local code of laws. "Instead of that," he wrote, "the Marquesas have been treated as one would treat a sub-prefecture of France in 1894."[52]

Tautain was unusually outspoken. In general, administrators were inhibited by officious criticism of their reports in Pape'ete and by a desire for promotion to a happier post. Their subordinates, especially the colonial gendarmes, were notorious for their lack of intelligence and their petty exactions. Lords of their islands and their charges, and costing about 15,000 francs a year each, they have been fittingly caricatured for their self-importance in Gendarme Guillot's autobiography, while their pluralistic offices were vilified by Gauguin.[53]

An attempt by a resident to register Marquesan usehold in 1889 failed for lack of courts or councils to hear claims, and the few titles lodged on his initiative were never published. By the end of the century, it was realized that there were no local chiefs who were still *tiohi fenua*—keepers of the land through whom a commission might work to decide the rights of each family. By a decree of 1902 all lands not claimed within a year became the property of the state, and Marquesans were forbidden to sell without permission.[54] When a titles commission began its hearings in 1904, no provision was made for any survey, and there was none before 1923.

The Taumotu and Mangareva were more closely supervised by retired naval officers in two residencies which cost about 50,000 francs each to run every year. The main concern of the administration had been to protect the lagoons as a major resource zone and to prevent chronic indebtedness from becoming a pretext for extensive land alienation. A scientific expedition was sent out from Paris in 1884 to advise on measures to promote the cultivation of mother-of-pearl oysters; and on the basis of G. Bouchon-Brandeley's reports, the policy of creating reserves which had been begun in the 1860s was applied throughout the archipelago.[55] The use of diving gear was prohibited in 1893, but limited use was allowed in eleven islands in 1902.

The main difficulty under the legislation of 1887 was to decide how far, if at all, lagoons were "communal property" and could be registered in the name of district councils in the Tuamotu. Numerous title claims were published from 1888 (though many were lost in 1903 and 1906 during flood and hurricane), but, on the whole, these were concerned with agricultural lands.[56] A projected decree arising from the Bouchon-Brandeley mission was examined by the General Council in 1888 and applauded for its conservation measures and attacked for permitting concessions of whole lagoons to European-financed diving teams.[57] Petitions from the Tuamotu in 1891 demanded recognition of the lagoons as council "domain," and a draft decree of 1904 moved toward this definition, but claims of the French state to shorelines prevented this solution. The question was complicated, moreover, by the rights of the Pomare family over the lagoons of certain islands and the need to continue the system of commercial exploitation which had become well established.

At Mangareva, resident officials were mainly concerned with preserving the population, not resources. There was a tendency to blame the Catholic mission for a situation which the administration did little to remedy, except for the introduction of a hundred or so Tuamotuans to replenish local stock. The Mangarevan code was abolished in 1887 in favor of legislation in force at Tahiti. Temporal control was transferred from the mission and a regency council to a French justice of the peace. Four chiefs were recognized for a population which had declined to about five hundred persons by the end of the century. Land registration was not attempted till 1897, but few claims resulted at such a distance from Pape'ete, except for the properties of the mission, and the whole exercise was repeated under a decree of 1902.

Even less was done at this date for the Austral group, though the French Civil Code was promulgated there in 1900 and 1901. Administration was left to three gendarmes who collected about 5,000 francs a year in taxes at Rapa, Tubuai, and Ra'ivavae. Rurutu and Rimatara with small populations of 800 and 400 persons each came under French protection from 1889, and they were the last islands of the territory to be annexed in 1900. Missionary laws were revised and adapted by a touring administrator; and except for land legislation, the code still guided the islanders till 1946.

By the date of final consolidation, then, French Polynesia consisted of a heterogeneous collection of archipelagoes grouped in six divisions. At the center, Tahiti and Mo'orea bore the brunt of experiments in assimilation and land registration. Representative and municipal institutions were set up after the models of French local government in other colonial territories. But the district councils were the merest parodies of metropolitan councils, and the authority of chiefs was sacrificed to the need for regular supervision at a period of intense political intrigue by Pape'ete politicians in the rural constituencies. With a few exceptions, the old nobility were replaced as effective agents by residents and gendarmes. The Tahitian land courts were not abolished, however, and the structure of the churches to some extent provided an alternative local government.

At the periphery, legal assimilation proved unworkable in the Marquesas and inapplicable in much of the Tuamotu. In the Leeward Islands and in part of the Australs, administrators fell back on the use of local judges and local laws, while attempting to register lands in the same way as at Tahiti.

In theory, the French posts in eastern Polynesia had become a unitary colony in 1903 after the abolition of the General Council and the assertion of central control through the governor's Administrative Council and government departments in Pape'ete. Colonial inspectors who toured the territory in 1909 and 1914 were not impressed with the attempt at conformity.[58] The Ministry of Colonies, too, was more sanguine about the legal assimilation attempted since annexation: "The global extension of French laws to the colonies has not always produced such good results in practice that one can now view without apprehension their application in certain territories of French Oceania, where the survival of older customs no longer presents great inconvenience or an obstacle to progress."[59]

It was finally established that if the 183 islands of the colony were roughly the size of a French department, they could not be administered like one. The attempt at "individualization" in land tenure was premature, and it would probably have been sufficient (as suggested in the General Council) to have registered in the name of households and make coproprietorship recognized in local law as it was in other parts of the French Empire. Nor should cadastral survey have lagged so far behind the disputes over claims.

But not everybody lost by this lengthy confusion. After 1887, *fari'ihau* lands were attributed to districts and the office of a district chief, and this transfer included some lands already claimed under the legislation of 1852. The Pomare family and a few chiefs of the Salmon-Brander lineage took the opportunity to make personal and family claims on district *fari'ihau*, using the To'ohitu to validate their "ancient" titles.

Thus, the bulk of worthwhile land belonging to the royal estates was allocated to the royal family (for example the Paofai estate at present situated in the commune of Papeete was *fari'ihau* of the district of Fa'a'a. It included the chief's residence, cemetery and the district school. It was claimed and adjudicated to the family of H. M. Pomare); and from among the district *fari'ihau* lands some were claimed by chiefs or their families, and others by the royal family. Moreover, lands which had been taken on the orders of the sovereign from the estates of important proprietors, or which had been given to the sovereign during residence in the districts *(fenua pupu hau)* and had been allocated as entail *(apanage)* to district chiefs, were claimed back in 1887 by their former proprietors or their descendants and were generally restored to them.[60]

The detailed list of lands which would be useful to substantiate this conclusion by *Inspecteur des Domaines* Roucaute is not provided in his study of Tahitian land tenure. But the *puta fariʻihau* for the western districts would appear to support the contention; and if he is correct, the total area of district communal land may well have been reduced after 1887 in conditions of speculation by senior island families who based their claims before the Toʻohitu on a mixture of genealogical evidence, partial registration in the 1850s and 1860s, past family titles, and their position as notable French subjects.

The social consequences of this consolidation of patrimony were considerable (and in some cases helped to compensate for loss of political authority). While the bulk of coproprietors held land in a condition of uncertain legal tenure, but de facto usehold, Euro-Polynesian notables and chiefs held land that was registered with fairly secure title and was used to support a series of commercial ventures in the expansive period of trade between 1887 and the 1920s. The precise extent of this consolidation in hectares is impossible to ascertain. But two sources—British consular records for the 1890s and the archives of the German SCO—provide a number of indications that the descendants of the *ariʻi*, especially in the Pomare and Salmon-Brander lines, knew how to make the law and the courts work for their benefit.[61] Some indication of this process of the definition and sale of Tahitian real estate can be gauged, too, from the amount of property declared as freehold and changing hands in the 1890s in the business center of Papeʻete, at Raʻiatea, and above all on the island of Makatea—possibly the best (or the worst) example of quick registration and sale of rights for economic development.

Thus while the formalities of French law on lease, sale, and contract made inroads into local concepts of property where rise in land values was greatest, the overall picture was one of very limited alienation. Would-be planters were few, and they acquired little through intermarriage with Tahitian families. In his *Tahitiens*, Patrick O'Reilly listed the biographies of some 129 European *colons* who left a record.[62] Most of them settled in the nineteenth century; and up till the First World War only thirty-six such proprietors would appear to have married Tahitians or other islanders. A large proportion of those who did so were soldier-settlers who were given small lots in Tahiti or the Marquesas by the administration. The rest would appear to have rented land or made a purchase by auction or private contract with Tahitians or one of the Euro-Tahitian families. A surprisingly large number contracted no legal marriage and left no legal descendants (though that fact is not a safe guide at a period of poorly kept registers and widespread cohabitation).

Professional and mercantile settlers with landed interests have left numerous Euro-Tahitian descent groups, though there are reservations to be made about their incidence in the nineteenth century. Of the twenty-six *"hommes d'affaires"* listed by O'Reilly as settlers prior to 1914, only six married Tahitians, though thirteen of their first generation of descendants did. But of the more prosperous of these merchants, engineers, and lawyers, some clearly owe part of their fortune to Tahitian connections. On the other hand, one of the *grands seigneurs* of Tahitian society, Auguste Goupil, bought his extensive estates from the well-established (and childless) George B. Orsmond, while making money from the most flourishing of Tahiti's professions—the law.

Social mobility in Tahiti was relatively easy with some education in English or French and a trade or profession. Nearer to the apex of local society, where income counted and titles helped, there were divisions on national, rather than racial, lines.* Numbering about two thousand by the end of the century, the settlers were grouped around British, American, French, and German firms, consulates, and social clubs, each with ramified connections with Tahitian society and with their own network of commercial and credit relationships. Officially, politics and government were French; but the informal influence exercised by business contracts and money-lending allocated a share of real power to the larger

---

* An exception to this generalization is the Chinese, whose numbers and position are discussed in Chapter 10.

merchant houses. Entry into these institutions was usually limited to nationals and some Tahitians who helped to extend the firm's clientage relations with smaller markets in the outer islands. Social rank depended, then, on success in making money, on generosity in spending it, on links with Tahiti's landed notables, and perhaps (though less dependably) on good connections with senior officials in the administration. Church institutions were closely identified through their educational, pastoral, and national services with business and administration. The more recent sects such as the Mormons and Kanitos were not even popular with their American consuls on whom they depended for protection from suspicious officials; these two sects tended to build up their churches among the rural populations of the outer islands.

It is hard to detect signs of a true proletariat or a landless laboring class in the making (except at Makatea from 1908). Tahitians were not hungry or poverty-stricken, though some Tuamotuans and Marquesans were. On the other hand, the most affluent did not appear to be very rich to an outside observer such as Henry Adams. Wealth by the end of the century lay in corporations engaged in trading and mining and not in plantations, retail stores, or even in the offices of busy barristers.

The politics of assimilation, then, did not result in any redistribution of power or a wholesale incorporation of Tahitians into the new institutions of administration. Rather, those institutions had either to be abandoned or modified to suit local needs. It was not till 1893 that Governor Lacascade managed to persuade the undersecretary of state for colonies to modify the system of examinations for entry into the executive grades of the administration and open places for successful Tahitians who could earn salaries ranging between 2,500 and 3,000 francs. But this was a very late development. Lacascade himself was a créole from the French West Indies. There is a certain irony that his appointment was announced to the first session of the General Council in 1886 by an acting governor who tactlessly regretted the absence of any "full-blooded" Tahitian, although Tati Salmon had been elected as a councillor and was probably present.

But no Tahitians rose to posts in the administrative service, except as district chiefs. Few had the level of education reached by Teri'itua (Joinville), who had spent two years in France, or of

Marau Salmon, who had been brought up in Sydney. In any case, the everyday language of Tahiti was not French but Tahitian or English, noted a colonial inspector: "The use of one or the other is constant, even in mixed Franco-Tahitian families, where it is common that a sentence begun in Maori is continued in English with a sprinkling of French expressions."[63]

In some parts of the territory French was deliberately avoided. Pomare IV had made a point of never understanding it. Governor Fawtier in his confidential instructions to his successor in 1915 located a potential source of opposition and Francophobia in Madame Marau Salmon, who refused to speak it.[64] And in the Leeward Islands, where Uturoa remained the "boulevard du protestantisme," neither French nor English was taught to recalcitrant Ra'iateans.[65]

Cultural resistance also took other forms, though both Protestants and Catholics found their converts curiously intelligent in their efforts to tease out the innermost meanings of religious texts. Such earnestness was not reflected in attitudes to imported rules of marriage. The fathers of the Sacred Hearts Congregation at Pape'ete found themselves locked in a complex debate with immigrant converts from the Tuamotu and the Leeward Islands who contracted Catholic and civil marriages at Tahiti without going through any of the formalities of divorce from Protestant spouses left behind. Such separations had become so customary

> that it would be difficult to find a man who had not been legally married to several successive wives, while the first was still alive. In general, from the 1st. January one is considered to be free from the engagement of the previous year, and many people make a new one. A number of these husbands come to reside in Tahiti; some ratify their union through the French administration; others prefer to keep their freedom to dismiss their wives and take others to live in concubinage which is tolerated with the greatest ease here. What is to be done when one of these Protestants becomes a Catholic?[66]

What indeed? It was a question, like the widespread practice of adoption, which no ruling from the Holy See could solve in terms which put an end to Tahitian and Ra'iatean arguments about the property rights of minors in such unions.[67] Nor did "illegitimacy" have much significance after a century of preaching, wrote a Mor-

mon missionary, in a community where "no distinction is made socially, or in business matters, or in office-holding, or church association, between the results of legal marriages and those who are
really bastards."[68]

In Tahiti, therefore, the wilder effusions of republican politicians and the earnest endeavors of moral reformers were tempered
by the behavior and institutions of communities that could not be
easily molded into the formal patterns of French citizenship. In
many ways Christianity, as taught by Europeans, provided a
secular overlay for other beliefs and responses. In the Tuamotu and
in Tahiti a few observers noted the widespread and persistent acceptance of ghosts, sorcery, and exorcism.[69] Even in the more
sedate circles of Pape'ete, Acting Consul George Miller, who had
lived all his life in Tahiti, attributed his failing health to "some ex-
traordinary secret powerful influence."[70] The rules of European ra-
tionalism looked less certain where *tupapa'u* stalked the consulate
grounds.

At a different level of discourse, there were tendencies in the intellectual life of Tahitian society which emphasized a vanished
past, rather than an uneasy present under alien rulers. Of the three
outstanding contributions made to our knowledge of the history
and legends of the eastern Polynesian Maori, two were scholarly
collections of oral traditions and the third was a work of pioneer
ethnography by a young French musicologist and historian. At a
period when it has become fashionable (indeed, obligatory) to recognize the legitimacy of such materials as evidence for the past of
preliterate peoples, the originality of these early works is striking.

The dedication of Teuira Henry in revising and editing her
grandfather's papers on Tahitian religion and social institutions
resulted in a corpus of local traditions which survived the indifference of most of the missionaries and later officials. The bulk of *Ancient Tahiti* derives from the eccentric curiosity of J. M. Orsmond,
and it was supplemented by a number of late-nineteenth-century
informants from among the Platt family on Ra'iatea, Mayor Cardella (who had been a counselor to Pomare V), Ta'areari'i Vahine,
Marau Salmon, and other Tahitian and Tuamotuan researchers.
The bulk of this composite text was completed when Teuira went to
teach in Honolulu (1890–1905), where she had access to collections not easily available in Tahiti. The work was offered to the

New Zealand Polynesian Society for publication in 1898, but it was not accepted (possibly because of its bulk and complexity). Teuira sent them a number of articles, however, and these appeared in the society's journal as a commentary on the status of the Pomare family among the *ari'i*. Orsmond's great collection was not published, therefore, till 1928, some thirty years after Teuira's death, by the Bernice P. Bishop Museum, unrevised and lacking the critical commentary that might have resolved some of its more difficult passages. That much of it was compiled in a changing vernacular and translated into English in the late 1890s is less surprising, however, than its relative inaccessibility to later generations of French Polynesians—until the Société des Océanistes in Paris translated and reissued the work in 1951.[71]

Although written for a different purpose, Henry Adams' *Memoirs of Arii Taimai* was undertaken in 1891 with the enthusiastic participation of the principal informants: Ari'itaimai Salmon, Marau Salmon, and Tati Salmon. The result was a second major corpus of traditions which are an expression of dynastic pride and contempt for rivals interspersed with Tahitian poetry and sections from European navigators. Altogether the *Memoirs* are a very uneven history of pre-European Tahiti.[72] But in his searching critique of the origins and successive adaptations of Adams' work, Pierre Lagayette has made the point that the informants had other ends in view. Authentication of the Teva's social and political rank was a useful cachet for a family descended from the chiefs of Papara—at the date when the American appeared on the scene to supply his aristocratic sympathy and literary talents.[73] Marau's divorce from Pomare had left her children cut off from claims that might have been made under the terms of the 1887 land legislation to district *fari'ihau* land. Ari'itaimai had been displaced from the Papara chieftaincy, which was only restored to her son in 1885, and had little to pass on to her daughter. The anti-Pomare bias is clear enough in the *Memoirs*. What is less certain is the use made of the special private edition of 1893 in prosecuting claims to a share of Pomare V's estate following his death in 1891.

The principal edition, published in 1901, continued to be revised and expanded with the collaboration of Adams and his informants into a thesis on the antiquity of the Teva and a somewhat inflated account of Ari'itaimai's share in peacemaking (1846–1847). It was also a unique statement of traditions that might otherwise have disappeared, as remembered and interpreted by a late-nineteenth-century titleholder from a senior Papara family. It was not the last time that European scholars were utilized to help publish the Teva version of their past: Marau prepared yet a third revision of the *Memoirs* with the assistance of Willowdean and Edward S. Craighill Handy of the Bishop Museum in 1922.[74]

There is, therefore, a considerable difference in the purpose and content of *Ancient Tahiti* and the Adams–Ari'itaimai–Marau *Memoirs*, though both have been well quarried by students seeking to understand the Tahitian past. Marau may well have supplied a small amount of material for the Orsmond manuscripts; but Teuira was discreet (or malicious) enough to present the genealogical origins of the Teva chiefs in full, while continuing to attribute the parentage of Marau's children to Pomare V.[75] She should, perhaps, be allowed to have the last word on the aims of the dramatis personae in such family histories:

> Owing to intermarriage all the chiefs of the realm were linked together in ties of relationship with one another, and it was the ambition of their daughters to strengthen and extend the interests of their own districts by becoming the wives and mothers of the chiefs of others, sometimes being the passive agents of their parents in doing so.[76]

No passive agent after her separation, Marau, seconded by her mother and brother, wrote with Adams an *oeuvre à thèse* embodying a whole corpus of oral tradition mixed with the evidence of printed sources. Henry (who was of British parentage and Tahitian sympathies) industriously salvaged her grandfather's passion for the past of a people he had come to transform, and she was able to expand his sources to include a number of French-Tahitian and Anglo-Tahitian informants. Both statements of tradition are notably silent on the period of French rule and its consequences for the society at large.

A contemporary verdict on that period of French rule was given, however, in the works of Eugène Caillot, who spent five months in Tahiti and the Tuamotu in 1900, collecting for his museum in Paris. He returned in 1912 for a brief period and published four works on the traditions and history of eastern Polynesia.[77] They still stand as the most able, if pessimistic, research by any observer of local society at the end of a century of change. There is a refreshing directness in Caillot's descriptions of fishing techniques, Taumotuan diving, and belief in spirit possession and his expert comments on dance and song. He was one of the few contemporaries who admitted that eastern Polynesia was only "French in name."[78] One would not agree with all his commentary on "assimilation" in French possessions, but it was a sufficient epitaph to the assumptions of a generation of officials and colonial politicians.

There were others whose writings perhaps owe more to Tahiti than they gave back in the form of accurate record. Robert Louis Stevenson spent three months in Tautira in 1888 and set down some of this experience in his book *In the South Seas*, published in 1896 as a mixture of acute observation and nostalgia. Louis Becke in his *Wild Life in the Southern Seas*, published a year later, wrote less well but provided sketches of the archetypal trader, missionary, and beachcomber who had begun to people the South Seas legend.

Another legend-maker was also at work in the last years of the century, a man with the mind of a *colon* and the eye of an artist. Journalist, polemicist, collector of folklore (from Moerenhout), and partial autobiographer, Paul Gauguin made some telling pictorial and written caricatures of Tahiti's administrative pretensions, but he did some of its personalities less than justice. In the district of Matai'ea he rediscovered Tahitian women, as many had done before him, and he dabbled in Tahitian myth from out-of-date texts. In 1896 he participated as a spectator in the expedition to subdue the Leeward Islands and accepted a grant of land from the Agricultural Bank to settle at Puna'auia. His period of newspaper warfare (1899–1900) is rich in aphorism but meager in painting. When he moved to the Marquesas in search of the "primitive," he found, instead, a complete degradation of material culture; and in its place he created and developed his own style of painting devoid of literary meanings. He made war on gendarmes and lived on credit from the SCO.

It is possible that Gauguin would have painted just as well somewhere else, had he never returned to Tahiti after the failure of his exposition in Paris in 1893 and 1895. But Tahitians would not have been incorporated so well by any other painter into the warm and subtle colors of a form which acknowledged their individuality without imposing any solution on their predicament: *D'où venons nous? Que sommes nous? Où allons nous?* Completed in 1897, before the artist attempted to take his own life, this single masterpiece which deliberately rejects the device of allegory stands as the antithesis of the policymaking, reform, and labored social engineering which Tahiti had been subjected to for nearly a century.

CHAPTER 9

MERCHANTS AND MINERS

WHILE THE HOTHOUSE POLITICS of Tahiti centered on the allocation of the small revenues available to the territory, the development of local markets was relatively unhindered by fiscal or monetary policies. Land registration probably assisted the transfer of blocks and the consolidation of a few plantations; it certainly assisted mining enterprise at Makatea, though, even there, there was insecurity of tenure which had to be removed by state intervention.

On the whole, the proprietors and cousers of land and marine resources in the territory were free to participate in cash crop markets, but on the terms of credit provided by European traders and brokers, just as they were free to sell their labor for wages without much compulsion by the administration. Within the limits of the overseas and local demand for staples, then, a local peasantry supplemented subsistence with cash returns throughout much of the nineteenth century, expressing a preference for market gardening and crop gathering, fishing and diving, rather than wage labor on local plantations or public works. Only toward the end of the century is there more evidence of Tahitian employment on the Pape'ete wharves or at Makatea, and much of this was casual.

While the broad base of agricultural producers expanded to include the whole of the territory as communications and demand improved, the turnover of produce and merchandise became concentrated in fewer hands in the three decades before the First World War. After a temporary recession in the late 1880s and early 1890s, the value and volume of trade continued to rise toward a peak value for total trade of 17.9 million francs in 1914. Some of this increase can be attributed to the phosphate industry at

Makatea, which exported 75,000 metric tons by that date. But much derived from the improved prices and quantities of a traditional variety of staples. These were supplied by a growing number of peasants and planters. But they were handled principally by three firms—J. R. Maxwell, Donald and Edinburgh, and the Société Commerciale de l'Océanie.

Foreign enterprise predominated, then, in a French territory; and less than 20 percent of trade was carried on by French firms.[1] About half the value of imports and exports was assigned to the United States, while New Zealand and Great Britain accounted for one quarter. The remaining trade values in official returns are assigned to Germany and France. But in practice many of the territory's exports were sent via New Zealand on Union Steamship Company vessels for a variety of European markets in London, Marseilles, Hamburg, and Amsterdam. The Oceanic Steamship Company transported produce to San Francisco for vegetable oil brokerages in the eastern states and Canada. Similarly, imports were of multiple origins, with British and American manufactures predominating. The "national" participation of different countries in the South Seas trade worried merchants much less than consuls and patriotic administrators.

It was not unusual for the SCO, for example, to import hardware and wines from Birmingham and Bordeaux and to consign vanilla and coconuts to San Francisco or Hamburg and oranges to Auckland.[2] The phosphates of Makatea were financed by British capital, mined by a French company, exported by British and German vessels, and marketed in North America, Europe, Australia, and New Zealand.

French Polynesia, then, and its predominantly peasant producers, were drawn into a worldwide network of markets at prices which depended on levels of consumption and manufacturing in Europe and North America. The pattern is familiar enough in Africa and Asia; and the pace of this change in the Pacific has been recognized but not very well measured for the late nineteenth century. While whaling, sandalwood, and sugar have their histories, the marketing of the major Pacific staple—the coconut and its derivatives—has yet to be described.[3]

What is clear, however, is that about 60 percent of the world consumption of copra by 1912 was accounted for by produce bro-

Pape'ete Town and Harbor about 1900.

kerages in Germany and France; and in Germany alone demand had increased between 1907 and 1912 from 50,000 to 180,000 tons. Remarkably little of this European tonnage was supplied by the colonies of either of the the two principal importers and manufacturers.[4] Some 16,000 tons was supplied from German Pacific territories, 8,000 tons from British and Australian Pacific colonies, and about 8,000 tons from French Polynesia (though not all of this was destined for Germany and France). By about 1910, too, a change from the use of cottonseed oil to coconut oil in the United States increased competition for supplies from American brokers.

In the eastern Pacific, the demand for copra was reflected in the spread of cash-cropping to remote atolls and the improvement of isolated stands and plantations begun earlier in the century. But after the experience of company enterprise at Atimaono, large-scale plantations were not a feature of this development; and although the planting of seed coconuts was undertaken nearly everywhere, there was little scientific guidance, no government agronomists, and no influx of Europeans to manage enterprises in the conditions which were typical of New Guinea, the New Hebrides, and Samoa. By 1906, when the territory was exporting nearly 6,000 tons of copra, only one-third of the tonnage came from Tahiti and Mo'orea; the remainder was produced in almost equal shares from smallholdings in the Leeward Islands, the Marquesas, and the atolls of the Tuamotu.[5] Indeed, Tuamotuan production increased more rapidly than in other groups, until it accounted for about half the bulk of total copra exports by 1914.

Furthermore, gross production throughout the territory was almost certainly higher than the export statistics suggest, "due to the fact that large quantities of coconuts are shipped monthly to San Francisco for manufacturing purposes, that at least 30% per annum of coconuts of a plantation are destroyed by rats, and that about another 30% is retained for home consumption and for feeding domestic animals."[6]

In 1904, a former American consul, J. Lamb Doty, founded a company with a capital of $50,000 in order to take advantage of this trend toward small-scale cash-cropping and the willingness of producers to participate in a cooperative venture for marketing.[7] The plan was simple enough—to bind members of the enterprise, as suppliers, for regular payments of merchandise; and as members of a "veritable agricultural and workers' union" they were forbidden to sell, on pain of a fine, at higher prices to other traders.[8] Since no legislation on such "cooperatives"* had been passed for the territory, the acting governor was uncertain about the legality of Doty's firm but decided that a precedent had been set already by the cooperative employment of diving teams in the Tuamotu. In 1905 the exports of the company amounted to one-sixth of the colony's total copra exports.

But this experiment in regimenting producers was unusual and depended on assured freight with the American Oceanic Steamship Company. It did not survive increased competition from other firms and the offer of higher prices to producers. Moore, Doty and Co. appear briefly among the debtors of the SCO in 1905 and 1906, and then disappear. Their overseas brokers were attracted to larger (and cheaper) suppliers in the highly competitive conditions prevailing after 1900; and the outer islands, where the company had sought to recruit low-priced cooperative members, were drawn into a relatively homogeneous price structure for the whole territory, based on the Pape'ete produce market.

For the SCO's commercial correspondence indicates that little distinction was made in prices offered for small consignments after 1900. Copra from different sources was bulked as "South Seas" whether it came from the company's own small plantations or from peasant producers.

On the other hand, careful distinctions were made, both in origins and in price, for pearl shell. The black-rimmed shell from the northern and northeastern Tuamotu was most highly prized, and

TABLE 6

Annual Average Prices (f.o.b. per kilo): 1880–1914

Period	Copra	Cotton	Vanilla	Shell
1880–1890	0 fr. 20	1 fr. 70	13 fr. 50	0 fr. 90
1891–1900	0 fr. 20–26	1 fr. – fr. 40	12 fr. 35	2 fr. 50
1901–1910	0 fr. 27–40	0 fr. 40	4 fr. 60	1 fr. 80
1911–1914	0 fr. 45–50	—	2 fr. 50	1 fr. 80

Sources: Calculated from monthly correspondence with Scharf & Kayser, Hamburg, in Staatsarchiv (Hamburg), SCO 5/1–8, 6/1–22. For cotton prices, Disp. USC 8, Doty, 7 July 1893.

---

*Strictly speaking Doty's firm aimed at a monopsony and was in no sense corporately owned by producers.

the best quality could command as much as 3,000 francs a ton, though the more usual market price was about half this amount. Low-quality Gambier (Mangareva) shell paid little more than 1,000 francs a ton. This was a highly specialized trade calling for considerable expertise and ability to collect supplies over a wide area in the diving season. The season was short, and there were annual variations in the London prices, just at the period when most of the local shell had already been gathered and sold through traders and merchants. The SCO made a loss in 1908 and 1909 on some varieties because their information was out of date and they paid producers at rates for a previous season.

Competition in the Tuamotu came mainly from J. R. Maxwell & Co. and the French traders V. L. Raoulx, L. Martin, and Émile Levy. The latter paid the highest prices, though this was not the only important feature of the trade. It was necessary to purchase poor-quality *piqué* (wormy) along with the best in order to make a bargain with diving teams or with small traders who would not grade their lots. There was, too, the relationship built up between firms and Tuamotuan communities: each was obliged to trust the other for advance of credit, transport, and adequate returns on the outlay without sale to a rival. From 1910, the SCO dealt directly with the diving teams:

> We have of course to convey these people and their relations on our schooners to the diving grounds and to transport them back home at the end of the season. If there were no trade we would simply leave our divers for another site . . . but hopefully, the relationship will prosper, for they are not only connected with us as pearl shell divers, but also as buyers of goods; for as we have often insisted, the produce and merchandise trades are not distinct.[9]

One source suggests that divers could earn up to 25 francs a day.[10] It is doubtful whether cash payments were usual, however, as advances of goods and more or less permanent indebtedness were endemic to the trade. When Maxwell's agents paid 1 franc 50 per kilo for shell in 1910, the SCO's manager reported that he had followed the new level, adding that profit from the company store on Hikueru had to be taken into the general calculation, as all his divers owed shell to it.[11]

There was still money to be made from pearls. Quantities sold are listed in the annual reports of the SCO (1888–1897) at variable amounts between 3,600 and 25,000 marks every year.[12] Then they disappear from the trade returns, though they are occasionally mentioned in monthly reports. Such sums for sales are consistent with the estimate made by Consul Rowley in 1909 that between £2,000 and £5,000 worth of pearls was exported annually, the best being purchased on the spot during the diving season by French buyers.[13] His predecessor regarded the pearl trade as a mixture of gambling and crime, though he judged that "nearly every properly built house owned by a Paumotu native has been purchased with the proceeds of the sale of this gem."[14] It is more likely, however, that such investments were financed from returns on the 500 or 600 tons of shell exported from the Tuamotu every year or from the sale of copra.

Some staples declined. Cotton, which was still being exported at the rate of 400 or 500 tons a year in the 1880s, was negligible in the 1890s. Its place was taken by vanilla; and exports of this crop expanded rapidly from under 10 tons a year before 1883 to 250 tons by 1910. Despite a sharp decline in price, it remained one of the colony's "windfall" crops and a ready source of cash income in small amounts.

Preparation of the vanilla beans purchased unripened from European and Tahitian growers had become a Chinese monopoly by about 1908. After a quick "sun cure" from five to six weeks, the beans were tinned and shipped out to San Francisco or Hamburg. The cultivation of the crop should have yielded much higher returns to the colony, though there were differing opinions about the reasons for the indifferent state of the local market:

> The native planter is as a rule in a chronic state of impecunity and in-debtedness, and as there exists in the country no system of assistance to the agriculturalists in the way of loans or advances on crops, the native planter is too easily tempted to fall into the arms of Chinese storekeepers who for months keep such natives going in tins of New Zealand canned beef and similar wares necessary to the latter's up-to-date tastes and false notions of civilized respectability. The conse-quence is that the wily Celestial lies in wait for his prey, and as soon as the native crop begins to mature, he puts on the screw and exacts his full pound of fat in green vanilla. This is the most treacherous pit-fall of the whole system, for the native, pressed by his creditor, and

hungry for more tins of canned beef, repairs to his so-called plantation armed with a huge chopping knife with which the whole crop is
hacked down mercilessly and regardless of the state of maturity of the
beans.[15]

There was doubtless a deal of truth in this commonplace caricature
of the marketing of a crop requiring much skill and patience to
bring the local variety of vanilla to the level of quality in other
French colonies. But there was more to the vanilla market than this
simplified debtor relationship with a Chinese storekeeper.

The commercial correspondence of the SCO suggests, rather,
that vanilla purchases owed as much to a Chinese "gamble" as to
Tahitian "impecunity" and depended on the availability of money
and goods from Chinese principals in Papeʻete or from the Bank of
Indo-China and such firms as the SCO. For example, one of the
SCO's own Tahitian customers sold 17 tons of vanilla to various
Chinese brokers in March 1912 at the high price of 6 francs 25 per
kilo. He had to accept promissory notes at three months until the
brokers could obtain sufficient funds as advances on preparation
and shipment.[16] For the rest of the season, reported Hoppenstedt,
"the greater part of all green vanilla will certainly be bought by
Chinese on three to four months' credit, during which period they
are able to give the Natives a large portion in goods, so that, finally, they do not have to pay out so much in cash." These goods, in
turn, were advanced by the merchants, Europeans, and Chinese,
sometimes in payment for past consignments overseas. From pro-
ducer to exporter, all were linked in a network of extended credit
which had been encouraged by the favorable prices of the 1890s
and which required larger and more frequent exports of the crop to
bring the same returns a decade later. The place of Chinese storekeepers in this market linkage was probably marginal to those who
specialized in the trade; and the initiative for the timing of sales
may well have come from producers at the beginning of the season.

THE SOCIÉTÉ COMMERCIALE DE L'OCÉANIE

Merchant houses that survived the recession of the late 1880s were
called on to play multiple roles in the local economy. They were
vertically integrated structures between overseas brokers, ex-
porters, bankers, and shipping companies, on the one hand, and the

smaller traders, retailers, and local producers, on the other. Before 1905, when a branch of the Bank of Indo-China was set up at Pape'ete, they also performed some of the functions of a monetary exchange, cashing drafts for customers, transferring their funds to European accounts, and making cash loans. The SCO made a useful profit of up to 70,000 francs a year on the importation and exchange of Chilean currency at a difficult period in the 1880s.

The growth of the German firm is important for the history of Tahiti, if only because its records have survived and reveal a good deal about the commercial life of island society. It engrossed, moreover, a good half of the colony's imports and exports. About two-thirds of French Polynesia's copra and a third of its shell were handled by the SCO, and it had a sizable share of the cotton and vanilla markets. Most of its profits, however, lay in trade in merchandise. Its annual turnover, by 1900, was about 2 million francs —a sum roughly equal to the colony's budget. In 1914, its assets were valued at over 4 million francs (£160,000).[17]

In the scale of Pacific enterprise, then, the SCO was no giant, though the firm's original capital of 1,400,000 marks was a good deal more than Soarès' Tahiti Cotton and Coffee Plantation Company in the 1860s and was equal to about half the sum required to float the Compagnie Française des Phosphates, in 1907, with a greater requirement for capital equipment.

It was well connected with other German Pacific commerce. The two Godeffroys, Johann César and his son, sat on the first board of directors, while a third son, Gustav Godeffroy, was one of two local directors. They held nearly half the shares; and in its more prosperous years the firm placed some of its reserves in the shares of the Deutsche Handels und Plantagen Gesellschaft.[18] Heinrich Schlubach, a son-in-law of John Brander with a wide experience of Pacific and Valparaiso business, joined the board for a few years after 1885. Other minority shareholders were Herman Meuel, who became a manager at Pape'ete, and C. Scharf, a principal of the Hamburg merchant house of Scharf & Kayser.

The firm had gained a foothold in French Polynesia in 1876 by buying out the firm of Wilkens & Co. in return for 115 shares valued at 575,000 marks. Wilkens had difficulty in keeping up his end of the management; and while the business was running close to a loss, his shares were bought up in 1888 by Schroeder & Co. of

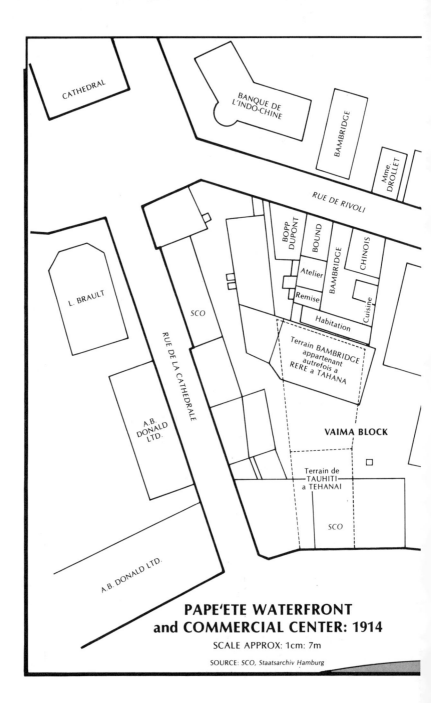

**PAPE'ETE WATERFRONT
and COMMERCIAL CENTER: 1914**

SCALE APPROX: 1cm: 7m

SOURCE: SCO, Staatsarchiv Hamburg

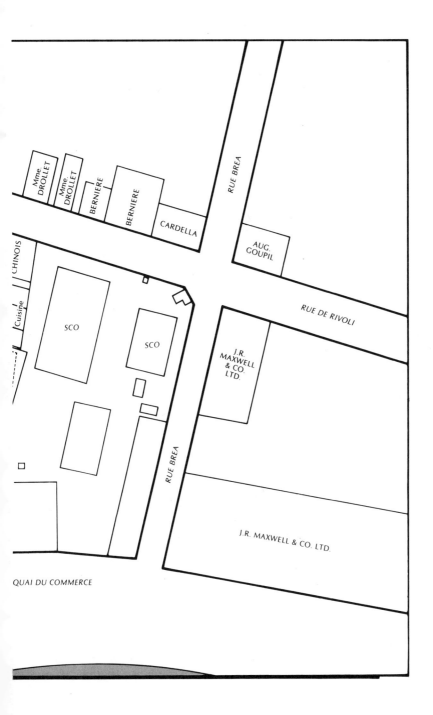

San Francisco. Total capital was cut back in 1893 to 500,000 marks, and the Kayser family, Scharf, Oscar Godeffroy, and Schlu- bach interests retained control of the firm, though the amount of capital shares in German hands was valued at only 288,000 marks by the time of the First World War.[19]

Thus the SCO gradually became a tropical branch of Scharf & Kayser, working closely with them as a commission house and us- ing the Hamburg firm from 1886 as a general agency. As trade with San Francisco grew, the SCO used the American firm of Wil- liams, Dimant & Co. to deal with brokers and shipbuilders in the United States, and from 1910 there were special accounts to record the volume of this business.[20]

But it was not easy to found a new enterprise in a French terri- tory in the early 1880s. Local managers began by acquiring a num- ber of small stores in Ra'iatea, the Marquesas, and at Rarotonga to increase the turnover of merchandise imported through Pape'ete. Very little was made from commission sales and export of produce. Overheads were low, but depreciation and insurance on the firm's small fleet of vessels were high. No dividend was paid in the early years, and the Scharf & Kayser directors concentrated on building up reserves. From 1903, shareholders were paid a dividend of 4 percent plus a bonus on profits which raised the dividend to be- tween 18 and 20 percent in the last four years of the company's commercial existence.[21] For the first time, in 1906, profits on pro- duce sales and consignments on commission were higher than prof- its on merchandise (see Table 7).

Part of the explanation for the early poor performance and later recovery of the firm lies with the strategies adopted by managers Meuel, Iorss, and Hoppenstedt in financing plantations and extend- ing credit to small traders. Losses in the Leeward Islands by a hur- ricane in 1878 were compounded by the policy of underwriting William Keane, a local manager and planter. The SCO defaulted on payments in 1881 and was only saved by its Hamburg creditors and a brisk sale of pearls.[22] Agencies in the Tuamotu were tempo- rarily suspended. The firm had also unwisely extended too much credit to David Byrnes, who owned Vaihiria plantation at Papeu- riri, where he had about 30 acres in sugarcane at a period of falling prices.[23] In the Marquesas, Gustav Godeffroy held shares for the SCO in John Hart's small agricultural company formed to exploit lands on Nukuhiva and Hiva Oa in 1877. William Keane was moved there from Ra'iatea to supervise the planting of coconuts and coffee trees. But, on the whole, the policy of the directors in Hamburg was to avoid large company landholdings and the special problems associated with plantations in a group where transport was irregular and labor costs high. Meuel was ordered to concentrate on building up the sales lost in the Leeward Islands through Keane's mismanagement, and Hoppenstedt was sent there to expand the merchandise side of the business.

The reason behind this policy was simple enough. Merchandise sales brought in a 50 percent return on cost prices—or $50,000 Chilean for a month's business at the Ra'iatea factory, compared with only $4,326 for small lots of copra and cotton consignments.[24] Moreover, credit in advances of goods provided the company with a lien over future produce exports and helped to plan the collection and bulking of staples in advance. Most of the smaller outer-island factories continued to show a profit through the 1880s, though the overall performance of the firm in Tahiti was modest despite its large turnover.

The annual lists of debtors (which are not complete in the records) continued to grow and were probably too large in the early 1890s. They were cut down and then, in the generous years after 1900, expanded again.

On these lists customers' names read like a social register of Tahiti. Most of the principal retailers ran accounts with the company, as one might expect, and so did administrators, lawyers, traders, and planters. Even the district of Afare'aitu on Mo'orea was advanced 1,565 francs for an *amuira'a himene* (a community singing) in 1906. A cooperative society at Papeto'ai had an advance of 5,344 francs. One of the firm's best clients in the Leeward group was a certain Hahe a Patamu; and there are numerous Polynesian names recorded for loans toward fitting out vessels and trading goods in the northwest Marquesas. As early as the 1880s, too, there is a sprinkling of Chinese names. By 1906, they account for 109,595 francs, or 15 percent of a very large annual credit total; but thereafter their share declines, as the bank and their own merchants offered alternative sources. Their names also change sufficiently every year to suggest that they cleared their debts regularly.

TABLE 7
SCO Profit and Loss Accounts (in francs)

Year	Profit on Produce	Sales of Merchandise	Profit on Merchandise	Listed Debtors	Net Profits	Net Loss*
1880	?	1,533,739	227,497		268,060	
1881	?	1,800,690	388,622		53,612	
1882	?	1,712,300	364,903		92,458	
1883	?	?	286,426		301,666	
1884	?	1,125,000	?		237,217	
1885	†	1,109,598	209,829	491,879		308,781
1886	†	898,322	207,201	536,162		382,663
1887		682,561	254,531	329,687		88,848
1888	28,966	1,361,000	225,565	422,485	72,518	
1889	†	?	355,166	542,132	1,149	
1890	196,093	?	353,828	?	129,188	
1891	39,188	1,464,003	442,628	?	109,738	
1892	142,379	1,401,037	319,369	696,462	30,827	
1893	(loss reported)	?	434,931	791,190	74,553	
1894	(loss reported)	1,588,000	397,657	762,471	(to reserves)	
1895	†	1,390,000	336,165	?	(to reserves)	
1896	†	1,201,000	361,568	?	(to reserves)	
1897	†	1,300,000	320,440	?	93,708	

Year					
1898	†	?	308,688	?	35,000
1899	†	?	308,314	?	57,500
1900	†	?	267,573	?	93,712
1901	†	?	237,549	?	91,839
1902	†	?	282,116	?	99,723
1903	61,274	1,394,287	170,332	333,000	115,713
1904	116,845	1,130,637	316,027	655,957	141,866
1905	83,057	1,393,174	247,976	661,012	87,216
1906	131,753	1,256,427	280,451	734,800	202,595
1907	202,928	1,528,988	339,018	860,319	131,328
1908	228,060	1,745,002	424,914	814,766	223,256
1909	493,247	1,758,385	685,588	706,480	436,748
1910	413,890	1,982,191	500,033	719,280	572,496
1911	†	?	771,391	572,585‡	441,561
1912	†	?	693,736	830,587‡	374,380
1913	†	?	766,612	871,953‡	421,613

* After salaries and overhead.
† Added to Profit on Merchandise.
‡ From balance sheets. The last annual report from Pape'ete was in April 1911 (for 1910).

Source: Staatsarchiv (Hamburg), SCO 11/1–2 (company accounts, 1895–1913); SCO 3 (annual reports, 1886–1930). Reports from Pape'ete do not always agree with the final balance sheets in Hamburg, and the latter have been preferred where there are discrepancies.

Increasing frequency in the lists of small loans to clients in the outer islands is one indication of the increasing incorporation of French Polynesians in Tahiti's total trade. In the Austral group a local entrepreneur, Tuere, owed 9,546 francs in 1907 on his schooner; and another, Taihoropua, owed 2,255 francs on goods for a small store. They were not in the same class, however, as W. Bardury and M. Sage, who borrowed 19,550 francs in 1910 to found the Casino de Paris at Pape'ete, or H. Hoffmann at Mangareva, who ran up a debt of 16,659 francs investing in the shell trade.

On the other hand, the number of Tuamotuan debtors reflects the direct entry of the SCO into this trade from 1910 (see Table 8). The names of divers and their "managers" appear on lists for Tikahau, Rangiroa, Kaukura, and Hao. A separate account was run for Hikueru, where there was a company store. By 1911, the SCO was also backing islanders in retail business in the Tuamotu, such as Mohi a Makitua (judged to be a good risk and "a very clever trader") at Takaroa and a certain Tufairai on Niau.[25]

Names that appear regularly in the annual reports of debtors belong mainly to members of the Salmon and Brander families. Apart from their connections by marriage with these notables (see Table 5), the directors and managers of the firm had good reason to

TABLE 8

SCO Abstract of Debtor Totals: 1909–1910

Debtor	Debtor Totals (francs)	
	1909	1910
Chinese	63,503	74,206
Traders	82,962	113,274
Private	52,206	75,477
Mo'orea	8,468	13,292
Leewards	62,430	58,799
Australs, Gambier	26,352	20,812
Tuamotu	130,936	147,298
Mortgages	17,209	18,098
"Douteux"	5,730	6,958
Opuhara Salmon	48,490	47,110
Nari'i Salmon	100.139	100,139
Sundry	53,070	22,020

Source: Staatsarchiv (Hamburg), SCO 3, Pape'ete Annual Reports. Totals are higher than the annual accounts in Hamburg. Categories of debtors are given as in the original balance sheets.

support Tati Salmon, Norman Brander, Nariʻi Salmon, and his nephew Opuhara Salmon from the 1890s. They provided an entry into the difficult local market for land and for diving concessions in the Tuamotu, both as holders of titles and mortgages and as organizers of plantation and diving labor. They were a group of Tahitian entrepreneurs (or "go-betweens," as Consul Rowley called them). And while there are such examples earlier in the protectorate period, the scale of their operations was much larger than occasional sugar plantations and copra schooners. Some of their activities bordered on fraud—such as the "lease" by Norman Brander of 250,000 coconut trees in the Tuamotu for "Copra Traders Ltd." in 1912.[26] But more usually they were a cover for other investors and had to be assisted with their debts.

By 1890, these debts were so great in Nariʻi Salmon's case that he merited a separate account to himself in the balance sheets of the SCO. Iorss and Hoppenstedt made a partnership contract with him, as the firm had previously done with Byrnes and Hart, and went on advancing goods and cash for copra and shell. In 1891, they added Tati Salmon to their list because he required assistance with a large mortgage he carried with the Agricultural Bank. They appointed him manager of Vaihiria plantation after Byrnes' death had given them control of title.

The indebtedness of the family grew when George Darsie (second husband of Titaua Brander) also got into difficulties and Nariʻi lost a court case against the successors of Pomare V for diving rights in the Tuamotu.[27] The case did not end there, and a bitter contest between the nephews of Hinoi Pomare, on the one hand, and the Salmons and Branders, on the other, ensued to determine the rights of Marau's children to the Pomare estate. It was decided that Marau should receive one-twelfth and Norman Brander one-twelfth of Tuamotuan and other interests. The remainder was not settled till 1900 by a compromise agreement to share costs and titles.[28] Hoppenstedt believed that this success on the part of Nariʻi's brother Norman and his sister Marau provided sufficient collateral in 1893 for further investment by the SCO in a diving venture at Hao and at Hikueru, where the Pomares had a monopoly of shell exploitation.

At this stage, too, Henry Adams was welcomed by the Salmon family, which was rich in titles but poor in liquid capital. The style of living at Tati's Papara estate or Marau's townhouse far exceeded their income. Nariʻi's business debts amounted to 220,000 francs in 1893; and Tati's situation was not improved when Byrnes' Tahitian widow contested his leasehold of three blocks of Vaihiria in 1894.[29] Adams provided literary skills and a sympathetic interest in the family's past history as justification for its contemporary status. He was also persuaded by Tati to make a loan of 50,000 francs in 1893 to cover mortgage payments and assist with Nariʻi's debts.[30] By 1900, Tati's son Opuhara, who was running the family property at Opunohu, Moʻorea (on a plantation developed by Alfred Hort), was also in trouble. Atwater, the American consul who had power of attorney for Adams, threatened legal action to recover principal and interest, but there is no evidence that Adams was willing to press the case against a brother by Tahitian adoption.[31]

Instead the SCO stepped in and paid off the interest owing to Atwater and part of the loan in return for title to Nariʻi's Tuamotuan property and Opunohu plantation. But this was not the end of Adams' largesse: in 1901 he came to Tati's rescue again when the SCO agreed to surrender claims for mortgage payments and legal costs in return for 26,841 francs.[32] This sum was extracted in 1903 after Tati, Atwater, and Adams himself had allowed their memories of the agreement to slip.

In Hamburg, the board was not in favor of acquiring an interest in Opunohu plantation. But the SCO had already taken over Hart's Marquesas plantations in 1895, and they had control of Vaihiria. When Nariʻi Salmon's creditors pressed him for more monies raised on the strength of the Salmon-Brander estates, the SCO covered his debts and made an inventory of his assets. These consisted of land at Papeʻete, Rarotonga, Moʻorea, Rangiroa, and Opunohu valued at 154,350 francs plus his access to three of the richest pearl shell lagoons at Hao, Hikueru, and Takapoto. Hoppenstedt set him up as "Nariʻi Salmon and Co." to make a new investment in diving. When his titles were cleared by the courts and permission was given to use diving gear in 1900, Nariʻi's reckless energy quickly expanded the firm's produce trade in shell. Opunohu remained his and Tati's, though heavily mortgaged. But his private debts mounted to 200,000 francs in 1903; Opuhara owed 40,000 francs; Atwater and Adams still owed 16,752 francs;

and Marau owed a modest 4,248 francs (which she promptly paid). Opunohu was leased on contract to the Tahiti Commercial & Sugar Co.—a San Francisco firm floated on a loan of 18,000 francs from the SCO in 1904 with the schooner *Roberta* as the only collateral.

When the sugar company failed to make a profit and the lease was in danger, Nari'i was persuaded to make over all his assets to the SCO in return for the liquidation of "Nari'i Salmon & Co." and a salary of 625 francs a month as captain of the SCO schooner *Eimeo*. Preparations were in hand for the end of this subsidiary in 1906 when a cyclone struck, and Nari'i, his son, and the *Eimeo* disappeared among the victims. His assets were then acquired remarkably cheaply by the SCO. At a cost of only 45,000 francs, by 1907 the firm held land at Fauta'ua, Paofai, on the Quai du Commerce, and at Opunohu. When the holdings of the firm were declared in 1914, the merchandise and consignment company had become a respectable property owner.[33]

Holding	Value (francs)
Shipping (schooners: *Moana, Roberta, Gauloise, Tiare, Apetahi, Vaitape,* and others)	210,500
Land in Pape'ete	195,000
Buildings in Pape'ete	102,500
Buildings in Ra'iatea	27,500
Buildings in Taiohae	37,900
Land in Tahauku	100,000
Land in Taiohae	50,000
Buildings in Tahauku	17,600
Land and buildings in Huahine	18,800
Opunohu plantation and cattle	500,000
Land and buildings of Nari'i Salmon	40,000
Business and stores in the Tuamotu	170,000
Factory at Ra'iatea	130,000
Factory at Taiohae	215,000
Factory at Tahauku	8,500
Total	1,822,800

Apart from these possessions of the company, there were numerous smaller retailers and traders, cash-croppers and divers, who depended on the stores in the outer islands. In the Marquesas alone, officials later listed twenty planters, storekeepers, and minor employees of the SCO who were forced to sell out when the firm's assets were sequestrated between 1915 and 1919. Among them were Frenchmen, Britons, a few Marquesans, and five Chinese retailers.

THE COMPAGNIE FRANÇAISE DES PHOSPHATES DE L'OCÉANIE

The colony's second-largest enterprise was founded in 1908 in conditions of feverish local speculation in land and administrative confusion over the supervision of the economic exploitation of Makatea Island. The isolation of this island some 135 miles northeast of Pape'ete made it an ideal site for mining phosphates. But it also meant that effective control of the conditions of extraction and export came under company managers, not under officials. The seat of government in the Tuamotu was at Fakarava, which was even farther away than Pape'ete; and although the administrator of this division was given a schooner in 1909 to tour his enormous archipelago, he was not always given instructions about the legal complications surrounding the development of mining. Too often the Pape'ete administration simply did not know what was going on.

Makatea's small population of 250 had been left to rule themselves with a chief and a district council. They were grouped in two small villages under the steep cliffs on the west and east shores of the island. Most of them had claims as coproprietors of sections of the shoreline and stands of coconut and fruit trees scattered over the elevated plateau inland. These claims had been registered (1890–1891) under the terms of the 1887 legislation and published in the *Journal Officiel*.[34] Like other such land registration, the areas ascribed to blocks were determined by guesswork, not by accurate survey. Indeed, if their superficial area is calculated, they amount to about twice the surface of Makatea. So far as is known, no one at Tahiti or elsewhere in the Tuamotu was sufficiently interested to make counterclaims. But none of the islanders troubled, either, to apply for title deeds at Pape'ete. Some unclaimed blocks reverted, under the terms of the 1887 decree, to the district council as communal land.

No one suspected the existence of phosphates in the 1890s; or if they did, they kept the knowledge to themselves. It is possible the mineral was not "discovered" in the conventional sense, but that an awareness of the peculiar geology of the island's coraliferous limestone merely awaited the correct conclusions to be drawn, samples to be taken, and the cost of extraction to be worked out.[35] The American geologist Alexander Agassiz, who led a scientific expedition to the Tuamotu and other parts of the Pacific in 1899, was more concerned with Makatea as an example of island formation by elevation than with its economic potential. Phosphates are not mentioned in the published records of the expedition. But he had discussed Makatea's structure with J. T. Arundel, who helped to found the Pacific Phosphate Company in 1902.

Arundel had been in the central and eastern Pacific as early as 1874 while still an employee of Houlder Bros. & Co. in London, who had leases to Caroline, Starbuck, Flint, and Christmas Islands to the northwest of French Polynesia.[36] He had leases of his own in some of these by the 1880s and planted coconuts, dug guano, and shipped out at least one cargo of the fertilizer to Hamburg through Peter Godeffroy. The missionary J. L. Green had visited his guano workings on Flint in November 1875 on Arundel's schooner the *Walker Glendening*; it seems that both Cook Islanders and Tuamotuans were recruited as labor there.[37] He was probably too busy with the affairs of the Pacific Islands Company (in which he had merged his own interests with those of Lord Stanmore) to do much about Agassiz' reports.[38] When the Pacific Phosphate Company was formed to exploit Nauru and Ocean Island, Arundel acted as its manager.

Arundel may well have been aware of the first tentative application by a Marseilles magnate, Eugène Salles, who requested the Ministry of Colonies for a phosphate concession in 1905 and claimed to have the backing of "Australian engineers."[39] The administration at Pape'ete and the resident administrator of the Tuamotu, Charles A. Marcadé, were taken by surprise and denied all knowledge of the existence of the mineral. But Arundel came to Tahiti in January and July 1906 to confer with lawyers and businessmen—E. Agache and Albert Goupil—and with the Public Works engineer, Étienne Touze. Early in 1907, the Société Française des Iles du Pacifique was formed with a modest capital of 125,000 francs and an Anglo-French board of directors which included Salles and Arundel as technical adviser. Its local agents were listed as Arundel, G. C. Ellis and J. E. Ellis (from the Pacific Phosphate Company), Agache, and Touze.

But, as yet, no one had really followed up the indications left by Agassiz. In July 1907, Goupil and Touze (who had just become his son-in-law) went to Makatea to obtain mining rights from proprietors. They were joined there for a few weeks by Arundel and his employees and a French geologist, L. Rozan. The extent of the deposits was confirmed—Rozan thought they covered about 400 hectares, or one-fifth of the island's surface. The SFIP was quickly registered at Pape'ete; and in October 1907 Goupil began to draw up the first of several hundred paper contracts with Makateans, offering 1 franc per ton and compensation for crops and trees in return for exclusive mining rights.

Already there were rival speculators in the field. Marau Salmon began to register her own series of contracts obtained by Norman Brander and the influence of her name (reported the British consul).[40] She also offered a higher royalty of 2 francs 25 per ton. The enmity between Goupil and Marau, as rival land-jobbers, persisted well into 1908; and it was not settled till Hoppenstedt and the SCO mediated between the two parties on behalf of the Pacific Phosphate Company.[41] Marau and Norman Brander were paid 70,000 francs each in cash and were allowed a royalty of 37 centimes per ton on exports for the surrender of all contracts to the SFIP. Albert Goupil also sold his "rights" and became a manager of the company at Makatea; his father became its legal counsel; and Étienne Touze resigned from Public Works to begin a long career as director for the company in the Pacific. As an extra precaution, Goupil also sold two contracts with the district councils of Makatea and Niau Island (where there were low-grade guano deposits) for the right to mine on communal land.

On this dubious foundation the SFIP felt secure enough to petition for legislation from the Ministry of Colonies in September 1908; to expand the capital base of the company to £240,000; and to change its name on 15 October to the Compagnie Française des Phosphates de l'Océanie. Most of the capital was British, and Arundel went to Paris at the end of 1908 to take a seat on the board of directors. The Ministry of Colonies refused to give any guarantees of title, however, because there was no mining legislation in force in French Polynesia.

This was serious, because a rival company, backed by German phosphate and shipping interests, had been hastily created in June

1908; and its lawyers and land-jobbers began to make spurious contracts of their own at Makatea in July by offering a royalty of 1 franc 50 per ton and a special price of 3,000 francs per hectare for outright sale of phosphate-bearing land. Some forty-six contracts were concluded; and a long series of court cases began at Pape'ete to determine prior rights of coproprietors.

Whatever the value of these rights, the CFPO was able to consolidate its position with working capital from the Pacific Phosphate Company and some of its technical experience. By August 1909, sections of the beach had been occupied; a wooden jetty and a tramway had been built at Mamao village; and a labor force of 250 men was engaged in construction work inland on the plateau.[42] Faced with this initiative, the Franco-German company ceased to make trouble in the courts and came to terms. Its principal shareholders were North-German Lloyd of Bremen and the Hanseatisches Südsee-Syndikat, which held concessions to phosphate deposits in German possessions. The shareholders were admitted into the CFPO as subscribers of increased capital which was raised to 8 million francs (£320,000). The British consul discerned "an arrangement intended to steady the Phosphate market by what might be called the Ocean–Nauru–Makatea–Angaur Combine."[43] This accommodation between the mining companies may well have been true, though Arundel resented Consul Simons drawing public attention to the amount of British participation in French Pacific phosphates in an article for the *Mining Journal* in 1908 and in his reports to the Foreign Office.[44]

The administration at Tahiti was still left with the problem of making local mining contracts legal. Colonial Inspector Fillon, who visited Makatea in 1909, severely criticized the failure of governors to supervise the activities of Goupil and Marau. He exposed the worthlessness of transfers made with proprietors who had no valid titles to blocks that had never been properly surveyed and had been "registered" in the *Journal Officiel* as claims long after the legal date permitted.[45] It was open to doubt, too, whether district councils could make contracts with private purchasers without the permission of the administrator of the Tuamotu or the governor at Pape'ete.

The Ministry of Colonies ordered Governor François to prepare legislation to cover the concession to the CFPO.[46] François set up a

Makatea: CFPO Installations.

small committee including Administrator Marcadé and the magistrate, Basquel, who were soon hopelessly at odds with the land registrar, Vermeersch, and the heads of the Interior and Public Works departments on the question of compensation to proprietors. The new governor, Bonhoure, was instructed to cut matters short by annulling the contract made by Goupil with the Makatea district council and making a concession of district land on behalf of the colony.

In December 1910, therefore, a new contract was passed between the governor and Étienne Touze transferring mining rights in lands acquired by the council under the legislation of 1887. The royalty of 1 franc per ton was to be paid to the administration; and the company was permitted to make roads and erect buildings.[47] Nobody knew precisely which blocks of land this contract applied to or how much phosphate lay in them.

At Pape'ete, a sharp lawyer, Jean Delpit, took up the claims of forty-six proprietors who argued that their lands were not part of "district domain" which was being generously conceded to the CFPO. A test case (*Hiti a Hiti* v. *the CFPO*) was lost before the Tahiti High Court in March 1911. Other cases were pleaded on behalf of the claimants who were excluded from a share of royalties because they had never registered coproprietor rights in lands on Makatea; these cases also were lost. The last hearing dragged on till 1920, when a petition from Hiti a Hiti was dismissed by the Council of State.

In France, other voices were raised to question the legality of the Goupil contracts. A French deputy, Maurice Violette, placed Makatea on the agenda of the Colonial Budget Commission in 1912. Governor Bonhoure wrote a well-documented reply contending that only the administration had the right to transfer district council lands to Europeans and (more doubtfully) that all royalties for coproprietors were held by the Caisse des Dépôts until their rights had been decided.[48]

Just how this was to be done was far from clear. The land registers were not accurate enough to determine the mathematics of claims; and phosphate-bearing lands were inextricably mixed with district domain and family usehold. The administration shrank from the idea of a completely new survey. There was no suggestion to pay all royalties into a common fund for the benefit of the islanders as a community.

The company, therefore, went ahead and opened up its first block in northern Makatea in January 1911. It was not really possible for the special agent, appointed by the administration, to keep track of the origins and tonnage of mineral extracted. Some compensation was paid. Families received about 200,000 francs for rent of lands and damage to crops up to 1913; and the administration (for the district council) received 150,000 francs in royalties. But these paltry sums, as a colonial inspector recognized in 1914, in no way absolved officials from settling the rights of proprietors who received nothing.[49]

In 1916, the Ministry of Colonies asked the governor whether there were still any land cases that might prejudice new legislation. After receiving his reply, a decree (based on a similar measure for New Caledonia) was ratified on 17 October 1917. A concession of up to 2,000 hectares was allowed to a private company, and Article 61 stipulated that an indemnity was to be paid for the occupation of nonphosphate lands near the diggings. Nothing was said of previous contracts or royalties. Accordingly, Étienne Touze made a formal request for a concession, and Governor Julien granted 2,000 hectares (or the northern two-thirds of Makatea without conditions, in October 1918, as published in the *Journal officiel de la République* (2 May 1919).

Much had been expected for the local budget from this enterprise. But it was not till 1918 that the administration was able to recover import duties from the company.[50] It could not be squeezed too hard in its early years because of the high capital outlay required to build up every type of facility at Makatea. In 1912, it was estimated that the CFPO was making only 2 francs per ton and had to compete with the Pacific Phosphate Company, which paid no duties on imports and only 6d. (60 centimes) on every ton exported. Consequently, the French administration kept the local export duty on phosphates down to 75 centimes despite the eagerness of the Administrative Council to extract more. The contribution of the company to revenues for many years was less than the export duty obtained from pearl shell.

A compromise also had to be reached on labor supplies. Up till the date of the formal concession in 1917, the company employed casual workers from Tahiti and the Tuamotu who had to be replaced constantly. In November 1919, they proposed to introduce Japanese labor, and both the Administrative Council and the governor's Privy Council opposed the suggestion. But Governor François and the Ministry of Colonies were in favor, though the company was cautioned to keep quiet about the numbers to be imported in order to avoid upsetting Europeans in Tahiti who were sensitive to the dangers of Asian immigration. Some 21 Japanese were employed in 1920, and 250 were brought in the following year.

THE TRIBUTARIES

While trade and commerce flourished in these decades before the First World War, the budget for administration and public works lagged far behind. Trade could not be taxed too heavily, for fear of driving merchants away. About half of local revenues came from customs, and less than 20 percent from other local taxes. The metropolitan subsidy remained steady at about 200,400 francs a year. The bulk of expenditure went toward the salaries and wages of officials. Public works, bridges and roads, absorbed less than 10 percent, which was not much more than the cost of sending officials to and from France every year. One of the largest items in the budget was the gendarmerie, which cost as much as education and grants to churches. One of the smallest was the health service (though the hospital and medical officers were paid for by France). Increasingly, the outer islands became more expensive to administer from Tahiti. They absorbed about 60 percent of expenditure in a budget which balanced at about 2 million francs in 1912.

The largest item of all was the cost of the Post Office, which included two subsidies of £6,240 and £720 to the Oceanic Steamship Company of San Francisco and the Union Steamship Company of New Zealand, while the equivalent of a further £2,000 was allowed for communications within the territory. There were vain attempts to end this dependency on overseas lines and apply French colonial navigation laws on the ownership of foreign vessels. But a concession had to be made in 1886 to allow German, British, and American captains into local cabotage.[51] In 1895 Governor Papinaud decreed that only French-owned vessels, under the command of French nationals, would be licensed to operate in interisland trade. British and German firms immediately protested that trade and postal communications would be wrecked, as would the system of credit advanced to French traders and to Polynesians in the outer groups. They hinted darkly that overseas communications might also cease. Papinaud replied at length in terms of the mercantilist advantage owed by colonies to national commerce. But it was no good. Foreign capital predominated; and no French merchants could be found to buy out local shipping. Another decree of 1911 demanded half French ownership of foreign vessels, but it was relaxed in favor of employing a few French captains and a number of Tahitians in the fleets operated by the largest merchant houses.

The attitude of Pape'ete politicians was ambivalent on this patriotic issue of national commerce and transport. In 1899, there was a serious proposal from Hecht Frères & Co. for a Pape'ete–Noumea line and a connection using Messageries vessels via the Far East. But the General Council rejected the total cost of 200,000 francs in extra subsidies.[52] As the secretary general summed up their plight: "We are at present the absolute tributaries of America through San Francisco and of England through Auckland. Not even our trade between groups within the colony itself is out of English hands, since their boats connect with the Marquesas, the Tuamotu and the Leeward Islands."[53]

But French merchants and traders within the General Council were not completely convinced by a metropolitan and imperial view of their predicament. In 1891, Governor Lacascade announced to them that the tariff policy of France was to be extended in varying degrees to all French overseas possessions; and the following year the famous Tariff Law of 9 May 1892 was promulgated locally. Colonies were divided into two classes. In the first, where metropolitan customs were to be applied, were the French West Indies, Indochina, Madagascar, and New Caledonia. Tahiti was included in the second class, in which full assimilation was avoided but where French goods were to enjoy an advantage over foreign imports of at least 18 percent of invoice values.

The General Council voted to make this preference as light as possible by recommending a general ad valorem duty of 10 percent. There was a list of exempted articles, and changes to the municipal tax *(octroi de mer)* were proposed to reduce the differential between goods of French and foreign origins. Taken together with higher freight charges for French imports, this system had the effect of neutralizing imperial preference.

Tahiti's location in the Pacific basin within a network of foreign commercial and maritime enterprise made such compromises with metropolitan imperial dogma inevitable. The administration itself imported flour, oil, wines, meat, and butter through Auckland and San Francisco—duty free when consumed by local officials and troops. On the other hand, luxury items from France, freighted through London, Liverpool, or New York, were taxed as goods of foreign origin. The main result was to raise local retail prices. Hardest hit were the small importers with insufficient capital to seek out the cheapest overseas markets; and they grew to depend more on larger houses such as the SCO.

One commercial group, however, resisted being driven under by the artificially high import prices. The small Chinese community in the 1890s, perhaps no more than three or four hundred, refused to pay a tax of 50 francs on all Chinese traders and merchants. They engaged a lawyer to show that it was contrary to agreements between France and China, and their protest was upheld in the Ministry of Colonies. Again, in 1908, as their numbers began to increase, they resisted attempts of the Chamber of Commerce to impose a discriminatory landing tax of 2,500 francs on Chinese immigrants and restrict the number of Chinese trading licenses. By that date, they were officially reckoned at 459, of whom there were 213 in Pape'ete. Some 46 of the 68 traders in the town were Chinese, including half the licensed butchers and all of the island's 32 bakers.[54]

While their commercial functions were appreciated, their enterprise was resented. The American consul in 1910 thought they had a monopoly of vanilla exports to all destinations and paid 40 percent of the invoice fees collected at his consulate alone. The *Océanie Française*, which spoke for French patriots, wanted more of them as labor, but not as traders.[55] Governor Fawtier thought they had grown in numbers to two thousand by 1914, though no detailed census of their community was made till after the war.

In one respect they had demonstrated they could change currency transactions in the colony. Chilean coin continued to depreciate through the last decades of the century; and while this was a source of profit to importers such as the SCO, it represented a loss to the administration in tax collection unless new exchange rates could be imposed. When this was threatened in 1909, the Chinese

> decided that they would have no more to do with the base coinage . . . as much a tribute to the soundness of their business principles as it is significant evidence of the importance and influence they have acquired over the destinies of local affairs. The action of the Chinese shopkeepers was brought about by a notice in the Official Gazette informing the public of the real silver value of the Chilean coins, which here were circulated at an enchanted value *[sic]*. The Chinese suspecting by this notice that a "coup" was being meditated by the local Government, held a secret meeting on the matter the result of which was that they got rid of all they held of Chilean coins and then declined to receive any more, consequently by this one single business action the much despised Chinese shopkeeper was able to eliminate, or bring to a head, a question which had been the cause of much local annoyance.[56]

The results were unexpected. Refusal of the Chilean *tara* led Tahitians to demand payment in U.S. equivalents, "franc and centimes having no significance to their dollar minds."[57] Instead of paying a laborer's wage at a daily rate of $1.50 Chilean, or 3 francs 35, the European population was asked to pay U.S. $1.50, or 7 francs 50.

Market produce followed the same inflated rates, and the economy of the town was thrown into disorder. There was a strike at the port by Tahitian laborers before a new wage level was fixed at about 5 francs a day. But produce prices did not come down, and there was a general rise of about 50 percent in retail prices. The fixed incomes of officials continued to shrink.

The question of local costs also had a bearing on evaluations of the future of the port of Pape'ete in 1912 and 1913. There is a surprisingly extensive literature on the economic development of the eastern Pacific in these years; and through it all shines the promise of Panama.[58] But the engineers and economists who tried to decide the place of Tahiti in this advance in maritime communications and commerce were forced to conclude that the probable price of coal made it uncertain whether much of the increased traffic across the Pacific would pass through French Polynesia.[59] Nevertheless, a careful plan for investment in local infrastructure was worked out, and a Public Works Commission of the Ministry of Colonies recommended widening the pass at Pape'ete, new dock-yards, coal stores, navigation aids, telegraphic communications, and improvements to the water supply. A financial bill for a state-guaranteed loan was prepared; but an interdepartmental commit-tee decided that the local administration was not competent to su-pervise such a large program and recommended a concession to a private company. If a coaling station could be built by private en-terprise, it was argued, other essential public works could be in-cluded in the deal. And if the price of coal at Pape'ete could be kept at 35 to 40 francs per ton (compared with 25 francs at Panama and 18 at Sydney), the port of call might still be marginally attractive for long-haul tonnages.

These plans were among the first colonial casualties of the war in 1914. Some stocks of coal were collected, but the guaranteed loan was not approved. The colony was left, instead, with a grow-ing sense of isolation in an ocean commanded by the navies of other powers. Governor Fawtier organized a small local militia of volunteers in August 1914 to supplement the garrison and reserves of about three hundred men. Command of the port was given to Captain Maxime Destremeau, who skillfully sited on shore the bat-teries of the gunboat *Zélée* and organized a motorized battery of six 37-mm guns to counter any landing parties. The German freighter *Walküre* was taken at Makatea and brought to Pape'ete with forty hostages.

On 22 September at about 6 A.M. the two German cruisers *Scharnhorst* and *Gneisenau* were sighted approaching Pape'ete from the west, accompanied by a merchant steamer. Warning charges were fired by one of Destremeau's hill batteries; and at 7 A.M., when the warships turned toward the harbor, two shells were fired short of them. The Germans hoisted battle ensigns, and the leading marks for entrance to the pass were destroyed by some of Destremeau's men. The rest took up positions along the shore.

It may have been Admiral von Spee's intention to land and seize stocks of coal and other provisions.[60] The whole episode in French records became shrouded in the controversy between Destremeau and Governor Fawtier which led to the captain's recall after an in-quiry by Admiral Huguet at the end of 1914. British consular re-ports indicate that the Germans concentrated on knocking out the batteries first and commenced firing at 8 A.M. from a distance of about a mile offshore. Some eighty shells landed in the hills behind the town. None of them damaged the guns. A couple of shells were also aimed at the British consulate and destroyed houses about a hundred yards to the rear. At 8:45 Admiral von Spee directed his fire on the *Zélée*, which was moored alongside the *Walküre*. The French gunboat was scuttled, and the *Walküre* was badly holed and sank. A number of shells went high and landed on the town behind the wharf, starting a fire which gutted the market and destroyed some stores, including the premises of Donald & Edinburgh.

Destremeau, early in the bombardment, ordered the coal stocks to be destroyed. (The consul says it was by order of Fawtier.) Some 2,000 tons at the naval dockyard were set alight and burned slowly, covering the town with a pall of black smoke. One report also suggests that Fawtier signaled to the warships that he had forty German hostages ashore, but this signal (if it was made) is not confirmed in German sources.[61] It would appear, rather, that the warships ceased firing at 9:15, when the *Zélée* sank, and moved away with their transport to the north under cover of a heavy squall. They proceeded to the Marquesas, where they requisitioned 89,000 francs worth of goods and cash from SCO stores at Taiohae and on Hiva Oa.[62] They left damage at Pape'ete estimated at £150,000. A Tahitian and a Chinese were killed.

On 24 September, two days after the bombardment, Fawtier decreed a war levy of a million francs (£40,000) on German nationals in the colony.[63] Most of the sum was paid by the SCO, whose stores and plantations were seized. Destremeau thought the levy far too little and began to play a brief and stormy role which led to his dismissal (though his name was subsequently given to one of Pape'ete's main thoroughfares).

The Pape'ete Chamber of Commerce also joined in the campaign, urging Fawtier to support the aims of the Colonial Commission set up at Bordeaux in October 1914 to link the economies of overseas territories more closely with the French war effort. They insisted on the need for a wireless telegraph (which could well have led to an early naval action with the German cruisers). A wireless station was opened at Ha'apape in 1915. More ominously, the chamber demanded that the vanilla market and copra market, formerly dominated by Hamburg and San Francisco, should be concentrated for French colonies in French brokerages by a system of colonial preferences. In order to decrease dependency on foreign firms, they demanded that German commerce be prohibited in the territory for as long as possible after the war.[64]

Thus in significant ways the easygoing balance of commercial cooperation between peasant producers and merchant firms was suddenly altered as a result of events in 1914. The starker overtones of nationalist conflict in Europe quickly encouraged the latent national animosities among Europeans in Tahiti. There was, too, a resentment of the preponderant position of German commercial finance and land ownership in the territory. The closure of accounts and eventual sequestration of the SCO's properties must have been viewed with a certain amount of relief by some of its more heavily indebted clients, as well as with genuine regret by others who were forced out of business for lack of a comparable supplier.

CHAPTER 10

FRENCH ASCENDANCY

In 1918 it was still possible for a French governor to describe his Pacific colony as a set of Polynesian and foreign communities linked by foreign trade and shipping with the outside world and administered by France without much compensation in terms of economic or strategic advantage.[1] Morale was at a low ebb. The promised public works program had been dropped; Papeʻete had been left open to German attack; the budget had been cut; and the price of copra fell during the war. There was even a rumor put about in 1920 that the whole territory might be sold to the United States.[2]

Twenty years later, as another international crisis threatened even the most distant possessions of the French empire, it was very unlikely that French Polynesia would be willingly ceded to any other Pacific power. There would also have been a genuine concern at such a possibility among the Tahitian population, especially in the ranks of the Franco-Tahitian bourgeoisie and plantocracy that emerged during the interwar period.

For that period is all too often treated as one of lethargy, interspersed with occasional scandals, in an insular colonial backwater —a fitting backdrop for the imaginative works of resident American novelists, occasional journalists, and wandering misanthropists such as Alain Gerbault. Tahiti, as never before, became a symbol for escapism from a dangerous Western civilization. And the necessary penetration of the tropical refuge by material and intellectual elements of that flawed civilization was, on the whole, described as a minor catastrophe by those in search of the "true" Polynesia. Superficially, there were grounds for concern if the attention was fixed for too long on the seedy waterfront of Papeʻete or on the depressed condition of islanders in the Marquesas and some atolls of the Tuamotu. But there is little evidence that the Polynesian population, on the whole, shared these misgivings or the disillusionment of European visitors. And the period was a source of two far-reaching changes: one in the structure of French Polynesian society, and the other in its total dependency on overseas markets for investment and trade.

Demographically, island communities began to recover from the long decline in population and admitted a larger proportion of immigrants of French and Asian origin. At the same time, the economic instability of markets in the 1920s and 1930s resulted in a greater intervention by France in the organization of copra and vanilla brokerages, improved metropolitan communications, and larger subsidies to the local budget.

For better or for worse, both these developments had their impact on the expression of new political interests among the second and third generations of Euro-Polynesian traders, planters, and businessmen who took a larger share in the management of the territory after 1945; and they also influenced the ways in which authority was concentrated, or shared, within the narrow framework of government permitted under French rule. The politics of the postwar period which were argued out under a new constitution were about questions of taxation, land tenure, the cost of living, and participation in decision-making—all of which had their origins in the interwar period, when they had been raised and suppressed or postponed.

Even Tahitians' changing attitudes which were given fuller expression after 1945 had already been rehearsed. The return of ex-servicemen in 1947 and their disappointment with economic and social opportunities for advancement were, in some ways, an echo of the return of Tahitian conscripts in 1919. There had been, moreover, many more of these called to the colors late in 1914, compared with the three hundred or so better-known volunteers of the 2nd Pacific Battalion.[3] No distinction was made between French nationals and the former subjects of Pomare V, and their names were chosen at random from the census records. Of the 1,589 recruits medically examined, 1,094 were accepted and sent overseas in six contingents from the beginning of 1915, first to New Caledonia and then to France. They fought in Salonika and on the Western Front. But compared with current research into the impact of the First World War on other colonies, little is known about these conscripts or their attitudes to their homeland and its status in the Pacific. At least one, Pouvanaa a Oopaa, was to be later active in politics.

But more immediately, the return of Tahitian conscripts from France in 1919 occasioned a crisis in labor relations at Pape'ete, where wartime inflation had reduced the purchasing power of wages. "A number worked a propaganda amongst the local native workmen," wrote Consul Williams, and started a strike of wharf laborers that "succeeded at all points."[4] Their wages of 7 francs 50 a day were raised to 2 francs 50 an hour for a working day of nine hours. Wages of ordinary day laborers followed this trend and were raised to 10 francs or 12 francs 50 per day. Plantation labor was paid between 75 and 100 francs a month and had their rates doubled. Henceforth a constant theme of economic debates in the Chamber of Commerce or the governor's Administrative Council was the shortage of workers at a price small planters and traders could afford.

This theme of high labor costs was taken up by Froment-Guieyesse's *Océanie Française*, founded in 1913 as a well-informed monthly that argued for French immigration, investment, and closer links between France and all French Pacific territories.[5] It was a theme just as eagerly denounced by Brunschwig's short-lived *Équité* in 1919 (founded after suppression of his newspaper, *Le Libéral*) because, like other settlers, he detected an administration plot to justify the importation of Asian labor. But few, if any, of the increasing numbers of Chinese immigrants were willing to work for very long as wage laborers; and on the whole it was left to Cook Islanders to fill a demand for indentured labor on Makatea during the war and then make their way to Tahiti, along with small numbers from the outer islands, to enter the lowest level of the wage labor market.[6]

The gap between the demand for low-cost casual workers and the supply from the rural peasantry was worsened, moreover, by the influenza epidemic of 1918. The disease was introduced at Pape'ete by the Union Steamship vessel *Navua*, on passage from San Francisco, when the town was crowded for armistice celebrations.[7] Governor Julien took no measures to provision the districts;

and despite the efforts of a number of volunteer relief workers organized by the U.S. consul, Layton, between three and four thousand
Tahitians, Mo'oreans, and Leeward Islanders died in the *ma'i rahi*.
Rigorous quarantine enforcement, however, prevented its spread to
the Marquesas, the Tuamotu, or the Austral group. It was the last
and the most serious of outbreaks of disease which left their mark
on the composition of a population whose resurgence was just
beginning to be appreciated.

THE DEMOGRAPHY OF SURVIVAL

Before the war, local studies of the population from census enumerations had still been pessimistic about the chances of "native" inhabitants holding their own in the long battle with infant mortality
rates, infertility, and low resistance to imported illnesses.[8] The in-
tercensal decline (1907–1911) in the total of "native" inhabitants
from 26,994 to 26,219 seemed to bear this suspicion out, though
some peculiar shifts in the detailed statistics for each group suggest
that faulty counts may also have been a factor (see Table 9). There
was less room for error about immigrants. The number of French
citizens of all origins, metropolitan and local, residing in Pape'ete
increased from 1,909 in 1907 to 2,153 in 1911; and the number of
Chinese appears to have doubled to 975 in the same period.[9] Police
records of the Chinese community in 1917 numbered them at
2,481.

A longer-term view of the population in 1914 argued, however,
that the Polynesian element was beginning to stabilize and was not
expected to decrease much further: "On the contrary, it has shown
evidence of an exceptional vitality, because it has been able to suffer the worst epidemics without decrease since 1829."[10] Unfortu-
nately, little statistical evidence was brought forward to support
this proposition. But one of the results of wartime conscription was
a thorough revision of the population registers, when it was found
that many of the districts, particularly in the Leeward Islands,
failed to record "illegitimate" births. This responsibility was subsequently taken out of the hands of district councils and pastors and
given to the gendarmerie and civil administrators.[11] Nevertheless,
there were other encouraging signs. On Tahiti and Mo'orea, between 1913 and 1917, all district registers, except two, showed an
excess of live births over deaths.

It is difficult to come to any firm conclusion about a "turning

TABLE 9
Population Enumerations

Region	1902	1907	1911	1921	1926	1931	1936	1941	1946
Tahiti	11,177	11,691	11,378	11,749	14,244	16,781	19,029	23,133	24,820
Mo'orea	1,558	1,564	1,616	1,826	1,837	2,011	2,251	2,279	2,838
Mai'ao	*	101	*	81	*	117	126	165	200
Makatea	*	*	866	628	1,086	1,160	992	1,248	1,826
Leewards	4,626	5,827	6,689	6,920	8,502	8,705	9,544	11,891	12,445
Marquesas	3,563	3,424	3,116	2,300	2,260	2,283	2,400	2,699	2,988
Australs	2,106	2,550	2,485	2,715*	3,170	*	3,456	3,621	3,921
Tuamotu	4,294	3,829	3,715	2,676	4,726	4,564	4,586	4,681	5,127
Mangareva	1,381†	1,533†	1,512†	*	*	1,501†	1,579†	1,504†	1,569†
Totals	28,705*	30,519*	31,376*	28,895*	35,456*	38,511	44,044	51,221	55,734

* Incomplete.
† Including some from the Tuamotu.

Sources: Valenziani 1949; McArthur (1968); Lyons (1968).

point" in the demographic history of the territory.[12] The crude enumerations of total population after 1900 indicate a dramatic upswing after the temporary setback of the 1918 epidemic (see Figure 1). Totals for Tahiti and Mo'orea dominate this pattern more than Leeward Islands totals, and probably more than totals for the Tuamotu, which show a decline before 1921 and then make a suspiciously striking recovery in 1926 (an increase of over two thousand in five years). There is more certainty about Marquesas totals, which continue to decline till the 1920s and then rise slowly. Some of the steepness in the rise of the demographic curve in the 1930s may also derive from undercounts and incomplete returns at the beginning of the century.

It is also difficult to separate net immigration gains from rates of increase in the resident Euro-Polynesian and Chinese communities in census years. Added to this problem is the mobility of islanders within the territory, which must have influenced some totals for island groups. (There is a good case, for example, for considering Tahiti, Mo'orea, and the Leeward Islands as a single demographic total.)

Up until 1907 it is possible to separate "indigenous" totals in the census from resident Europeans, Chinese, and other minor immigrant groups. The results suggest the beginnings of recovery for Tahiti, Mo'orea, and Leeward Islands population and a continued decline for the Marquesas. The particularly valuable census of 1907 is the last to confirm this pattern. Thereafter, in the interwar years, the distinction between metropolitan and local French citizens is not always clear; and Polynesian French citizens (from Tahiti, Mo'orea, and the Tuamotu, plus any others who had gained this status by war service or education) include categories of long-resident settlers of European origin. French "subjects" (all those not formerly subjects of Pomare V) numbered 10,021 in 1926, compared with 19,242 French "citizens"; and they, too, may have included immigrant Polynesians from the Cook Islands, descendants of nineteenth-century immigrant labor from the Gilbert Islands, and others in transition between the numerous *"population flottante"* and those with resident status.

Given this ambiguity in the classification of census groups, a doubt must persist about the exact contribution of the "Polynesian" element—certainly the largest—to the overall increase of the

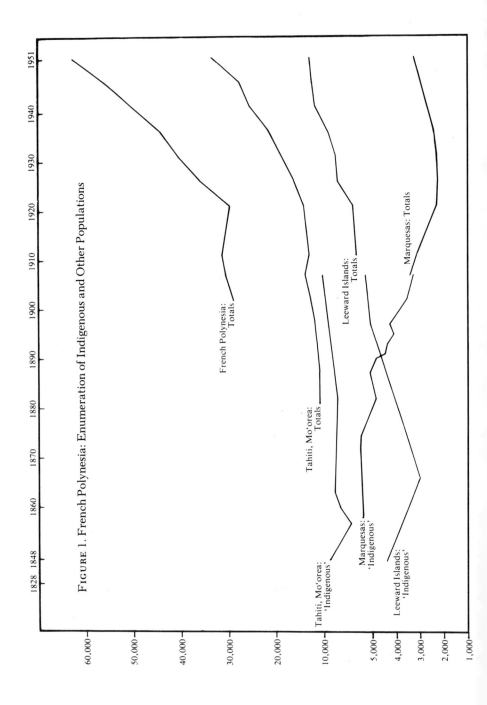

FIGURE 1. French Polynesia: Enumeration of Indigenous and Other Populations

1920s and 1930s. It has been shown, by extrapolation from the detailed census of 1956, that the effects of the *ma'i rahi* of 1918 on the birth cohorts for 1917 to 1921 in Tahiti and Mo'orea are evident throughout the period, but very attenuated.[13] Apart from this reduction, the standard rate of mortality for the territory as a whole would not seem to be different from that obtaining for other Pacific communities in the interwar period; and the fertility rate was certainly higher than some by the 1950s.

But an increase there certainly was, both among peasants and the small numbers of wage earners, salary earners, and others not directly dependent on subsistence and cash crops for their livelihood. Miscegenation, for long an important feature of island society, also continued, though we have no way of telling its incidence.

Differentiation within this demographically mobile society in the interwar years was probably accelerated by immigrant groups, rather than by a rigid division between occupation groups. These immigrant groups were predominantly made up of European officials and settlers and Asians. All were highly concentrated in the township of Pape'ete, whose population more than doubled between 1911 and 1936, at a faster rate than the increase for the territory as a whole. Nearly a third of the population of Tahiti lived within the boundaries of the commune, and another third inhabited the nearby districts of Arue, Pirae, Fa'a'a, and Papara as early as 1897. By 1936, these districts contained 44 percent of Tahiti's population on the edge of a small Pacific capital which had already begun to expand from the harbor area to Nu'utere in the west and the Fauta'ua Valley in the east.[14] In Tahiti, as in other Pacific ports, urbanization is a relatively old phenomenon.

One other trend among the increased numbers of immigrants was politically important. There is a distinct reversal in the proportions of metropolitan French, compared with other foreigners, by the end of the 1930s and the Second World War (see Table 10). American and British subjects numbered between three and four hundred by 1926 and did not expand further; and the "foreigners" also included 496 Vietnamese in the total count by that date.

The increased Asian element in the territory's population was frequently recorded and cited, but it was subject to wide fluctuations when considered in terms of net immigration. Over the whole period 1905 to 1946, there was a gain of arrivals over departures

TABLE 10

Metropolitan French, Chinese, and Foreign Nationals

Year	French Polynesia			Pape'ete (all groups)
	Metropolitan French	Foreign Nationals	Chinese	
1881	991	615	447	3,224
1907	850	858	459	3,617
1911	*	1,611	991	4,282
1921	*	*	2,687	4,601
1926	870	1,830	3,989	5,569
1931	*	1,992	4,030	6,274
1936	[2,170]†	1,261	4,569	7,456
1946	3,200	771	6,593	7,595

* Not stated.
† Estimate from Lyons (1968:40) and FO 687/19 (consular estimates).

Sources: Valenziani (1949:95); Lyons (1968:31–32); Recensement général (Décembre 1956), 7; Teissier (1953:13).

of nearly three thousand Chinese before a large exodus of 689 in 1948. By then, there were some 6,600 Chinese resident in the territory; thus about half this population derived from natural increase from within the Chinese community.

The two principal periods of Chinese immigration when there were substantial gains in the immigrant Asian population were 1909–1914 and 1922–1925 (see Figure 2). There were always some female Chinese immigrants during this period, though generally fewer than males before 1918. But they did not provide the labor the colony required for Makatea or for plantations and public works. In 1920 an immigration service was set up to assist recruitment from African, Asian, and Pacific sources, at the recruiter's expense, and wages were fixed at 45 francs a year for males and 35 francs for females.[15] The CFPO struggled through the war years with some two hundred Japanese workers supplemented by seventy to eighty Tahitian and Leeward Islanders and a few dozen Cook Islanders.[16] The latter caused increasing difficulties over the terms of their contracts, especially those from Aitutaki who were imported in 1917.[17] Accordingly, the CFPO was one of the first enterprises to take advantage of the new system of recruitment organized through the colonial government in Saigon with the participation of the Bank of Indo-China. The first contingent of Vietnamese arrived at Pape'ete in August 1925 and numbered 345. Of

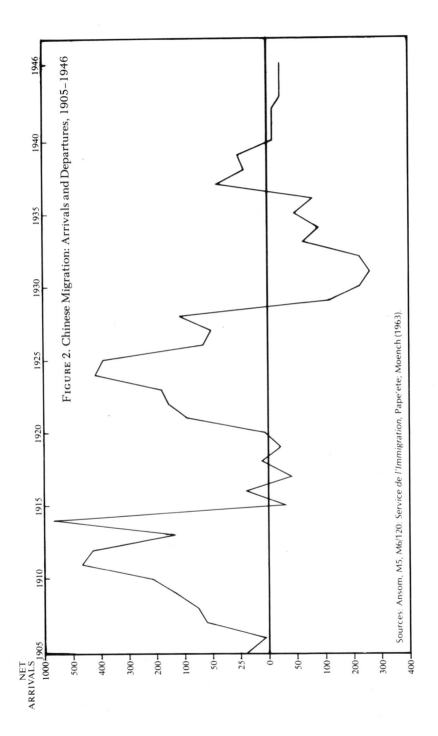

FIGURE 2. Chinese Migration: Arrivals and Departures, 1905–1946

NET
ARRIVALS

Sources: Ansom, M5, M6/120. *Service de l'Immigration,* Pape'ete; Moench (1963).

these, 287 were hired for Makatea, along with 272 Chinese brought in from Hong Kong. The employment of Polynesians from Tahiti, Tuamotu, and the Leeward Islands was stepped up to over two hundred a year by the end of the 1920s. A few dozen Japanese were also hired from 1930.

It is not possible to cite the cumulative totals of labor immigration throughout the territory. The population census for Makatea gives totals of about a thousand inhabitants in the 1930s, and these had nearly doubled by 1946. But there were also repatriations of Vietnamese labor in Tahiti for economic rather than social reasons. The rate of exchange of the franc deteriorated against the Saigon piastre, and all contracts were concluded in terms of this currency. Labor costs rose; and the Chamber of Commerce asked the administration to stabilize wages and allowances for rations and clothing at the levels prevailing when the Vietnamese arrived in the colony. This request was refused after correspondence with Saigon. And in 1930, when a decree was passed to induce the Vietnamese to sign on for a further five years, the wage levels were too expensive for most local employers.[18] By 1938, their numbers had dwindled to 83 in Tahiti and 104 in Makatea.

By then, too, there had been a reversal in policy toward Chinese immigration. Under pressure from the Chamber of Commerce, the administration issued a decree in 1929 which demanded a return fare of 4,500 francs from foreign settlers landing at Pape'ete.[19] The large net gains in arrivals during the 1920s soon turned into net losses by departures to San Francisco, China, or islands in the Pacific.[20]

But like other immigrant groups, the Chinese were well entrenched economically; and they had freely intermarried with the Polynesian population. Many learned Tahitian and knew no French.[21] For a brief period between 1928 and 1933 it was possible for a small number to acquire French nationality before this avenue was closed until after the Second World War.[22] In general, it was no easier for Chinese children of a Tahitian mother to claim French nationality than any other group of foreign settlers whose descendants could prove that a legal marriage had been contracted (and that their mother was Tahitian). On the whole, the Chinese remained economically integrated and socially distinctive with separate legal status.

Social differentiation within the Euro-Tahitian population turned increasingly on educational and economic criteria. The term *demi* (or *afa popaʻa*) is hardly encountered in contemporary popular or official literature in the interwar period, though the term *métis* often is. To some degree most Tahitians or Moʻoreans might be considered as the products of a heavily miscegenated society over a period of a century and a half. But it is possible to distinguish a sharpening line between those Polynesians (whether French citizens or subjects) who remained predominantly peasants and occasional wage earners, speaking Tahitian, and a transitional group of mixed parentage, speaking some French, which moved between rural and urban employment for regular monetary income from agriculture, business, and the professions. Consul Rowley had once termed them "go-betweens" before the First World War, when many of them were Anglo-Tahitians. The postwar generation of *demis*, by parentage and by education, still spoke Tahitian, but they were more closely identified with the commerce and administration of the metropolitan power.

The distinction between this Franco-Tahitian group and the bulk of the population was, in the first place, a function of the success of the elementary and secondary education system in providing facilities for a limited number of pupils at Papeʻete and its failure to give more than an education in the vernacular in the districts and outer islands.[23] By the 1920s, hopes of raising the level of elementary education had faded before the realities of a restricted budget and the problem of instruction in a foreign language in a rural environment where the teachers and most of the pupils did not use French in their daily lives. Of the four thousand government primary school children in the territory, only sixty attended the École Centrale at Papeʻete on bursaries. Another 1,200 attended private (mission) schools; and a small group of 120 went on to "higher" primary education by the Protestant or Catholic missions in Papeʻete. Some eighty or ninety primary certificates were obtained by pupils who completed classes in the rural schools every year, and some fifty were awarded to pupils from Papeʻete schools. The higher primary certificate *(brévet supérieur)*, which was also an elementary teaching qualification, was awarded to fifteen or so candidates every year. There were also two elementary industrial schools at Fakarava and Papeʻete; and a school for executive personnel was started at Taravao in 1929 to train clerical staff for the administration and business. There were two Chinese schools which taught French.

There were, moreover, by the beginning of the 1930s, official doubts about the utility of French in the rural district schools. Tahitian was returned officially to the curriculum (unofficially it had never disappeared), and this patronage of the vernacular was assisted by the appearance of a number of government newspapers — *Te vea a te hau* (1922–1924) and *Te Vea Maohi* (1930–1946).

This latter monthly, which recognized the distinct cultural identity of Tahitian-speakers (as the missions had for a much longer period), was first and foremost an *oeuvre de vulgarisation*, as well as a news sheet, and had a circulation of about 1,600 in the 1930s. It was inspired by Governors Bouge and Jore, both of whom took an intelligent interest in the history and customs of Polynesia and produced works of scholarship on Oceania. Notices of employment, instructions on civil registration, warnings against alcohol, songs, shipping timetables, reports of governors' tours—a miscellany of information filled its pages. *Te Vea Maohi* aimed at social change as well as information; and there were rigorous explanations about the problem of name-changing among Tahitians and the use of patronymics, the legal implications of *fa'amu* adoption under French law, and some potted history of the islands stressing the "validity" of French occupation. It was also through *Te Vea*, by prodigious translation, that many Tahitians were introduced to current affairs in the 1930s in articles on the Munich crisis, the Sino-Japanese conflict, and the outbreak of the war in Europe.

At a different level of patronage, the administration sponsored the Société des Études Océaniennes, begun by Governor Julien in 1917 with the purpose of studying "the anthropology, ethnology, philology, archeology, history, institutions, customs and traditions of the Maoris of eastern Polynesia." This brave initiative attracted some three hundred members who founded a small journal, began a museum, and depended heavily on the contributions of a few devoted students of local society to keep going through the lean years of the budget. Missionaries remained its principal patrons and supporters.

But missionaries, too, had begun to pose questions about the future of Tahitians within the framework of the churches they had helped to create. Old doctrinal battles between the sects began to appear less relevant as greater demands were placed on the capability of their converts to meet the changing economic and administrative conditions of a competitive society in Tahiti. Monsignor Mazé, who was consecrated bishop in 1939, had spent most of his missionary life in the Tuamotu, studying at first hand the problems of adaptation from a subsistence to a cash crop economy. He had seen his mission expand into Protestant fiefs in the Leeward Islands and the Australs and reopen in the Marquesas. His main ambition in 1939 was to give greater emphasis to training Polynesian adolescents as technicians and teachers; and he began (for the first time in the congregation's history in Tahiti) to plan for a Catholic Tahitian clergy.[24]

Among the Protestants, the SMÉ already depended, like the Mormons and Kanitos, on an indigenous pastorate to keep its congregations alive while it exercised close supervision through the pastoral conferences. Both sets of European missionaries recorded wide differences in outlook between their congregations and themselves on the relevance of biblical teaching to everyday conduct.[25] Some of the Kanitos elders went to the United States in 1929 and 1931, but they returned with their ideas unchanged and their interpretation of negative prohibitions, as laid down by their American mentors, as elastic as ever. In 1940, Charles Vernier looked back over the previous 130 years of the Tahitian Protestant churches in a survey which stressed the frustrations of European leadership of institutions "to which we remain foreign, we who are at their head with our White man's mentality, with our concepts and reactions which are so different from those of the natives, and which make it so difficult for us to enter the Tahitian soul."[26] For this metaphysical purpose, he reported, courses on theology were not enough; and the usual "trunk-and-branch" sermons with their symbolic formalism did not meet the needs of congregations whose Protestant children required a better education than the SMÉ schools at Papeʻete could provide.[27]

It was another Protestant missionary, too, who turned a perceptive mind, trained in other Pacific societies, on Tahiti and discerned that the pace of social and economic change in the interwar years had resulted in a noticeable status differential between rural Tahitians and immigrant groups. Pastor Maurice Leenhardt toured the island and its churches and schools in 1926 and found they did not give sufficient training to secure for Tahitians a place in the occupational structure commensurate with their position as *ta'ata fenua*—occupiers of the land:

> From the position of landed proprietor that he once was, the Tahitian citizen has gradually allowed himself to slip into second place, to become no more than an employee, perhaps one day, a proletarian. But this population is changing. Ceaseless intermarriage with Europeans or Chinese has miscegenated the race. . . . The half-caste, while not giving up any of the privileges of landed wealth which he can hold through his mother, takes pride, on the other hand, in the white man's blood that flows in his veins and takes advantage of it at the expense of the unmiscegenated Tahitian. It is he who flatters the inclination of the whites to look on the Tahitian as something of a native, and he who compromises with Catholicism and encourages the prejudice that the Tahitian Protestant Church is the church of the people; he who wishes desperately for French for his children and a European culture and who thereby thinks that is opposed to the old Christian traditions of the island.[28]

Although it is open to doubt whether the religious alignment of Tahitians and Tahitian-*demis* was as polarized as Leenhardt suggested, the correlation of property and economic functions among the widening social group of educated intermediaries of mixed parentage is attested in other sources. Apart from education, much of this change came about because of the unstable economic conditions of the 1920s and 1930s and the increasing patronage of the colonial government and the French state for entrepreneurs and producers who were French citizens.

THE ECONOMIC CRISIS

Tahiti and its dependencies emerged from the war into a long period of rising retail prices and a deterioration of the profitable returns from produce exports that had marked its progress from the 1890s. The malaise deepened the profound mistrust of the foreign community which the administration shared with French traders, planters, and merchants who sat in the Municipal Council, the Chamber of Commerce, and the Administrative Council. The success of foreign enterprise during the years of prosperity only served to heighten resentment in the years of uncertainty. As a reminder of the consequences of vulnerability, the wreck of the *Zélée* lay in the harbor, a monument to Tahiti's brief experience of war. The *Walküre* was sold to an American contractor, raised, repaired, and sailed away.

All of the five governors and temporary governors who found themselves in office between 1916 and 1921 wrote appreciations of the foreign settlers in varying tones of patriotism, suspicion, and mild hostility. W. J. Williams, a local dentist and acting British consul (occasionally U.S. consul as well), was singled out for particular attention. Most of the German community was interned and deported, unless married to French Tahitians. An increasing number of Americans in search of an island paradise were refused entry: for the foreign colony, the day of the beachcomber was over. "Its members," wrote Governor Julien, "are not the best types; they are made up of the indifferent, or the disappointed, sometimes the mentally disturbed, and rarely those who are well-balanced; they come to the Pacific to find the easy-going and sensual way of life described by the first navigators."[29] He would have none of them; and his successor, Simoneau, who was also head of the judiciary, made an example of several by expelling them.

But this xenophobia could not be carried too far. The bulk of business and trade in the 1920s was still with the United States and New Zealand; and while the colony depended on indirect taxes for its revenue and foreign shipping for its mails, patriotism had to be muted. When the largest prize of the war—confiscated property —came up for auction, it was not even certain that Frenchmen, rather than the foreign community, would be among the principal beneficiaries.

The properties of German nationals which had been sequestrated and closed down were finally sold in 1924. They consisted of plantations owned by three Germans on Ra'iatea, Ra'ivavae, and in the Marquesas, the lands and stores of six traders at Pape'ete, and the lands, stores, and goods of the SCO in twenty-two separate lots.[30] The details of the auction were sent back to Hamburg, where the SCO was still making claims for compensation from the German government, but Germans were excluded from participation in the sale. The purchasers were headed by Chin Foo.

Property	Purchaser	Price (francs)
Fauta'ua plantation (20 hectares)	Chin Foo	19,000
Stores (Gustav and Hermann Meuel)	Chin Foo	250,000
	Chin Yen	425,000
SCO stores and warehouses	Chin Foo	800,500
SCO stores (Ra'iatea)	"Chinese"	(not stated)
Allgoewer property (Taunoa)	Ralph Hart	30,000
Meuel property (Taunoa)	Louis Palmer	113,000
Koeppen property (Taravao)	E. W. Vivish	170,000

The SCO's correspondent described Chin Foo as "a Banker in Tahiti and proprietor of several lots in town, including old Cardella's place, where he has built himself a fine home. [He] was 20 years ago a baker in Mataiea, where he used to peddle his loaves along the road for coconuts. He made his money in vanilla."[31] In fact, Chin (Tchung Fo Chong) came from a family of Cantonese traders to Tahiti in about 1897 and had established himself as a restaurant owner and vanilla merchant. He founded a bank in 1924 and was prominent in the affairs of the Sin Ngi Tong property company, set up before the war, and was instrumental in keeping its funds separate from a rival association which favored support for the Kuomintang. The ability of Chin and his associate, Chin Yen, to raise nearly 1½ million francs to speculate in the auction is ample commentary on the place they had achieved in local business.

The other purchasers were Ralph Hart, son of SCO's one-time indebted partner, John Hart, and a planter and pilot at Ra'iatea; Louis Palmer was an American schooner captain and trader; and Edwin Vivish was an Englishman who had made his money working for Coppenrath in the Tuamotu and at Rurutu. The most valuable property—the 900-hectare plantation at Opunohu with its 11,600 coconut trees, beehives, copra drier, pastures, fruit trees, and bungalow—was bought by an American, Medford Kellum. The SCO's plantation at Tahauku, Hiva Oa, was not sold till 1932 and was purchased by a French settler, Émile Rauzy.

Thus the demise of Tahiti's largest nineteenth-century merchant enterprise served mainly to further Chinese and other foreign investment in the 1920s. But no single firm again dominated local trade in the manner of the SCO. There appeared, instead, two moderate-sized British firms, the Compagnie Navale de l'Océanie (a commission house for the Maison Ballande of Bordeaux), several interlocking Chinese firms linked with one of the two or three Chinese associations in Pape'ete, and a number of smaller French traders linked to the merchants. The valuable waterfront property of the SCO on the Quai du Commerce was sold (or leased) to a partnership consisting of an American journalist, Charles Brown-Petersen, and two Franco-Tahitian businessmen, George Bambridge and Émile Martin. But they lacked the capital, knowledge, and overseas connections required to run a merchant house, and the buildings were sublet to retailers.

This nest of shops in the Vaima block was flanked by the firms of J. R. Maxwell on one side and A. B. Donald on the other. Maxwell's made their money out of copra concessions on Flint, Caroline, and Vostock Islands, which were visited from Tahiti every four months and worked by small parties of Tahitians and Cook Islanders on two-year contracts. Donald's (formerly Donald & Edinburgh) had its base in Auckland and was the Dominion Fruit Company in Suva. The Tahiti branch came under increasing pressure from the administration and French merchants represented in the Chamber of Commerce in the 1930s; and it was obliged to register as a French company, Établissements Donald, while its shipping interests in local interisland trade were registered as the Compagnie Française Maritime de Tahiti to meet the letter of local laws. By 1938, the firm's annual imports were valued at 13 million francs a year (less than 10 percent of local import values) and it paid taxes and duties amounting to 2 million francs (or about one-seventh of local revenues).[32] By then, too, the personnel of the firm were mostly French or Franco-Tahitian—some seventy employees and agents under the direction of a second-generation settler, Clément Coppenrath.

While one British firm adapted, the other, J. R. Maxwell, went into voluntary liquidation and sold off its schooners and trading posts to Chinese and French buyers in 1935. In 1944 its remaining interests were taken over by a Franco-Tahitian entrepreneur, A. P. (Tony) Tetuanui Pootahi Bambridge—shopkeeper, film magnate, merchant, planter, and politician.

Bambridge's rise was typical of advances made by the Franco-Tahitian community in the interwar years. A number led by Henri Grand and Pedro Miller (natural son of the British consul) formed small partnerships and were bought out by Comptoirs Français de l'Océanie, a French commission house which disappeared in the 1930s. They then went back to planting copra and vanilla, or they became employees of larger firms. Thus G. and H. Malardé (second-generation settlers) were traders and landed proprietors, while a third-generation member of the family became manager of Donald's. Émile Martin, son of a nineteenth-century trader, was educated in San Francisco and Paris to become the colony's most important industrial entrepreneur and, like Bambridge, a politician and member of the governor's council. Alfred Poroi, a third-generation Franco-Tahitian, became branch manager for the Union Steamship Company. A local-born Frenchman, Marcel Tixier, worked for all three major companies—the CFPO, the Compagnie Navale, and A. B. Donald—in the 1920s and 1930s before trading on his own account.

There was much less room for failure than there had been in the late nineteenth century. But it was still possible for relatively minor traders such as Henri Bodin, who had been a shell buyer in the Tuamotu, to become a member of the Chamber of Commerce and the Economic and Financial Delegations of the 1930s. There were signs, too, of a professionalism in the arrival of Robert Hervé, who came from Marseille in 1934 with legal and commercial degrees to work for his uncle's Paris firm of vanilla brokers, and in the appointment of Jules Niuhitoa Millaud (a Tahitian ex-serviceman) as an official of the Bank of Indo-China, after a career in Paris, Saigon, and Pondichéry.

Foreigners did not enter easily into this community of French and Tahitian interests. Robert MacKitrick of Liverpool, who worked for both the Compagnie Navale and for Donald's in the Marquesas, was obliged to become a French national. There was less room, too, for commercial buccaneers of the stamp of Stewart, Brander, and Hort, though one survived in the colossal form of Emmanuel Rougier, ex-Catholic missionary, plantation manager, *grand seigneur* of Papeʻete society from 1931, and president of nearly all its many civic bodies.

The second most important group of merchants, traders,and retailers—the Chinese—had also begun to move from the status of shopkeepers and market gardeners into the import-export business. Their progress is uncertain in any quantifiable terms in the inter-

Tahiti: Copra-loading.

war years, though there are three identifiable *Tungka* (principals) —Chin Foo, Siu Kung Po, and Wong Hen—who were all established early in the period. Undoubtedly there were others with their own clients in the outer islands, but they have not so far been recorded by students of the Tahitian Chinese, and there is no account given of the share of exports and imports passing through Chinese merchant houses.[33] The fate of the Kong Ah company, whose directors were connected with the Kuomintang's local association and which owned a small fleet of schooners and acted as a copra and vanilla brokerage, has tended to obscure less spectacular, but probably more successful, Chinese firms.

The institutions through which metropolitan French officials and the Franco-Tahitian community defended and enlarged their share of the local market were not greatly changed from the prewar period. The governor's Administrative Council of seven officials and a few nominated notables continued the work of the old General Council as a strictly consultative body. It was enlarged in 1930 to include three Tahitian members. Suggestions for a return to the General Council or to some other elected representation ran into the old problem that the electoral consequences of assimilation would have led to a majority based on the districts and outer islands, not on Pape'ete.

Legislation on nationality, adopted locally in 1921, while recognizing that citizenship had been granted to the subjects of Pomare V, was suitably vague on whether this included the Tuamotu and the Austral Islands.[34] The concession made in 1880 was never formally abolished; but the conditions of citizenship which obtained in other colonies—literacy in French, public office, or wartime service—were accepted as criteria for a change of status from "subject" to "citizen." And as they became part of official thinking, any expanded franchise was rejected, while Tahitian-French "citizenship" became a second-class status unless the Tahitian possessed sufficient education in French or was employed by the administration.

Not everybody was satisfied with this tacit compromise with the legacy of nineteenth-century "assimilation." When, in 1921, Governor Guédès tried to balance the budget by imposing a tax on business turnover and new import duties, the Chamber of Commerce transformed itself into a settlers' assembly and a committee for the defense of taxpayers organized a popular demonstration against the impost.[35] The tax was abolished and Guédès was recalled. Not the least objection to his policy locally was his decrease of Tahitian head taxes from 18 francs to 6 and his refusal to introduce a tax on unimproved land. His successor, Governor Louis Rivet, refused to countenance the wilder claims of the settlers to elected representation on an exclusively metropolitan franchise; and henceforth it was the Chamber of Commerce which spoke as the most influential French pressure group and united French planters, traders, merchants, and shipowners.

Rivet, moreover, brought with him from Indochina, where he had been an administrator, a number of ideas favored by Sarrault's Ministry of Colonies for closer links between New Caledonia, Tahiti, and French possessions in the Far East.[36] Communications, financial aid, indentured labor, and medical assistants and teachers from Hanoi University were to flow along the Saigon–Nouméa–Vila–Papeʻete axis. There was even a plan for a quasi-federal governor generalship to counter "foreign pressure" from America and Australasia. While not all French settlers went that far, the promise of 15 million francs for the port of Papeʻete was welcomed; and Dr. Lucien Sasportas, a medical administrator who was also president of the local Syndicat d'Initiative, saw the linkage as a way of importing rice, cement, and French manufactures along with French Indochina policies on plantations and land.[37]

The practical results of this effort to end the isolation of French Pacific territories were seen in shipping subsidies and local land tenure legislation. The Union Steamship cargo and passenger service continued to receive a small grant for carrying mails to San Francisco. At the same time the Ministry of Colonies negotiated with Messageries Maritimes in 1922 to connect France, Fort de France in the West Indies, Papeʻete, and Nouméa, thus completing the French colonial route between the Caribbean, the Pacific, and the Indian Ocean.[38] The *Ville de Tamatave* made a pilot voyage at the slow rate of 11 knots and became the first vessel to link Tahiti directly with France since the war. Regular Messageries vessels began to call every two months from May 1924.

It was not always easy to provide cargo space for the colony's produce: Tahiti had to take whatever was available after loading at Vila and Nouméa. But when the colony's San Francisco and Auckland services were threatened in the 1930s by the intense competition between American lines and Union Steamship, an alternative route which did not depend on foreign contracts was available. Loss of copra cargoes to the United States in 1934 and 1935 finally determined Union Steamship to end their passenger and cargo run from Sydney to San Francisco via Auckland and Papeʻete, in 1936, though the company continued to send occasional freighters from

Australian and New Zealand ports. Messageries Maritimes increased its tonnages to cope with the extra business.

Rivet's land legislation of 1923 lowered fees for the issue of property titles based on published claims. It left intact the appeals procedure through district councils and the Tahitian Appeals Court; but it also introduced the possibility of the legal auction and sale of lands in "joint ownership" *(licitation)* instead of fractioning automatically the share of each coproprietor. If one proprietor wished to sell, "group transfers became the rule, and division in kind the exception."[39]

The full implications of this encouragement of land transfer were not immediately realized, and they depended on local investment in land. In the 1920s and early 1930s, the market for certain types of land in Tahiti, Mo'orea, and the Leeward Islands improved. The rich littoral with its possibilities for coconut stands, vanilla crops, and coffee was most in demand. By 1932, Acting Governor Bouchet considered that land alienation had gone far enough and passed a decree extending administrative control over all land transactions, even those between French citizens.[40] More rigid regulations on development before approval of title were also introduced to discourage speculation. In 1933 there were further signs of serious land shortage among rural Tahitians, and the administration took the unusual step of purchasing sections of valley and plateau land as public domain for redistribution by sale and donation to heads of families and returned servicemen.[41] The following year, a new decree by Governor Montagné reaffirmed the regulatory role of the administration in preventing alienation for indebtedness (ostensibly to Chinese); and at the same time Article 7 of the decree made it easier for a coproprietor to dispose of inherited rights in land.

As one study of Tahitian land tenure has pointed out, this adaptation of the French Civil Code differed from metropolitan practice in that the text of local legislation permitted sales "even if this inheritance only covers one or several properties of the Estate or of the original co-proprietorship *(indivision)* and not the whole."[42] It was now possible to "pick the eyes" out of a suitable set of blocks by making a generous offer to one inheritor (who may not even have lived in the district); and if the family titles rested solely on a published claim without title deeds, the inheritor could obtain a court order for an auction of group assets.

The permutations of land alienation have never been fully examined in French Polynesia (least of all by the administration); but from postwar surveys of particular districts and from the records of Land Office registers, some indications of the general pattern of change are possible.[43] In Afareʻaitu and Papeari districts it has been noticed by researchers that a large percentage of transfers of land in the period 1890 to 1940 was by sale arising from *licitation* procedure or by simple contract *(sous seing privé)* to *demis*, French citizens, and foreigners.[44] The area of coconut plantation land is especially large in these transactions, and there is a high incidence of transfers before 1930, when produce prices were still fair and credit easier than in the period of the depression. In the example of Afareʻaitu district in Moʻorea, C. Rignon discerns speculation and property accumulation by Franco-Tahitians:

> These families are for the most part the product of marriages between an immigrant and a local village woman. The properties are as much as from 20 to more than 80 hectares. The families have acquired in the space of thirty years nearly 220 ha. in 48 lots, which makes up one third of the total superficial area of Afareʻaitu and its valley, and one half of the lots that have been property transactions. But in area these 48 lots make up 62 per cent of lots sold; 30 of the lots are situated in the coastal zone and on the south slope of the valley.[45]

In Papeari district, the largest percentage of all lands registered had already been alienated by the early 1950s.[46] Of forty-seven transfers negotiated before 1930, thirty-nine were with nonresidents of the district; and this "absenteeism" helps to account for the widespread practices of squatting and sharecropping for vanilla and copra. In Punaʻauia and Paʻea districts, it is claimed that "the *demis* hold the largest share in the form of large estates. These properties, acquired between 1880 and 1920, make up the great coconut plantations of the coastal plain and are evidence of an older urban influence [from Papeʻete] on real estate development and agricultural investment as indirect proof of claims."[47]

A partial examination of district registers for sales, donations, and inheritance for Punaʻauia confirms the antiquity and the latter-day intensity of land alienation in specific resource zones of high value.[48] Of some 133 property titles traced through the intricacies of multiple transfers, some 78 went back to the original registration and claims system of the 1850s and 1860s; the remainder had passed through at least three or four proprietors between the 1890s and the period of examination (1961). Typical of European and *demi* holdings were the 9 hectares bought (with the governor's permission) by Charles Nordhoff as thirteen adjacent lots in 1936. These had been transferred, in turn, by sale and by inheritance by both French settlers and Tahitians in the 1920s in four main "accumulations" of title registration. Some lots went farther back in time to short-lived speculations by settlers in the nineteenth century and to acquisitions made by the Caisse Agricole in the 1860s. But not all such titles were acquired so easily. In another example, a land block (Atitupua) sold to a Franco-Tahitian family in 1942 was traced back through two sales and three legacies (all by Tahitians) to a disputed inheritance of land already registered and sold in the nineteenth century.[49]

Land records are also a measure of social mobility, as well as a tribute to the legal ingenuity of officials and settlers to circumvent or work through the system of multiple-claims tenure obtaining in Tahiti. In general, it is possible to argue that the pattern of land tenure changes begun by the French administration between 1852 and 1887, and again in the early 1930s, had the effect of safeguarding islanders' tenure rights by enshrining multiple inheritance in the archives. And this claim would seem to be supported by the archaic state of land tenure survey and registration immediately after the Second World War (see Table 11). They were also saved from loss of land by an unwillingness to make large colonial concessions; a plan by Rivet for an agricultural company on Nukuhiva in 1927 was not approved by the Ministry of Colonies.[50]

But island computations of tenure are blunt instruments for discerning historical patterns of change. All that can be said of the state of registration by the end of the Second World War is that there were remarkably wide differences from group to group in the amount of land surveyed by the Service des Domaines. Nearly all the Leeward Islands had been completed and very little of the Tuamotu. The number of titles issued for Tahiti and Mo'orea, between 1852 and the 1940s, numbered 18,700.[51] Only half these claims had been surveyed; and it would be safe to say that the nine thousand or so "private properties" represented in this cumulative effort to equate ownership with area were mostly for estates in Pape'ete and around the fertile shoreline.

TABLE 11

French Polynesia: Land Tenure Survey, 1950

Division	Total Area (hectares)	Hectares Surveyed	%	Number of Surveyed Lots	Number of Unsurveyed Lots
Tahiti, Mo'orea, dependencies	122,385	47,485	38.79	9,306	10,060
Leewards	41,455	39,255	94.89	3,306	3
Australs	15,775	6,800	43.1	2,567	2,376
Marquesas	97,540	32,000	33.83	708	4,570
Tuamotu	75,700	3,000	3.96	995	20,152
Mangareva	13,170	nil	nil	nil	4,435
Totals	366,325	129,540	35.36	16,882	41,596

Source: Bureau des Terres (Pape'ete): Tableaux comparatifs (MS).

But as later surveys recognized (particularly that made by Jean Roucaute in 1951), there were other forms of usehold tolerated and operating by unwritten agreement between Tahitian families of co-proprietors, between absentee proprietors and *métayers*, and between proprietors and squatters. Moreover, it is clear that the market for produce and land which encouraged investment from the 1890s (and earlier for sugar and cotton) also encouraged cash-cropping by Tahitians and a great deal of redistribution in limited and specific produce zones. The administration was aware of this piecemeal transfer to French settlers, foreign settlers, and Franco-Tahitians and attempted to slow it down in the early 1930s. Many of the new Franco-Tahitian proprietors also mitigated the economic effects of transfer by refraining from dispossessing squatters and arranging sharecropping.

The objective of much of this later French legislation was also to prevent indebtedness to Chinese and foreclosures arising from the failure of produce prices after 1930. Other decrees in 1926 had limited the rate of interest on loans to 8 percent and stipulated that credit agreements had to be notarized and pass through the Bank of Indo-China or the Caisse Agricole or, finally, through the offices of divisional administrators. There was even a measure to require all accounts to be kept in French, but this had to be relaxed after protests by the Chinese community.[52]

Yet it is far from clear that the Chinese were the principal beneficiaries of land transfers in the first half of the century, apart from the auction of SCO properties. A better indication of the distribution of agricultural wealth in terms of production (and political power) can be found in the measures taken by the administration, in conjunction with local government bodies, to meet the economic crisis of the 1930s.

The territory's trade and revenues continued to depend on a narrow range of exports throughout the interwar years.[53] Copra production and export for sale followed a steadily rising curve from 1910 to 1940, with two important price falls in 1921–1922 and 1927–1936. A rise in internal consumption of coconut production also decreased slightly the amount of copra available for export. In general, deteriorating prices from 1929 onward fell to about one-quarter the level for 1900, allowing for devaluation of the franc. But much of this loss in the terms of trade was made up by the quadrupling of copra tonnages between 1900 and 1940 (see Figure 3). Vanilla exports and prices were wildly erratic over the whole period. Production fell, and so did exports, between 1910 and 1930, and then rose quite sharply in the decade before 1940.[54] The price at constant dollar level (1934) was as high as $21.20 per ton in 1924 and as low as $1.33 in 1933. Taken together with copra, vanilla made up the bulk of receipts from annual exports of produce.

F.o.b. Values	1910	1913	1924	1932	1942
% from vanilla	24	40	38	44	42
% from copra	53	44	52	50	38
% from other produce	23	16	10	6	14

Source: After C. Robineau in *Travaux et Documents d'ORSTOM*, 24.

Of the other resources from island markets, shell provided a decreasing return. Though the quantities exported sometimes reached as much as a thousand tons, they were usually between 300 and 600 tons annually. Not till 1930 did phosphates make much impact on the balance of trade, when this export accounted for 20 percent of f.o.b. values and rose to 36 percent in 1940.

The annual budget of the administration also continued to squeeze as much as possible from indirect taxes on trade, but it did not keep pace with the value of total trade in the 1920s (because of political resistance). Despite some increase of duties, more particularly on phosphates, and a new tax on dwellings (constructed from imported materials) in 1930, the budget had a deficit of 5 million francs in 1931.[55] The cost of general administration had risen to 18 million francs (at current values), mainly because of the excessive numbers of metropolitan and local officials recruited since the war. Tahiti's promised share of a 15 million franc loan to carry out the port expansion planned in 1913 was placed in jeopardy because of the high cost of servicing the loan.

Worse, by the end of 1931 the full effects of the world recession were beginning to be felt. The Chamber of Commerce came out against increased duties and warned that "poverty" *(misère)*, as measured by its own estimate of the retail index, was spreading among the rural population of the territory.[56] Governor Jore made an unusually outspoken critique of past incompetence, while the deficit rose by another million francs. In 1932, Colonial Inspector

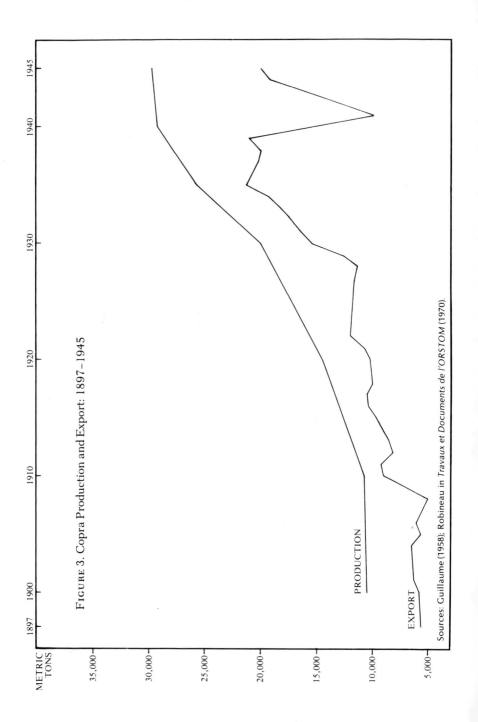

FIGURE 3. Copra Production and Export: 1897–1945

Sources: Guillaume (1958); Robineau in *Travaux et Documents de l'ORSTOM* (1970).

Caseaux met the chamber and struck a bargain: in return for an agreed rise in import and export duties from the trading community in order to service the loan for public works, he urged that French Polynesia participate in the new system of protective tariffs for French colonial produce, as outlined in the law of 31 March 1931. At the same time, insistence on more adequate representation of French interests, without sacrificing them to the uncertainties of General Council elections, produced a plan for Economic and Financial Delegations of seven members from the municipality, the Chambers of Commerce and Agriculture, the Uturoa Municipal Council, three officials from the Marquesas, the Tuamotu, and Mo'orea, and three members elected by the district councils of Tahiti, Mo'orea, and the Tuamotu.[57]

The loan was finally approved in 1933, though little of this money was available for local contracts till two years later. But outright subsidies to the budget amounting to 13 million francs were paid by France between 1932 and 1934, and smaller credits of around 300,000 francs a year continued to assist the colony till 1940. This was not the only advantage of the metropolitan connection. Messageries Maritimes was obliged to lower its freight rates to 250 francs a ton in 1930. An agricultural cooperative with credits from the Bank of Indo-China began to handle bulk exports of copra and vanilla for small growers in 1930, amounting to just over 1 million francs in value for the first year.[58] All of this was sent to France on the *Ville de Verdun*, and the copra amounted to 1,700 tons (11 percent of copra exports).

The trend toward French protection and a monopoly of the local market was confirmed by Caseaux's negotiations and an agreement in 1933 that 60 percent of French Polynesian copra would go to France in return for a system of bonus payments *(primes)* to be paid to producers from the proceeds of high import duties in France on produce of foreign origin.[59] At the end of the first year of payment in 1934, producers got an extra 90 francs per ton (£1.10s. Australian). This was not as much as had been agreed—New Caledonia and the New Hebrides received higher bonuses—and there were difficulties in deciding how much should be shared with the local budget. There had also been some stockpiling as a speculation against future prices and a rise in the bonus; but it was paid to all producers, large and small, and not just to French nationals. By

1936, the bonus had risen to 120 francs a ton and the local French support price for the Pape'ete market was 90 to 95 centimes per kilo (£16 Australian per ton), enough to make local producers the envy of the British Pacific.[60]

For the first time, in 1932, the French metropolitan share of the local export of produce amounted to 40.28 percent of current values, compared with 24.7 percent exported to the United States.[61] In 1936 this share rose to 70.8 percent as France took all copra and most of the vanilla. Imports from France also rose to a third of invoice values (though much of this was materials for the public works program).

Compared with this neomercantilist underpinning, the antics of the administration during the collapse of the Kong Ah company in 1933, or the allegations of bribery and corruption following the arrest and imprisonment of Emmanuel Rougier in 1936, are marginal to the interests of local metropolitan and Franco-Tahitian groups.[62] Very few, if any, of the local politicians were implicated in these affairs; and even within the Chinese community, while the bankruptcy divided the Kuomintang association, it did not reduce the philanthropic or economic position of merchants associated with Chin Foo or the Sin Ngi Tong association. Equally marginal, compared with the politics of economic dependency on France, were the occasional elections of deputies to the Conseil Supérieur—unknown candidates from Corsica or French Guiana who attracted no more than a few thousand votes from electors in the territory.

The local assembly formed from the colony's commercial interest groups had no more than consultative powers over the budget, but it had two advantages not shared by previous representative bodies. Its permanent commission, meeting between sessions of the Economic and Financial Delegations, was used by the administration to assist in the allocation of produce bonuses through the "Copra Conference" of 1935 and 1936. It also contained a small indirectly elected element from the district councils; and these members were responsible, at a lower level, for pressure for *primes* from the producers.

The composition of district councils, moreover, had greatly changed from the late-nineteenth-century chiefs, or presidents, and *ra'atira* (Table 12). Five of the council presidents and a little under

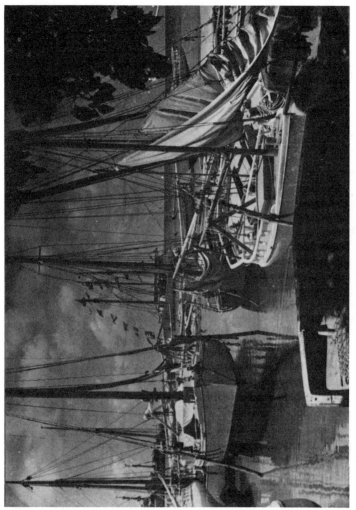

Tuamotu: Shell-diving and Trading Craft.

TABLE 12
District Council Membership: 1933–1939

	Presidents		Members *(Memo Tauturu* and *Tumu)*	
District	French Europeans*	French Tahitians	French Europeans*	French Tahitians
Tahiti				
Fa'a'a	1		3	1
Puna'auia		1	3	1
Pa'ea	1		3	1
Papara		1	2	2
Matai'ea		1	1	3
Papeari		1†	2	2
Afa'ahiti	1		4	
Vairao	1			4
Teahupo'o		1	2	2
Tautira		1		4
Pueu		1	1	3
Hitia'a-Fa'aone		1	1	3
Tiarei-Maha'ena		1		4
Papeno'o		1		4
Mahina		1	1	3
Arue		1	1	3
Pirae		1	3	1
Mo'orea				
Afare'aitu		1		4
Ha'apiti	1		2	2
Papeto'ai		1		4
Teavaro-Teaharoa		1	2	2
Totals	5	16	31	53

* First or second generation.
† Chinese.

a third of the "ordinary" and "assistant" members were Europeans, usually of one or two generations standing in the community and all Tahitian-speakers. Other presidents were identifiably Tahitian or *demis*. One was a *demi* of Chinese-Tahitian parentage who had fought in the First World War and served on the Papeari council from 1919 to 1953.* Among the ordinary and assistant members there are six identifiable *demis*.

The main qualification for membership was the status of *fatu fenua* (landowner). The term *ra'atira* with its connotation of pre-

---

* Cho Chong Ah Min (1896–1962), *Médaille Militaire* and *Légion d'Honneur*.

scribed status within extended families was dropped. There were still a few chiefs, such as Teri'iero'o of Puna'auia, though none of the Salmon or Brander or Pomare titleholders of the nineteenth century survived into the structure of patronage politics and elected representation that was founded on transfer of land and dependency on French brokerages, communications, and subsidies by the late 1930s.

THE POLITICAL CRISIS

More closely linked than it had ever been to metropolitan France, Tahiti registered immediately the shock waves of events in Europe from September 1939. Governor Chastenet de Géry, who had been two years in the colony, continued the public works program and hurried through the coordination of the education and health services which an improved budget allowed. But he had meager defenses at his command.[63] If anything, Tahiti was in a weaker position than in 1914. There were, in theory, five thousand reservists, but there were no arms for them, and none were called up for local duties as Governor Fawtier had done. There was a small force of Colonial Infantry—some two hundred men, the old sailing vessel *Zélée* resurrected as a gunboat, two 65-mm batteries, and a 47-mm gun "on a small truck."[64] The naval airbase on Fare Ute had two twin-engined seaplanes (CAMS 55) and a single-engined CAMS 37, operational since 1937. For much of the period up till early July 1940, a small 2,000-ton sloop of war, the *Dumont d'Urville*, under the command of Captain Toussaint de Quiévrecourt, was on station as part of a tour of duty in the Pacific from Saigon. But the outer islands and the phosphate works at Makatea were reported to be "defenceless."[65]

The fall of France in May 1940 and the armistice of 23 June left French governors in the Pacific nominally responsible to Pétain's new government at Bordeaux. It was far from clear whether they would accept the implication of Vichy's compromise with the late enemy, but in the immediate trauma of defeat they temporized until the consequences might become clear.[66] Neither in Tahiti nor in New Caledonia was there any immediate response to the appeal made by an unknown soldier, General de Gaulle, on 18 June.[67] Under pressure from Quiévrecourt and the naval commandant, Grange, Chastenet de Géry issued a proclamation on 24 June promising to continue the fight alongside Great Britain; this statement was followed by a more ambiguous "Notice" the following day urging calm and patience.[68]

At the British consulate, Consul F. Edmonds kept open channels with London and Wellington through a better radio transmitter than the one possessed by the administration. He had his own peculiar appreciation of de Géry's situation, a mixture of sympathy for the man and contempt for his government; and he requested Wellington to send a warship "with a view to fostering present pro-British as against anti-American feeling."[69] From 27 June he was aware that the Germans had been using French naval codes in the name of Admiral Darlan and he passed on this information to the governor.[70] While it is unlikely that this is the explanation for Darlan's order to continue the fight, issued on 20 June, naval intelligence at Wellington and the New Zealand government were cautious about commiting Union Steamship vessels to the eastern Pacific without a clarification of the intentions of the commander of the *Dumont d'Urville.*

This strategic consideration for the safety of communications received no satisfactory answer from Tahiti, where a Foreign Office circular of 27 June urged French territories to ally with the British Empire—on the grounds that the Vichy government was without a "mandate" to surrender them to the Germans—and promised to "cover the payment of salaries and pensions" of civil and military officials.[71] But Chastenet de Géry (through Edmonds) wanted to know what sort of "French government" existed outside of France and what kind of assistance was required. To this the Foreign Office replied that the British government recognized de Gaulle "as leader of all Free Frenchmen":

> This statement does not mean that General de Gaulle has been recognised as the head or organiser of an alternative government or that His Majesty's Government have ceased to have dealings with the French Chargé d'Affaires in London who still represents the Bordeaux Government.[72]

It was not difficult for de Géry to take shelter behind this equivocal statement through the early part of July and to refuse any outright adherence to a military resistance which the British government itself seemed hesitant to recognize. But this was not the last word on the subject (as Chastenet de Géry has implied in his personal account of events in 1940).[73] For, on 3 July, the Foreign Office clarified British views and left the question of political support for de Gaulle to be decided by Frenchmen in overseas territories.[74] This test of local opinion was not acceptable to de Géry, who looked on the exiled general as "an upstart and a traitor to his country."[75]

More immediately, there were pressing questions of supply to be settled. Edmonds showed the governor cables* from the senior naval staff officer, Wellington, stating that the *Dumont d'Urville* would not be stopped and that Allied shipping would proceed to Tahiti, providing the governor would give an assurance that Pape'ete was a "safe port." Unless this was given, it was made clear that there would be no oil for French vessels at Suva in transit to Nouméa and Tahiti. Edmonds extracted a signed statement from de Géry and de Quiévrecourt that British shipping would not be attacked; and it was agreed to unload a cargo of nickel ore from the *Ville d'Amiens* (whose Senegalese crew had not been paid and were to cause trouble for everybody in the weeks that followed).

On 6 July, the *Dumont d'Urville* cleared for sea, her destination New Caledonia, though this was not generally known at Tahiti. De Géry managed to confirm arrangements made at Sydney to open the colony's sterling account (held in London) and to purchase supplies. These were held up, and de Géry, "utterly exhausted, mentally and physically," complied with instructions from Vichy and ordered the British consulate to be closed on 20 July, though he did not go so far as to intern the consul or seize his codes.[76] Edmonds retired to a house outside Pape'ete. He was allowed to cable Canberra, but not Wellington, and he continued to receive the governor socially.[77] He informed the Australian government in two short, naive, and misleading reports that the population at large would welcome British intervention and a protectorate "similar to that enjoyed by Tonga."[78]

In these conditions there was no "gentleman's agreement" with the British Pacific dominions (as the governor has since claimed).[79] Throughout July and August there was uncertainty about supplies which did not arrive, and there existed a political vacuum left by

---

* Not all of these cables are reproduced in de Géry's book.

de Géry's irresoluteness which amateur politicians attempted to fill.

For beneath the tragicomic events of Tahiti's *ralliement* in 1940 there were deeper issues which the fall of France threw into relief. The excessive centralization of an administration which depended so closely on Paris had been compounded by the decline of representative institutions since the late nineteenth century and by the gap between the bulk of the population and French officials at Pape'ete. To some extent the channels of communication had been improved by official Tahitian newspapers; and in the marketing of island produce, welfare projects, and public works, there had been a considerable advance in French official patronage. But, on the whole, "representation" at an official level was limited to French commercial interests through the formal institutions of the delegations and within the municipality of Pape'ete, together with some informal influence from the hierarchies of the Protestant and Catholic churches. When a crisis arose which called for a consensus after explanation and debate, few officials had the administrative will to offer their policies to public scrutiny through the means available to them.

There were, too, deep divisions of opinion imported with metropolitan officials from the troubled capital of the Third Republic. The compromises of the Popular Front were not acceptable to all service chiefs and departmental heads, many of whom (especially in the local medical corps) leaned towards the anticommunist and antisemitic program of patriotic revival and self-assertion which merged into Pétain's "National Revolution." It was possible, moreover, for French patriots of very different political convictions to take opposing standpoints on how to preserve France from chaos during the occupation. Memories of 1871 competed with instinctive reactions to the shame of capitulation. But if Vichy had to bargain and the French metropolitan civil service carried on as best it could, were officials in French colonies to follow this lead? When the City fell, who was to say where authority lay?

Different French territories gave different answers to this question. The history of their reactions to the fall of France is, as yet, unwritten, compared with the historiography of the occupation; but much would seem to have depended on the attitudes and personalities of local governors. In the New Hebrides, at Port Vila, the

French resident commissioner, Henri Sautot, had no difficulty in rallying his half of the Anglo-French condominium on 18 June. Following the Churchill–de Gaulle agreement of 27 August, most of the Equatorial African territories declared for the Free French movement, but Senegal did not, and the Allied naval operation at Dakar in September failed to capture this French West African center. On 19 September, in the Pacific, an Australian warship assisted Sautot and pro–de Gaulle settlers to neutralize and remove a pro-Vichy administration at Nouméa and encourage the withdrawal of the *Dumont d'Urville* from New Caledonian waters to Saigon.[80]

At Tahiti, Governor Chastenet de Géry was temperamentally incapable of seeking any kind of mandate for his authority within the structure of representation allowed by the governor's council and the delegations. Such a consultation could hardly have been interpreted as "autonomist"; and it would have done much to break down the isolation of the executive from the opinions debated by other sectors of the community. In the tomblike silence of Government House, other voices, less informed, were listened to instead.

On about 10 August a Pétainist "Comité des Français d'Océanie" issued a wild proclamation rallying patriots and condemning Jews and Freemasons.[81] A few days later, the *Wairuna* arrived from Sydney with three months' supplies which raised morale at Pape'ete and relieved pressure on the executive for a commitment to the Allies and de Gaulle. For a time officials could still temporize, and the *Journal Officiel* printed decrees emanating from both the Pétain and the Daladier-Réynaud administrations, while a local pro-Vichy committee inscribed some sixty names in its support.

But on 19 August, when the Economic and Financial Delegations met, there was a sharp reaction against official apathy. By unvoiced agreement, the officials, settlers, and chiefs present dispensed with the formal definition of their role as a purely consultative body and widened the area of discussion to include the pressing political issues of the day. Chastenet de Géry withdrew from the debate; and although the delegations did not pronounce on his authority, the way was left open for the formation of a Free French Committee from about 26 August which forced the policies of the executive into the open.

The composition of the committee reflected both the extent and the limits of local support for de Gaulle.[82] It included the three civilian members of the governor's council, Édouard Ahnne, Émile Martin, G. Bambridge (also mayor of Papeʻete), and G. Lagarde, five municipal councillors, the president of the Chamber of Agriculture, and the four chiefs who represented Tahiti, Moʻorea, and the Tuamotu in the delegations. There were four departmental heads *(chefs de service)*, the administrator, M. Sénac, and the medical administrator, Émile de Curton. In addition, there were ten or so settlers, retired officials, and others, some of whom provided effective leadership. In particular, Jean Gilbert, a reserve naval pilot and son-in-law of Martin, a communist mechanic named Davio, and a future Tahitian politician, Pouvanaʻa, were instrumental at different levels in securing support or neutralizing potential opposition. But none of the senior naval or military officers joined the movement, and the bulk of the corps of medical administrators was openly hostile to it.

On 25 August, de Géry showed his hand by proclaiming a Vichy law of 13 August 1940 against illegal associations and requesting the withdrawal of administrators such as de Curton and Sénac from the embryonic Gaullist movement. On 30 August, a deputation consisting of the civilian members of the governor's council and the unofficial members of the delegations confronted de Géry and secured his reluctant permission for a referendum. This was followed up by a petition on 31 August—headed by Teriʻi Nui O Tahiti (Marau's eldest daughter), some thirty or so civic personalities, and a signatory for the unruly crew of the *Ville d'Amiens*—requesting adherence to de Gaulle.

The "referendum" was hastily organized on 1 September by Sénac, and a militia was formed from Tahitians and others who donned a uniform of workers' overalls and called themselves *les bleus*. The result of this essay in public consultation produced 5,564 votes for de Gaulle and 18 against.

Following this, on 2 September, Ahnne, Lagarde, Martin, and Bambridge formed a "Provisional Government," issuing their own proclamation to explain their aims, and called a meeting with the departmental heads of the administration. The aged Édouard Ahnne quietened their fears, and all the fourteen senior officials of the colony agreed to continue as usual. The naval commandant, Grange, refused and was replaced by Jean Gilbert, who won over the naval air arm officers and men and the crew of the *Zélée*. The naval armory was seized by Quartermasters Pommier and Vachot. But the attitude of the commander of the Colonial Infantry, Captain Félix Broche, who also had control of the police, was still a critical factor. His decision on 3 September to give the new administration his qualified support, in return for authority to form an infantry battalion, set the seal on de Géry's term of office.[83]

The *ralliement* was completed by a telegram to de Gaulle on 2 September which was relayed by Edmonds' consulate. De Gaulle replied on 7 September and the local military intendant, Mansard, was appointed governor. De Géry and a few naval officers who had not supported the coup embarked for Vancouver and France on 13 September.

It was not the first time a governor had been forced to leave Tahiti; but it was a novel expression of popular sentiment and clandestine organization through the unofficial Free French Committee and its fringe groups, combined with the civilians and businessmen of the governor's council. The presence of Ahnne lent a dignity and stability to the proceedings and helped to secure the Protestant Tahitian population. Great use was made of *Te Vea Maohi* to explain exactly who *Tenerara* de Gaulle was; Captain Broche used its pages to call up those eligible for military service; and there were long explanations of the significance of the Berlin Pact and the roles of Laval and Pétain in France. There had not been so much consultation with the districts since the years of elections for the General Council in the 1890s.

The economic situation of the colony, however, was still precarious. The New Zealand government held back Union Steamship vessels from calling, after the *Wairuna*, until the consulate was reopened. Without prior invitation, the cruiser *Achilles* appeared at Tahiti on 10 to 13 July with a government representative, R. T. G. Patrick, who made a careful inquiry into the conduct of Edmonds and his relationship with de Géry. A retired consul general, George Gorton, was called up from Taravao to act as official link between the consulate and the provisional government. But New Zealand could not offer a market for the territory's produce. As stocks of copra accumulated, the local price fell to 35 centimes a kilo. A way out was not found till offers to buy were received from American brokers: "The credit for the present move in the right direction," reported the British consul, "should go to the Chinese who took the initiative by direct negotiations with their Chinese confrères in America. European firms are now following suit and meeting the market, such as it is,"[84] At the same time, pressure on the Établissements Donald for requisitions of stock and price controls increased.

For, by the beginning of 1941, Mansard had retired from ill health and had been replaced by Dr. de Curton. Sénac organized the *bleus* into an armed militia, and some of the enthusiasm for the new regime began to wane when the corps of medical officers was placed under arrest along with three magistrates and a few minor officials. The Free French Committee melted away, and the delegations were not called together.[85] Plots real and imagined provoked stricter regulations during the ferment of political discussion among the French and *demi* population—but no clear proposals emerged for constitutional reform to end the state of emergency. In March 1941 an American squadron of two cruisers and four destroyers called unannounced and was well received. In April, three hundred Tahitian volunteers left on the *Monowai* to form part of the Pacific Battalion under Broche, which sailed for the Middle East from New Caledonia, along with other contingents, in May 1941.

But another crisis was in the making because of a deteriorating financial situation and some ill-conceived schemes by Sénac for a government monopoly of produce marketing to the exclusion of the Chinese community.[86] By March 1941, there were still 20,000 tons of copra and 160,000 tons of phosphate awaiting shipping; the Union Steamship subsidy of 325,000 francs had not been paid; and the exchange rate with sterling had not been fixed. The New Zealand representative, though he got on well enough with de Curton, had no powers to supply the kind of financial aid Tahiti had become accustomed to receiving from France. The possibility that New Zealand would send a fiscal officer before any such assistance was given only deepened the mistrust between Pape'ete and Wellington. French territory could not be treated like the Cook Islands.

The uneasy relationship was not improved by a "raid" on the British consulate on 30 May, when codes were endangered and Gorton temporarily replaced Edmonds (though this move was later approved by the Foreign Office).

More important from the point of view of internal support for the government was its policy over local resources. Sénac's plans for an administrative cooperative with its own fleet of schooners was promoted at the worst possible time—in the midst of the economic disarray of the territory's markets—and could not be financed except by increasing export duties on phosphates and by demanding "repatriation" of funds from phosphate sales overseas.

At this point, therefore, de Curton's administration would appear to have alienated influential supporters such as the Bambridge family and Lagarde. High Commissioner Sautot, who had been given a general authority over Free French interests in the Pacific, alerted the Western Pacific High Commission in Fiji and de Gaulle's Free French government in London. De Gaulle sent out Governor General Richard Brunot (who had "rallied" in the Cameroons) on a mission of inspection in June 1941. On his own initiative this professional proconsul assumed full powers, appointed his own officials, dissolved the Municipal Council, and arrested and interned on Mo'orea de Curton, Sénac, and other members of the administration. A new state of emergency was declared and Brunot took over the militia, which he expanded and formed into a personal praetorian guard—the Légion Valmy. Temporary Consul Gorton was also arrested, and Edmonds returned briefly to his post.

This fiasco was terminated by the arrival of Admiral d'Argenlieu, as Pacific high commissioner, on the *Triomphant* on 23 September, with orders to secure communications and defenses in eastern Polynesia. De Curton was sent to London, where he was cleared of Brunot's unreasonable and unfounded allegations; Brunot himself was hastily retired. With the entry of Japan and the United States into the war, there was no room for comic opera in the wings.

Brunot's replacement was Lieutenant-Colonel Georges Orselli, who ran the territory for just over four years till December 1945— one of the longest governorships and in many ways one of the most effective. He ruled with a firm hand, keeping the Légion Valmy up to strength by creating a special uniform and paying its legionaries 45 francs a day. A unit was sent to Borabora in 1943 to keep order during the construction of the U.S. airbase on the island. Internal security was also tightened up, and Consuls Archer and Cameron reported to the Prime Minister's Department in Wellington on suspects with contacts in San Francisco and Saigon.[87]

Moreover, with a rise in commodity prices in 1943 there was a rapid improvement in the colony's balance of payments. Orselli revived the Economic and Financial Delegations to plan the budget, and he arranged for the sale of all copra to the United States and Canada. Trade quickly recovered to prewar levels; and with far fewer personnel in the administration, hard-currency reserves were built up. The interisland medical services were restored, and money was available for investment in agriculture.

Toward the end of the war in Europe, there was, too, a promise of political advancement when the French Provisional National Committee met in Algiers in January 1944. There colonial reforms and a rather far-fetched project for imperial federation were debated. Orselli went to Algiers and returned in August to announce plans for a decentralization of powers from Paris to local governors, a locally elected assembly, recruitment of Tahitians to administrative posts, and the expansion of health and education services. He also negotiated new copra and vanilla agreements in Europe and the United States when the price rose to $67 per ton and the exchange rate was finally stabilized at 200 francs to the pound sterling. Prospects for political change and economic development had never looked better.

* * * * *

Judgments on the promise and fulfillment of these prospects for French Polynesia must be made in later studies of the territory. It will be for other historians, too, to decide how far there was a structural change in the institutions and organization of Tahitian society after 1945, or how far Tahitian folk memories of their immediate past in the nineteenth century account for elements of Tahitian "nationalism" at a later date.

The threads of historic continuity are many, though not always easily analyzed. Public ceremonial offers some evidence. September 1942 marked the centenary of French occupation of Tahiti, and the event was hardly remembered at all as a public occasion in French Polynesia. It was as though a whole series of official symbols, for so long accepted as a necessary part of Tahiti's political life and an expression of the formal cohesion of the many islands of the territory with Pape'ete and with France, suddenly seemed irrelevant. *Te Vea Maohi* devoted several pages instead to the two-year-old anniversary of the *ralliement* of 2 September, and not a line to the French protectorate of 1842 or to the Pomares.

It is possible that a new tradition and a new identity were in the making. For, on 9 September 1942, the first casualty list of the dead lost at Bir Hacheim was published. The names of one Franco-Tahitian and four Polynesians were printed in a short notice in the *Bulletin Officiel*. By the end of the war, the number had risen to ninety-four. The battalion had fought at El Alamein, in Italy, in northern France, and in the Vosges. In September 1945 they formed part of General Koenig's honor guard and took part in the ceremonial march through Paris.

The protectorate, therefore, was remembered in other ways. In 1943, Princess Teri'i Nui O Tahiti, one of the last tenuous links with the nineteenth-century *ari'i*, presented "with official sanction" a silken replica of the old Tahitian flag—red, white, and red—to the Tahitian contingent overseas, where it was flown as a battle flag with the Cross of Lorraine. After a hundred years, the Pomares were remembered by commitment to action and not by the dusty platitudes of a public anniversary. The flag returned as a potent symbol in local politics after the war.

But much else had survived from that distant past. The language had grown into a regional dialect, supplanting other dialects, and was itself transformed from an esoteric and unrecorded speech to the language of the churches, the markets, and (to a lesser extent) administration and politics. The hierarchy of priests and chiefs who once used it as an instrument of Tahitian religion and government had disappeared, giving way to a new elite which emerged in the late nineteenth century as the *ari'i* declined. There, too, the ranks of the old Anglo-Tahitian coterie had been broadened into a Franco-Tahitian segment of a population which began to recover demographically and which was geographically and socially mobile at the end of the interwar period.

The springs of these developments lay, for the most part, in the growth of commodity markets, in the market for land, and in the less commercial but persistent importation of ideas and religious institutions encouraged by traders, missionaries, and settlers. Islanders accepted these changes, where possible on their own terms, retaining at first the innovations and political structure of missionary and *ari'i* cooperation. When their terms concerning settlement, land values, and the pace of change were not accepted, the tensions of European contact were resolved by force, resulting in a redistribution of authority between chiefs and French naval officers. In practice, the theories of "protection" or "assimilation" were, perhaps, less important than the encouragement of continuous market exchanges. French rule provided a framework for an orderly penetration of capital, some technology, and some new ideas on political organization within a part of Oceania which was centered on Tahiti and its port. On the whole, too, the market for land had less serious results for the bulk of the island peasantry, if only because cash-cropping was preferred to wage labor. Through mismanaged policies, as much as by official protection, most productive resource zones, with the exception of some plantation land and mines at Makatea, still remained in the hands of the *Ta'ata fenua*.

But among this predominantly rural population both alien and evolved segments filled the place of the old leaders of Tahitian society as commercial and administrative intermediaries. By the Second World War they included a wide variety of immigrants from the outer islands, from Asia, and from Europe. As in other spheres of social behavior earlier in the market for goods and ideas, "assimilation" in French Polynesia has meant an incorporation of alien settlers into local folkways—so much so that the term "Tahitian" has gained an extensive and inclusive denotation, certainly by the 1940s, and perhaps earlier, which reflects this process of adjustment on the main island at several different levels of organization. The actions of the missionaries in the nineteenth century in consolidating both temporal and spiritual authority in Tahitian institutions under Pomare II gave a certain impetus to this process, though the relative autonomy of district and island churches ran counter, in practice, to the homogeneity suggested by the terms "kingdom" or "Etaretia." Government was an oligarchy of chiefs on each island, although the written codes and the Scriptures were adopted through eastern Polynesia and Tahitian pastors and deacons were influential well beyond their own shores. The elaboration of the Tahitian Synod, after the establishment of nominal French control in most islands of the territory, was a further step toward centralization. The Catholic Church, however, remained divided between two bishoprics and was much less of a supplement to French administration than might be expected from the early history of its foundation in the region. Mormons and Kanitos furthered the tendency to structural centralization, similar to the Protestant conferences and the legal and financial departments of French colonial government. But all the pressures of European direction, it might be argued, sat fairly lightly on the shoulders of church congregations, chiefs and peasantry, and those island entrepreneurs deep in debt to traders.

There were variations because of distance and proximity to the capital. The administration itself was inevitably Tahitian-centered after the initial experiment in the Marquesas. Policies tried out in Tahiti were extended through Tahitian *mutoi* in the Tuamotu and the Austral Islands and through officials and magistrates who looked to Pape'ete's offices and courts for guidance and promotion. Land tenure legislation was a fairly good example of the consequences of a slavish adoption of Tahitian examples and the practical limits to this functional and legal "assimilation" of the periphery to the center.

Tahiti was also a central market. The network of commerce and debt that were features of a relatively underdeveloped economy had been extended by traders, schooner captains, and islanders to the remotest atolls since the 1830s. The impetus given to the production of a few staples by the availability of cash, credit, and merchandise resulted in a secondary dependency on Pape'ete by every other inhabited portion of the territory (and even by some islands outside the area of formal French rule). Interisland trade also increased the mobility that had existed since the late eighteenth century and had been a feature of the recruitment of islanders as whaling crews in the 1840s. There were Tuamotuan enclaves in Tahiti from the early nineteenth century, and large numbers of Leeward Islanders from the 1880s. Along with Chinese, some Vietnamese, Gilbert Islanders, and a large number of European settlers, immigrant Polynesians from the outliers gradually made Tahiti a local metropolis and transformed Pape'ete from a roadstead for shipping into a municipality of heterogeneous cultures.

That municipality and its subordinate districts, moreover, came under European control at a relatively early date in the history of European expansion in the South Pacific. Only New Zealand had been annexed prior to 1842; and other comparable island groups went through a longer transitional period of informal empire before partition and formal occupation. The protectorate itself was a novelty in French imperial experience—a compromise adapted from a British example in the Mediterranean and applied to a Pacific archipelago to satisfy the legal and diplomatic proprieties of European powers.

It was a difficult formula to apply in practice, not merely because it ran counter to French colonial experience elsewhere in the nineteenth century but more because the local society could not be isolated from other sources of social and economic change. What if the protected executive, paid for from French funds, chose to be assisted by advisers who were not French? Annexed status, too, and the experiment in legal and institutional assimilation were compromised by the existence of French settlers as an enclave in a foreign and Polynesian community. The political logic of assimilation stopped short of allowing the new "citizens" a preponderant voice in the General Council or other organs of representative government. Legal formulas were, in any case, a very inexact definition of the changing relationship between a huge area of islands which was open to foreign trade and a distant metropolitan power which was unwilling to withdraw and unable to speed up the pace of social change by education and employment in the conditions of local finance and investment.

For much of the period, therefore, French overrule looks like a caretaker government for the trading houses and shipping companies of the United States, the British colonies, and Germany. On any rough cost-benefit analysis it is hard to see what France gained in the classic terms of "economic imperialism" or even for the more atavistic urges of the "national prestige" school of French expansionists. Most French capital came in the form of support costs for the officials and materials required to establish the post by war, and to maintain it, on a reduced scale, throughout the long decades of marginal development by foreign entrepreneurs. For the sterling equivalent of a few thousand pounds a year (including naval defense in the Pacific), the French government underwrote a market for foreign enterprise, missionary conversions, and the islanders' access to the material goods and ideas of the outside world.

This pattern of evolution and its assumptions were disrupted by the First World War, which hardened French attitudes to foreign trading houses and eliminated the largest of them. Moreover, the economic crisis of the 1930s accelerated the creation of metropolitan and imperial links with France and other French possessions in the Far East and the Pacific. The neomercantilism implicit in much of France's late-nineteenth-century fiscal legislation, and avoided by French patriots in Tahiti, was applied and accepted to protect local producers in 1931. The budget deficit was reduced by a series of grants-in-aid that matched the outlay for the posts in 1843. The emergence of a new segment of Franco-Tahitian planters and businessmen who had taken advantage of land transfers from the 1890s assisted this late gallicization of the colony's economic structure.

The events of 1940 severely tested these new links and the loyalties of islanders to a defeated power. Alternative markets were found; but there was no suggestion for an alternative European administration, provided the implications of widened consultation between government and Euro-Tahitian interest groups were accepted, though, at the same time, a new awareness of a "Tahitian" identity probably crystallized in the turbulent debate that led to the overthrow of the executive and in the experience of Tahitian servicemen abroad.

NOTES

ABBREVIATIONS

AAÉ	Archives des Affaires Étrangères [2]
Adm.	Admiralty [18]
AM	Archives de la Marine [1]
AMP	Archives Musée de Pape'ete [4]
ANSOM	Archives Nationales, Section Outre-mer [3]
Arrêté	*Les Arrêtés du Gouverneur des Établissements français de l'Océanie*
BM	British Museum [7]
BOÉFO	*Bulletin officiel des ÉFO*
CMA	Calvinistic Methodist Archives [9]
CSC	Congrégation des Sacrés-Coeurs [10]
CO	Colonial Office [18]
Disp. USC	Dispatches from United States Consuls [11]
FO	Foreign Office [6] [18]
HL	Hocken Library [13]
HLUH	Hamilton Library, University of Hawaii [11]
HMCSL	Hawaiian Mission Children's Society Library [12]
HRA	*Historical Records of Australia*
JOÉFO	*Journal officiel des Établissements français de l'Océanie*
JORF	*Journal officiel de la Republique française*
JSMÉ	*Journal de la Société des Missions Évangéliques*
JSO	*Journal de la Société des Océanistes*
LMS	London Missionary Society [15]

ML   Mitchell Library [16]
MAÉ   Ministère des Affaires Étrangères
PMB   Pacific Manuscripts Bureau [11]
SCO   Société Commerciale de l'Océanie [20]
SMÉ   Société des Missions Évangéliques [19]
SS   South Seas (LMS series) [15]
TBCP   Tahiti British Consulate Papers [6] [16]

Chapter 1: THE MARKET AT MATAVAI BAY

1. Or *Ma'ohi*. The term is recorded in Davies' *Tahitian and English Dictionary* (1851), but I have not seen it used in other nineteenth-century records, prior to a letter by Bishop Jaussen dated 10 February 1850: CSC/58. Even thereafter the more usual term was Kanaka *(Ta'ata)* for Tahitians and other islanders. For a definition of *Ma'ohi*, see Oliver (1974:6); and for a discussion of such terms, see O'Reilly (1975:33).

2. Oliver (1974:588).

3. Corney (1915:5–6).

4. Morrison (1935:201); Oliver (1974:213).

5. Turnbull (1813:262). Turnbull states that the tribute was paid to Pomare.

6. Oliver (1974:1083–1090).

7. Journal of William Wales, in Beaglehole (1961:799).

8. Robertson (1948:142–143).

9. Robertson (1948:243).

10. By Purea and Amo of Papara in Teva-i-uta (Adams 1901:109); for the significance of this incorporation, see Cook in Oliver (1974:1215, 1233).

11. Robertson (1948:185).

12. Journal of William Wales, in Beaglehole (1961:794).

13. Robertson (1948:146).

14. Robertson (1948:200).

15. Adm. 53/335: W. J. Stone, Journal, entry for 8 January 1792. There are some early lists of exports to Tahiti in Customs 8/19 for the 1820s, indicating the consistency of types of trade goods.

16. Beaglehole (1955:118).

17. Beaglehole (1961:800).

18. Beaglehole (1955:118).

19. Corney (1915:127).

20. Beaglehole (1961:411).

21. Jacquier (1960:117–146).

22. Beaglehole (1967:pt. I, 223).

23. For a discussion of this staple, see Oliver (1974:270–275).

24. Ellis (1829:II, 284–286); Oliver (1974:304–305); Corney (1915: 272–273, 282–284).

25. Adm. 55/6: Lt. Portlock MS "Remarks," f. 138; Vancouver (1801: 334).

26. Vancouver (1801:II, 38–41); [William House], *A Letter from the South Seas* . . . 1792; Maude (1968:178–232).

27. Maude (1968:227–232).

28. Beaglehole (1967:pt. II, 239); Bligh (1937:I, 394).

29. Maude (1968:208–211); compare the more cautious assessment of Oliver (1974:1281–1287).

30. Maude (1968:224).

31. Adm. 55/6: Lt. Portlock MS "Remarks," 11 April 1792, f. 134.

32. *HRA*, Series 1, 1914–1915: 3, Pomare to King, 10 August 1801, 333.

33. *HRA*, Series 1, 1914–1915: 3, Jefferson to King, 9 August 1802, 725–726.

34. Turnbull (1813:270).

35. Turnbull (1813:307–308).

36. For a more detailed account of their influence, see Oliver (1974: chap. 28).

37. Morrison (1935). There were also offspring of at least four of the mutineers, and their wives were known to Vancouver's officers.

38. Davies (1961:108 n.).

39. Turnbull (1813:292–295).

40. Roe (1967:xlvii–xlix).

41. Corney (1915:128).

42. Beaglehole (1961:799, 805).

43. Corney (1919:32–33).

44. Corney (1919:98).

45. Turnbull (1813:332).

46. Turnbull (1813:337).

47. Or Toerero. Adm. 55/32: Lt. Baker, Log, f. 96; and [Bell], Journal, f. 108. He had been to England on a vessel employed in the fur trade and had two years' schooling.

48. Turnbull (1813:262, 266–267).

49. Bligh, in Oliver (1974:1284); compare [Bell], Journal, f. 116.

50. Turnbull (1813:136).

51. Oliver (1974:1286–1287).

52. Apart from the sources surveyed in Oliver (1974), this section is based on the manuscripts listed in Newbury (1967b:"Calendar of Docu-

ments") and some materials in the unpublished journals of Bligh and Vancouver's officers; for the period after 1797, the LMS journals and correspondence provide the main evidence.

53. Corney (1913:307).

54. Corney (1913:319).

55. Newbury (1967b:490); Oliver (1974:993–1014).

56. Oliver (1974:1234).

57. Newbury (1967b:487). Ha'amanemane (Tutaha, Mauri) arrived in 1788.

58. SS 8/2, Platt, 1 August 1831; Chesnau (1928).

59. Newbury (1967b:492–497).

60. BM Add. MSS, 32641, Menzies, Journal, f. 160; compare Vancouver (1801:I, 141).

61. BM Add. MSS, 17545, Puget, Log, v. 46.

62. [Bell], Journal, f. 122.

63. SS 4/2, Crook, 3 October 1823.

64. Henry (1928:70).

65. Ellis (1829:II, 377).

66. SS 3/1, Hayward, 1819. See, too, Panoff (1970:261–262).

67. Ellis (1829:I, 120).

68. Beaglehole (1961:1796).

69. See "Land and Territory" in Chapter 8; and PMB 70, "Parau no te mau fenua Arue e te tahi atua mau matainaa" *[sic]*, 1855.

70. See Broughton (1804); Turnbull (1813); Wilson (1799); Myers (1817).

71. SS 1/1, Jefferson, 12 December 1800.

72. SS, Thomson, f. 28.

73. Davies (1961:chap. 2).

74. SS, Thomson, f. 36. The murder of Ha'amanemane gave great offense to the chiefs of Ra'iatea, but Tenania and the *'arioi* visited Mo'orea and Matavai in 1799. Ibid., f. 33.

75. Oliver (1974:1309) (italics in original).

76. Turnbull (1813:322). This was not in August 1803, and it was prior to the death of Teari'inavahoroa (Ari'ipaea) on 18 June 1803.

77. SS, Thomson, ff. 68–70.

78. Oliver (1974:1316).

79. Davies, Youl, and others cited in Oliver (1974:1317); SS, Thomson, f. 82.

80. SS, Journals/1, Hayward, Nott, Scott, Wilson, entry, 3 December 1808.

81. Oliver (1974:1325).

82. Davies (1961:103).

83. Oliver (1974:34–35).

84. LMS *Transactions*, 1819: Davies, Tour of Tahiti, 29 October 1816, 325–326.

Chapter 2: THE EVANGELICAL IMPACT

1. LMS *Reports*, 1810: Davies, 12 November 1808, 356.

2. Davies (1961:144 n.).

3. Davies (1810).

4. Elder in Davies (1961:31–32 n.).

5. Davies (1961): missionaries to Pomare, 29 April 1809, 133.

6. LMS Australia/1, Marsden to missionaries, 4 October 1810.

7. LMS Australia/1, Marsden to directors, 23 November 1811; LMS *Reports*, 1811, 369.

8. LMS Board Minutes 1, 156–157, and memoranda on expenditure, 1797–1812. The second largest expenditure was on stations in South Africa.

9. SS/2, Nott to directors, 28 July 1812; Maude (1968:216–219); Davies (1961:73 n.).

10. LMS *Transactions*, 1817:6.

11. Davies (1961:164).

12. Davies (1961:88, 349). Pomare I's earlier letters were written by Jefferson.

13. LMS *Reports*, 1812: Davies and others, 17 September 1811, 435.

14. PMB 73, Pomare to Missionary Society, 1 January 1807; LMS *Reports*, 1808:273–275.

15. LMS *Reports*, 1812: Pomare to Henry, 8 November [1810], 435–437. This letter would appear to be wrongly dated 1811.

16. LMS *Transactions*, 1818, IV: Pomare to missionaries, 25 September, 8 October 1812, 8–10; and SS/2 (copy).

17. LMS *Transactions*, 1818, IV: Henry to directors, 12 June 1813, 12.

18. Davies (1961:174); SS 3/4, Pomare to Burder, 15 February 1824; LMS Australia/2, Elder to Waugh, 10 March 1824.

19. Turnbull (1813:331).

20. Oliver (1974:1320).

21. Davies (1961:168).

22. Davies (1961:158).

23. SS 2/1, missionaries to directors, 14 January 1815; Newbury (1967b:492–497) for the chronology of Pomare's movements.

24. Takau Pomare (1971:252–253, 260).

25. LMS *Transactions*, 1818, IV:95–96; SS 2/4, Davies to Cowper, 30 March 1816.

26. SS 2/4, Pomare to directors, 19 February 1816; Davies (1961: 198–199).

27. Ellis (1829:I, 246–254).

28. Moerenhout (1942:II, 464–468).

29. Takau Pomare (1971:253).

30. Davies (1961:197).

31. SS 3/1, summary of interviews and notes, 1819.

32. Ibid.

33. LMS Australia/2, Elder to Waugh, 10 March 1824.

34. Ibid.

35. LMS *Transactions*, 1819:321–326.

36. LMS *Transactions*, 1818:305.

37. SS 3/1, Hayward, 1819.

38. LMS *Transactions*, 1819:329.

39. SS Journals, Crook, April–December 1824 *[sic]*, Taiarapu, entry for 21 November 1825.

40. LMS *Transactions*, 1818:15.

41. SS 3/1, Bicknell to directors, 31 July 1819.

42. Davies (1961:205 ff.).

43. SS 2/7, Pomare to Haweis, 3 October 1818.

44. Davies (1961:203); SS 2/7, Pomare to Haweis, 3 October 1818.

45. Davies (1961:app. II); Tagupa (1974); Bouge (1952).

46. LMS Home Odds/10, Tyerman and Bennet, 3 October 1823.

47. SS 3/2, Darling, 5 June 1820; SS Journals, Crook, 30 October 1820; 17 February, 6 July, 31 July, 3 August 1821.

48. Davies (1961:246, 258); Tyerman and Bennet (1840:40).

49. CMA, Davies to Hughes, 18 May 1821.

50. SS Journals/4, Crook, 1820–1821.

51. Orsmond MS, cited in Davies (1961:351).

52. Ellis (1829:I, 419–420).

53. SS/1, Hayward, 1819.

54. SS 3/1, Bicknell, 31 July 1819.

55. SS 3/2, for copies of correspondence with Eagar, Henry, Bicknell; and LMS Australia/2; Stevens (1965:274–275); and for Williams' version of these events, see SS 3/9, 10 March 1822.

56. Compare Maude (1968:218); she was later run by John Dibbs for Pomare III.

57. SS 3/9, Williams, 10 March 1822.

58. SS 3/5, Capt. Grimes, 18 June 1821.

59. SS Journals/4, Crook, 17 April 1821.

60. SS Journals/4, Crook, 21 April 1821.

61. SS Journals/4, Crook, 3 December 1821.

62. SS 3/1, Bicknell, 31 July 1819; Orsmond, Williams, Threlkeld, 30 August 1819; LMS Australia 2/2, Marsden to Burder, 15 August 1818.

63. LMS Australia 2/2, Hassall, Eyre, Smith to Burder, 15 August 1818. They had left the society's employment by this date.

64. SS 3/1, Darling, 9 August 1819.

65. SS 3/1, cited in Darling, 9 August 1819.

66. LMS Australia 2/2, Marsden, 21 March 1821.

67. Davies (1961:224); SS Journals/4, Crook, 25 August 1821.

68. Tyerman and Bennet (1840:30–31).

69. SS Journals/4, Crook, 1821, f. 23.

70. O'Reilly MSS no. 32, Orsmond, 6 September 1819.

71. CMA, Davies, 19 April 1824.

72. Tyerman and Bennet (1840:28).

73. SS Journals, Crook, April–December 1824.

74. SS Journals/5, Crook, January–July 1827.

75. SS 4/1, Henry and Platt, 6 March 1823; Blossom, 23 August 1823; SS 4/2, Crook, 3 October 1823; SS 5/5, Henry, 9 February 1826.

76. SS 4/5, Williams, 24 December 1824.

77. SS 4/5, Williams and Threlkeld, 24 March 1824.

78. O'Reilly MSS, Platt, 28 September 1827; Platt to Tyerman, 28 May 1828, 24 August 1829.

79. SS 5/3, Williams, 12 November 1825.

80. SS Journals/5, Crook, Tahiti, 10 April 1826.

81. SS Journals/5, Crook, Journal, 10 May 1827.

82. Ellis (1829:II, 426–440).

83. LMS Home Odds, Tyerman and Bennet, 3 October 1823.

84. SS Journals/5, Crook, August 1827–February 1828.

85. SS Journals/5, Crook, 24 September 1828.

86. SS 8/2, Platt, 1 August 1831.

87. SS 8/6, Blossom, 16 December 1832; SS 9/1, Armitage, 12 January 1833; Wilson, 16 May 1833.

88. SS 9/1, Darling, 4 January 1833.

89. SS 9/5, Darling, 10 April 1833; SS 9/1, Simpson, 18 May 1833. Simpson states that fifty or sixty were killed.

90. Stewart (1832:262).

91. Olmstead (1844:83).

92. SS 10/6, Orsmond, 5 October 1836.

93. Cited in Davies (1961:app. II, 375).

94. Heath, cited in Davies (1961:337).

95. SS 10/5, Armitage, 25 March 1836.

96. SS 14/2, Stevens, 5 July 1841.

97. Ibid.

98. Davies (1961:328–331).

99. SS 14/2, Stevens, 5 July 1841.

100. SS 15/2, 30 September 1842.

101. SS 16/1, Howe, 22 February 1843.

102. SS 17/2, Howe, 19 June 1844; students to directors, 20 August 1844.

103. Dening (1974:19).

104. Dening (1974:20).

105. LMS, Thomson, "The Marquesas Islands" MS; Gracia (1843).

106. HLUH, "Report of the Deputation to the Georgian, Society and Marquesan Islands" [1832–1833]. I am indebted to William Tagupa, University of Hawaii, for drawing my attention to this manuscript.

107. LMS, Thomson; SS Journals/9, for Stallworthy, Marquesas, 1837–1838, 1838–1839; Rodgerson, 1838; Heath, Marquesas, 1840.

108. SS Journals/9, Stallworthy, 1838–1839.

109. Ibid.

110. SS 12/8, Stallworthy, 20 February 1839.

Chapter 3: *THE MARKET EXPANDED*

1. SS 9/1, Darling, 18 May 1833 (enclosing copies of bills).

2. Wilkes (1844:II, 48).

3. Wilkes (1844:II, 4–8).

4. These values are calculated from consular returns in TBCP/2, 1834–1843; ANSOM J 1/64, J 6/55 (1836–1844); Disp. USC 1 (1836–1841). The U.S. silver dollar varied in its rate of exchange against the pound sterling from $4.30 in Hawaii, $4.80 at Sydney, and $5.20 at Valparaiso. Wilkes (1844:V, 485–486). At Tahiti in the late 1830s the U.S. 25-cent piece was exchanged against the piastre (worth 20 cents in the U.S.A.), and the British sovereign was exchanged for $5 Chilean. Spanish doubloons were valued at $16.80 U.S. I have averaged exchange rates at $4 Chilean or $4 U.S. to the pound for this early period. See also Wilkes (1844:II, 36–48).

5. Harlow (1952 and 1964:passim); and for the late eighteenth century, see Roe (1967:xv ff.).

6. Wilkes (1844:V, 485–486).

7. ANSOM J 2/56, for reports by Dupetit-Thouars, 1839; Dupetit-Thouars (1843:III, 375–380).

8. Disp. USC 5, Vandor, report for 1866.

9. PMB 205, whaling logs, especially for *Pallas, George and Susan, Tybee, Emerald.* There is additional trade information in *Records Relating*

to U.S. Exploring Expedition, MS microfilm, HLUH, 5 (1836–1842), Wilkes to secretary of navy, 24 September 1839. See, too, Stackpole (1953) for early whaling voyages.

10. Faivre (1953:362–363).

11. Findlay (1851:II, 1225–1317).

12. FO 58/14, "Treaty of Commerce," enclosure in Elley to FO, 12 December 1826; Morrell (1960:65).

13. FO 58/14; TBCP Pomare, FO to Pomare, 14 February 1837; Fitz-Roy (1839:506–557).

14. Bach (1963:chap. 2).

15. Faivre (1953:343).

16. Dunmore (1969:II, 284); Faivre (1953:408–410).

17. Especially TBCP Miscellaneous; and consulate files in FO 687/46 (registers of mortgages and sales, complaints, shipping, wrecks, estates, wills, and deeds).

18. Lucett (1851:passim).

19. O'Reilly and Teissier (1975:268).

20. TBCP Miscellaneous, Henry to Nicolas, 24 March 1843.

21. Davies (1961:liii).

22. SS 3/8, Williams, 13 November 1822.

23. SS 3/8, Williams, 13 November 1822.

24. SS 5/9, Williams, 5 January 1822.

25. SS 3/2, Williams, 13 November 1822.

26. LMS Australia 2/4, Marsden, 26 February 1824; SS 4/4, Williams and Threlkeld, 24 March 1824.

27. SS 4/4, Williams, 24 March 1824.

28. SS 4/5, Williams, 20 December 1824.

29. SS 5/1, Darling, 1 February 1825.

30. SS 5/5, Pritchard, 9 January 1825.

31. SS 7/2, Darling, 17 April 1829.

32. SS 6/5, Wilson, 22 April 1828.

33. SS 6/5, Blossom, 25 September 1828.

34. SS 5/5, Blossom, 12 February 1826.

35. SS 7/2, Darling, 17 April 1829.

36. SS 9/1, Darling, 18 May 1833.

37. SS 7/6, Nott, 25 October 1830.

38. SS 11/5, Rodgerson, 25 August 1837.

39. Their complaints are confirmed by price lists for imports on the *Camden* in Capt. R. C. Morgan, 1840, in SS 13/3.

40. SS 15/1, Smee, 4 March 1842.

41. SS 13/3, Darling to Wilson, 20 December 1840.

42. SS 11/2, Orsmond, 25 December 1837.

43. SS 9/4, enclosures: accounts for W. Henry for 1833 ($168.70) and G. Platt ($151.00). It is clear that Henry also purchased from Moerenhout on this account.

44. SS 9/4, Pritchard to Ellis, 31 January 1834.

45. SS 11/2, Pritchard, 30 December 1837.

46. SS 9/1, Davies, 13 May 1833.

47. SS 9/4, Darling, 27 January 1834.

48. SS 11/2, Darling, 4 December 1837.

49. SS 15/2, Charter, 12 July 1842.

50. SS 15/2, Charter, 12 July 1842.

51. SS 15/2, Rodgerson, 11 July 1842.

52. SS 6/1, Pritchard, 6 January 1827.

53. Disp. USC 1; AM BB4/1005, Moerenhout to minister of marine, 21 July 1840.

54. ANSOM A8/1, Moerenhout to Duperré, 1 June 1841.

55. Disp. USC 1, Blackler, 31 October 1840; 5 June 1841.

56. SS Journals/4, Crook, May–August 1823, 5 July 1823.

57. FO 687; TBCP Pomare.

58. FO 687/4, Atea to Ari'ifa'aite, 28 May 1841; Uata to consul, 15 February 1842; Paraita to Wilson, 16 May 1842.

59. TBCP 2, Uata to Wilson, 14 March 1842.

60. SS 15/2, Jesson, Journal (extracts for April–September 1842); *Code Tahitien, 1842.*

61. FO 687/4, Wilson to Uata, 2 April 1842.

62. FO 687/4 (for the Tahitian version, 1842); and TBCP 2.

63. FO 687/9, Mauruc, Fergus, Smith to Uata and Pomare, 26 April 1842.

64. ANSOM A 4/1, Dubouzet to Dupetit-Thouars, 11 July 1842.

65. Wilkes (1844:I, 141).

66. ANSOM A 11/1, Lefèvre (to Moerenhout?), 25 December 1841; O'Reilly and Teissier (1975:328).

67. FO 687/4, for a grant to Henry by Judges Ta'aroa and U'opai, 30 October 1842; FO 687/3, statement by Judges Rotea, Paete, Paofai, Poroi, 3 September 1840; land grant to Capt. Cotton, 28 June 1838, by Teremoemoe (Claims Part I, 1838–1873).

68. TBCP 2, Deas Thompson to Wilson, 11 July 1842; TBCP 8, Wilson to CO, 20 March 1842. The Sydney superintendent of police found all parties guilty of fraud in a written opinion but had no jurisdiction over the case.

69. ANSOM A 4/1, Dubouzet to Dupetit-Thouars, 11 July 1842.

70. TBCP 8, Wilson to Pritchard, 27 May 1841.

71. Blue (1933:85–99); Faivre (1953:288–290); Dunmore (1969:II, 263–264).

72. SS 5/9, Loomis to LMS, 19 August 1826.

73. For the background to this missionary venture, see Laval (1968:xiii ff.).

74. SS 9/4, Wilson to Allis, 16 April 1834.

75. SS 6/7, Crook, 31 December 1838; Pritchard, 21 September 1838.

76. Morrell (1960:77).

77. SS 10/1, Armitage, 23 June 1835; 10/2, Henry, 15 July 1835; Davies, 8 October 1835.

78. Disp. USC 1, Moerenhout, 24 December 1836.

79. SS 11/1, Pritchard to Moerenhout, 3 December 1836, enclosure in Pritchard to Ellis, 25 March 1837.

80. Dunmore (1969:II, 304–307); Disp. USC 1, 15 March 1839. Moerenhout was informed he was replaced in a letter which arrived with Consul Blackler dated 28 July 1837.

81. SS 11/5, "Report of a Meeting held at Papara on Wednesday 7th November 1838 to establish a law with a view to prevent the Priests of the Roman Catholic faith from teaching their peculiar doctrines should they arrive at Tahiti," 9 November 1838.

82. The Tahitian text has *fa'anavenave* (seducing).

83. *Sic: fa'autu'a:* "condemned" (sentenced).

84. FO 58/15, "No te faatupu raa i te parau au ore i te Evenelia mau roa," enclosure in Pritchard to Palmerston, 9 November 1838. The translation is in the hand of Pritchard.

85. SS 11/5, Rodgerson, 9 November 1838.

86. SS 12/1, Stevens, 25 July 1839.

87. FO 58/16, Paraita, Tati, Hitoti, Paete, August 1841, enclosure in Admiralty to FO, 6 May 1842.

88. FO 58/16, Paraita to Consul Cunningham, 21 August 1841, enclosure in Admiralty to FO, 6 May 1842.

89. FO 687/2, Matamoe's case, 1840–1842.

90. ANSOM A 4/1, Dubouzet, "Rapport," 4 June 1842.

91. TBCP 8, Wilson to Rouse, 15 August 1841.

92. ANSOM A 4/1, Dubouzet to Dupetit-Thouars, 11 July 1842.

93. ANSOM A 4/1, *ibid.*

Chapter 4: OCCUPATION AND RESISTANCE

1. ANSOM A 71/14, Orsmond, "Look Again! Or a Few Observations on the affairs of Tahiti from 1845 to 1849 by an Eye Witness and Cast at the feet of the Protectorate."

2. Guizot (1867:8, 41).

3. Dunmore (1969:II, 389).

4. Dunmore-Lang, "New Zealand in 1839," HL, 4, 1839–1847; Rev. Henry Williams, "Apprehension of New Zealand being seized by the French Government," HL, MSS, 53/28. This theme is emphasized in Brookes (1941:passim) and Jore (1959).

5. Grattan (1963:216–220); Perbal (1939:passim).

6. Morrell (1960:88).

7. Faivre (1953:502–503).

8. Takau Pomare (1971); Salmon (1964:chap. 10).

9. Pomare wrote five petitions to Queen Victoria between 1843 and 1844, and Teri'itaria wrote two. For the "Appeal of the Natives of Tahiti to the Governments of Great Britain and America," 12 January 1846, in Adm. I/5561, see Newbury (1973:21–25).

10. ANSOM A 52/9, Guizot to minister of marine, 23 June 1847.

11. Salmon (1964:31).

12. SS 11/2, Darling, 4 December 1837.

13. ANSOM B 3/40, Laplace to Duperré, 15 July 1839.

14. Duchêne (1928:189).

15. ANSOM A 7/1, extracts from correspondence from Desvault to Dupetit-Thouars, Vaitahu, 14 January 1839.

16. ANSOM A 7/1, "Note sur les îles Marquises et sur les avantages qu'elles offrent comme lieu de déportation," 22 August 1839; AAÉ Nouvelle-Zélande I (for duplicate reports and minutes).

17. ANSOM A 12/31, "Mémoire sur l'Océanie," 4 November 1839.

18. Dupetit-Thouars (1843:3, 375–380).

19. AM BB4/1010, Soult to Rosamel, 23 January 1839; Buick (1928: passim).

20. AAÉ Nouvelle-Zélande I, Duperré to Lavaud, 14 January 1840.

21. ANSOM A 7/1, Duperré to Dupetit-Thouars, 15 October 1841; AAÉ Océanie I, Duperré to Guizot, 14 March 1842.

22. AAÉ Sydney I, Faramond to Guizot, 17 September 1841.

23. ANSOM A 12/31, Duperré to Lucas, 27 April 1842.

24. ANSOM A 12/31, Buglet to Pomare, 25 January 1842.

25. AAÉ Océanie I, and ANSOM A 10/1, Dupetit-Thouars to Duperré, 18 June 1842; and A 13/28 for acts of possession.

26. AAÉ Océanie 2, Dupetit-Thouars to Duperré, 20 June 1842.

27. ANSOM A 15/2, Dupetit-Thouars to Ministry of Marine, 1 July 1842.

28. AAÉ Océanie 2, Dupetit-Thouars to Duperré, 19 January 1843.

29. ANSOM A 10/1, Cugnet to Dupetit-Thouars, 3 November 1842.

30. ANSOM A 11/1, Dupetit-Thouars to Ministry of Marine, 25 September 1842 and enclosures.

31. ANSOM A 12/31, Lucas, "Enquête sur les Évènements de l'Océanie de 1837 à 1847"; A 11/1, Dupetit-Thouars to Ministry of Marine, 25 September 1842; SS 15/2, Howe and Simpson, 27 September 1842.

32. ANSOM A 11/1, "Déclaration," 8 September 1842; *Parliamentary Papers*, 1843(61):8–11.

33. Disp. USC 2, MS copy enclosed in Blackler, 10 September 1842 (*sic:* 9 September 1842). Consul Wilson did not report events till a dispatch of 15 September 1842 to Sir George Gipps: TBCP 8.

34. *Parl. Papers*, 1843(61):14–18.

35. ANSOM A 12/31, Lucas, "Enquête."

36. AAÉ Sydney I, Faramond to Guizot, 22 October 1842.

37. Adm. I/5530, Nicolas to Thomas, 13 January 1844, enclosure in Thomas to Admiralty, 8 May 1844.

38. Adm. I/5530, Nicolas to Moerenhout, Reine, de Carpegna, 7 May 1843.

39. TBCP 2, FO to Pritchard, 25 September 1843. These orders arrived via Honolulu and were given no publicity.

40. LMS "French Aggressions upon Tahiti," circular, 25 March 1843; *Journal des Débats politiques et littéraires*, 17 March 1843; Baldwin (1938:213); Morrell (1960:83–88).

41. ANSOM A 15/2, Dupetit-Thouars to Ministry of Marine, 3 November 1842.

42. ANSOM A 15/2, "Résumé de motifs exposés par M. l'Amiral Du Petit-Thouars," n.d. (Roussin?).

43. ANSOM F 1/58, Desclozeaux, "Rapport, fait au ministre de la marine et des colonies par une commission spéciale, chargée de la révision du projet d'ordonnance concernant l'administration des Iles Marquises"; and "Ordonnance," 20 April 1843.

44. ANSOM A 16/2, Roussin, "Instructions pour le Gouverneur Bruat," 28 April 1843.

45. ANSOM A 16/2, ibid.

46. CO 135/186, Maitland to CO, 1 March and 7 May 1817.

47. ANSOM A 16/2, "Note pour le commandant Bruat," 3 February 1843.

48. *Moniteur universel*, 11 June 1843; and A 14/28 for debates and reports to the chamber.

49. *Moniteur universel*, 19 September 1843; Duchêne (1938:217).

50. AAÉ Océanie 1, Roussin to Bruat, 20 July 1843.

51. ANSOM A 60/29, Mackau to Bruat and Hamelin, 18 August 1845.

52. ANSOM A 16/*bis* 2, "Règlement sur le service administratif," 14 October 1843.

53. ANSOM A 12/31, Lucas, "Enquête"; Lucett (1851:II, 17, 193).

54. ANSOM A 16/*bis* 2, Bruat to Ministry of Marine, 16 January 1844; Newbury (1973:10–11).

55. LMS South Seas, Odds, "The Old Orsmond MS, 1849."

56. Newbury (1973:10 n.).

57. ANSOM A 35/7, *Conseil de gouvernement*, minutes, 31 December 1845. Other sources suggest Atiau surrendered in March 1845. Salmon (1964) does not discuss her role in the war. See also Teissier (1978:10–11) for an accurate account.

58. ANSOM A 35/7, Bruat to minister of marine, 6 April 1845.

59. ANSOM A 35/7, LMS to Orsmond, 16 January 1845, copy enclosed in Bruat to Ministry of Marine, 21 August 1845.

60. ANSOM A 35/7, Bruat to Ministry of Marine, 17 January 1845.

61. ANSOM A 24/5, Bruat to Ministry of Marine, 22 January 1844; 25 February 1845.

62. Newbury (1967b); and for French reports on the Leeward Islands, see ANSOM A 34/8 and FO 58/38, Adm. I/5561, and TBCP 3.

63. ANSOM A 39/4, Bruat to de Mackau, 21 September 1845.

64. TBCP 8, G. Miller to Consul-General Miller, 15 December 1845.

65. Lucett (1851:II, 147).

66. SS 21/1, Thomson, 9 January 1847.

67. BM Add. MSS 41472, Martin Papers, cxxvii, journal, 29 October 1846, f. 70.

68. ANSOM A 52/9, Pomare to Bruat, 25 March 1847, enclosure in Bruat to Ministry of Marine, 28 March 1847.

69. ANSOM G 1/32, G 3–5.

70. TBCP Annual Reports 2, 1841–1850.

71. SS 20/2, Simpson, 24 July 1847.

72. SS 20/2, Johnston, 11 May 1847.

73. SS 20/2, Charter, 25 October 1847.

74. ANSOM A 52/9, Bruat, "Mémoire adressé au capitaine de vaisseau Lavaud," May 1849; and Table 2 in this chapter.

75. ANSOM A 52/9, Bruat, "Mémoire."

76. ANSOM A 52/9, Bruat, "Mémoire."

77. ANSOM A 52/9, Convention, 5 August 1847, enclosure in Lavaud to Ministry of Marine, 9 August 1847.

78. *Arrêtés* (1846): Decrees 49 and 50, 1845.

79. ANSOM A 52/9, Convention, 5 August 1847, Art. 9.

80. ANSOM A 54/9, Guizot to Ministry of Marine, 17 January 1848.

81. ANSOM A 62/2, Arago to Lavaud, 1 May 1848.

82. ANSOM E 11/31, "Lois revisées dans l'Assemblée des Législateurs, mars 1848, pour la conduite de tous sous le Gouvernement du Protectorat dans les Terres de la Société"; and minutes, 24 March 1848.

83. *Océanie Française*, 25 April 1844.

84. "Lois revisées . . . 1848," 7.

85. ANSOM E 11/31, minutes, 24 March 1848, enclosure in Lavaud to Ministry of Marine, 29 March 1848.

86. SS 20/2, Howe, 15 October 1847.

87. *Messager de Tahiti*, 9 June 1861 (for results of the census, 1848–1861); see, too, *Annuaire*, 1863, 334–335.

Chapter 5: CHURCHES AND STATE

1. ANSOM A 57/10, Lavaud to Ministry of Marine, 20 March 1848.

2. ANSOM A 57/10, Lavaud to Ministry of Marine, 19 May 1849.

3. O'Reilly and Reitman (1967:526–527).

4. ANSOM A 75/14, Saisset to Ministry for Algeria and Colonies, 15 February 1859.

5. ANSOM H 3/43, Bruat to Ministry of Marine, 2 October 1948.

6. ANSOM H 4/43, Ta'atari'i, Tari'iri'i (Vaira'atoa), Hitoti (adopted son of Hitoti), Motu (son of Peueue), Ta'ua, Niuhi (son of Paraita).

7. ANSOM H 8/107, Lavaud to Ministry of Marine; H 4/43, Lavaud, "Mémoire sur le Protectorat de la France à Taiti, ses relations et son influence en Océanie, laissée à M. Bonard," 6 March 1850.

8. CSC Tahiti, R. P. Venance Prat, "Vie de Mgr. Jaussen, évêque d'Axieri," pt. 2, chaps. 2, 4; CSC Tahiti 58/2 (Jaussen); 59/10 (Heurtel); 59/11 (Collette).

9. *BOÉFO*, 1850–1852: 312; ANSOM E 11/31, Bonard to Ministry of Marine, 7 May 1852; SS 26, Barff, "A Brief Statement regarding the Tahitian and Society Island Mission," July 1855; Vernier (1948:178–180).

10. TBCP 9, *Arrêté*, 27 May 1852.

11. It was submitted to a tribunal consisting of Alexander Salmon, Robert de Rougement, and Capt. de Kersenson. O'Reilly and Reitman (1967:53).

12. ANSOM H 10/106, La Richerie to Ministry of Marine, 1 June 1858.

13. "Projet de loi sur le culte national," 11 May 1860, *Messager de Tahiti*, 8 July 1860; ANSOM A 78/16, "Petition de l'Assemblée Indienne," 15 May 1860, signed by Maheanu'u, president, Tamuta, vice-president, Ta'atari-Tairapa, secretary, Mano, Paofai, Moeori, enclosure in La Richerie to Ministry for Algeria and Colonies, 16 October 1860.

14. SS 28, Howe, 16 August 1860.

15. ANSOM H 12/106, La Richerie to Ministry of Marine, 25 February 1861.

16. Arbousset (1864).

17. SMÉ, Correspondence, Atger, 2 July 1865; *JSMÉ* 40(1865):12–55.

18. SMÉ, Correspondence, Atger, 4 March 1867.

19. SMÉ, Correspondence, Atger and Vernier to Director of Native Affairs, enclosure in Atger to Casalis, 24 August 1868. The candidate was probably Father Bruno Schuten or Father Fierens on Ana'a; CSC Tuamotu 72/3. They were faced with an influx of pastors from Taha'a Pastoral School at this period.

20. SMÉ Correspondence, 1869–1872, Viénot, 2 September 1869; LMS to SMÉ, 25 September 1872; SS 32, Green, 18 October 1870.

21. SMÉ Correspondence, 1873–1875, Viénot, 5 January 1874.

22. *JSMÉ* 51(1876):290–293; SMÉ Correspondence, 1873–1875, Viénot to Gilbert-Pierre, 3 February 1876; Gilbert-Pierre to Synod Committee, 25 February 1875; PMB 38, J. L. Green Papers; *Messager de Tahiti*, 24 October 1879, 6 February 1880; Décret, 23 January 1884, *JORF*, 3 February 1884; *Arrêté* (and Decree), *JOÉFO*, 8 May 1884; *Ture tumu na te mau Etaretia Tahiti*, *JOÉFO*, 12 June 1884.

23. SS 36, Green, 30 September 1880; Green was instrumental in reforming the training of pastors on Taha'a and Ra'iatea and remained there and in Tahiti, 1870–1886.

24. *Ture tumu na te mau Etaretia Tahiti*, *JOÉFO*, 12 June 1884. The internal regulations of the Etaretia were based on *Synode des Églises tahitiennes, Statuts et règlements*, in *Messager de Tahiti*, 21 November 1873.

25. "Comité de la Société des Missions," 8 June 1865, *JSMÉ*, 1883: 390.

26. CSC, "Correspondance Verdier," 1 April 1884.

27. *Ui Katorika (pope) o te Vikario raa apotoro i Tahiti* (Pape'ete?: 1851); Jaussen (1861); Moing (1885?).

28. CSC 58/3, Jaussen, 13 October 1852.

29. CSC 58/3, Jaussen, 13 October 1852.

30. For details of this architecture, see Laval (1968:cxi ff.).

31. Laval (1968:cxl–cxli).

32. Laval (1968:lxix–lxxxvii).

33. CSC 47/2, Dordillon, 2 October 1864, 1 July 1865.

34. CSC 47/2, Dordillon, 26 March 1879; 49/10, Fournon, 21 March 1879. The income was estimated at 15,000 to 20,000 piastres (100,000 francs) in 1879.

35. CSC 49/10, Fournon, 24 July 1870.

36. CSC 47/2, Dordillon, 14 March 1880.

37. CSC 49/10, Fournon, 14 June 1880, 9 August 1880.

38. CSC 47/5, Martin, 13 December 1883.

39. Ellsworth (1959:6–30).

40. Ellsworth (1959:20).

41. O'Reilly and Teissier (1975:469).

42. CSC 72/9, Jaussen, 30 September 1852.

43. CSC 72/9; the internal correspondence between gendarmes and island authorities is in CSC 72/9 and is more extensive than extant official reports in ANSOM F 14/59 (Justice, Police).

44. TBCP 9, Miller to Moresby, 17 November 1852, 29 January 1853.

45. HMCSL, Kekela's correspondence in Tagupa (n.d.): "Soliloquies from the Surviving: Missionary Notes from the Marquesas Islands, 1853–1868." I am grateful to William Tagupa for the use of this unpublished paper.

46. SS 26, Lind, 23 January 1855.

47. SS 27, Chisholm, 29 September 1857; SS 33, Saville, 14 September 1871.

48. LMS, Personal 1, Alfred F. Saville, "Diary, Huahine and Society Islands" (1867–1871).

49. SS 31, Vivian, 6 March 1866.

50. SS 30, Vivian, 30 November 1865; SS 32, Vivian, 11 July 1867.

51. SS 35, Green, 5 December 1876.

52. Wilmot (1888:29).

53. C. W. Wandell, Claud Roger, Sydney, January 1874, in *The True Latterday Saints' Herald*, 1874, 296.

54. Smith to Joseph, 1 March 1885, *Saints' Herald*, 1885: 309.

55. Smith to Joseph, 15 April 1885, *Saints' Herald*, 1885: 402.

56. Laval (1968:passim).

57. CSC 47/5, Martin, 11 March 1888.

58. CSC 58/9, Verdier, 20 September 1885.

59. *Messager de Tahiti*, 5 January 1879; SMÉ Correspondence, 1877–1879, Viénot, 13 January 1879.

60. Smith, 23 March 1885, *Saints' Herald*, 1885: 384. See *Te Heheuraa api* (from 1878) and *Te Orometua* (from 1897).

61. Vernier (1948:254).

62. SMÉ Correspondence, 29 December 1873.

63. Disp. USC 8, Burton to Doty, 10 August 1904.

64. ANSOM Q 5/66, Revel to Ministry of Colonies, 25 June 1914.

Chapter 6: THE SEARCH FOR STAPLES

1. Compiled from TBCP 8 Annual Reports; ANSOM J and K; *Annuaire*, 1863, 1885, 1917.

2. *Annuaire*, 1863: "État des Batiments de commerce," 340–341.

3. TBCP 8 Annual Reports; Kelly (1885:40).

4. *Annuaire*, 1863: 92.

5. *Annuaire*, 1863: 96. A "chaloupe" was built on the lines of a whaleboat with a broad beam.

6. ANSOM J 13/57, "Mouvement du Port de Papeete," 1838–1858; Robillard (1845:17).

7. Laval (1968:table, lxxiii).

8. Ricardi (1845:passim); *Annuaire*, 1863: 97–98.

9. *Annuaire*, 1863: 99.

10. *Messager de Tahiti*, 2 July 1854.

11. Laval (1968:lxxiv).

12. CSC 73/13, Montiton, 1 July 1851.

13. Brassey (1878:670).

14. ANSOM E 26/57, Carrey to La Roncière, 23 June 1868.

15. ANSOM E 26/57, Carrey to La Roncière, 23 June 1868.

16. *Messager de Tahiti*, 15 August 1868; Wilmot (1888:passim).

17. *Messager de Tahiti*, 19 September 1873.

18. Kelly (1885); Newbury (1972a:149).

19. Newbury (1972a:149).

20. TBCP 8, Miller, 19 November 1876.

21. *Messager de Tahiti*, 27 January 1876.

22. *Messager de Tahiti*, 1 June 1872 (values at San Francisco prices).

23. *Annuaire*, 1865: 320; *Messager de Tahiti*, 1 June 1872; FO 687/15.

24. La Richerie to Committee for Agriculture and Commerce, in *Messager de Tahiti*, 30 January 1864.

25. Ibid.

26. ANSOM A 68/13, Bonard to Ministry of Marine, 16 July 1850.

27. ANSOM A 71/13, Du Bouzet to Ministry of Marine, 10 December 1855.

28. ANSOM A 75/14, Saisset to Ministry for Algeria and Colonies, 15 February 1859.

29. *BOÉFO*, 1850–1852: 235, 253. For details, Newbury (1960:125–132).

30. "Loi tahitienne sur l'enregistrement des terres," 24 March 1852, *BOÉFO*, 1850–1852: 314; ANSOM E 11/31, "Procès-verbaux de l'Assemblée des législateurs," 1852.

31. Bureau des Terres (Service des Domaines); Newbury (1960:126).

32. ANSOM F 25/57, Faucompré to Hubert, 20 August 1863.

33. Newbury (1972a:152–157).

34. TBCP 8, Miller, 19 November 1866.

35. ML, *Rapport fait à M. le Commandant commissaire impérial par la Commission d'inspection des cultures*, Papeʻete, 1866.

36. ANSOM E 23/53, "Procès-verbaux du conseil d'administration," 12 January 1863, enclosure in La Richerie to Chasseloup-Laubat, 2 October 1863.

37. ANSOM E 23/53, Chasseloup-Laubat to La Richerie, 24 August 1863. The 39 hectares reported were probably lots 71–73 and 77–78, marked in the margin of the Punaʻauia *puta tomite* as sold in 1862 and 1863 to the "comité agricole": Bureau des Terres.

38. TBCP 5, Stewart to FO, 18 April 1865, enclosure in FO to Miller, 1 November 1865.

39. ANSOM E 16/71, E 25/57, "Procès-verbaux du conseil d'administration," November 1862.

40. ML, J. L. Young, "Atimaono"; and PMB 23, J. L. Young Papers; Ramsden (1946:187–214); Langdon (1959:185–195).

41. ANSOM E 25/57, Chasseloup-Laubat to La Richerie, 15 January 1864.

42. *Messager de Tahiti*, 5 March 1864: Trastour to the district councils of Mataiʻea and Atimaono-Papara, 11 January 1861 [1864].

43. PMB 23, J. L. Young Papers; FO 687/4, Miscellaneous, 1849–1899 (Tahiti Cotton and Coffee Plantation); 687/8, Estates, Wills, Deeds, Part III, 1866–1875/9, Tahiti Cotton and Coffee Plantation Co. Ltd.; Part V, 1888–1900/12, William Stewart.

44. TBCP 5, Stewart to Miller, 7 March 1864; Brander to Miller, 13 March 1864; Stewart to FO, 8 April 1865.

45. ANSOM M 1/35. Tongareva lies about 600 miles northwest of Tahiti. The immigrants were 33 men, 22 women, 27 boys, and 17 girls collected by a contractor named Parker who was paid for only 50 of the shipload. There is no record of repatriation.

46. ANSOM M 1/35, "contrat de travail," 9 June 1863.

47. *Messager de Tahiti*, 11 November, 17 November 1865; Candelot (1870:12–14).

48. Candelot (1870:14).

49. "Tahitian Slavery," *San Francisco Times*, 30 June 1867; "Letter from Tahiti," *Daily Herald* (San Francisco), 7 June 1867; compare Stewart, "An Outline of how it Came to Pass that so Many Absurd Stories have been Circulated about the Cotton Plantation on Terre Eugénie, Tahiti," in ANSOM E 25/57; TBCP Miscellaneous, Walter to FO, 27 January 1870.

50. The episode is a Pacific classic. The barque *Moaroa* under Capt. Blackett had been chartered by Stewart in 1869 to bring laborers from the

Gilbert Islands. Blackett took over the human cargo of another black-birder—the *Annie* (or *Anaa*). These broke out on the voyage to Tahiti and murdered the captain, mate, and some of the crew. The others saved themselves by blowing up a section of the ship. TBCP 6, Miller to FO, 30 September 1869.

51. ANSOM F 22/58, La Roncière to Ministry of Marine, 7 August 1868 (and enclosures for all documents on the case); Jacolliot (1869:30–39).

52. ANSOM E 25/57, "Consultation pour la Compagnie Tahiti Cotton and Coffee Plantation" (an inquiry by judges of the Imperial Court against James Stewart).

53. Martiny, "Comité d'agriculture et de commerce," 7 August 1878, *Messager de Tahiti*, 6 September 1878.

54. Newbury (1972a:154–155).

55. ANSOM E 25/57, Boyer, "La Vérité sur Tahiti," 12 January 1869.

56. *Messager de Tahiti*, 17 April 1869.

57. Ernest Davillé, second husband of Marion Brander, would appear to be the first. It is not clear to me why titles from Atiau Vahine passed through Marau Salmon, rather than through another senior male or female of the lineage.

58. [Admiral Layrle] (1933:307–318).

59. "Arrêté fixant les tarifs des taxes locales," 21 December 1864, *BOÉFO*, 1864:458.

60. *Arrêté*, 28 December 1871; *Messager de Tahiti*, 10 February 1872. Strictly speaking the *octroi* was a tax on consumer goods levied by a municipality (which did not, as yet, legally exist at Tahiti).

61. ANSOM A 108/20, SCO to Ministry of Marine and Colonies, 18 December 1877.

Chapter 7: QUEEN POMARE'S PROTECTORATE

1. Perkins (1854:424).

2. Brassey (1878:674).

3. Hort (1891:13).

4. ANSOM A 75/14, La Richerie to Chasseloup-Laubat, 12 November 1860.

5. ANSOM A 71/13, Ducos, "Note sur Taiti," 1854.

6. ANSOM E 30/141, Chasseloup-Laubat, "Historique," n.d.

7. ANSOM A 75/14, La Richerie to Chasseloup-Laubat, 31 August 1864; E 16/73-4, "Procès-verbaux du conseil d'administration," June, December 1876. For details of the budgets at this period, see Newbury (1960:passim).

8. For a portrait of the Tahitian court, see O'Reilly (1975:17–19).

9. *Annuaire*, 1863: Ribourt, 310; Bureau des Terres, *puta fari'ihau*; PMB 70, "Parau no te mau fenua Arue e te tahi atua mau mataiaa" *[sic]*, 1855.

10. Bureau des Terres, *puta tomite*, and other land registers. For the legal aspects of tenure, see Roucaute (1951:passim) and the thoughtful interpretation by Panoff (1970:236 ff.).

11. ANSOM A 71/13, Page to Ducos, 7 November 1854.

12. ANSOM A 71/13, Du Bouzet to Ducos, 3 December 1854.

13. ANSOM A 71/13, "Procès-verbaux du conseil d'administration," 21 October 1854.

14. TBCP 10, Miller to Salmon, 27 September 1859; Salmon (1964: 116).

15. Salmon (1858:9).

16. ANSOM A 75/14, Ari'itaimai to La Roncière, October 1867; *Messager de Tahiti*, 19 October 1867. Compare Teissier (1978:89).

17. ANSOM A 75/14, Bonet to Ari'itaimai, 7 November 1867. I have seen no evidence she was the daughter of a "foreigner."

18. ANSOM A 57/10, Pomare to Lavaud, 28 August 1851, 22 June 1852.

19. ANSOM D 7/13, Page to Hamelin, 18 February 1856.

20. ANSOM A 75/14, La Richerie to Chasseloup-Laubat, 12 November 1860.

21. ANSOM E 11/31, E 15/16 for minutes of assembly meetings; O'Reilly and Reitman (1969:720–721) for printed proceedings.

22. *Arrêté*, 16 March 1869; *Messager de Tahiti*, 27 March 1869.

23. ANSOM A 97/17, Rigault de Genouilly, "Rapport à l'Empereur," 25 December 1869; A 87/18 (for general correspondence on the case).

24. *Messager de Tahiti*, 14 and 19 May 1869; ANSOM A 96/19, La Roncière to Ministry of Marine, 12 May 1869.

25. ANSOM A 96/19, Décret, 25 May 1869, enclosure in Jouslard to Ministry of Marine, 8 July 1869.

26. ANSOM A 96/19, La Roncière to Ministry of Marine, 25 June 1869.

27. *Messager de Tahiti*, 13 November, 11 December 1869.

28. TBCP 11, Miller to FO, 13 November 1869.

29. ANSOM E 25/57, Boyer, "La vérité sur Tahiti," 12 January 1869.

30. "Loi sur l'organisation du service judiciaire tahitien," 28 March 1866, *BOÉFO*, 1866: 40; *Messager de Tahiti*, 19 May 1866.

31. ANSOM E 30/141; Pomare (n.d. [1870]).

32. *Messager de Tahiti*, December 1869–January 1871: "Appels au cour de cassation," cases 276–433.

33. "Loi tahitienne," 30 November 1855, *BOÉFO*, 1859: 4.

34. Case 370, *Messager de Tahiti*, 9 July 1870; case 387, *Messager de Tahiti*, 23 July 1870; case 338, *Messager de Tahiti*, 14 May 1870.

35. Case 363, *Messager de Tahiti*, 18 June 1870.

36. "Rua a Rerii *v.* Hupehupe a Teamai," 2 September 1875, enclosure in Gilbert-Pierre to MMC, 5 December 1875.

37. ANSOM A 97/17, Rigault de Genouilly, "Note sur le développement de Tahiti," September 1869.

38. ANSOM A 91/17, Cloué to Genouilly, 2 December 1869.

39. Adm. I/5561, Barff to Seymour, 9 November 1845.

40. SS 45, Green, 23 August 1876; PMB 38, J. L. Green Papers, entries for 1875.

41. O'Reilly MSS, "Jugement de divorce," 17 July 1887.

42. ANSOM A 106/20, Jallout, "Note confidentielle," 4 October 1875.

43. Wandell and Roger, *Saints' Herald*, no. 6, 1874.

44. PMB 38, J. L. Green Papers, entry 11 September 1877; TBCP 12, Miller to FO, 16 September 1877; compare Salmon (1964:171–172).

45. SS 35, Green, 7 May 1878.

46. ANSOM A 109/131, Planche to Montaignac, 6 March 1878.

47. ANSOM E 30/141, Q 2/32, Le Clos to MMC, 15 August 1874 (with marginal notes by Inspector Jore).

48. Ibid.

49. ANSOM A 107/35, Michaux to MMC, 28 May 1877; "Procès-verbaux," 4 December 1876, February–April 1877.

50. ANSOM A 107/35, "Projet d'organisation coloniale pour Tahiti," enclosure in Planche to MMC, 15 October 1878.

51. ANSOM A 102/20, Ezymé to Gilbert-Pierre, 26 January 1875.

52. SS 25, Barff to Ellis, 21 July 1853.

53. TBCP 4, Miller to FO, 17 July 1852.

54. FO 687/7 and TBCP A/III, "Resolutions," Ra'iatea, 8 January 1861. The price of coconuts was fixed at $1 per hundred, oil at $0.50 per gallon ("the true gallon of the land, no other gallon to be used"); and credit sales were prohibited.

55. Disp. USC 4, Owner, 27 April 1858; TBCP 4, Chisholm to FO, 25 December 1858.

56. TBCP 6, Tamatoa and chiefs of Taha'a to Miller, 11 February 1867.

57. LMS Personal 1, Saville, Diary, July 1868.

58. SS 34, Pearse, 10 July 1873. Teari'imaevarua died in 1873.

59. SCO/2, *Statuten*; SCO 1/1, Board of Directors, 1875.

60. Hamburg, Staatsarchiv, Naval and Consular: XIII/1, Godeffroy to AA, 11 June 1878; SCO 1/1, Board of Directors, 9 July 1879.

61. Hamburg, Staatsarchiv, Naval and Consular, XII/2, 1879–1880; SCO 7/1 (Ra'iatea); TBCP 6, Miller to FO, 10 May 1879; SS 35, Green, 10 May 1879.

62. SCO 11, 7/1.

63. ANSOM A 114/21, Planche to MMC, 6 March 1878, 12 June 1879.

64. ANSOM A 114/21, Michaux to Jauréguiberry, 31 May 1879.

65. ANSOM A 114/21, Jauréguiberry to MAÉ, 19 July 1879.

66. ANSOM A 114/21, Jauréguiberry to MAÉ, 19 August 1879.

67. *Messager de Tahiti*, 28 January 1881.

68. SMÉ Correspondence, 1879–1880, Vernier, 11 February 1880; AAÉ Océanie 5, Chessé, "Note sur les Iles Sous leVent," 23 January 1882.

69. SMÉ Correspondence, 1879–1880, Planche to Vernier, 11 October 1879, enclosure in Vernier, 11 November 1879.

70. SMÉ Correspondence, 1879–1880, Vernier, 11 March 1880; ANSOM A 123/21, Jauréguiberry to Admiral Landolfe, 23 September 1882.

71. TBCP 12, Godeffroy to Miller, 18 April 1880, enclosure in Miller to FO, 24 April 1880; *Messager de Tahiti*, 23 April 1880.

72. *Documents Diplomatiques Français* (1st series), III, 1880–1881: 47, 186.

73. "Proclamation de Pomare V aux Tahitiens," *Messager de Tahiti*, 2 July 1880.

74. TBCP 12, Miller to Chessé, 29 June 1880.

75. SMÉ Correspondence, 1879–1880, Vernier, 23 December 1880.

76. "Loi," 30 December 1880, *Messager de Tahiti*, 25 March 1881.

Chapter 8: THE POLITICS OF ASSIMILATION

1. McKay (1943:214–237); Murphy (1948:16–30); Varigny (1881:390–414); Vignon (1886:159–163); Deschanel (1884:passim).

2. D'Ingremard (1889).

3. Mager (1889:279–281); and see his *Le monde polynésien* (1902:233–237).

4. For further discussion of this theme, see Newbury (1967a); de Saussure, (1899:28); and de Thozée (1902:222). There is a similar conclusion in West (1961:83–86); compare Newbury (1956:245–246).

5. Goupil in *Océanie Française*, 13 May 1884.

6. "Décret concernant le gouvernement des Établissements Français de l'Océanie, 28 décembre 1885," in *Documents concernant le gouvernement de la colonie et l'institution d'un conseil général* (1886), 5.

7. Gauguin, *Le Sourire*, 13 October 1899.

8. "Décret instituant un conseil général dans les ÉFO, 28 décembre

1885," *Documents concernant le gouvernement de la colonie: Annuaire des ÉFO*, 1891, 186–187.

9. *Océanie Française*, 12 August 1884; *Messager de Tahiti*, 18 August 1884.

10. *Océanie Française*, 21 August, 25 September, 30 October 1883.

11. *Arrêté*, 30 September 1884; *JOÉFO*, 2 September 1884.

12. *Procès-verbaux des séances du conseil général*, 1886–1887, 85, 127–128.

13. ANSOM E 41/101, d'Ingremard to MMC, 15 November 1889.

14. ANSOM E 47/50, "Procès-verbaux du conseil privé," 15 February 1900.

15. CSC 58/10, Verdier, 26 January 1894; 28 March 1894.

16. ANSOM E 45/102, Gallet to MC, 14 December 1898.

17. *Procès-verbaux des séances du conseil général*, 1898–1899: 85, 127–128.

18. Ibid.: 1901: 106, Decrais to Petit, 2 November 1901 (cited in minutes).

19. ANSOM E 52/51, MC to Petit, 13 June 1903; *Décret*, 19 May 1903, *Journal officiel des É.F.O.* 1903.

20. ANSOM E 30/116, Michaux, minute, 28 September 1882.

21. *Océanie Française*, 17 April 1883, 22 and 29 April 1884.

22. Morau to General Council, 1 September 1884, cited in *Océanie Française*, 9 September 1884.

23. SMÉ Correspondence, 1883–1884, Vernier to Morau, 18 March 1884.

24. ANSOM A 133/21, Puaux to MMC, 25 August 1887.

25. *Messager de Tahiti*, 2 November 1887.

26. ANSOM E 44/48, "Procès-verbaux du conseil privé," October 1890.

27. ANSOM A 155/23, Petit to MC, 31 March 1901.

28. ANSOM A 133/21, Poroi to Puaux, n.d., cited in Puaux, "Note sur Tahiti," 11 February 1887.

29. ANSOM E 35/116.

30. PMB 71, Biography of Teri'iero'o.

31. *Océanie Française*, 18 September 1883.

32. *Le Petit Tahitien*, 25 December 1882.

33. Bureau des Terres, *puta tomite*, 1875, Pare no. 110; *La Cloche*, 25 March 1887 (for a report on the court case). The block had been owned within the family of Paraita's wife; the nephew, Hiamahupo'o, paid costs and a 50-franc fine to Pare council for "unlawful" registration.

34. ANSOM E 16/75, "Procès-verbaux du conseil d'administration," August 1884.

35. ANSOM E 32/121 and E 40/80.

36. *Décret*, 24 August 1887, *BOÉFO*, 1887: 390.

37. *Procès-verbaux des séances du conseil général*, 1895–1896: 136.

38. I base this rough estimate on later surveys by the Service des Domaines; Roucaute (1951); and the published claims in the *BOÉFO*. But the precise distribution of different types of usehold and registered claims cannot be demonstrated prior to 1945.

39. *La Tribune de Tahiti*, 1 January 1914.

40. SS 40, Richards, 2 February 1888.

41. SS 39, Cooper, 27 December 1889.

42. *JSMÉ* 66 (1889):69; 70 (1895):76–77; and for details of the insurrection, see Caillot (1909:107–288).

43. FO 27/3056, Hawes to FO, 14 February 1891; 27/3098, Hawes to FO, 26 December 1892; FO 687/4, Teraupoʻo to Hawes, 28 September 1891.

44. CSC, Marquesas, 47/7, Martin, 6 February 1901. Fire-walking episodes by Ita and others (from Huahine) are recorded in CSC 47/7, Martin, 11 March 1896.

45. Cited from Caillot in O'Reilly and Teissier (1975:552).

46. Caillot (1909:185).

47. SCO 6/4–6 1895–1897; the unsettled conditions in Raʻiatea are mentioned but not discussed in detail.

48. Bracconi (1906b:330); O'Reilly MSS, "Documents sur l'administration des Iles-Sous-le-Vent," 1895–1904.

49. O'Reilly MSS, "Documents," Laborde, "Affaire Taʻamotu," November 1904.

50. O'Reilly MSS, Bellisle, "Archipel des Marquises. Rapport d'ensemble pour l'année 1920."

51. Tautain in Bommier, 22 April 1893, cited in Bellisle, "Archipel des Marquises."

52. Ibid.

53. Guillot (1935:passim) for Ua Pou and Nukuhiva in 1889 and 1894–1901; Gauguin to Morice, February 1903, in Malingue (1946:314).

54. *Décret*, 31 May 1902, in Roucaute (1951).

55. Bouchon-Brandeley (1885:passim).

56. Bureau des Terres, Doucet, 1950.

57. Porlier (1929) for the legal status of the lagoons.

58. ANSOM Q 4/65, Fillon, 1909; Q 5/66, Revel, 25 June 1914.

59. ANSOM A 174/104, Instructions to Governor Fawtier, 27 June 1913.

60. Roucaute (1951:55).

61. FO 687/46, 1885–1920, mortgages; 687/8, estates, wills, and deeds, 1888–1904; 687/16, reports to Intelligence Branch, Board of Trade; SCO 5/3–8, 1896–1906 (Papeʻete correspondence).

62. O'Reilly and Teissier (1975:674).

63. ANSOM Q 5/66, Revel to MC, 25 June 1914.

64. ANSOM A 178/105, Fawtier to Julien, 22 October 1915, enclosure in Fawtier to MC, 22 October 1915.

65. ANSOM Q 5/66, Revel to MC, 25 June 1914.

66. CSC 58/9, Verdier, 15 July 1884.

67. Roucaute (1951: "l'adoption Faamu," chap. 6).

68. Smith in *Saints' Herald*, 1887: 34.

69. Caillot (1909:56–58).

70. FO 27/3013, Miller to FO, 6 January 1890. His father, George Miller, had retired to San Francisco.

71. Henry (1928; 1951).

72. Arii Taimai (1893; 1901; 1964); for bibliographical notes on these works, see O'Reilly and Reitman (1967:586–587).

73. Lagayette (n.d.:168).

74. Lagayette (n.d.:111–113). This version was published after Marau's death by Takau Pomare.

75. Henry (1928:270–272).

76. Henry (1928:272).

77. Caillot (1909:59; chap. 4).

78. Caillot (1909:84).

Chapter 9: MERCHANTS AND MINERS

1. Much of the statistical evidence is contained in the *Annuaire des Établissements français de l'Océanie* (1885–1917) and *Statistiques décennales du commerce des colonies françaises* (1896–1905). While these are useful for general orders of magnitude, I do not think (for reasons explained in Chapter 6) that they are accurate for details of entrepôt traffic, and I have not reproduced them in full. They have been supplemented by other descriptions of trade in FO 687 (consular reports) and SCO 19, which present a more precise, if narrower, focus on the pattern of imports and exports.

2. SCO 4/2 (correspondence with European firms); SCO 6/1–22 (monthly and quarterly correspondence with Pape'ete by Scharf & Kayser, 1886–1914); SCO 14/1–11, 1899–1910, gives inventories of goods in stock (including a large selection of Chinese goods from 1890 on).

3. SCO 19, "Denkschrift," 1912, on German trade. There is much historical information on the copra market for the immediate prewar period in the excellent articles by R. E. P. Dwyer, *New Guinea Agricultural Gazette*, especially vol. 2, no. 2, October 1936; see also numbers of *Tropenpflanzer: Der Zeitschrift für tropische Landwirtschaft* (Berlin,

1899–1914) for a continuous commentary on production and marketing of staples, including copra.

4. Most of the imported copra came from British dependencies (Malaya and Ceylon) and the Philippines and Netherlands East Indies. British market consumption reached 35,000 tons in 1911. SCO 19, "Denkschrift," 1912.

5. *Rapport d'ensemble*, Pape'ete, 1907: 10–15, 22–25.

6. FO 687/16, Rowley, trade report, 15 April 1910.

7. Disp. USC, 1903–1906. He had been consul at Tahiti (1888–1902) and became vice-president of the Moore, Doty produce brokerage in San Francisco.

8. ANSOM A 164/23, Cor to MMC, 5 November 1904.

9. SCO 6/15, Hoppenstedt, 5 December 1911.

10. Vernier in *JSMÉ*, 1886: 74.

11. SCO 6/15, Hoppenstedt, 19 August 1910.

12. SCO 5/3.

13. FO 687/15, Rowley to Bauer and Schaumer (London), 17 August 1909.

14. FO 687/15, Simons, trade report for 1907.

15. FO 687/16, Rowley to FO, 5 April 1910.

16. SCO 6/17–19, especially Hoppenstedt to Sharf & Kayser, 29 March 1912.

17. SCO 19. More exactly, at 4,441,040 francs, or 3,597,242 marks (£177,641). The evaluation is slightly inflated by outstanding debts and the war levy paid to the Tahiti administration.

18. SCO 1/1, Board of Directors, 15 June 1904.

19. SCO 19. The remainder were bearer shares and difficult to trace by 1915. But see SCO 8, SCO to CFPO, Paris, 10 March 1912, where it is stated that 262 "old" shares were still held by T. Henry Schröder & Co., London.

20. SCO 16, accounts and ledgers, 1910–1915.

21. SCO 11/1–2, accounts, 1895–1913.

22. SCO 4/1, Meuel to Scharf & Kayser, 10 January 1881.

23. SCO 4/1, Meuel to Scharf & Kayser, 14 September 1880.

24. SCO 4/1, Meuel to SCO, 7 February 1881.

25. SCO 3, report, 15 April 1911.

26. FO 687/16, Rowley to Intelligence Branch, Board of Trade, 18 November 1912; Richards to Board of Trade, 11 October 1913 (affairs of the Tropical Exploitation Syndicate Ltd.).

27. SCO 5/2, Hoppenstedt, 30 August 1893.

28. SCO 5/5, ff. 37–38; ANSOM E 53/122, Salmon, 3 December 1901.

29. SCO 5/2, Langomazino to Tati Salmon, 1 December 1894.

30. SCO 5/5, f. 103.

31. SCO 5/5, f. 117.

32. SCO 5/6, Hoppenstedt to Adams, 30 August 1903.

33. SCO 19, enclosure in SCO to Auswärtiges Amt, 3 January 1915.

34. ANSOM J 32/124. For details of the phosphate lands and their location, see Newbury (1972b:167–188).

35. For the geology, see Agassiz (1903:56–64); on the taxonomy of mineral "discoveries," see the suggestive article by Blainey (1970:298–313).

36. Morrell (1960:264); and for his visits to Tahiti, PMB 38, J. L. Green Papers.

37. PMB 14, H. I. M. Moouga, "Diary of a Guano Digger at Flint Island, Eastern Pacific," 2 vols. for 1889–1891. This consists mostly of short entries on work tasks and daily events, lists of gangs, health, and so forth. The commentary or note accompanying it is inaccurate in claiming it is one of the few manuscripts in Tahitian at this period.

38. PMB 492, John T. Arundel Correspondence, 1897–1912. I deduce his movements from the correspondence and the list of reports appended. His valuable diaries are illegible on microfilm. See also Langdon (1974:59–61).

39. ANSOM E 56/123, MC to Jullien, 28 August 1905.

40. FO 687/16, Simons to FO, 3 October 1908.

41. SCO 5/8, Hoppenstedt, 23 March 1908.

42. ANSOM J 28/123, Charlier to MC, 17 August 1908.

43. FO 687/16, Simons, 3 October 1909.

44. PMB 492, John T. Arundel Correspondence, 1897–1912, Stanmore to Arundel, 3 December 1908. Lord Stanmore (Sir Arthur Gordon) took the view that Simons was bound to report what he knew and that it was "quite accurate."

45. ANSOM J 30/134, Fillon to MC, 21 July 1909 (especially his confidential enclosures 46 and 47).

46. ANSOM E 62/122, Trouillot to François, 25 March 1910.

47. ANSOM E 62/122, contract, 29 December 1910; J 30/134, Bonhoure to MC, 13 January 1911.

48. ANSOM J 32/124, Bonhoure to MC, 16 March 1912.

49. ANSOM E 62/22, Revel to MC, 30 May 1914.

50. ANSOM J 29/123; E 63/121 for decision of the Council of State, 11 May 1917.

51. SCO 22, especially SCO to Papinaud, 17 December 1894.

52. *Procès-verbaux des séances du conseil général*, 1898–1899, 8 March 1899.

53. Ibid.

54. ANSOM M 2/35 and M 5/125; FO 687/16, Rowley, report for 1910.

55. *Océanie Française*, 1914: 166.

56. FO 682/16, Rowley to FO, 9 April 1910.

57. Ibid.

58. O'Reilly and Reitman (1967:757–758, 773).

59. ANSOM K 60/126, "Rapport de la mission chargée d'étudier les conséquences de l'ouverture du canal de Panama en ce qui concerne les colonies françaises des Antilles et d'Océanie," Paris, 1913; and "Note sommaire," 24 October 1912.

60. FO 687/17, report, 1 October 1914; ANSOM O 29 and 30/105; *Océanie Française*, 1916: 213; Pochhammer (1918:passim).

61. *Océanie Française*, 1916: 213.

62. SCO 8, SCO to Navy, Kiel, 22 October 1915. The value of the naval requisition was eventually refunded at the rate of 323,739.47 marks in 1920.

63. SCO 19, SCO to Auswärtiges Amt, 24 November 1914. The firm paid 850,000 francs and the rest was levied from Hoppenstedt, Krisch, Barmeister, Krämer, Muth, Allgoever, and Koeppen.

64. ANSOM F 65/120; SCO 19, copy Minutes of the Pape'ete Chamber of Commerce, 5 December 1914. The SCO was kept remarkably well informed of events in Tahiti during the war by local correspondents.

Chapter 10: FRENCH ASCENDANCY

1. ANSOM A 128/105, Fawtier to Hostein, confidential, 6 April 1912; Fawtier to MC, 22 October 1915; Julien to MC, 14 April 1919.

2. FO 687/18, Consul-General, San Francisco, and "Commercial," 1920.

3. For a history of local conscripts, see Basquel and Delmont (1922:153–160, 225–236); ANSOM K 57/127.

4. FO 687/18, Williams to FO, 14 September 1919.

5. *Océanie Française*, 1917: 54; 1922: 124.

6. FO 687/17 (files on Cook Islands labor).

7. FO 687/18, Williams to FO, 1 February 1919.

8. *Océanie Française*, 1913: 34, 66; 1914: 76.

9. ANSOM M 6/120 (immigration).

10. Léon Reallon in *Océanie Française*, 1914:76.

11. *Océanie Française*, 1916:249; 1917: 25.

12. See McArthur (1968:232–243); Lyons (1968:passim).

13. McArthur (1968:328–331).

14. Auzelle (1950:81–128 and plans).

15. ANSOM M 8/120; *Océanie Française*, 1920: 5.

16. FO 687/17 (contracts for Manihiki); see also, "Makatea," in *JSO* 15(1959):202–203.

17. FO 687/17, Touze to Commissioner, 12 July 1917; Marama to "the Resident Commissioner," Pape'ete, 10 June 1917.

18. *Océanie Française*, 1930: 117.

19. *JOÉFO*, 13 February 1929.

20. Coppenrath (1967:annex I).

21. Ibid., 66.

22. Ibid., 92–94.

23. ANSOM H 43 and 44/98 and 132.

24. CSC 59/5 and 59/6 for Mazé; see also O'Reilly and Teissier (1975:371).

25. *Saints' Herald* 63(1916):410–411.

26. *JSMÉ*, 1940: 112–113.

27. G. Preiss in *JSMÉ*, 1940: 120–124.

28. *JSMÉ*, 1926: 329–333.

29. ANSOM A 174/104, Julien to MC, confidential, 14 April 1919.

30. *ÉFO. Liquidation des biens séquestrés. Avis de vente, avec admission des étrangers autres que les ressortissants des anciennes puissances ennemies* (Pape'ete, 1924); SCO 19.

31. SCO 19, enclosure in SCO to Reichsfinanzministerium, 11 December 1924. For an article based on some of this material, see O'Reilly (1976); for Chin Foo, see O'Reilly and Teissier (1975:113–114); Coppenrath (1967:59–60).

32. FO 687/21, Donald's to Edmonds, 17 December 1940.

33. Coppenrath (1967:76–78); and Moench (1963:passim).

34. *Océanie Française*, 1921: 112.

35. ANSOM E 65/120; G 83/110; Coppenrath, *JSO* 15(1959):241.

36. *Courrier Colonial*, 9 June 1922 in ANSOM A 174/104; *Océanie Française*, 1922: 103.

37. *Océanie Française*, 1923: 17–18; ANSOM E 76/121 (for decree, 25 March 1923).

38. ANSOM K 65/126; *Revue du Pacifique*, 1931: 628–643.

39. Roucaute (1951:17).

40. *Océanie Française*, 1932: 119; 1933: 113.

41. *Océanie Française*, 1933: 53.

42. Roucaute (1951:17).

43. Bureau des Terres, registers for Puna'auia (examined 1955, 1964); C. Ringon and F. Ravault in *Travaux et Documents d'ORSTOM* (n.d.).

44. *Travaux et Documents d'ORSTOM*, 17, 119.

45. Ibid., 77–78.

46. Ibid., 119.
47. Ibid., 159.
48. Bureau des Terres, *Puta monora'a, Puta ho'ora'a* (for Puna'auia).
49. Ibid., *Puta tomite*, 1883 [*sic* 1853]: Atitupua, no. 130; and compare *Puta fa'ahurura'a* no. 7,13.
50. ANSOM A 174/104; *Océanie Française*, 1929: 74.
51. Bureaux des Terres, "Tableaux comparatifs," MS.
52. Coppenrath (1967:82).
53. Guillaume (1958:279–299, 448–457, 558–629); *Travaux et Documents d'ORSTOM*, 22.
54. *Travaux et Documents d'ORSTOM*, 24.
55. ANSOM G 83/110; *Océanie Française*, 1932: 26.
56. *Bulletin de la Chambre de Commerce de Papeete*, 1931, in ANSOM C 91/149; *Océanie Française*, 1931: 72.
57. Coppenrath (1959:245); and for the first meetings, 1933–1935, ANSOM E 65/121 (mimeographed minutes).
58. *Océanie Française*, 1930: 76; 1931: 100.
59. ANSOM J 35/125; *Océanie Française*, 1935: 22, 91, 92; see, too, *Pacific Islands Monthly*, October 1931.
60. *Pacific Islands Monthly*, March 1936: 18.
61. These percentages are calculated from customs returns printed in surveys of trade in *Océanie Française*, 1931–1940.
62. Coppenrath (1959:246–249).
63. Chastenet de Géry (1975:399).
64. FO 687/21, Edmonds to Naval Intelligence, Wellington, 15 May 1940.
65. FO 687/21, "Defences," 1940–1941.
66. For New Caledonia, see Lawrey (1975:64–81); for Vichy France, see Paxton (1972:passim).
67. FO 687/21, Edmonds to Naval Intelligence, 18 June 1940; Edmonds to High Commissioner, Western Pacific, 24 June 1940; compare Chastenet de Géry (1975:401).
68. Émile de Curton (1973:*annexe* 2). De Curton cites only the second of these documents.
69. FO 687/21, Edmonds to Naval Intelligence, 18 June 1940.
70. Chastenet de Géry (1975:400–401).
71. FO 687/21, FO to Edmonds, 27 June 1940; compare Chastenet de Géry (1975:402, doc. 4). This was in no sense an "ultimatum."
72. FO 687/21, FO to Edmonds, 1 July 1940; Chastenet de Géry (1975:doc. 6).
73. Chastenet de Géry (1975:404).

74. FO 687/21, FO to Edmonds, 3 July 1940.

75. FO 687/21, Edmonds, consular report for 24 January to 24 July 1940. The phrase is Edmonds', reporting de Géry.

76. Ibid. The closure of the consulate is not mentioned by de Géry, though it may be inferred from doc. 9. It was reopened on 1 September.

77. FO 687/21, Edmonds to Prime Minister's Department, Canberra, 20 July 1940.

78. Ibid.

79. Chastenet de Géry (1975:406).

80. Lawrey (1975:80–82).

81. De Curton (1973:*annexe* 3 (unsigned)). The copy in FO 687/21 is signed by Dr. Florisson, Lainey, Buillard, Constant, and Alain Gerbault.

82. De Curton (1973:75–77).

83. Ibid., *annexe* 13.

84. FO 687/21, consul (unsigned copy) to Prime Minister's Department, Wellington, 13 January 1941.

85. De Curton (1973:134). It is not explained why popular consultation was suddenly abandoned.

86. FO 681/21, Edmonds, Secret. Consular report, 13 January 1941, Secret. De Curton to Prime Minister, Wellington, 14 March 1941; De Curton (1973:151 ff.); consul to Naval Intelligence, 31 March 1941.

87. FO 687/21, Archer to Shanahan, 9 October 1941; Cameron, reports to New Zealand Naval Board; 687/22, "Political and Economic Reports," 1943, and "Bora Bora Island, 1943."

REFERENCES

The following series are no more than the title suggests. For a guide to printed materials, see Patrick O'Reilly and Édouard Reitman, *Bibliographie de Tahiti et de la Polynésie française* (Publications de la Société des Océanistes, no. 14, Musée de l'Homme, Paris, 1967).

UNPUBLISHED SOURCES, ARCHIVES, AND PRIVATE COLLECTIONS

[1]   Archives de la Marine (Archives Nationales). Paris.

> Series: BB4, as under: Voyages et découvertes, 1003–1009; Nouvelle-Zélande, Océanie, 1010–1023.

[2]   Archives des Affaires Étrangères (Ministère des Affaires Étrangères). Paris.

> Series: *Correspondance commerciale*, I Sydney (1842–1847); *Océanie, Mémoires et Documents*, I *Lettres et pièces diverses* (1822–1843); 2 *Occupation des Iles Marquises* (1841–1843); *Nouvelle-Zélande*, 1 (1772–1839).

[3]   Archives Nationales, Section Outre-mer (formerly Ministère de la France Outre-mer, Ministère des Colonies). Rue Oudinot, Paris.

> For a detailed inventory, see Étienne Taillemite, "Inventaire du fonds Océanie (Polynésie française) conservé aux archives du Ministère de la France d'Outre-mer," *Journal de la Société des Océanistes* 15(1959):267–320.
>
> The following series were used: A (Affaires politiques, Correspondance générale); B (Relations extérieures, Colonies étrangères); C, D (Explorations, missions, voyages, mémoires); E (Administration générale et municipale); F (Justice); G (Finances); H (Instruction publique); I (Santé publique); J (Affaires économ-

iques); K (Navigation, communications); L (Travaux publiques); M (Travail et main d'oeuvre, Immigration); N, O (Approvisionnement, Affaires militaires); P (Personnel); Q (Contrôle et inspection).

[4]   Archives, Société des Études Océaniennes, Musée de Pape'ete.

Letter-books and inward correspondence of the protectorate administration, 1842–1851. The SÉO is also repository for a number of archives formerly located under O'Reilly MSS and PMB collections cited below.

[5]   Bibliothèque Nationale. Paris.

Nouvelles Acquisitions Françaises, as under: Océanie, Nouvelle-Zélande, 9446; Iles Marquises, Pritchard, 9447.

[6]   British Consulate. Pape'ete.

Tahiti British Consulate papers, registers, and correspondence were examined in the consulate office in 1954. After closure of the consulate, these records were transferred to the Public Record Office, London, and have been cited under series FO 687/1–47 (1826–1948). Registers of British subjects, mortgages, wills, and shipping begin at FO 687/25. See also Mitchell Library below.

[7]   British Museum. London.

Additional MSS: 17542–17543 (W. R. Broughton, Log Book of the *Chatham*, 1791–1792); 17545 (Lt. Peter Puget, Log Book of the *Discovery*, August 1791–January 1792. These are entries and portions of a rough journal; further fragments for Tahiti are found in 17546–17548 and 17549–17550); 32641 (Archibald Menzies, Journal of Vancouver's Voyage, 1790–1794); 41472 (Martin Papers).

[8]   Bureau des Terres (Service des Domaines). Pape'ete.

Land registers and committee books; Tableaux comparatifs pour toutes les îles du Territoire des É.F.O., 1950; Cadastre des Tuamotu, Rapport Doucet, 30 June 1950.

[9]   Calvinistic Methodist Archives, National Library of Wales. Aberystwyth.

A series of manuscript letters by John Davies (in Welsh) to the Rev. John Hughes and others.

[10]   Congrégation des Sacrés-Coeurs. Rome.

For the Pacific series, see Amerigo Cools, "Répertoire des Ar-chives des Pères des Sacrés-Coeurs concernant l'Océanie," *Jour-nal de la Société des Océanistes* 25(1969):354–357. There is a selective microfilm series under Hamilton Library 4351 which does not contain all the items listed in the congregation ar-chives.

[11]   Hamilton Library, University of Hawaii. Honolulu.

Location for (1) dispatches from United States Consuls in Tahiti (microfilm), vols. 1–10, 1836–1906; (2) Pacific Manuscripts Bureau, Australian National University, microfilm series; (3) records relating to the U.S. Exploring Expedition under com-mand of Lt. Charles Wilkes, 1836–1842.

[12]   Hawaiian Mission Children's Society Library. Honolulu.

Correspondence from missionaries in the Marquesas.

[13]   Hocken Library, University of Otago.

New Zealand pamphlets; manuscript letters, 53/28.

[14]   India Office Library. London.

Thomas Godsell, second officer's journal on board the ship *Duff*, 1796–1798, 407A.

[15]   London Missionary Society (Livingstone House and School of Oriental and African Studies). London.

Series: South Seas; Correspondence; Journals; Australia; Per-sonal; Home Odds; Board Minutes; Robert Thomson MS "History of Tahiti" (three parts).

[16]   Mitchell Library. Sydney.

W. W. Bolton MSS, Old Time Tahiti, A 3375; Despatches to Governors of New South Wales, August–December 1842; Capt. A. S. Hamond, "Remark Book of Captain A. S. Hamond, H.M.S. *Salamander*, April 1844–January1845"; Letter-Book of Capt. Hamond, H.M.S. *Salamander*, An 138.

Tahiti British Consulate Papers, as under: Pomare, 1826–1843; 2 In-Letters, 1834–1843; 3 In-Letters, 1844–1850; 4 In-Letters, 1851–1856; 5 In-Letters, 1857–1866; 6 In-Letters, 1867–1873; 8 Out-Letters, 1833–1846; 9 Out-Letters, 1847–

1853; 10 Out-Letters, 1854–1864; 11 Out-Letters, 1865–1876; 12 Out-Letters, 1877–1878; Letters to Local Authorities, 1853–1863; Despatches to Foreign Office, 1852–1863, 1863–1866; Annual Reports, 1838–1882.

George Tobin, Journal of H.M.S. *Providence*, 1791–1793, A 562.

[17] O'Reilly MSS (formerly André Ropiteau and Patrick O'Reilly collection). Paris.

Administration des Marquises. Reports and correspondence of Poyen Bellisle; Documents sur l'administration des Iles-Sous-le-Vent, 1896–1904; Letters from English Missionaries at Tahiti, 1807–1897. Some of this collection is now located in the Musée de Pape'ete and on microfilm under PMB 70 and 73 (see O'Reilly 1969 below).

[18] Public Record Office. London.

Series: Admiralty I (for dispatches from British naval officers in the Pacific); Admiralty 50 (for the journals of Admirals Sir G. F. Seymour, P. Hornby, R. Thomas); Admiralty 51, 53, 55 (for logbooks of the officers of H.M.S. *Chatham* and *Discovery*, 1791–1792, H.M.S. *Providence*, 1791–1793, and H.M.S. *Assistant*, 1791–1793.

Colonial Office 136 (for Ionian Islands Protectorate).

Customs 8.

Foreign Office 58/(dispatches from consuls in the Pacific); 27/(for diplomatic and consular correspondence concerning the Leeward Islands and Tahiti).

[19] Société des Missions Évangéliques. Paris.

Correspondence, 1860–1894 (for letters from missionaries in Tahiti).

[20] Staatsarchiv. Hamburg.

German Naval and Consular Correspondence: Pacific 1860–1883; Société Commerciale de l'Océanie. For an inventory of this series, see *Journal de la Société des Océanistes* 17(1961): 59–61.

[21] Turnbull Library. Wellington.

[Edward Bell], Journal of Voyage in Chatham, 1791–1794 (ff. 69–126 concern Tahiti).

PUBLISHED SOURCES

GOVERNMENT PUBLICATIONS

French:

Annuaire des ÉFO, 1863. Pape'ete, 1863.

Annuaire des ÉFO, 1885–1917. Pape'ete.

Les Arrêtés du Gouverneur des Établissements français de l'Océanie. I (1843–1845). Pape'ete, 1846.

Bulletin officiel des ÉFO, 1860–1902. Pape'ete.

Code Tahitien, 1842. Livre des lois pour la conduite du gouvernement de Pomare-Vahine 1er. Pape'ete, 1845.

Documents concernant le gouvernement de la colonie et l'institution d'un conseil général. Pape'ete, 1886.

Documents Diplomatiques Français, 1er. série. Vol. 3, 1880–1881. Paris, 1931.

ÉFO Liquidation des biens séquestrés. Avis de vente, avec admission des étrangers autres que les ressortissants des anciennes puissances ennemies. Pape'ete, 1924.

Journal officiel de la République française. Paris, 1884.

Journal officiel des Établissements français de l'Océanie, 1884–. Pape'ete, 1884–. (See also *Messager de Tahiti.*)

Municipalité de Papeete. Décrets du mai 1890 instituant la Commune de Papeete. Pape'ete, 1890.

Procès-verbaux des séances du conseil général, 1886–1887, 1887–1902. Pape'ete.

Rapport d'ensemble sur la situation générale de la colonie. Année 1907. Pape'ete, 1908.

Rapport fait à M. le Commandant commissaire impérial par la Commission d'inspection des cultures. Pape'ete, 1866.

Statistiques décennales du commerce des colonies françaises, 1896–1905. 3 vols. Paris, 1914.

British:

Parliamentary Papers. As under: 1843 (61), 475, Correspondence relative to the proceedings of the French at Tahiti, 1825–1843; 1844 (51), 529, Correspondence relative to the Society Islands; 1847 (70), 841, Papers relative to Tahiti and the Leeward or Society Islands.

Australian:

Historical Records of Australia. Edited by F. Watson. Series 1, Governors' Despatches, vols. 1–3. Sydney, 1914–1915.

MISSIONARY PUBLICATIONS

Journal des Missions Évangéliques. Paris, 1824–.

Quarterly Chronicle of the Transactions of the London Missionary Society, 1815–1832. 4 vols. London, 1821–1833.

Reports of the London Missionary Society. London, 1820–.

Te Heheuraa api. Pape'ete, 1907–.

Te Orometua. Te ve'a Sanito te Ekaresia a Jesu Mesia. Pape'ete and USA, 1897–.

Transactions of the Missionary Society, 1795–1817. 4 vols. London, 1804–1818.

The True Latterday Saints' Herald, 1874–1933. PMB 93.

Ui Katorika (pope) o te Vikario raa apotoro i Tahiti. Pape'ete (?), 1851.

NEWSPAPERS AND PERIODICALS

La Cloche. Pape'ete, 1886–1887.

Le Courrier Colonial. (Used for 1922.)

Daily Herald. San Francisco. (Used for 1867.)

La Dépêche de Tahiti. Pape'ete. (Used for 1976.)

Journal des Débats politiques et littéraires. Paris. (Used for 1843 and 1869.)

Messager de Tahiti (Journal officiel des Établissements français de l'Océanie). Pape'ete, 1852–1884.

Messager de Tahiti (Te Vea no Tahiti). Pape'ete, 1884–1889.

Moniteur universel. Paris. (Used for 1842–1846.)

Océanie Française. Pape'ete, 1844–1845; 1883–1887; 1911–1940.

Pacific Islands Monthly. Sydney.

Le Petit Tahitien. Pape'ete, 1882.

Revue du Pacifique. (Used for 1931.)

San Francisco Times. (Used for 1867.)

Le Sourire. Pape'ete, 1899–1900.

Te Vea Maohi. Pape'ete, 1930–1946.

Te Vea no Tahiti. Pape'ete, 1850–1859.

La Tribune de Tahiti. Pape'ete, 1912–1915.

Tropenpflanzer: Der Zeitschrift für tropische Landwirtschaft. Berlin, 1899–1914.

BOOKS AND ARTICLES

Agassiz, A.
  1903 *Reports on the Scientific Results of the Expedition to the Tropical Pacific, in the Charge of Alexander Agassiz, by the U.S. Fish Commission Steamer "Albatross," from August 1899 to March 1900, Commander F. Moser, U.S.N., Com-*

manding. Vol. 4, *The Coral Reefs of the Tropical Pacific.* Cambridge, Mass.

Arbousset, Thomas
> 1864 *Te maa vaorua na te mau ekalesia.* Papeʻete: Government Press.

Arii Taimai
> 1893 *Memoirs of Marau Taaroa, Last Queen of Tahiti.* Washington. Privately printed.
> 1901 *Memoirs of Arii Taimai E Marama of Eimeo, Teriirere of Tooarai, Teriinui o Tahiti.* Paris, privately printed.
> 1964 *Mémoires d'Arii Taimai.* Publications de la Société des Océanistes, no 12. Paris: Musée de l'Homme.

Auzelle, Robert
> 1950 *Plan directeur d'aménagement de l'agglomération de Papeete.* Paris: Ministère de la France d'Outre-mer.

Bach, J. P. S.
> 1963 "The Royal Navy in the South Pacific, 1826–1876." Ph.D. thesis, University of New South Wales.

Baldwin, J. R.
> 1938 "England and the French Seizure of the Society Islands." *Journal of Modern History* 10:212–231.

Basquel, Victor, and Alcide Delmont
> 1922 *Le livre d'or de l'effort colonial français pendant la Grande Guerre 1914–1918.* Vol. 1. Paris: Institut colonial français.

Beaglehole, John C. (ed.)
> 1955 *The Journals of Captain James Cook on His Voyages of Discovery.* Vol. 1. Hakluyt Society, Extra Series, no. 34. London: Cambridge University Press.
> 1961 *The Journals of Captain James Cook on His Voyages of Discovery.* Vol. 2. Hakluyt Society, Extra Series, no. 35. London: Cambridge University Press.
> 1962 *The Endeavour Journal of Joseph Banks 1768–1771.* 2 vols. Sydney: Angus and Robertson.
> 1967 *The Journals of Captain James Cook on His Voyages of Discovery.* Vol. 3, pts. 1 and 2. Hakluyt Society, Extra Series, no. 36. London: Cambridge University Press.

Beechey, Frederick William
> 1833 *Narrative of a Voyage to the Pacific and Beering's Strait, to*

Co-operate with the Polar Expeditions: Performed in His Majesty's Ship Blossom under the Command of Captain F. W. Beechey in the Years 1825 . . . 1828. London: H. Colburn and R. Bentley.

Bennett, F. D.
1840   *Narrative of a Whaling Voyage round the Globe, from the year 1833 to 1836, comprising sketches of Polynesia, California, the Indian Archipelago, etc. with an account of Southern Wales, the spermwhale fishery and the natural history of the climates visited.* London: R. Bentley.

Blainey, G.
1970   "A Theory of Mineral Discovery: Australia in the Nineteenth Century." *Economic History Review* 23:298–313.

Bligh, William
1792   *A Voyage to the South Sea, Undertaken by Command of His Majesty, for the Purpose of Conveying the Breadfruit Tree to the West Indies, in His Majesty's Ship the Bounty, Including an Account of the Mutiny on Board the Said Ship.* 2 vols. London: G. Nicol.
1937   *The Log of the Bounty. Being Lieutenant William Bligh's Log of the Proceedings of His Majesty's Armed Vessel Bounty in a Voyage to the South Seas, to Take the Breadfruit from the Society Islands to the West Indies.* 2 vols. London: Golden Cockerel Press.

Blue, G. V.
1933   "The Project for a French Settlement in the Hawaiian Islands, 1824–1832." *Pacific Historical Review* 2:85–99.

Bonhoure, René
1915   "La Propriété foncière dans les Établissements français de l'Océanie." Thèse pour doctorat, Université de Paris.

Bouchon-Brandeley, G.
1885   *Rapport de M. Bouchon-Brandeley sur sa mission à Tahiti. Les Pêcheries des îles Tuamotu.* Papeʻete: Government Press.

Bougainville, Louis Antoine de
1771   *Voyage autour du monde, par la frégate du Roi, la Flûte l'Étoile: en 1766 . . . 1769.* Paris: Saillant and Nyon.

Bouge, L. J.
1952   "Prémière législation tahitienne. Le Code Pomaré de 1819.

Historique et traduction." *Journal de la Société des Océanistes* 8:5–26.

Bovis, Edmond de
1863 "État de la société tahitienne, à l'arrivée des Européens." *Annuaire des ÉFO* (Pape'ete), pp. 217–310.

Bracconi, P.
1906a "La colonisation française à Tahiti," *Questions diplomatiques et coloniales* 224:807–818.
1906b "Les Iles-Sous-le-Vent de Tahiti et le régime de l'indigénant." *Questions diplomatiques et coloniales* 230:231–333.

Brassey, Thomas
1878 "Round the World in the *Sunbeam*." *The Nineteenth Century* 3(14):667–686.

Brookes, Jean Ingram
1941 *International Rivalry in the Pacific Islands, 1800–1875*. Berkeley and Los Angeles: University of California Press.

Broughton, William Robert
1804 *A Voyage of Discovery to the North Pacific Ocean . . . performed in His Majesty's sloop Providence, and her tender in the years 1795 . . . 1798*. London: T. Cadell and W. Davies.

Buick, T. Lindsay
1928 *The French at Akaroa: An Adventure in Colonization*. Wellington: Government Printer.

Caillot, A. C. E.
1909 *Les Polynésiens orientaux au contact de la civilisation*. Paris: E. Leroux.
1910 *Histoire de la Polynésie orientale*. Paris: E. Leroux.
1914 *Mythes, légendes et traditions des Polynésiens*. Paris: E. Leroux.
1932 *Histoire de l'île Oparo ou Rapa*. Paris: E. Leroux.

Candelot, M.
1870 *Plantation de coton de Tahiti. Compagnie "Tahiti Cotton and Coffee Plantation."* Paris: Balitout, Questroy & Co.

Chastenet de Géry, J.
1975 *Les derniers jours de la troisième république à Tahiti 1938–1940*. Société des Océanistes. Paris: Musée de l'Homme.

Chesnau, Henri
    1928   "Histoire de Huahine et autres îles Sous-le-Vent." *Bulletin de la Société d'Études océaniennes* 3:57–67.

Coppenrath, Gérald
    1959   "Évolution politique de la Polynésie française depuis la Première Guerre mondiale." *Journal de la Société des Océanistes* 15:237–265.
    1967   *Les Chinois de Tahiti: De l'aversion à l'assimilation 1865–1966.* Publications de la Société des Océanistes, no. 21. Paris: Musée de l'Homme.

Corney, Bolton Glanville (ed.)
    1913   *The Quest and Occupation of Tahiti by Emissaries of Spain during the Years 1772–1776.* Vol. 1. London: Cambridge University Press.
    1915   *The Quest and Occupation of Tahiti.* Vol. 2. London: Cambridge University Press.
    1919   *The Quest and Occupation of Tahiti.* Vol. 3. London: Cambridge University Press.

Cottez, J.
    1955   "Tahiti il y a cent ans. Aperçu rétrospectif des Cadres Maoris des Iles Tahiti et Moorea vers 1855." *Bulletin de la Société des Études océaniennes* 112:434–460.

Curton, Émile de
    1973   *Tahiti 40. Récit du ralliement à la France libre des Établissements français d'Océanie.* Publications de la Société des Océanistes, no. 31. Paris: Musée de l'Homme.

Davies, John
    1810   *Te Aebi No Taheiti. E Te Parou Mata Mua I Parou Hapi Iaitea Te Perini E Te Ridini Te Parou No Taheiti.* London.
    1851   *A Tahitian and English Dictionary and a Short Grammar of the Tahitian Dialect.* Tahiti: Missionary Press.
    1961   *The History of the Tahitian Mission 1799–1830.* Edited by C. W. Newbury. Hakluyt Society, Second Series, no. 116. London: Cambridge University Press.

Dening, G. M. (ed.)
    1974   *The Marquesan Journal of Edward Robarts 1797–1824.* Pacific History Series, no. 6. Honolulu: The University Press of Hawaii.

Deschanel, Paul
    1884   *La politique française en Océanie à propos du canal de Panama.* Paris: Berger-Levrault.
    1888   *Les intérêts français dans l'Océan Pacifique.* Paris.

Duchêne, Albert
    1928   *La politique coloniale de la France. Le Ministère des Colonies depuis Richelieu.* Paris.
    1938   *Histoire des finances coloniales de la France.* Paris.

Dunmore, John
    1965   *French Explorers in the Pacific.* Vol. 1: *The Eighteenth Century.* Oxford: Clarendon Press.
    1969   *French Explorers in the Pacific.* Vol. 2: *The Nineteenth Century.* Oxford: Clarendon Press.

Dupetit-Thouars, Abel A.
    1843   *Voyage autour du monde sur la frégate la Vénus pendant les années 1836 . . . 1839.* 4 vols. Paris: Gide.

Dwyer, R. E. P.
    1936   "A Survey of the Coco-nut Industry in the Mandated Territory of New Guinea." *New Guinea Agricultural Gazette* 2:1–72.

Ellis, William
    1829   *Polynesian Researches.* 2 vols. London: Fisher, Son and Jackson; 1831, 2nd ed. 4 vols. London: Fisher, Son and Jackson.

Ellsworth, S. George
    1959   *Zion in Paradise: Early Mormons in the South Seas.* Logan: Utah State University Press.

Faivre, Jean Paul
    1953   *L'Expansion Française dans le Pacifique de 1800 à 1842.* Paris: Nouvelles Éditions Latines.

Findlay, A. G.
    1851   *A Directory for the Navigation of the South Pacific Ocean.* London: R. H. Lawrie.

Finney, Ben
    1964   "Polynesian Peasants and Proletarians: Socioeconomic Change in the Society Islands." Ph.D. dissertation, Harvard University, Cambridge, Mass.

FitzRoy, Robert
    1839   *Narrative of the Surveying Voyages of His Majesty's Ships Adventure and Beagle, between the Years 1826 and 1836.* Vol. 2. London: H. Colburn.

Gracia, Father Mathias
    1843   *Lettres sur les Iles Marquises ou Mémoires pour servir à l'étude religieuse, morale, politique et statistique des Iles Marquises et de l'Océanie Orientale.* Paris: Gaume Frères.

Grattan, Hartley C.
    1963   *The Southwest Pacific to 1900: A Modern History. Australia, New Zealand, The Islands, Antarctica.* Ann Arbor: University of Michigan Press.

Guillaume, M.
    1958   "Économie rurale de l'Océanie française. Esquisse de développement agricole." *Agronomie tropicale* 13:279–299, 448–457, 558–629.

Guillot, François
    1935   *Souvenirs d'un colonial en Océanie. Taïti, Iles Marquises, Tubuai et Tuamotu (1888–1911).* Annecy: L. Dépollier.

Guizot, François P. G.
    1867   *Mémoires pour servir à l'histoire de mon temps.* 8 vols. Paris.

Gunson, Niel
    1977   *Messengers of Grace: Evangelical Missionaries in the South Seas 1797–1860.* Melbourne: Oxford University Press.

Hanson, F. Allan
    1973   *Rapa. Une île polynésienne hier et aujourd'hui.* Publications de la Société des Océanistes, no. 33. Paris: Musée de l'Homme.

Harlow, V. T.
    1952, *The Founding of the Second British Empire 1763–1792.* 2
    1964   vols. London.

Henry, Teuira
    1928   *Ancient Tahiti.* Bernice P. Bishop Museum Bulletin no. 48. Honolulu.
    1951   *Tahiti aux temps anciens.* Société des Océanistes, no. 1, Paris: Musée de l'Homme.

Hort, Dora
    1891   *Tahiti, the Garden of the Pacific.* London: T. Fisher Unwin.

[House, William]
    1792   *A Letter from the South Seas, by a Voyager on the Daedalus, 1792.* Edited by John Earnshaw. Cremorne, NSW: Talkarra Press.

Ingremard, Maurice d'
    1889   *Discours prononcé à l'ouverture de la session extraordinaire du Conseil général.* Pape'ete: Government Press.

Jacolliot, Louis
    1869   *La vérité sur Taïti. Affaire de la Roncière.* Paris: Librarie internationale.

Jacquier, Henri
    1960   "Énumeration des plantes introduites à Tahiti depuis la découverte jusqu'en 1885." *Bulletin de la Société d'Études océaniennes* 130:117–146.

Jaussen, Mgr. Florentin Étienne (Tepano)
    1861   *Grammaire tahitienne.* Saint-Germain-en-Laye: L. Toinon.

Jore, Léonce
    1959   *L'Océan Pacifique au temps de la Restauration et de la Monarchie de Juillet, 1815–1848.* Paris: G. P. Maisonneuve.

Kelly, John L.
    1885   *The South Sea Islands: Possibilities of Trade with New Zealand . . . Tonga, Samoa, Rarotonga, and Tahiti.* Auckland: H. Brett.

Lagayette, Pierre
    n.d.   *Henry Adams et les mers du sud: "The Memoirs of Arii Taimai."* Doctorat de Troisième Cycle, University of Pau et les Pays de l'Adour.

Langdon, Robert
    1959   *Island of Love.* London: Cassell.

    1974   "Arundel the Shy Cecil Rhodes of the Pacific Islands." *Pacific Islands Monthly* 45(4):59–61.

Laval, Honoré
    1968   *Mémoires pour servir à l'histoire de Mangareva ère chrétienne 1834–1871.* Edited by C. W. Newbury and

P. O'Reilly. Publications de la Société des Océanistes, no. 15. Paris: Musée de l'Homme.

Lawrey, John
    1975   "A Catch on the Boundary: Australia and the Free French Movement in 1940." *Journal of Pacific History* 10:64–81.

[Layrle, Admiral]
    1933   "L'Océanie en 1870, d'après le journal d'un officier de marine." *Revue de l'histoire des colonies françaises* 21: 307–318.

Levy, Robert I.
    1975   *Tahitians: Mind and Experience in the Society Islands.* Chicago:University of Chicago Press.

[Lucett, Edward]
    1851   *Rovings in the Pacific, from 1837 to 1849; with a Glance at California. By a Merchant long resident at Tahiti.* 2 vols. London: Longman, Brown, Green and Longmans.

Lyons, Robin Ray
    1968   *"Population Structure in French Polynesia: Ethnic and Economic Patterns."* M.S. thesis, Brigham Young University.

McArthur, Norma
    1968   *Island Populations of the Pacific.* Honolulu: The University Press of Hawaii.

McKay, D.
    1943   "Colonialism and the French Geographical Movement," *Geographical Review* 33:214–237.

Mager, Henri
    1889   "Un vieux tahitien." *Cahiers coloniaux de 1889.* Paris: Colin.
    1902   *Le monde polynésien.* Paris: Schleicher frères.

Malingue, Maurice (ed.)
    1946   *Lettres de Gauguin à sa femme et à ses amis.* Paris: B. Grasset.

Maude, H. E.
    1968   *Of Islands and Men: Studies in Pacific History.* Melbourne: Oxford University Press.

Moench, Richard A.
1963   *"Economic Relations of the Chinese in the Society Islands."*
Ph.D. thesis, Harvard University, Cambridge, Mass.

Moerenhout, Jacques-Antoine
1942   *Voyages aux îles du Grand Océan, contenant des documens nouveaux sur la géographie physique et politique, la langue, la littérature, la religion, les moeurs, les usages et les coutumes de leurs habitans; et des considérations générales sur leur commerce, leur histoire et leur gouvernement, depuis les temps les plus reculés jusqu'à nos jours.* 2 vols. 2nd ed. Paris: A. Bertrand.

Moing, Richard Le
1885? *Te aveia no te mau tamarii Tahiti ia haapii i te reo Farani.*
Pape'ete: Government Press.

Morrell, William Parker
1960   *Britain in the Pacific Islands.* Oxford: Clarendon Press.

Morrison, James
1935   *The Journal of James Morrison, Boatswain's Mate of the Bounty, Describing the Mutiny and Subsequent Misfortunes of the Mutineers, together with an Account of the Island of Tahiti.* Edited by Owen Rutter. London: Golden Cockerel Press.

Murphy, Agnes
1948   *The Ideology of French Imperialism, 1871–1881.* Washington: Catholic University of America Press.

Myers, John
1817   *The Life, Voyages and Travels of Capt. John Myers, Detailing His Adventures during Four Voyages round the World . . .* London: Longman, Hurst, Rees.

Newbury, Colin W.
1956   "The Administration of French Oceania, 1842–1906." Ph.D. thesis, Australian National University, Canberra.
1960   "L'administration de l'Océanie française de 1849 à 1866." *Revue française d'histoire d'outre-mer* 46:97–157.
1967a "Aspects of Cultural Change in French Polynesia: The Decline of the Ari'i." *Journal of the Polynesian Society* 76:7–26.

1967b "Te Hau Pahu Rahi: Pomare II and the Concept of Inter-Island Government in Eastern Polynesia." *Journal of the Polynesian Society* 76:477–514.

1972a "Trade and Plantations in Eastern Polynesia: The Emergence of a Dependent Economy." In R. Gerard Ward (ed.), *Man in the Pacific Islands: Essays on Geographical Change in the Pacific Islands.* Oxford: Clarendon Press.

1972b "The Makatea Phosphate Concession." In R. Gerard Ward (ed.), *Man in the Pacific Islands: Essays on Geographical Change in the Pacific Islands.* Oxford: Clarendon Press.

1973 "Resistance and Collaboration in French Polynesia: The Tahitian War: 1844–7." *Journal of the Polynesian Society* 82:5–27.

Oliver, Douglas L.
1974 *Ancient Tahitian Society.* 3 vols. Honolulu: The University Press of Hawaii.

Olmstead, Francis Allyn
1841 *Incidents of a Whaling Voyage.* New York: D. Appleton.

O'Reilly, Patrick, and Édouard Reitman
1967 *Bibliographie de Tahiti et de la Polynésie française.* Publications de la Société des Océanistes, no. 14. Paris: Musée de l'Homme.

1969 *Tahiti et la Polynésie française 1768–1964: lettres, manuscrits et documents.* Vente aux enchères publiques à Paris le 2 juin 1969. Le Havre: Ancienne imprimerie Étaix.

1975 *La vie à Tahiti au temps de la reine Pomaré.* Société des Océanistes. Paris: Musée de l'Homme.

1976 "Petite histoire du vieux bloc Vaima," *La Dèpeche de Tahiti* 27 December 1976.

O'Reilly, Patrick, and Raoul Teissier
1975 *Tahitiens: Répertoire biographique de la Polynésie.* Publications de la Société des Océanistes, no. 36. Paris: Musée de l'Homme.

Panoff, Michel
1970 *La terre et l'organisation sociale en Polynésie.* Paris: Payot.

Paxton, Robert O.
1972 *Vichy France: Old Guard and New Order, 1940–1944.* New York: Knopf.

Perbal, R. P.
    1939   *Les missionnaires français et le nationalisme.* Paris: Librairie de l'Arc.

Perkins, Edward
    1854   *Na Motu: Or, Reef-Rovings in the South Seas.* New York: Pudney and Russell.

Pochhammer, Hans
    1918   *Graf Spees letzte Fahrt. Erinnerungen an die Kreuzergeschwader.* Berlin: Dom-Verlag.

Porlier, Louis
    1929   *Documentation sur les lagons des îles Tuamotu propriété communale des districts.* Pape'ete: Imprimerie de l'Océanie.

Ramsden, Eric
    1946   "William Stewart and the Introduction of Chinese Labour in Tahiti." *Journal of the Polynesian Society* 55:187–214.

Ricardi, T.
    1845   "Les îles Pomotou." *Nouvelles annales des voyages* (Paris) 4:244–250.

Robertson, George
    1948   *The Discovery of Tahiti.* Edited by Hugh Carrington. London: Hakluyt Society.

Robillard, H. de
    1845   *Mouvement commercial des Établissements français de l'Océanie pendant l'année 1845.* Pape'ete: Government Press.

Roe, Michael (ed.)
    1967   *The Journal and Letters of Captain Charles Bishop on the North-West Coast of America, in the Pacific and in New South Wales 1794–1799.* Hakluyt Society, Second Series, no. 131. London: Cambridge University Press.

Roucaute, J.
    1951   *Étude sur la situation juridique, dans les É.F.O., des dépendances naturelles du domaine public, telles qu'elles sont énumérées dans l'article 538 du Code Civil (et plus particulièrement les rivages et les eaux des lagons, et de la mer, ainsi que les récifs).* Pape'ete: Service des Domaines.

Salmon, Alexander
  1858   *Lettre concernant l'état actuel de Tahiti adressée à Sa Majesté Napoléon III.* London: Effingham Wilson.

Salmon, Ernest
  1964   *Alexandre Salmon, 1820–1866, et sa femme Ariitaimai 1821–1897: Deux figures de Tahiti à l'époque du Protectorat.* Publications de la Société des Océanistes, no. 11. Paris: Musée de l'Homme.

Saussure, Léopold de
  1899   *Psychologie de la colonisation française dans ses rapports avec les sociétés indigènes.* Paris.

Stackpole, Edouard A.
  1953   *The Sea-Hunters: The New England Whalemen during Two Centuries, 1635–1835.* New York: Lippincott.

Stevens, Margaret
  1965   *Merchant Campbell 1769–1846: A Study of Colonial Trade.* Melbourne: Oxford University Press.

Stewart, Charles Samuel
  1832   *A Visit to the South Seas in the U.S. Ship Vincennes, during the years 1829 & 1830, with scenes in Brazil, Peru, Manilla, the Cape of Good Hope, and St. Helena.* London: Fisher, Son & Jackson.

Tagupa, William E.
  1974   "Legal Concepts and Crises in Tahiti, 1819–1838." *Hawaiian Journal of History* 8:111–120.
  1978   "Soliloquies from the Surviving: Missionary Notes from the Marquesas Islands, 1853–1868." *Journal de la Société des Océanistes* 34:110–115.

Takau Pomare
  1971   *Mémoires de Marau Taaroa dernière reine de Tahiti traduits par sa fille la Princesse Ariimanihinihini Takau Pomare.* Publications de la Société des Océanistes, no. 27. Paris: Musée de l'Homme.

Teissier, Raoul
  1953   "Étude démographique sur les Établissements français de l'Océanie, de Cook au recensement des 17–18 septembre 1951." *Bulletin de la Société d'Études océaniennes* 102: 6–31.

1978   "Chefs et notables des Établissements Français de l'Océanie au temps du Protectorat 1842–1880." *Bulletin de la Société d'Études océaniennes* 202:1–139.

Thozée, Pety de, C. and R.
1902   *Théories de la colonisation au XIXe. siècle et rôle de l'État dans le développement des colonies.* Bruxelles.
1970   *Travaux et documents de l'ORSTOM. Tahiti et Moorea. Études sur la Société, l'Économie et l'Utilisation de l'Espace.* 2 vols. Paris: ORSTOM.

Turnbull, John
1813   *A Voyage round the World in the Years 1800 . . . 1804, in Which the Author Visited Madeira, the Brazils, Cape of Good Hope, the English Settlements of Botany Bay and Norfolk Island, and the Principal Islands in the Pacific Ocean, With a Continuation of their History to the Present Period.* 2nd ed. London: A. Maxwell.

Tyerman, Daniel, and George Bennet
1840   *Voyages and Travels Round the World, by the Rev. Daniel Tyerman and George Bennet Esq., Deputed from the London Missionary Society to Visit Their Various Stations in the South Sea Islands, Australia, China, India, Madagascar, and South Africa, between the Years 1821 and 1829.* Edited by James Montgomery. 2nd ed. London: John Snow.

Valenziani, Carlo
1949   "Enquête démographique en Océanie française." *Bulletin de la Société d'Études océaniennes* 7:658–684.

Vancouver, George
1801   *A Voyage of Discovery to the North Pacific Ocean, and Round the World.* 6 vols. 2nd ed. London: J. Stockdale.

Varigny, Charles de
1881   "La France dans l'Océan Pacifique: Tahiti." *Revue des deux mondes* (Paris) 44:400–408.
1888   *L'Océan Pacifique.* Paris.

Vernier, Charles
1948   *Tahitiens d'hier et d'aujourd'hui.* 2nd ed. Paris.

Vignon, Louis
1886   *Les Colonies françaises.* Paris.

West, Francis J.
1961   *Political Advancement in the South Pacific: A Comparative Study of Colonial Practise in Fiji, Tahiti and American Samoa.* Melbourne: Oxford University Press.

Wilkes, Charles
1844   *Narrative of the United States Exploring Expedition during the Years 1838 . . . 1842.* 5 vols. and atlas. London.

Wilmot, C.
1888   *Notice sur l'archipel des Tuamotu . . . publié sous les auspices du Conseil général.* Pape'ete: Government Press.

Wilson, James
1799   *A Missionary Voyage to the Southern Pacific Ocean, Performed in the Years 1796, 1797, 1798, in the Ship Duff, Commanded by Captain James Wilson.* London: T. Chapman.

INDEX

🎴 Production Notes

This book was designed by Roger Eggers
and typeset on the Unified Composing System
by the design and production staff of
The University Press of Hawaii.

The text typeface is Compugraphic
Caledonia and the display typeface
is Tiffany.

Offset presswork and binding were
done by Halliday Lithograph. Text paper is
Glatfelter P & S Offset, basis 55.

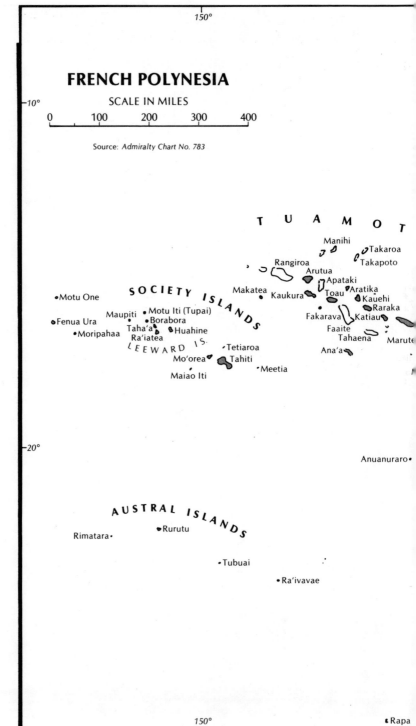

FRENCH POLYNESIA

SCALE IN MILES

| 0 | 100 | 200 | 300 | 400 |

Source: *Admiralty Chart No. 783*

T U A M O T

Manihi

Takaroa

Takapoto

Rangiroa

Arutua

Apataki

Aratika

Makatea

Toau

Kauehi

S O C I E T Y   I S L A N D S

Kaukura

Raraka

Motu One

Fakarava

Katiau

Maupiti

Motu Iti (Tupai)

Faaite

Fenua Ura

Borabora

Tahaena

Marute

Taha'a

Huahine

Moripahaa

Ra'iatea

Ana'a

L E E W A R D   I S.

Tetiaroa

Mo'orea

Tahiti

Meetia

Maiao Iti

20°

Anuanuraro

A U S T R A L   I S L A N D S

Rurutu

Rimatara

Tubuai

Ra'ivavae

150°

Rapa